CHILD WELL-BEING
AND NONRESIDENT PARENTS

CHILDREN'S ISSUES, LAWS AND PROGRAMS

Additional books in this series can be found on Nova's website
under the Series tab.

Additional E-books in this series can be found on Nova's website
under the E-books tab.

SOCIAL ISSUES, JUSTICE AND STATUS

Additional books in this series can be found on Nova's website
under the Series tab.

Additional E-books in this series can be found on Nova's website
under the E-books tab.

CHILDREN'S ISSUES, LAWS AND PROGRAMS

CHILD WELL-BEING
AND NONRESIDENT PARENTS

LAURA M. FERNANDES
EDITOR

Nova Science Publishers, Inc.
New York

NOTICE TO THE READER

The Publisher has taken reasonable care in the preparation of this book, but makes no expressed or implied warranty of any kind and assumes no responsibility for any errors or omissions. No liability is assumed for incidental or consequential damages in connection with or arising out of information contained in this book. The Publisher shall not be liable for any special, consequential, or exemplary damages resulting, in whole or in part, from the readers' use of, or reliance upon, this material. Any parts of this book based on government reports are so indicated and copyright is claimed for those parts to the extent applicable to compilations of such works.

Independent verification should be sought for any data, advice or recommendations contained in this book. In addition, no responsibility is assumed by the publisher for any injury and/or damage to persons or property arising from any methods, products, instructions, ideas or otherwise contained in this publication.

This publication is designed to provide accurate and authoritative information with regard to the subject matter covered herein. It is sold with the clear understanding that the Publisher is not engaged in rendering legal or any other professional services. If legal or any other expert assistance is required, the services of a competent person should be sought. FROM A DECLARATION OF PARTICIPANTS JOINTLY ADOPTED BY A COMMITTEE OF THE AMERICAN BAR ASSOCIATION AND A COMMITTEE OF PUBLISHERS.

Additional color graphics may be available in the e-book version of this book.

LIBRARY OF CONGRESS CATALOGING-IN-PUBLICATION DATA

Child well-being and nonresident parents / editor, Laura M. Fernandes.
    p. cm.
 Includes index.
 ISBN 978-1-60692-382-5 (hbk.)
 1. Child welfare--United States. 2. Children--United States--Social conditions. 3. Absentee fathers--United States. 4. Absentee mothers--United States. 5. Single parent families--United States. I. Fernandes, Laura M.
 HV741.C53585 2011
 362.7--dc22
                            2011001305

Published by Nova Science Publishers, Inc. † New York

CONTENTS

PREFACE

The nation's future depends to a larger extent on its children's ability to develop into contributing adult members of society. For that reason, and for what many would consider a society's moral obligation to care for the young and vulnerable, Congress and the nation take an interest in promoting children's well-being. Their well-being and ability to develop into productive adults in an increasingly competitive global economy is influenced by a variety of factors and public policies. This new book discusses topics such as child well-being and the noncustodial father; child support enforcement and ex-offenders; parents in prison and their minor children, as well as child welfare agencies' efforts to identify, locate and involve nonresident fathers.

Chapter 1- The structure of a family plays an important role in children's well-being. A contributing factor to the high rates of child poverty over the long-term, and the increase in child poverty during the period from 2001-2007, was the increasing likelihood of children living in families headed by a single female. In 2009, about one-third of all children lived in families without their biological father present. According to some estimates, about 50% of children (who are currently under age 18) will spend or have spent a significant portion of their childhood in a home without their biological father.

Chapter 2- According to recent estimates, about 1.7 million children in the United States have parents who are currently incarcerated in state or federal prisons. Among the approximately 700,000 persons who are released from prison each year about 400,000 of them are fathers and mothers. The current economic crisis together with overcrowded prisons and state budget shortfalls are likely to result in a significant number of inmates convicted of nonviolent offenses getting early release dispensations. How these former inmates reconnect to their families impacts not only the children involved but society at large and is of great interest to Congress and the nation.

Chapter 3- An estimated 809,800 prisoners of the 1,518,535 held in the nation's prisons at midyear 2007 were parents of minor children, or children under age 18. Parents held in the nation's prisons—52% of state inmates and 63% of federal inmates—reported having an estimated 1,706,600 minor children, accounting for 2.3% of the U.S. resident population under age 18. Unless otherwise specified in this report, the word *parent* refers to state and federal prisoners who reported having minor children. The word *children* refers to youth under age 18.

Chapter 4- Over the past decade an interest in fathers and their contributions to family stability and children's healthy development has heightened the attention paid within the child welfare field to identifying, locating, and involving fathers. Many of the children served by child welfare agencies have nonresident fathers. In addition, the Adoption and Safe Families Act of 1997 renewed focus on expediting permanency for children in out-of-home placement. Engaging fathers of foster children can be important not only for the potential benefit of a child-father relationship (when such a relationship does not pose a risk to the child's safety or well-being), but also for making placement decisions and gaining access to resources for the child. Permanency may be expedited by placing children with their nonresident fathers or paternal kin, or through early relinquishment or termination of the father's parental rights. Through engaging fathers, agencies may learn important medical information and/or that the child is the recipient of certain benefits, such as health insurance, survivor benefits, or child support. Apart from the father's potential as a caregiver, such resources might support a reunification goal or a relative guardianship and therefore enhance permanency options for the child.

In: Child Well-Being and Nonresident Parents
Editor: Laura M. Fernandes

ISBN: 978-1-60692-382-5
© 2011 Nova Science Publishers, Inc.

Chatper 1

CHILD WELL-BEING AND NONCUSTODIAL FATHERS

Carmen Solomon-Fears, Gene Falk and Adrienne L. Fernandes-Alcantara

SUMMARY

The structure of a family plays an important role in children's well-being. A contributing factor to the high rates of child poverty over the long-term, and the increase in child poverty during the period from 2001-2007, was the increasing likelihood of children living in families headed by a single female. In 2009, about one-third of all children lived in families without their biological father present. According to some estimates, about 50% of children (who are currently under age 18) will spend or have spent a significant portion of their childhood in a home without their biological father.

In 2008, the poverty rate for children living in female-headed families (usually headed by a single mother) was 43%, compared to 10% for children living in married-couple families. Policies enacted in the mid-1990s focused on moving single mothers from the welfare rolls to work; with these policies in place and the economic expansion of the late 1990s, child poverty rates fell. However, these gains in the economic well-being of children were limited and temporary, as child poverty increased again in the period from 2001 to 2007, even before the onset of "the Great Recession."

An option to improve the well-being of children living in single-mother families is to seek greater financial and social contributions from fathers, particularly noncustodial fathers. However, the ability of noncustodial fathers to support their children has been complicated by certain economic and social trends. Over the past three decades, changes in the labor market have led to less employment and lower typical wages for men. The wages of men with lower levels of educational attainment have fallen since the mid-1970s. Criminal justice policies have changed, leading to increases in the rate of incarceration of men. These trends, while affecting all racial and ethnic groups, had a disproportionate impact on African American men. "The Great Recession," which began in December 2007, has hit men's employment hard; and it has hit employment of young, African American men particularly hard.

Although social science research and analysis acknowledge a father's influence on the overall well-being of his children, federal welfare programs have to a large extent minimized or underplayed the role of fathers in the lives of children. Noncustodial fathers and other men are largely invisible to these programs as clients or recipients. They become visible only in their role as family income producers (e.g., payers of child support). Other federal programs and/or systems that have included many men on their rolls (such as employment and training programs and the criminal justice system) have not fully addressed the unique needs and circumstances of fathers, particularly those who do not have custody of their children.

Social policy programs could be used to help noncustodial parents stay connected to their children and thereby improve the well-being of their children. Potential policy options include establishing an Innovation Fund that provides services to both noncustodial and custodial parents; examining strategies for reducing child support arrearages; changing the financing structure of Child Support Enforcement (CSE) access and visitation programs for noncustodial parents; modifying the earned income tax credit (EITC) to make noncustodial parents eligible; enhancing or expanding job training and education programs to assist low-income men and youth, which in turn can help them in providing for their (current or future) families; and redefining eligibility for certain programs so that disadvantaged young adults can receive more holistic training and other services that can better prepare them for adulthood.

INTRODUCTION

The nation's future depends in large part on its children's ability to develop into contributing adult members of society. For that reason, and for what many would consider a society's moral obligation to care for the young and vulnerable, Congress and the nation take an interest in promoting children's well-being. It can be argued that children are the nation's most valuable resource, constituting the next generation of workers, taxpayers, and parents. Their well-being and ability to develop into productive adults in an increasingly competitive global economy is influenced by a variety of factors, and public policies can affect these factors to varying degrees.[1]

Parents and family life exert a primary influence on children's well-being throughout their development and into adulthood. The family is the place where children develop their first attachments to other people—usually to their parent(s) as their primary care giver(s). Early attachments have been shown to have consistent and enduring influences on children's social and emotional development. The family is also the economic unit that obtains and manages the resources that meet a child's basic needs, while also playing a significant role in stimulating the child's cognitive, social, and emotional development.[2]

The structure of a family plays an important role in children's well-being. Divorce, the loss of a parent due to death or incarceration, or being born to a single parent can change or create a family's composition and character and ultimately affect children's well-being.[3] According to some estimates, about 50% of children (who are currently under age 18) will spend or have spent a significant portion of their childhood in a home without their biological fathers.[4] In 2009, 23% of the 74.5 million U.S. children (under age 18) were living in families headed by their mothers, with their fathers not present. In that year, one-third of all children lived apart from their biological fathers.

A broad array of social science research and analysis[5] indicates that although most children who grow up in single-parent families become well-adjusted, productive adults, children raised in mother-only families (or with a mother and stepfather[6]) are more likely than children raised with both biological parents to do poorly in school,[7] have emotional and behavioral problems,[8] become teenage parents,[9] and have poverty-level incomes.[10]

There is widespread agreement that the negative outcomes associated with living in a single- parent family compared to living with both biological parents are primarily due to the low income of the family and the poor quality of the parent-child relationships. Single-parent families are more likely to be poor than two-parent families, especially if the lone parent is the mother. Public policy research and programs have generally focused on children and their single mothers, especially those on the lower end of the income and asset continuum, because these families tend to be impoverished, which generally translates into poorer outcomes and less well-being for children. During the welfare reform era, public policy initiatives were enacted to require low- income mothers to participate in the workforce, and to provide work supports for them. Welfareto-work efforts might have succeeded in their primary goals of reducing the welfare rolls and spurring more work among single mothers. However, these families often remained poor; the work efforts of the single mother alone often failed to increase incomes as their low wages merely replaced low welfare benefits.[11] Since reaching an all-time low in 1969, the growth in the number of single-parent families, which tend to have a high incidence of poverty, has contributed to higher rates of child poverty overall.

Another way to address poverty in single-parent families and improve child well-being is through the fathers of these children (nearly all noncustodial parents are fathers). Even though there is general agreement among policymakers and the public regarding the importance of the father in improving the well-being of his children, federal *welfare* programs have to a large extent minimized or underplayed the role of fathers in the lives of children. Moreover, other federal programs and/or systems that serve or involve men—such as employment and training programs and the criminal justice system—have not fully addressed the unique needs and circumstances of fathers, particularly those who do not have custody of their children.

In some cases (of child abuse and/or domestic violence), a father's involvement with his children may do more harm than good. However, in most cases, involving fathers in the lives of their children is generally regarded as a worthy policy goal. A myriad of studies indicate that an active and nurturing style of fathering is associated with better verbal skills, intellectual functioning, and academic achievement among adolescents. These studies suggest that fathers who are involved, nurturing, and playful with their infants have children with higher IQs, as well as better linguistic and cognitive capacities. Girls with involved, respectful fathers see how they should expect men to treat them and are less likely to become involved in violent or unhealthy relationships. According to some research, even from birth, children who have an involved father are more likely to be emotionally secure, be confident to explore their surroundings, and, as they grow older, have better social connections with peers. These children are also less likely to get in trouble at home, school, or in the neighborhood. It is also reported that children who grow up with involved fathers are more comfortable exploring the world around them and more likely to exhibit self control and pro-social behavior.[12] According to sociologist Dr. David Popenoe, "Fathers are far more than just 'second adults' in the home ... Involved fathers bring positive benefits to their children that no other person is as likely to bring."[13] The financial and emotional commitment of fathers to their children is a crucial factor in child well-being.

It may be that the next era of welfare reform will incorporate the new thinking in this area—that both parents are important to their children. The issues raised by father absence—and the social and economic context affecting men's abilities to be responsible fathers—spans a wide spectrum of social policy domains including income support, employment and training, housing, and the criminal justice system. Over recent decades, the wages of men have stagnated and even fallen. While women and single mothers increased their labor force participation, work and labor force participation among men actually declined. Additionally, incarceration rates for men, especially low-income men, have risen considerably over the past several decades. Efforts to help fathers, especially low-income fathers, play a successful role in improving the well-being of their children may prove to be challenging given that the financial situation of many men is precarious and their living situations are often complicated. In FY2009, roughly 14 million[14] noncustodial fathers in the United States had children on the Child Support Enforcement (CSE) rolls. Data from the Urban Institute's 1997 National Survey of American Families (NSAF; the most recent available) found that two-thirds of nonresident fathers did not formally pay child support.[15] Nearly all (90%) poor fathers did not pay, compared to just over half (5 6%) of non-poor fathers. Further, of the poor, nonpaying fathers who were not institutionalized (mostly in prison), 43% did not work.

Proponents maintain that social policy could help to stabilize low-income noncustodial fathers[16] so that they can be positively involved, both financially and emotionally, in the lives of their children. Social policy could play a role across several domains: (1) economic assistance programs (Temporary Assistance for Needy Families (TANF) block grant, the Earned Income Tax Credit (EITC), and the Supplemental Nutrition Assistance Program (SNAP)); (2) family support (the Child Support Enforcement (CSE) program and the Healthy Marriage and Responsible Fatherhood programs); and (3) human capital (workforce programs). This report provides information on these programs and also examines federal programs that have the purposes of preventing teen pregnancy and helping disadvantaged youth obtain the skills and support they need to become positive, productive, self-sufficient members of their communities. These programs, if fully utilized, are seen as having the potential to keep young people from getting "off-track" because of drug use/abuse, an unintended pregnancy, or failure to complete high school. The underlying premise is that the aid or services received from these programs by low- income, disadvantaged men[17] may help them overcome economic and emotional barriers and aid them in becoming productive members of society in a number of ways—by giving them job training and employment opportunities (and thereby the ability to make regular child support payments), educational information and emotional support to promote positive interaction between them and their children, and supportive services and counseling to help them avoid criminal activity.

This report displays and discusses some of the data related to the poverty of children and their living arrangements and data on male employment and earnings, educational attainment, and incarceration. It also presents several public policy approaches being considered by the policy community that might improve the lives of low-income noncustodial fathers and their children. This report is a starting point for discussions on how social policy can assist low-income noncustodial fathers in (1) meeting their financial commitments to their children, and (2) supporting their children emotionally and being a positive presence in the lives of their children.

BACKGROUND: SOCIAL AND ECONOMIC TRENDS

There is a scarcity of data on the economic and demographic characteristics of noncustodial fathers. The Census Bureau's major household surveys that produce official employment and income statistics, the Current Population Survey (CPS) and the American Community Survey (ACS) do not capture information to determine whether a man living in a household without children is a noncustodial father. The most recent snapshot of noncustodial fathers was taken through the Urban Institute's National Survey of American Families (NSAF), discussed above, which was part of the Institute's Assessing New Federalism project initiated in the wake of the 1996 welfare reform law and privately funded through foundations.

Given the lack of recent and consistent trend information on noncustodial fathers, this report talks about men in general to provide a sense of the economic and social context in which noncustodial fathers live. That is, the report does not provide information on the characteristics of noncustodial fathers, but rather provides the economic and social trends generally affecting men that have a bearing on the ability of noncustodial fathers to help support their children.

Child Poverty Rates

Persistently high rates of child poverty have long been a social policy concern. In 2009, the official poverty rate for children was 20.7%, meaning that one in five children were classified as poor. Child poverty rates vary dramatically by family setting. In 2009, the child poverty rate for related children in female-headed families (usually headed by a single mother) was 44.4%. For children living in families headed by a married couple, the poverty rate was 11.0%.

Female-headed families have historically been the focus of policies for disadvantaged families with children. The reasons for this focus include the following:

- the high rates of poverty among children living in families headed by a single woman, indicating high rates of economic disadvantage among such families;
- cash welfare for needy families was, for many years, legally restricted to families with either an absent or disabled father; even when these legal restrictions were relaxed, the cash welfare rolls were still dominated by families headed by single parents, at least until recently; and
- the desire to reduce the welfare rolls, both because of the view that welfare receipt itself helped promote disadvantage and to save taxpayer money.

Figure 1 shows the trend in child poverty rates from 1959 (the first year for which official poverty statistics are available) through 2009. It includes the poverty rate both for all children and for children living in female-headed families. The female head is usually a single mother. It shows that improvements in child poverty rates generally occurred through the 1960s. However, the child poverty rate for all children reached a low point in 1969, increased somewhat through the 1970s, and rose sharply beginning in 1979. The poverty rate for children in female-headed families declined until 1979. In the 1980s, the overall child poverty rate generally fluctuated around the 20% mark. Poverty among children in female-headed families failed to drop below 50% during that decade.

The mid-1990s saw major changes in policies affecting families with children. Tax legislation in 1993 significantly expanded the Earned Income Tax Credit (EITC) for families with children and with workers. The 1996 welfare reform law (The Personal Responsibility and Work Opportunity Reconciliation Act of 1996, P.L. 104-193) made major changes to cash welfare that sought to require work and reduce welfare "dependency." The 1996 welfare law also further expanded aid to the working poor by substantially increasing child care subsidies. It also made major changes to the Child Support Enforcement (CSE) program. A year later, the Balanced Budget Act of 1995 (P.L. 105-35) created the State Children's Health Insurance Program (SCHIP), which provided health coverage to the children of the working poor.

In the wake of these policy changes, which occurred during an economic expansion, the cash welfare rolls declined precipitously and employment among single mothers increased. The child poverty rate also declined, falling from 22.7% in 1993 to 16.2% in 2000. The poverty rate for children in female-headed families fell 14 percentage points, from 53.7% in 1993 to 39.3% in 2001.

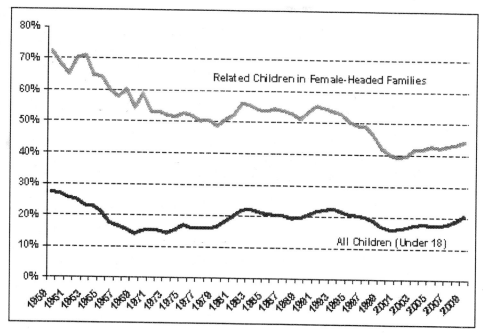

Source. Congressional Research Service (CRS), based on data from the U.S. Census Bureau.

Figure 1. Poverty Rates for Children, by Family Type: 1959-2009.

The improvements in poverty rates for children in the late 1990s were limited. In 2000, the child poverty rate had declined to 16.2%, its lowest rate since 1978 but still above the 14.0% rate of 1969. The poverty rate for children living in families headed by single parents reached 39.3% in 2001, its all-time low over the period for which official poverty statistics are available but still representing two in five such children living in poverty. Moreover, the improvements did not last. During the 2000s, child poverty rates increased again. This increase occurred even *before* the onset of the deep recession that began in December 2007.

Living Arrangements of Children

A contributing factor to the high rates of child poverty over the long term, and the increase in child poverty during the period from 2001 to 2007, was the increasing likelihood of children living in families headed by a single female. **Figure 2** shows that in 1959, less than 1 in 10 children (9%) lived in families headed by a single female. This proportion increased almost every year until the mid-1990s, reaching 24.0% in 1995. The share of children living in female-headed families fell slightly during the remainder of the 1 990s, before rising again in the 2001-2009 period.

The proportion of children born to unmarried mothers reached 40.6% in 2008—the highest level during the period for which these data are available. [18] The period from 2001 to 2008 saw particularly steep increases in the share of children born to unmarried mothers. In 2001, 33.2% of all births were to unmarried mothers.

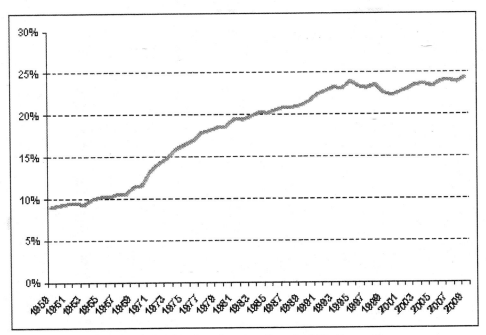

Source. Congressional Research Service, based on data from the U.S. Census Bureau.

Figure 2. Percent of all Related Children Under Age 18 Living in Single-Parent, Female-Headed Families, 1959-2009.

The living situations of children are complex. In 2009, almost 6 in 10 children lived with both their biological parents, who were married to each other. However, this means 4 in 10 children were living in other situations. A small share of children (about 3%) lived with both their biological parents who were unmarried. Another relatively small share of children lived with their biological fathers without their biological mothers. However, about one-third of all children lived in families without their biological fathers present.

Although little is known (empirically, in aggregate) about the men who spend years living apart from their biological children, anecdotal evidence suggests that some of these men are in relationships with women who have children fathered by other men. The advent of multiple relationships that produce children, often referred to as multiple partner fertility (i.e., when mothers and fathers have had children with more than one partner), generally complicates the family situation of children. Thus, many fathers may not be living with their own biological children but rather with the children of another man. In short, noncustodial and surrogate fathers play a large part in the family lives of children, but most federal programs have minimal official contact with them and therefore little is known about their characteristics.

Challenges of Increasing Involvement of Noncustodial Parents with their Children

A father's involvement with his children may be influenced by a number of factors. Over the past three decades, changes in the labor market have led to less employment and lower typical wages for men. Criminal justice policies have changed, leading to increases in the rate of incarceration of men. What has not changed much over this period is that men living apart from their biological children have not been a primary focus of policies to assist men, or their biological children, who are economically disadvantaged. Though there are likely to be financial and nonfinancial benefits of increasing the involvement of noncustodial fathers with their children, policies to promote such engagement face an uphill battle given these economic and social trends.

Earnings

The earnings of typical full-time, full-year workers are a key indicator to how they are faring in the workforce. **Figure 3** displays the median annual earnings of men and women from 1960 to 2009 (in inflation-adjusted dollars) who worked full-time during an entire year. When adjusted for inflation, the median annual earnings for a man working full-time, full-year peaked in 1973. While there have been fluctuations in the real wages of men since then, the inflation-adjusted median annual earnings for men in 2009 was lower than it was in 1973 by 4.3%. The median annual earnings for men reached their post-1973 low point in 1996 at 9% below the 1973 level. Real wage growth in the late 1990s and the early 2000s made up for some of the lost ground in men's earnings, but this period of growth was short-lived. In contrast to the trend for men, the median wage for women who work full-time, full-year generally increased after 1973.

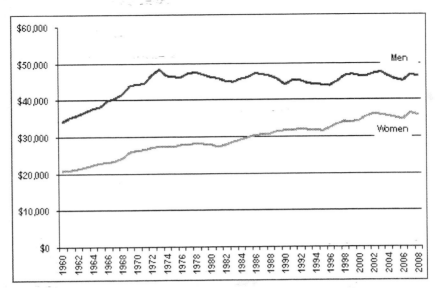

Source. Congressional Research Service, based on data from the U.S. Census Bureau.
Notes. Constant dollars were computed using the Consumer Price Index (CPI) for all Urban Consumers (CPI-U-RS).

Figure 3. Median Annual Earnings of Men and Women Who Work Full-Time, Full-Year: 1960-2009 In 2009 (inflation-adjusted) dollars.

The trend in typical earnings for men varied markedly by education status. Figure 4 shows the average inflation-adjusted earnings for men by educational attainment from 1975 to 2008. Since the late 1970s, inflation-adjusted earnings have increased for men with college degrees. The greatest payoff in recent years has been for men with advanced degrees, who have earned an average of more than $100,000 in each year since 1995. However, for men lacking a high school diploma, inflation-adjusted earnings fell substantially. In 2008, the average earnings for a man lacking a high school diploma was $24,831, 17% below the 1979 level when such a man earned on average around $30,000 a year. The inflation-adjusted earnings of men with a high school diploma declined by less, but they were still lower in 2008 than they were in 1979.

Employment

Wages alone do not tell the full story about how individuals of working age are faring in the labor market. Whether they are actually employed is perhaps a more telling indicator of their economic well-being. The increase in labor force participation and employment among women during the post-World War II period is well known. However, during this period, the rate of employment among men declined. **Figure 5** shows the employment rate for men and women over the period from 1948 to 2009. Men began the period with an employment rate over 80%. Women began the period with an employment rate around 30%. By 2007 (generally before the recession that began in December of that year), the employment rate for men had declined to 69.8%, while the employment rate for women had risen to 56.6%. The recession caused drops in the employment rate for both men and women, though the decline was more pronounced for men (to 64.5%, a decline of 5.3 percentage points, compared to 54.4% for women, a decline of 2.2 percentage points).

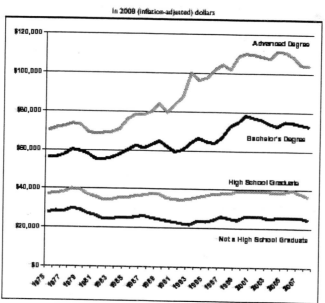

Source. Congressional Research Service, based on data from the U.S. Census Bureau.
Notes. Inflation adjustment made using the CPI-U-RS.

Figure 4. Average Inflation-Adjusted Earnings for Men Aged 18 and Older, by Education Level: 1975-
2008.

The decline in the employment rate for men stems from several factors, including the aging of the population, retirements, and the increasing prevalence of early retirements. However, it also reflects declining employment rates among both prime-aged men (ages 25 to 54) and young men. **Figure 6** shows the employment rates for men by age. As shown, employment rates declined among all groups represented in the figure. In 1948, over 90% of prime-aged men were employed, a rate that fell into the 80% range before the onset of the recession in December 2007. The employment rate had also declined for the younger groups. For teens, employment rates that were in the mid-50% range at the beginning of the period had fallen to just above 30% in 2007. For young adults (20 to 24 years old), employment rates fell from around 80% to 70%. Employment rates for older men also fell, though they are not shown in the figure (presumably, many of these men are not fathers of children under age 18).

The long-term decline in employment rates for teens and young adults partially reflects increases in school enrollment among these age groups.[19] Thus, these trends can partially be viewed as a consequence of a positive social trend. However, not all of these trends reflect a tendency toward voluntary withdrawal from the workforce to complete schooling. Unemployment rates among teens and young men tend to be high. Moreover, the recession that began in December 2007 disproportionately affected young men. The impact of this recession on men in general and on men by age is discussed in the next section.

The Great Recession

The recession that began in December 2007, sometimes called "the Great Recession," has disproportionately affected men. **Figure 7** shows unemployment rates for men and women, and the gap in the unemployment rate between men and women from 1948 to 2010. Unemployment reflects the number of people actively looking for, but unable to find, work.

During the period from December 2007 through May 2010, the unemployment rate for men reached a high of 11.4% in October 2009. That was the highest unemployment rate for men in the entire 1948-2010 period. The peak unemployment rate for women during this period was 8.8% (April 2010 and May 2010). The gap in the unemployment rate between men and women reached historical highs in the months since December 2007. For the period from March 2009 to April 2010, the gap in the unemployment rates between men and women exceeded two percentage points.

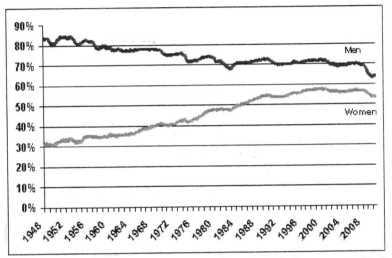

Source. Congressional Research Service, based on data from the U.S. Department of Labor, Bureau of Labor Statistics (BLS).

Figure 5. Employment Rates for Men and Women Ages 16 and Older, 1948-2010.

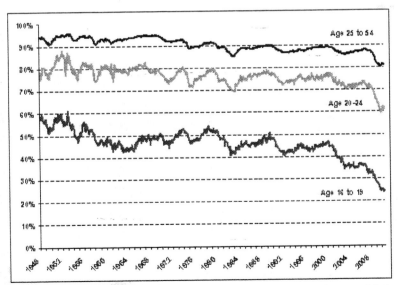

Source. Congressional Research Service, based on data from the U.S. Department of Labor, Bureau of Labor Statistics (BLS).

Figure 6. Employment Rates for Men by Age, 1948-2010.

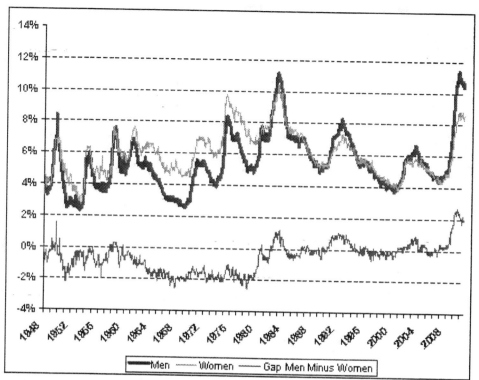

Source. Congressional Research Service, based on data from the U.S. Department of Labor, Bureau of Labor Statistics.

Figure 7. Unemployment Rates for Men and Women and the Gap in Rates Between Men and Women, 1948-20 10.

Incarceration Rates

Incarceration has affected the ability of men to participate in the labor market and the lives of their children. At the end of 2008, 1.6 million persons, of whom 1.5 million were men, were imprisoned in federal or state facilities. Incarceration rates in the United States have increased in recent decades. The growth of the prison population, which is predominately male, poses another challenge in attempting to increase financial and social support from noncustodial fathers to their children.

Figure 8 shows the growth in incarceration rates from 1995 to 2008 for men and women with sentences of at least one year. These rates have grown for both men and women, but incarceration is clearly a phenomenon that mostly affects men. The chart shows that incarceration rates grew more rapidly during the late 1990s than during the 2000 to 2008 period. In 2008, 952 out of 100,000 men (almost 1% of all men) were incarcerated by federal or state authorities, compared to 68 out of 100,000 women.

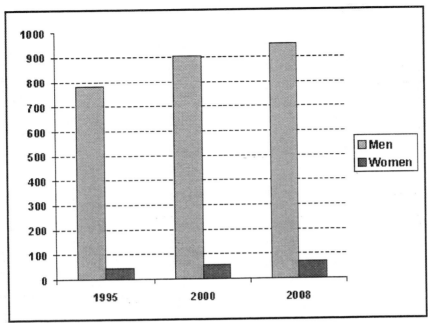

Source. For 2000 and 2008, U.S. Department of Justice, Office of Justice Programs, Bureau of Justice Statistics, Prisoners 2008, revised April 1, 2010. For 1995, U.S. Department of Justice, *State and Federal Prisons Report Record Growth in Last 12 Months*, December 3, 1995.

Notes. The 2000 and 2008 data represent incarceration rates as of December 31 of the year. The 1995 rate represents data as of June 30, 1995. Rates represent the number of prisoners with sentences of more than one year per 100,000 in the population.

Figure 8. Incarceration Rates for Selected Years, by Gender, 1995 to 2008 (Rates per 100,000 in the population).

African American Families

The social and economic conditions in the labor force and with respect to incarceration, while occurring in the population as a whole and across racial and ethnic groups, have disproportionately affected African American families. In 2008, the poverty rate for African American children was 34.7%, compared to 19% of all children.[20] In the population as a whole, one-third of all children lived in households that lacked their biological fathers. Among African American children, nearly two-thirds (65%) lived apart from their biological fathers.

The relatively high rates of economic disadvantage and father absence among African American children occur despite improvements in some social indicators for African American men, reflecting a long history of relative disadvantage. However, African American men are still relatively worse off than white men and, on some measures, Hispanic men.

For example, the educational attainment level for African American men has increased. In 1965, 25% of African American men ages 25 and older had completed four years of high school, compared with 50% of white men ages 25 and older. The proportion of men with at least that level of schooling increased for both white men and African American men, with greater improvement for African American men. However, **Figure 9** shows that despite this improvement in educational attainment, the percentage of African American men who lack a high school diploma was still higher than that of white men—1 6% of African American men lack a high school diploma compared to only 8.6% of white men. (Hispanic men had the highest rate of lacking a high school diploma.) African American men ages 18 to 24 were also far less likely than their white counterparts to have a high school diploma.

Moreover, African American men without a high school diploma typically earn less than other men without a high school diploma. **Figure 10** shows the average earnings for men without a high school diploma in 1975 and 2008 (the 1975 earnings data are adjusted for inflation to 2008 dollars). In real terms, the average earnings for white men without a high school diploma declined and average earnings for Hispanic men without a high school diploma increased; there was little change in real earnings for African American men without a high school diploma. These trends left African American men who lacked a high school diploma with the lowest earnings of the three racial/ethnic groups shown in the figure in 2008, with average annual earnings of $22,344, compared to $25,386 for white men and $24,340 for Hispanic men without a high school diploma.

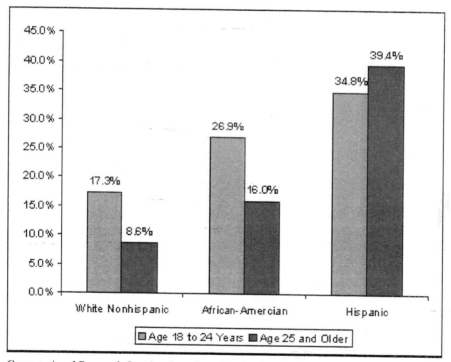

Source. Congressional Research Service, based on data from the U.S. Census Bureau.

Figure 9. Percent of Men Who Lack a High School Diploma, by Race/Ethnicity, 2009.

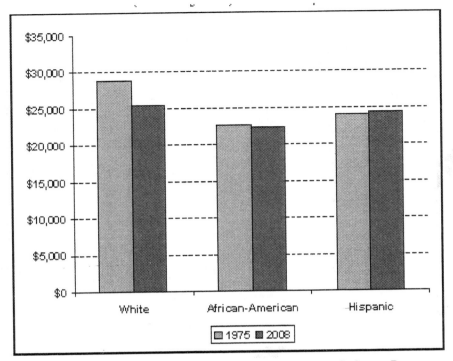

Source. Congressional Research Service (CRS) based on data from the U.S. Census Bureau.
Notes. Inflation adjustment is based on the CPI-U-RS.

Figure 1 0. Average Earnings for Men without a High School Diploma, by Race/Ethnicity, 1975 and 2008 (1975 earnings are adjusted for inflation).

The most telling indicator of the poor employment outcomes for African American men without a high school diploma is the employment rate. **Table 1** shows the employment rates for men without a high school diploma in March of selected years by race and ethnicity for two groups: youth (ages 16 to 24) who were not enrolled in school, and all men ages 25 to 54. Over the past two decades, the employment rate for African American men without a high school diploma has declined. In 2007 (before the recession), less than 3 in 10 African American men ages 16 to 24 who lacked a high school diploma and were not in school were employed. This proportion changed little during the recession—though the overall employment rate for African American men declined between 2007 and 2009, a higher rate of these men were enrolled in school in 2009.

While the decline in employment rates for young African Americans has been noted elsewhere, employment rates for prime-aged African American men (ages 25 to 54) who lack a high school diploma also fell. While employment rates for other racial and ethnic groups also declined, Hispanic men without a high school diploma maintained high rates of employment.

Table 1. Employment Rates in March of Selected Years for Men without a High School Diploma, by Race/Ethnicity and Age (1989, 2000, 2007, 2009).

	1989	2000	2007	2009
Ages 16 to 24 (and not in school)				
African American	54.9	40.8	28.7	31.4
White Nonhispanic	81.3	72.3	55.0	44.8
Hispanic	81.7	80.2	74.0	73.5
Ages 25 to 54				
African American	69.9	59.9	53.6	40.6
White Nonhispanic	83.8	71.2	68.2	62.1
Hispanic	84.5	85.0	83.9	75.5

Source. Congressional Research Service tabulations of the March Current Population Survey for selected years.

One of the most stark indicators of disadvantage for African American men is their high incarceration rate. **Figure 11** shows incarceration rates (with sentences of one year or more) for men by race and ethnicity at the end of 2008. At that point in time, there were 3,161 African American men imprisoned per 100,000 in the population (3.1% of the population), compared to 487 white men and 1,200 Hispanic men per 100,000 in the population.

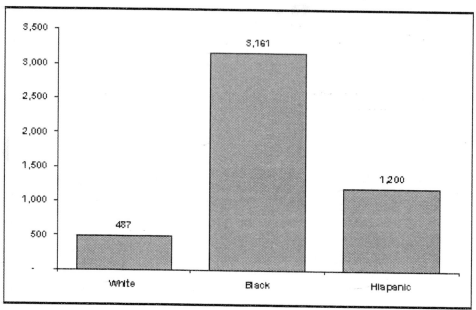

Source. U.S. Department of Justice, Office of Justice Programs, Bureau of Justice Statistics, Prisoners 2008, revised April 1, 2010.

Notes. Rates represent the number of prisoners with sentences of more than one year per 100,000 in the population.

Figure 11. Incarceration Rate for Men in 2008, by Race/Ethnicity (Rates per 100,000 in the population).

SELECTED FEDERAL PROGRAMS: BARRIERS ENCOUNTERED BY NONCUSTODIAL FATHERS AND OTHER MEN

The focus of social policies for disadvantaged children has been on families headed by single mothers. These long-standing policies have provided cash and non-cash assistance to mothers. Yet noncustodial fathers, many of whom are low-income, could benefit from policies that would help them be positively involved in the lives of their children. Social policy might play a role across several policy domains: (1) economic assistance (Temporary Assistance for Needy Families (TANF) block grant, the Earned Income Tax Credit (EITC), and the Supplemental Nutrition Assistance Program (SNAP)); (2) family support (the Child Support Enforcement (CSE) program and the Healthy Marriage and Responsible Fatherhood programs); and (3) human capital (workforce programs). This section provides information on these programs and also examines federal programs that have the purposes of preventing teen pregnancy and helping disadvantaged youth obtain the skills and support they need to become positive, productive, self-sufficient members of their communities. As noted earlier, the underlying premise is that the aid or services received from these programs by low-income, disadvantaged men may help them overcome economic and emotional barriers and aid them in becoming productive members of society in a number of ways—by giving them job training and employment opportunities (and thereby the ability to make regular child support payments), educational information and emotional support to promote positive interaction between them and their children, and supportive services and counseling that can help them stay connected to their communities and families (and thereby avoid criminal activity).

Economic Assistance Programs

Economic assistance is designed to supplement the income of poor families to help them meet their basic needs. Noncustodial parents have either been ineligible for economic assistance based on low income because they do not live with their children, or they have not been a large population within low-income assistance programs.

In the early 1900s, states established "mothers' pension" programs, assistance programs that aided widows so that they could care for their children at home rather than institutionalizing children. The Social Security Act of 1935 (P.L. 74-271) provided federal funding for these programs. President Franklin Roosevelt's Committee on Economic Security justified proposing federal financial assistance for mothers' pensions as follows:

> The very phrases "mothers' aid" and "mothers' pensions" place an emphasis equivalent to misconstruction of the intention of the laws. These are not primarily aids to mothers but defense measures for children. They are designed to release from the wage-earning role the person whose natural function is to give her children the physical and affectionate guardianship necessary not alone to keep them from falling into social misfortune, but more affirmatively to rear them into citizens capable of contributing to society.

The Social Security Act established social insurance programs (Old Age and Unemployment Insurance) for those expected to work to have them earn benefits for old age and temporary unemployment. It established need-tested cash benefits for two groups (at that time) not expected to work—the aged and families with children with a single mother or with an incapacitated father. While other groups (particularly the disabled) were subsequently granted benefits under the act, non-aged, able-bodied adult men were excluded from need-tested cash benefit programs as they were expected to work. Of course, the sentiment expressed in the committee's report—that single mothers were not supposed to work but rather to raise children—conflicted with the major social changes of the second half of the 20th Century, which saw increases in mothers' participation in the labor force and expectations that mothers should work.

The program established in the Social Security Act to provide need-tested aid to families with children was first called Aid to Dependent Children (ADC); it was renamed Aid to Families with Dependent Children (AFDC) in 1962. Until 1961, federal funds were only provided to aid families with a single mother or an incapacitated father; in 1961, states were given the *option* to aid families with two able-bodied parents if one parent was unemployed. Even with this mandate, AFDC for families with an unemployed parent paid on more restrictive terms than those that existed for single-parent families or families with an incapacitated parent. Medicaid, the major health care program for the poor, was tied to the receipt of AFDC and thus also became a benefit primarily for families headed by a single parent.

The fact that AFDC generally restricted aid to single-parent families caused concern among policymakers that cash welfare provided an incentive for some families to break up, contributing to the growing number of children living in single-parent, female-headed families. New need-tested benefit programs, designed during the 1960s and 1970s, generally did not restrict aid to families with children based on the absence of a parent. The Food Stamp program (now known as SNAP), created in the 1960s but expanded nationwide in the 1970s, provided aid based on national eligibility standards without regard to family structure. The Earned Income Tax Credit (EITC), first created in 1975, did not legally restrict benefits to single-parent families with children, though it did require that a child be in the tax unit to be eligible for the credit. The Family Support Act of 1988 (P.L. 100-485) converted the state option to aid families with two parents, one unemployed, to a mandate effective October 1, 1990.

The mid-1990s saw major changes in aid to low-income persons and families, including substantial increases in aid to the working poor through expansions of the EITC, increased funding for subsidized child care, and the establishment of the State Children's Health Insurance Program (SCHIP). A small EITC was added for tax filers without children, though the bulk of the EITC expansions were for families with tax filers who had dependent children.

There were also changes that curtailed benefits for those who did not work. The 1996 welfare reform law (Personal Responsibility and Work Opportunity Reconciliation Act of 1996, P.L. 104-193) ended AFDC and its federal rules for determining financial and nonfinancial eligibility for cash welfare, replacing it with the Temporary Assistance for Needy Families (TANF) block grant. States were granted additional latitude in designing their cash assistance programs and were also given the authority to use TANF funds for a wide range of activities beyond those of traditional cash welfare programs. (TANF included some federal requirements, such as work standards and time limits for adult recipients of cash welfare.) The 1996 law also curtailed food stamps for recipients who are able-bodied adults (ages 18 to 50) without dependents (ABAWD). This rule, known as the ABAWD rule, restricts assistance to adults who are not working or participating in a work or training program to three months of assistance in a 36-month period.

Following these changes, cash welfare spending declined substantially. EITC grew, and in the 2000s the food stamp program also grew so that these two programs far surpassed TANF cash welfare as the major sources of cash aid for low-income families.

Eligibility restrictions have generally been lifted for families where the father lives with his children, and such families can be eligible for work supports such as earnings supplements from the EITC or benefits from SNAP. However, noncustodial fathers still face some programmatic barriers in receiving aid from economic assistance programs. Below are descriptions of the major features of three major economic assistance programs—TANF, EITC, and the Supplemental Nutrition Assistance Program (SNAP, the new name for the program formerly called food stamps)—and a discussion about how they relate to noncustodial parents.

Cross-Cutting Issues Affecting Economic Assistance Programs

There are two major issues that affect noncustodial parents across all cash and near-cash need- tested programs. The first centers on the financial incentives and disincentives for the noncustodial parent to join the household and live with their children, for those who have this option. In tax policy, this issue is known as the "marriage penalty"—where a couple is financially better off if two people live apart rather than marry. (However, in terms of the federal income tax, whether a couple is financially better off if they marry or not depends on the circumstances of each individual, so there are both marriage penalties and marriage "bonuses."[21])

There is an analogous situation in need-tested programs. If a noncustodial parent brings income to a family or household, need-tested benefits to that household can be reduced or even eliminated if the noncustodial parent's income puts a family over the income eligibility threshold. Yet this increase in income may not necessarily make the family economically better off than it would be if it was receiving benefits.

The second major issue is whether a noncustodial parent's payment of child support improves the economic well-being of the custodial parent and the children if the custodial parent's family or household receives need-tested aid. If child support income is considered countable income in a need-tested program, it can also reduce or end eligibility for the need-tested benefit. Thus, the noncustodial parent's paying of child support might not fully benefit his children, which reduces the willingness of the noncustodial parent to pay.

TANF

The TANF block grant, while best known as a program that helps states fund cash welfare for needy families with children, helps fund a wide range of benefits and services that help to ameliorate the effects, or address the root causes, of economic disadvantage among families with children. The forms of economic aid include ongoing cash assistance (what most consider traditional welfare), non-recurrent short-term aid, and refundable tax credits for low-income families.

TANF provides states with a set block grant amount that can be used to help achieve its broad goals. The basic block grant is $16.5 billion per year, an amount that has remained the same since its establishment in 1996. There are also supplemental grants to states and contingency funds. The American Recovery and Reinvestment Act of 2009 (P.L. 111-5) established a temporary Emergency Contingency Fund (ECF) for FY2009 and FY20 10 that reimburses states for 80% of the increase in costs of providing basic assistance, short-term non-recurrent aid, and subsidized employment. In addition to federal funds, states have to contribute from their own funds a minimum amount each year (totaling $10.4 billion nationwide).

Under TANF, as under AFDC before 1996, states determine the income and financial resource levels that make a family eligible for cash assistance, as well as the benefit amount. States are free to determine nonfinancial eligibility rules—there are no federal rules restricting aid to two-parent families. Additionally, TANF law and regulations do not define what constitutes a "family," permitting states to include noncustodial parents as part of the "family," thus making them eligible for assistance.

Monthly TANF cash benefit amounts represent only a fraction of poverty-level income in all states. In 2008 for a family of three, benefits ranged from about half of poverty-level income in Alaska ($928 per month; Alaska has a higher poverty level than the 48 contiguous states and the District of Columbia) and California ($723 per month) to 12% of poverty-level income in Mississippi ($170 per month). Moreover, receipt of cash benefits triggers a number of requirements. Families with an adult cash welfare recipient are limited to 60 months of federally funded benefits. These families also are included in determining whether the state meets federal work participation standards (though the work requirements that apply to individual recipients are determined by the state). Custodial parents must also cooperate with the child support enforcement system and assign (i.e., legally turn over rights) to the state any child support received as reimbursement for cash welfare.

In 2009, TANF cash welfare totaled $10 billion. Yet, TANF cash assistance serves only a small fraction of all families with poor children. In 2008, there were 14.1 million poor children, but only a monthly average of 3.1 million children were in families receiving cash assistance. As mentioned above, noncustodial parents can be included in a family (or represent a family on their own) receiving TANF assistance, but this is very rare. In FY2008, there were 70 noncustodial fathers receiving TANF assistance.

Table 2. Earned Income Tax Credits: Maximum Credits and Income Eligibility Amounts for Filers With and Without Children, 2010 (Filers with qualifying children are those filing as head of household, representing a single parent).

	Childless Filers	One Qualifying Child	Two Qualifying Children	Three or More (Temporary, through 2010 only)
Maximum credit	$457	$3,050	$5,036	$5,666
Income threshold for credit eligibility	$13,460	$35,535	$40,363	$43,352
Income threshold as a percent of earnings for a worker at the federal minimum wage working full-time	89%	236%	268%	287%

Source. CRS Report RS2 1352, *The Earned Income Tax Credit (EITC): Changes for 2009 and 2010*, by Christine Scott.

States can also use TANF funds for a wide range of activities other than cash assistance, with few rules or restrictions regarding the design of such benefits and services other than that they be aimed at achieving a TANF goal. This includes economic assistance, such as earnings supplements through refundable tax credits and non-recurrent short-term benefits. For example, New York has used TANF funds to pay for the refundable portion of a "noncustodial Earned Income Tax Credit" that provides a wage supplement to noncustodial parents who pay child support (this will be discussed later in the report under policy options). Noncustodial parents can also benefit from non-recurrent short-term aid—benefits designed to meet needs expected to last four months or less.

Earned Income Tax Credit (EITC)

The EITC was first created in 1975 as a temporary measure to offset payroll taxes for low-income families with children. It was made permanent by the Revenue Act of 1978 (P.L. 95-600), and expanded several times since then. An expansion of the EITC in 1993 was a major component of the strategy to "make work pay" more than welfare. The 1993 expansion also included extending the EITC to tax filers without children, though (as shown below) this credit is small relative to that for filers with children and is available only to those with very low earnings.

As part of the tax code, the budgetary costs of the EITC are realized as foregone tax revenue available to the federal budget. EITC rules are uniform nationwide. The EITC has become the largest form of need-tested cash aid, with credits totaling $50.7 billion for tax year 2008.[22] Of this, the bulk of aid is for families with qualifying children (that is, taxpayers residing with children). EITC credits totaled under $1.4 billion for tax filers without qualifying children.

Table 2 compares EITC rules for childless filers and for single parents with children. As shown in the table, the maximum credit available for childless filers (including noncustodial parents not living with any of their children) is $457, compared to $3,050 for those with one qualifying child and maximum credits over $5,000 for filers with two or more qualifying children. Moreover, the EITC for childless filers is restricted to those with very low earnings. A childless filer becomes ineligible for any EITC credit once his income reaches $13,460. A person who works 40 hours per week at the 2010 federal minimum wage of $7.25 an hour would earn $15,080 annually. Thus, a childless filer who works 40 hours per week at the federal minimum wage for the entire year is *ineligible* for the EITC. In contrast, a single parent who earns more than two times the minimum wage is eligible for the EITC.

Supplemental Nutrition Assistance Program (SNAP)

SNAP, formerly known as food stamps, provides help to low-income families for purchasing food. Like the EITC, it reaches many more families and persons than does cash welfare. In 2009, $50 billion in benefits were paid to 33.7 million persons in 15.2 million households. Federal funds pay 100% of SNAP benefit costs; the federal government and the states share the cost of administering the program.

Low-income households are eligible for SNAP regardless of family type, though in permanent SNAP law there are restrictions for able-bodied adults without dependents (ABAWDS), a group that would include most low-income noncustodial parents. Benefits are determined in federal law and are uniform nationally.[23] For a household consisting of a single person, the maximum monthly SNAP benefit in FY2010 is $200 per month; for a family of three, the maximum monthly benefit is $526 per month.

Though SNAP eligibility is generally not restricted by household type, most SNAP households have members who are elderly, disabled, or children. In FY2008, 51% of all SNAP households included children, 19% had an elderly member, and 23% had a disabled member. Only 17% of SNAP households, totaling 2.2 million, had only nonelderly, able-bodied adults.

The 1996 welfare reform law established the ABAWD rule noted above, which affects able- bodied noncustodial parents who do not live in households with children. The ABAWD rule establishes a time limit for able-bodied adults ages 18 to 50 without dependents who do not work or work less than 20 hours per week, and who are not participating in an education training program. The time limit is three months in a 36-month period. An additional three months of benefits may be paid in the 36-month period if a person becomes employed, works at least 80 hours in a 30-day period, and then becomes unemployed again. The ABAWD rule was suspended for FY2009 and FY2010 under the American Recovery and Reinvestment Act (P.L. 111-5).

Family Support

In addition to economic assistance programs, a number of federal programs are designed to provide other forms of support to families. Three federal programs in particular—Child Support Enforcement, Healthy Marriage, and Responsible Fatherhood—seek to assist men in providing financial and other support to their children or future children. The Child Support Enforcement (CSE) program focuses on collecting child support payments from noncustodial parents for the purpose of contributing to the payment of childrearing costs; however, it also promotes visitation and better relations between custodial and noncustodial parents through grants to states. Eligible activities under the CSE Access and Visitation program include but are not limited to mediation, counseling, education, development of parenting plans, visitation enforcement, and development of guidelines for visitation and alternative custody arrangements. Separately, the Healthy Marriage program recognizes that child well-being is associated with a child living with two parents. The program funds counseling and education initiatives targeted primarily to low-income individuals that seek to facilitate healthy relationships, with the ultimate goal of providing better outcomes for children. The Responsible Fatherhood program focuses on the financial and personal responsibility of noncustodial parents for their children, with the goal of increasing the participation of fathers in their children's lives. Some responsible fatherhood initiatives help noncustodial parents strengthen their parenting skills. Other initiatives try to discourage young men from becoming fathers until they are married and ready for the responsibility.

Child Support Enforcement (CSE)

The CSE program was enacted in 1975 as a federal-state program (Title IV-D of the Social Security Act) to help strengthen families by securing financial support for children from their noncustodial parent on a consistent and continuing basis and by helping some families to remain self-sufficient and off public assistance. Child support payments enable parents who do not live with their children to fulfill their financial responsibility to their children by contributing to the payment of childrearing costs. The CSE program is one of only a few federal programs that specifically interact with men based on their status as fathers.

The CSE program provides seven major services on behalf of children: (1) locating absent parents, (2) establishing paternity, (3) establishing child support orders, (4) reviewing and modifying child support orders, (5) collecting child support payments, (6) distributing child support payments, and (7) establishing and enforcing support for children's medical needs. All 50 states and four jurisdictions (the District of Columbia, Guam, Puerto Rico, and the U.S. Virgin Islands) operate CSE programs.[24] The CSE program is administered by the federal Office of Child Support Enforcement (OCSE), which is in the Department of Health and Human Services' Administration for Children and Families (ACF). The federal government and the states share CSE program costs at the rate of 66% and 34%, respectively. The federal government also gives states an incentive payment to encourage them to operate effective CSE programs.[25] Federal law requires states to reinvest CSE incentive payments back into the CSE program or related activities.

The CSE program serves both poor families (including those who receive TANF benefits) and non-poor families.[26] Child support collected on behalf of non-welfare families goes to the family, usually through the state disbursement unit. However, most child support collections on behalf of families receiving TANF benefits are used to reimburse state and federal governments for TANF payments made to the family.[27]

For low-income, TANF-receipt families, child support payments may not reach the children. This may be a disincentive to pay child support. The rules are complex and may leave the family with little to no benefit over and above the TANF benefit. CSE distribution rules determine which claim is paid first when a child support collection occurs. The order of payment of the child support collection is important because in many cases arrearages are never fully paid. While a family receives TANF cash benefits, the states and federal government retain any current child support and any assigned child support arrearages collected on behalf of that family up to the cumulative amount of TANF benefits paid to the family. While states may pay their share of collections to the family, they must pay the federal government its share of child support collections collected on behalf of TANF families. P.L. 109-171 (the Deficit Reduction Act of 2005, enacted February 8, 2006) helped states pay for the cost of their CSE pass-through and disregard policies by requiring the federal government to share in the costs of the entire amount (up to $100 per month for one child, up to $200 per month for two or more children) of child support collections passed through and disregarded by states (this provision took effect on October 1, 2008).[28] This means that both states and the federal government share in the cost of child support passed through to families (and disregarded by the state in determining the family's TANF cash benefit). Based on June 2009 data, 19 states and the District of Columbia have a child support pass-through and disregard policy, and 31 states do not.[29]

States must distribute the following child support collections to former TANF families first before the state and federal government are reimbursed (the "family-first" policy): (1) all current child support, (2) any child support arrearages that accrue after the family leaves TANF (these arrearages are called never-assigned arrearages), plus (3) any arrearages that accrued before the family began receiving TANF benefits. An exception to this rule occurs when child support arrearages are collected via the federal income tax refund offset program—those collections are divided between the state and federal government.[30] (Any child support arrearages that accrue during the time the family is on TANF belong to the state and federal government.) If a family has never received TANF benefits, the entire amount of the child support payment collected by the state from the noncustodial parent goes to the custodial parent via the state disbursement unit.

In FY2009, about 14% of the CSE caseload[31] consisted of TANF families; about 44% were families who had at some point been on the TANF program, and 43% were families that had never received TANF benefits. In FY2009, the CSE program collected $26.4 billion in child support payments from noncustodial parents and served nearly 15.8 million child support cases.[32] Of the $26.4 billion collected in child support payments, about 92% went to families, 7% went to state and federal governments, and 1% consisted of medical support payments or fees paid to states. On average, in FY2009 the CSE program collected $4.78 in child support payments for each $1 spent on the program. In FY2009, total CSE expenditures amounted to $5.8 billion.

The CSE Program and Noncustodial Fathers

There is a growing consensus that the CSE program is one of the financial keys to helping families become and remain self-sufficient. According to the most recent data available, child support on average constitutes about 17% of family income for households that receive it. Among poor households that receive it, child support constitutes about 30% of family income. [33] Moreover, data indicate that parents who make regular child support payments have better family relationships than those who do not (e.g., they have more interaction with their children).[34]

The CSE program has the potential to impact more children and for longer periods of time than most other federal programs. According to Census Bureau data, in 2007 13.7 million parents had custody of nearly 22 million children under age 21[35] while the other parent lived somewhere else. Of those 13.7 million custodial parents, 35% received child support, 21% received food stamp (SNAP) benefits, 19% received Medicaid benefits, 10% received pubic housing assistance, and 4% received TANF benefits.[36] In many cases, the CSE program may interact with parents and children for 18 years, and in some cases for up to 30 years if the noncustodial parent owes past-due child support.[37]

Over the last 10-15 years, the CSE program has expanded its mission beyond its initial welfare cost-recovery goal to focus on providing its clients with more effective and efficient CSE services and fostering parental responsibility. In FY2009, there were 17.4 million children in the CSE program. Given that most of these children had a living mother and father and that most of them were living with their mother,[38] there were roughly 14 million noncustodial fathers with children on the CSE rolls in FY2009.[39]

Work Programs

To receive federal matching funds, states are required, among other things, to establish and implement a number of child support enforcement tools. One such tool requires state child support officials to have the authority to seek a judicial or administrative order that directs any noncustodial parent owing past-due support to a child receiving TANF benefits to pay that child support in accordance with a plan approved by the court or to participate in appropriate work activities.[40] This enforcement tool, which was mandated by the 1996 welfare reform law (P.L. 104-193), reflected Congress' acknowledgement that many noncustodial parents lack the education and skills necessary to obtain a job. The purpose of the CSE work-activities provision is to provide some noncustodial fathers of children receiving TANF cash assistance with employment opportunities so that they can meet their child support obligations by passing on some of their earnings to their children.[41] The tool allows judges to remand nonpaying noncustodial parents (of a child receiving TANF benefits) to a TANF work program, with the mandate to participate in the program, pay the child support owed, or be confined in jail. This obligation can be monitored to ensure compliance by the noncustodial parent. If the parent is in fact working surreptitiously, it is likely that the work program will conflict with his or her other job, forcing the parent to admit to having earnings and thereby to pay child support. If the noncustodial parent really is jobless, the program can help him or her get a job.[42] One example of a child support-driven employment project is the Texas Noncustodial Parent Choices Program.[43]

In addition, a number of state CSE programs have established employment programs in partnership with state and local workforce development boards and local courts for noncustodial parents regardless of whether the child is enrolled in the TANF program.[44]

Access and Visitation

A noncustodial parent's right to visit with his or her children is commonly referred to as visitation or child access. State family or domestic relations law almost universally treats child support and visitation as completely separate issues. Although a noncustodial parent's right to visit with his or her children and receipt of child support payments by custodial parents are legally separate issues, Census Bureau data indicate it is more likely that noncustodial parents will make payments of child support if they have either joint custody or visitation rights.[45] Also, according to an Urban Institute study, fathers who pay child support (as compared to those who do not) are more likely to visit their children.[46] The Parents' Fair Share (PFS) demonstration, a large-scale demonstration project conducted between 1994 and 1996, was designed to increase support payments, employment and earnings, and parental involvement. The study found that PFS did not generally lead to increases in the frequency or length of contact that noncustodial parents had with their children. However, PFS was effective at increasing the occurrence of regular visits at sites where it served families with relatively low visitation rates (i.e., significant results were seen at the two sites whose level of noncustodial parental involvement was extremely low at the outset of the demonstration program).[47]

Federal and state policymakers have increasingly promoted efforts that address child support and access and visitation in the same forum. In order to promote visitation and better relations between custodial and noncustodial parents, the 1996 welfare reform law (P.L. 104-193) provided $10 million per year for grants to states for access and visitation programs.[48] An annual entitlement of $10 million from the federal CSE budget account is available to states for these grants. Eligible activities include but are not limited to mediation, counseling, education, development of parenting plans, visitation enforcement, and development of guidelines for visitation and alternative custody arrangements.

According to data from the federal Office of Child Support Enforcement (OCSE), all 50 states plus the District of Columbia, Guam, Puerto Rico, and the Virgin Islands have provided access and visitation services to over 500,000 noncustodial parents and their families since the program became operational in FY1998. Most participating noncustodial parents have received parenting education, supervised visitation services, mediation services, and help in developing parenting plans. According to a report on the grant program for FY2008, states contracted with over 374 court and/or community- and faith-based nonprofit service providers for the delivery of access and visitation services to noncustodial parents and their families. The report indicated that over 85,000 individuals were served by the grant program, compared to 20,000 who were served by the grant program during its first year of operation in FY1998.[49]

Modification of Child Support Obligations[50]

In FY2009, $107.6 billion in child support arrearages was owed to families receiving CSE services, but less than 7% ($7.5 billion) of those arrearages was actually paid. Still, 63% of obligors continued to make payments on their child support arrearages. One interpretation of this information is that many noncustodial parents simply have too many financial obligations (e.g., food and shelter for themselves) to cover with their limited incomes; therefore, they may always be a little or a lot behind in meeting their child support obligations.

An Urban Institute study revealed the following findings on those with child support arrearages: (1) high debtors were expected to pay a larger percentage of their income for current child support orders—the median child support order for high debtors (i.e., noncustodial parents who owed $30,000 or more in child support arrearages) was 55% of their income compared to 13% for non-debtors and 22% for those who owed less than $30,000 in child support arrearages; (2) high debtors with a current support order tended to have older orders than other obligors; (3) high debtors were more likely to have multiple current child support orders than non-debtors; (4) high debtors were less likely to pay support than non-debtors; (5) high debtors were less likely to have a known address; and (6) high debtors were twice as likely to have an interstate child support case as a non-debtor.[51]

Under the CSE program, states are given significant latitude regarding modifications and reviews of child support orders.[52] Federal law requires that states give both parents the opportunity to request a review of their child support order at least once every three years, and states are required to notify the parents of this right. In order to prevent child support arrearages, especially for noncustodial parents who are unemployed or in prison, some analysts argue that child support modification laws should be changed so that they are more sensitive to periods of incarceration, unemployment, or injury/illness during which the noncustodial parent's ability to pay child support decreases. They contend that it is virtually impossible for most low-income noncustodial parents with those types of barriers to stay current in meeting their monthly child support payments.

Child Support and Ex-Offenders

About 1.7 million children (under the age of 18) in the United States have parents who are currently incarcerated[53] and more than 10 million U.S. children are separated from one of their parents during a portion of their childhood because of the parent's incarceration.[54]

According to the Bureau of Justice Statistics, of the 1.5 million inmates held in the nation's prisons (federal and state) in mid-2007, approximately 809,800 of them (53%) were parents of minor children. Of the estimated 700,000 persons who are released from prison each year,[55] about 400,000 of them are fathers and mothers.[56] Many of these former inmates have formal child support obligations. Although the proportion of incarcerated noncustodial parents in state and federal prisons is only roughly 5% of the CSE caseload[57] at any one point in time, the cumulative impact is much higher. States indicate that 30%-40% of their "hard to collect from" cases consist of noncustodial parents who have a criminal record.[58]

Pursuant to P.L. 107-273, the Department of Justice (DOJ) and state and local law enforcement agencies have been developing programs to assist with successful re-entry for the thousands of people being released from state and federal prisons each year.[59] Also, HHS, primarily through its federal Office of Child Support Enforcement (OCSE) and state and local CSE agencies, has been approving program waivers and providing demonstration funds that foster effective methods of working with incarcerated and recently released parents and with re-entry programs. HHS has indicated that there are several reasons why CSE agencies should be concerned about ex- offenders and prisoner re-entry programs:

> One is the large number of parents in the child support caseload with a criminal background. Another is the likelihood that their children are recipients of public assistance and are vulnerable to a variety of negative outcomes. A third reason is that these parents are accessible in prison settings and respond positively to outreach efforts by child support personnel. Finally, 16 to 18 percent of child support arrears, which exceeded $107 billion in Fiscal Year (FY) 2007, are held by incarcerated or recently released obligors.[60]

Moreover, given the current economic crisis, states are looking to find creative ways to maximize the use of their resources. State and federal prison officials and CSE officials may find that it is mutually beneficial to work together on behalf of inmates who are parents.[61] Some analysts have suggested that state and federal prisons can strengthen their re-entry programs by incorporating information on CSE obligations and services. Further, CSE programs can make their programs more successful by identifying parents with child support obligations while they are in prison so that parents are better able to avoid the accumulation of excessive child support arrearages and so that information can be provided to prisoners that highlights the benefits of including child support payments in their post-release plans.[62]

Several strategies have been suggested that would involve both the criminal justice system and the CSE program in proactively addressing the reality that more ex-offenders are being released back into local communities. They include (1) making inquiries about a prisoner's parental status and whether or not he or she is required to pay child support as part of the prison intake process; (2) encouraging prisoners to contact the CSE agency regarding questions about the paternity and child support order establishment rules, due process procedures, collection methods, and other concerns; (3) informing inmates about how they can have their child support orders modified so that they do not incur high child support debt while in prison; (4) encouraging inmates to maintain contact with their children while they are in prison; and (5) helping former inmates develop a plan to pay their child support obligations.[63] It has also been suggested that prison intake procedures include an automated data match or weekly population list exchange among corrections and CSE agencies, and that policies be implemented to assist with the child support modification process, such as providing noncustodial parents with forms, addressed envelopes, and postage.[64]

Healthy Marriage Programs

The current healthy marriage initiative (which was part of P.L. 109-171, the Deficit Reduction Act of 2005; enacted February 8, 2006) resulted from two parallel developments.[65] First, in the late 1980s and early 1990s states and local communities came together to develop strategies to strengthen marriage and reduce divorce rates, with the goal of improving child well-being. Most of the early initiatives were targeted toward middle-income persons and focused on educating people on why marriage matters and on providing them with the knowledge and skills necessary to form and sustain a healthy marriage. Second, during the welfare reform debate in the mid-1990s, Congress and the Clinton Administration expressed their concerns about the high cost of nonmarital childbearing and its adverse affect on child well-being. Subsequently, the 1996 welfare reform law (P.L. 104-193) stipulated that TANF funds were to be expended to achieve four statutory goals. One of the goals is to promote the formation and maintenance of two-parent families. Another of the goals is to end the dependence of needy parents on government benefits through work, job preparation, and marriage. [66] In the early 2000s, the George W. Bush Administration directed specific federal agencies[67] to test different ways of strengthening couple relationships and encouraging marriage to stabilize families.[68] The federally funded healthy marriage initiatives implemented after 1996 have been targeted primarily to low-income persons.

From the outset, information from HHS about the healthy marriage initiative proposed by President George W. Bush indicated that the healthy marriage initiative was not about (1) telling people that they should be married, (2) trapping people in abusive marriages, or (3) withdrawing support for single mothers.[69] In proclaiming November 24-30, 2002, as National Family Week, President Bush stated:

> We know that by helping couples to build and sustain strong, two-parent families, we will contribute to the well-being of our children and the strength of our society.... My welfare reform agenda also will strengthen families. We plan on continuing to provide historically high levels of support for childcare and child support enforcement. And we will continue to encourage strong marriages and two-parent married families as a worthy policy goal.[70]

In proclaiming October 12-18, 2003, as Marriage Protection Week, President Bush stated:

> To encourage marriage and promote the well-being of children, I have proposed a healthy marriage initiative to help couples develop the skills and knowledge to form and sustain healthy marriages. Research has shown that, on average, children raised in households headed by married parents fare better than children who grow up in other family structures. Through education and counseling programs, faith-based, community, and government organizations promote healthy marriages and a better quality of life for children. By supporting responsible child-rearing and strong families, my Administration is seeking to ensure that every child can grow up in a safe and loving home.[71]

P.L. 109-171 established within TANF a new categorical grant for healthy marriage promotion initiatives.[72] The healthy marriage promotion initiative is funded at approximately $100 million per year (FY2006-FY2010), to be spent through grants awarded by HHS to support research and demonstration projects by public or private entities, and technical assistance provided to states, Indian tribes and tribal organizations, and other entities.

The activities supported by the DRA healthy marriage initiatives are programs to promote marriage to the general population, such as public advertising campaigns on the value of marriage and education; education on "social skills" (e.g., marriage education, marriage skills, conflict resolution, and relationship skills) for engaged couples, those interested in marriage, or married couples; and programs that reduce the financial disincentive to marry, if combined with educational or other marriage promotion activities. Entities that apply for marriage promotion grants must ensure that participation in such activities is voluntary and that domestic violence concerns are addressed (e.g., through consultations with experts on domestic violence). Although healthy marriage programs are not income-based, the emphasis has been on providing such programs to low-income persons. In 2006, pursuant to the DRA, the HHS Office of Family Assistance (OFA) awarded healthy marriage grants to 123 grantees. The grantees were awarded five-year contracts to implement healthy marriage programs. In FY2009, the contracts (in aggregate) amounted to about $93 million.[73]

The DRA requires healthy marriage grantees to evaluate their programs. The evaluations must identify project milestones and expected outcomes, and describe the services and activities that were implemented in the program. HHS is currently overseeing three large-scale, multi-site longitudinal, scientific evaluations of approaches to providing healthy marriage education services.[74] The final results of the studies are expected between 2011 and 2013.[75] In addition, a comprehensive process and output evaluation of selected ACF healthy marriage projects that serve Hispanic families will be conducted for programs operating during the period from September 2007 through September 2012.[76]

Healthy Marriage Programs and Child Well-Being

A 2008 report examines the economic costs associated with the decline in marriage (which the authors contend increases the number of children and adults eligible for and in need of government services).[77] The authors of the report maintain that the decline in marriage is a product of both divorce and unmarried childbearing. The report estimates that combined, the high rates of divorce and nonmarital childbearing costs U.S. taxpayers at least $112 billion per year in federal, state, and local costs—$70.1 billion of which is federal costs.[78] It states that "these costs arise from increased taxpayer expenditures for antipoverty, criminal justice, and education programs, and through lower levels of taxes paid by individuals who, as adults, earn less because of reduced opportunities as a result of having been more likely to grow up in poverty."[79]

Another study examined the impact of nonmarital childbearing on poverty by using a regression analysis that was based on hypothetically matching single women and men in the population on the basis of factors such as age, education, and race. It found that if the share of children living with two parents in 2000 was increased to what it had been in 1970, the child poverty rate in 2000 would have declined by about 29% compared to the actual decline of 4.5%.[80] If that analysis is applied to 2007 data, 3.7 million fewer children would be in poverty.[81]

Although the DRA healthy marriage program grants are funded through the TANF title of the Social Security Act, the statute makes it clear that the healthy marriage grants are not targeted exclusively to low-income clients. Some observers of the healthy marriage program contend that by encompassing middle-income persons as part of its clientele, the focus of promoting marriage as a poverty-reduction strategy for low-income persons is substantially diminished and thereby activities and services (i.e., program components) that could potentially help persons, especially low-income persons, become more employable[82] (e.g., financial literacy, anger and stress management, self-awareness, emotional control, and respect for others) may not be offered by the program. [83]

Critics of marriage promotion programs caution that government must be careful about supporting programs that cajole individuals into marrying.[84] They note the problems associated with child-bride marriages (i.e., women marrying young) and the short-term and often unhappy nature of the so-called "shotgun" marriage (i.e., marriage hastened by pregnancy).[85] Others contend that marriage promotion programs could encourage women to stay in abusive relationships, that they minimize the excellent job that many single parents do in raising good children, and that marriage is a private rather than a government affair.[86] Some supporters of healthy marriage programs remark that many long-lasting marriages were based on financial alliances (e.g., to increase economic status, family wealth, status in the community, etc.). They assert that policies or programs designed to promote healthy marriages are not intended to force anyone into unwanted, unhealthy relationships, trap women in abusive relationships, or withdraw support from single mothers. Supporters maintain that a relationship is not healthy if it is not safe. They also maintain that marriage is a proven path out of poverty for women. [87]

Nonetheless, many observers are concerned about the impact of healthy marriage promotion programs on survivors of domestic violence or those still in abusive relationships. They assert that all marriage promotion programs must identify and respond to domestic violence issues in a manner that is effective for the individual program in question.[88] Some observers contend that policymakers should focus healthy marriage programs on couples who want to get married, couples who are free from substance abuse problems and/or violent tendencies, and couples who do not have any children by other partners.[89] Others note that the phrase "healthy marriage" is specifically used because healthy marriage initiatives do not tolerate violence of any sort and instead educate couples on effective ways to resolve conflict and successful approaches to forming and sustaining committed and loving long-term marriages.

Early Impact Findings from the Building Strong Families (BSF) Project

The Building Strong Families project is one of the centerpieces of a broad policy strategy to support healthy marriage. The project, which is funded by HHS, seeks to determine whether well-designed interventions can help interested unwed parents realize their hopes for a healthy marriage and thus enhance the well-being of their children. The findings from a recently released evaluation of the short-term impacts of the BSF program were not very encouraging. As indicated above, the BSF project was designed to answer the question of whether relationship-skills education could be effective in improving relationship communication and satisfaction among low-income couples, and whether improving a couple's relationship will enhance the well-being of their children. The BSF project provided relationship and marriage education, case management, and referrals to other services. The 15-month impact evaluation of the stability and quality of the couples' relationships found:

> When results are averaged across all programs, BSF did not make couples more likely to stay together or get married. In addition, it did not improve couples' relationship quality.[90]

In seven of the eight programs evaluated,[91] the BSF program failed to yield better outcomes for program participants than for a control group that did not have access to the program. The evaluation measured the living arrangements, relationship status, relationship quality, extent of father involvement with his child, domestic violence, and economic well-being of approximately 5,000 couples who were randomly assigned to either a control group or a group that had access to a BSF program.[92]

The Obama Administration has indicated that the BSF program was not comprehensive enough to improve the stability of couples and the well-being of children. They contend that the approach outlined in their proposed Fatherhood, Marriage, and Family Innovation Fund initiative will encompass a broader effort that "will provide the comprehensive support that parents and couples need to succeed in their relationships as well as in their roles as workers, providers, and engaged parents."[93]

Other analysts note that some of the findings of the evaluation were confusing. For example, it indicated that the BSF program had negative effects on couples' relationships in Baltimore (where 92% of the couples were African American).[94] But, it also indicated that the BSF program improved the relationship quality of African American couples. Some commentators mention that program implementation problems and inconsistent participation are often reasons for unfavorable outcomes in scientific evaluations of social programs.[95]

The authors of the evaluation point out that early and interim impacts are not always the same as the final results. They also note that the final follow-up survey will examine effects on child wellbeing. The final impact study is expected in 2012.

Responsible Fatherhood Programs

The federal government has also sought to engage men in the lives of their children through what are known as responsible fatherhood programs. These programs recognize that committed, involved, and responsible fathers are important in the lives of their children. These programs seek to promote the financial and personal responsibility of noncustodial parents for their children and increase the participation of fathers in their children's lives.[96] Some responsible fatherhood programs help noncustodial parents strengthen their parenting skills. Other programs try to discourage young men from becoming fathers until they are married and ready for the responsibility.[97]

Even before the federal government became interested in responsible fatherhood programs, many states [98] and localities, private organizations, and nonprofit agencies had been operating responsible fatherhood programs since the early 1990s.[99] From the start, many CSE agencies recognized the importance of cultivating a collaborative relationship with these responsible fatherhood programs. During these early years, it was not always easy to form amicable connections, in part because there had been a longstanding tension between noncustodial parents and the CSE program. Noncustodial parents often claimed that by exclusively focusing on financial support, the CSE system devalued their role as a nurturer, disciplinarian, and mentor. Nonetheless, most responsible fatherhood programs clearly explained the goals and duties of the CSE program and encouraged noncustodial parents to interact with CSE agencies in a proactive manner.

During the 106th Congress, then-Representative Nancy Johnson, chair of the Ways and Means Subcommittee on Human Resources, stated, "to take the next step in welfare reform we must find a way to help children by providing them with more than a working mother and sporadic child support." She noted that many low-income fathers have problems similar to those of mothers on welfare—namely, they are likely to have dropped out of high school, to have little work experience, and to have significant barriers that lessen their ability to find or keep a job. She also asserted that in many cases these men are "dead broke" rather than "deadbeats" and that the federal government should help these noncustodial fathers meet both their financial and emotional obligations to their children.[100] During this same time period, research indicating that father absence had a profound negative impact on children became more widely accepted.

As indicated above, the advantages and disadvantages of having federally funded responsible fatherhood programs have been debated in Congress since the 106th Congress (1999), but it was not until the Deficit Reduction Act of 2005 (P.L. 109-171) that specific funding was provided for these programs.[101] P.L. 109-171 included a provision that provides up to $50 million per year (for each of FY2006-FY20 10) in competitive grants to states, territories, Indian tribes and tribal organizations, and public and nonprofit community organizations (including religious organizations) for responsible fatherhood programs.[102]

Most responsible fatherhood programs include parenting education; training in responsible decision-making, conflict resolution, and coping with stress; mediation services for both parents; problem-solving skills; peer support; and job-training opportunities. Like healthy marriage promotion programs, responsible fatherhood programs are not income-based, but the emphasis has been on providing such programs to low-income persons. According to data from ACF, 99 grantees were awarded five-year contracts to implement responsible fatherhood programs. In FY2009, the contracts (in aggregate) amounted to about $45 million.[103]

An evaluation of responsible fatherhood programs sponsored by HHS—the National Evaluation of the Responsible Fatherhood, Marriage and Family Strengthening Grants for Incarcerated and Reentering Fathers and Their Partners (MFS-IP)—began in 2006 and is still enrolling participants. The evaluation is a multiyear (quasi-experimental) study that is expected to run from 2006 through 2013. A final report on the impact of the program is expected between 2011 and 2013.[104]

Responsible fatherhood programs, in affirming the importance of fathers to their children's wellbeing, have to a certain extent encouraged open communication between noncustodial parents and the CSE program.[105] It is generally agreed that positive, constructive communication between noncustodial parents and CSE agencies sometimes leads to more child support for children.[106] Moreover, findings from several of the demonstration projects that provided noncustodial fathers with employment and supportive services indicate that partnerships between the CSE programs and employment programs can result in significant, sustained increases in the amount of child support paid to custodial parents on behalf of dependent children.[107] Given that recruitment of noncustodial parents to responsible fatherhood programs has been a challenge for many of these programs, some observers contend that it is important to integrate the CSE agency into fatherhood programs because they have more leverage than other agencies or entities in persuading noncustodial parents to participate.[108] They also note that the involvement of the CSE agency provides an improved knowledge base about the program to both staff and participants, and that the CSE agency has the unique ability to implement "realistic" child support order amounts and develop strategies to address noncustodial parents with large amounts of accumulated debt.[109]

Many commentators contend that to help fathers and mothers successfully meet their parental responsibilities, responsible fatherhood programs must be expanded to include broad-based collaborative strategies that include schools, employment programs, prison systems, churches, community organizations, and the health care system.[110] The role of these entities would be to recruit noncustodial parents to the programs and/or provide relevant information, and if appropriate, services, to existing programs. Some child welfare,[111] Head Start,[112] and prisoner reentry programs have included responsible fatherhood initiatives or components in their programs.

Human Capital Programs

Unlike economic assistance programs that seek to support family consumption, and family support programs aimed at nurturing family relationships, human capital programs are focused on helping individuals develop the skills necessary to obtain employment and realize their economic potential. Several human capital programs are specifically designed to enhance employability and earnings.

Though dated, an Urban Institute report from 1997 shows that nearly all noncustodial low-income fathers did not pay child support, and of those who were not in prison, almost half did not work.[113] Further, among the fathers who worked, most held a full-time job but only worked part of the year, leading to low annual earnings of about $5,600. These fathers were far less likely than poor custodial mothers to participate in job search and job training and education programs. The mothers had access to these programs through their enrollment in TANF.

While existing federal workforce development programs do not directly target noncustodial fathers per se, they can play a role in providing these fathers (and others) with opportunities to secure employment, which in turn can help them meet their obligations to their children. These programs provide a combination of job search assistance, education, and training services to prepare individuals for work or improve individuals' labor market performance. In the broadest sense, workforce development includes secondary and postsecondary education, private employer training, and the publicly funded system of job training and employment services. The federal government provides workforce development activities through programs authorized under the Workforce Investment Act (WIA) of 1998 (P.L. 105-220). Workforce development may include activities such as job search assistance, career counseling, occupational skill training, classroom training, or on-the-job training. Title I of WIA provides job training and related services to unemployed and underemployed individuals. Title I programs are administered by the U.S. Department of Labor (DOL), primarily through its Employment and Training Administration (ETA), and carried out by states and localities through what are known as workforce investment boards. Although WIA authorized funding through September 30, 2003, WIA programs continue to be funded through annual appropriations. In FY20 10, programs and activities authorized under Title I of WIA are funded at $5.5 billion, including $3.0 billion for state formula grants for youth, adult, and dislocated worker training and employment activities. The remaining funding is for multiple national programs.

WIA does not expressly provide services to noncustodial parents and it is not clear the extent to which Title I programs reach noncustodial parents, since data are not kept on the parenting status of participants (except whether they are single parents). Generally speaking,

Title I seeks to benefit all participants by increasing their employment, job wages, and occupational skills. As stated in the purpose of Title I, more skilled workers can "improve the quality of the workforce, reduce welfare dependency, and enhance the productivity and competitiveness of the Nation."[114] For noncustodial parents, attachment to the workforce and increased wages can improve their ability to provide for their children. Recent initiatives under WIA to engage prisoners re-entering the community may particularly benefit prisoners who are noncustodial parents and face difficulty in meeting their financial obligations upon re-entry.

One-Stop Delivery System

One of the innovations of WIA was the establishment of the "One-Stop delivery system" (hereinafter, "One-Stop") to provide coordinated access to a range of employment and support services. WIA requires each state to establish a One-Stop delivery system to provide "core" services (i.e., intake and job search assistance) and provide access to "intensive" (i.e., individual employment plans, group counseling, etc.) and "training" (i.e., on-the-job training, skill upgrading and retraining services, etc.) among other services.

Each local workforce investment area in a state is required to have at least one physical One-Stop center in which the aforementioned programs and services are accessible. In addition, a state One- Stop delivery system may provide access to programs and services through a network of affiliated sites and through a network of One-Stop partners linked electronically. As noted, one of the characteristics of the WIA One-Stop system is to provide a central point of service for those seeking employment, training, and related services. To this end, WIA requires multiple partner programs and allows additional programs to operate in the One-Stop system. Some of these programs, including TANF and SNAP, are targeted to low-income individuals.[115]

WIA State Formula Grant Programs

Three formula grant programs for youth, adults, and dislocated workers provide funding for employment and training activities carried out by the national system of One-Stop Career Centers. Funds are distributed to states by statutory formulas based on measures of unemployment and poverty status for youth and adult allocations, and unemployment measures for dislocated worker allocations.[116] States in turn distribute funds to local workforce investment boards (WIBs), which administer and oversee local workforce development activities funded by WIA. There are no eligibility requirements for participation in services funded by the Adult Activities and Dislocated Worker Activities programs, but a youth must be low-income and have a barrier to employment (i.e., be a school dropout, in foster care, etc.) in order to participate in Youth Activities-funded services. However, Section 134(d)(4)(E) of WIA instructs local WIBs to give priority to recipients of public assistance and other low-income individuals for training and intensive services when funds are limited.

The state formula grant programs are the following:

- The Youth Activities program, discussed further under "Youth Activities," below, provides training and related services to low-income youth ages 14 through 21 through formula grants allocated to states, which in turn allocate funds to local entities. Programs funded under the youth activities chapter of WIA provide 10 "program elements" that consist of strategies to complete secondary school, alternative secondary school services, summer employment, work experience, occupational skill training, leadership development opportunities, supportive services, adult mentoring, follow-up services, and comprehensive guidance and counseling. In FY20 10, funding for state grants for Youth Activities is $924 million.

- The Adult Activities program provides training and related services to individuals ages 18 and older through formula grants allocated to states, which in turn allocate funds to local entities. There are no income requirements to participate in WIA Adult Activities programs. Participation in the adult program is based on a "sequential service" strategy that consists of three levels of services. Any individual may receive "core" services, which primarily encompass job search assistance. To receive "intensive" services, including individual career planning and prevocational services (i.e., interview skills, development of learning skills, etc.), an individual must have received core services and need intensive services to become employed or to obtain or retain employment that allows for self- sufficiency. To receive training services— including on-the-job training, skill upgrading, and retraining—an individual must have received intensive services and need training services to become employed or to obtain or retain employment that allows for self-sufficiency. In FY20 10, funding for state grants for Adult Activities is $862 million.

- A majority of WIA Dislocated Worker Activities funds are allocated by formula grants to states, which in turn allocate funds to local entities to provide training and related services to individuals who have lost their jobs and are unlikely to return to those jobs or similar jobs in the same industry. As in the Adult Activities program, there are no income requirements to participate in the WIA Dislocated Worker Activities program. The remainder of the appropriation is reserved by DOL for a National Reserve account, which in part provides for National Emergency Grants[117] to states or local entities (as specified under Section 173).[118] In FY2010, funding is $1.2 billion for state grants for Dislocated Worker Activities and $229 million for the National Reserve.[119]

Detailed WIA data on demographics and services received are based on the concept of program "exiters." An exiter is a participant who received a service funded by WIA or a partner program, has not received the service for 90 consecutive calendar days, and is not scheduled to receive future services.[120]

Of the three programs, the Adult Activities program serves the most individuals. In the most recent program year for which data are available (PY2008), 849,738 adults exited the Adult Activities program. Notably, about 6 out of 10 exiters received only core services, which are generally limited to job search assistance and do not include education and job training. Of the approximately 40% of exiters who went on to receive more specialized services, including job training,

- 14.7% were single parents,
- 44.1% were low-income,
- 16.4% were recipients of public assistance,
- 5.7% were offenders, and

- 14.6% did not hold high school degrees.

Reintegration of Ex-Offenders Program

In addition to state formula grants, WIA authorizes funding for several national programs—Job Corps, Native American programs, Migrant and Seasonal Farmworker programs, Veterans' Workforce Investment programs, Demonstration and Pilot programs, National Emergency Grants, and YouthBuild. Funding for these national programs combined is $2.3 billion in FY2010. Within the national programs, WIA Section 171 (Demonstration and Pilot programs) provides funding for more targeted populations. In general, Section 171 authorizes the Secretary of Labor to provide grants or contracts to carry out projects that address training and employment needs. One of the services implemented under Section 171 of WIA (and Section 212 of the Second Chance Act of 2007, P.L. 110-199) is the Reintegration of Ex-Offenders program (REO). This program is the most relevant to low-income and noncustodial males.

The Reintegration of Ex-Offenders program consolidated funding from two previous demonstration projects, the Prisoner Reentry Initiative (PRI) and the Responsible Reintegration of Youthful Offenders (RRYO). PRI, which was first funded in FY2005, funds faith-based and community organizations that help recently released prisoners find work when they return to their communities. RRYO, first funded in FY2000, supports projects that serve young offenders and youth at risk of becoming involved in the juvenile justice system. In FY2008, the Reintegration of Ex-Offenders program combined the PRI and RRYO into a single funding stream. In FY2010, funding for this single program is $108.5 million.

In the FY2010 budget, the Administration indicated that new grants under the REO program "may prioritize programs which include transitional job strategies" and that the Employment and Training Administration, which is responsible for administering the REO program, may fund programs that prepare ex-offenders for employment in green industries and other high-demand fields.[121] In addition, ETA plans "to coordinate" with other relevant social service programs, such as responsible fatherhood initiatives.[122]

Youth Programs

The nation's future depends on today's young people leaving school prepared for college or the workplace and beginning to make positive contributions to society. Some youth, however, face barriers to becoming taxpayers, workers, and participants in civic life. They may also disengage from their own families, including their children. Social science research indicates that many low-income, disadvantaged youth come from families in which their father was absent from the home. Single-parent households tend to have less income and other resources than two-parent households. Having fewer resources lowers children's school performance, decreases their labor force participation, and contributes to early childbearing.[123] For example, multiple studies of births among teenagers show that teens in single-parent households are more likely to have children and to do so outside of marriage compared to those in two-parent families.[124]

While the federal government does not have a single approach or policy for serving disadvantaged young people, select youth programs seek to ameliorate the negative outcomes they may experience. [125] The goals of these federal programs are not necessarily to engage teens and young adults in the lives of their children—if in fact they have children—but rather, to ensure that these young people are adequately prepared for adulthood. Three types of programs in particular focus on delaying early family formation or engaging young people in productive activities as they transition to adulthood: teenage pregnancy prevention programs, youth employment programs, and education programs. (Notably, the workforce programs include education services and the education programs include workforce elements.) Yet by preparing youth for adulthood, these programs may ultimately put teenagers and young adults in a better position to provide for and be involved in the lives of their (current or future) children.

Teenage Pregnancy Prevention Programs

In 2008, 10.2% of all U.S. births and 21.8% of nonmarital births were to teens.[126] Although the birth rate for U.S. teens has dropped in 15 of the last 17 years, it remains higher than the teenage birth rate of most industrialized nations.[127]

The high volume of pregnancies and birth rates among teenage and never-married women is often attributed to a liberal view of sexual activity. [128] Some analysts also contend that contraceptive advancements have afforded women a false sense of security, thereby contributing to increased sexual activity and more pregnancies. The academic and professional communities also maintain that teen parenthood is one of the negative consequences of growing up without a father present in the household. [129] Moreover, policymakers suggest that, prior to its reform, "welfare" was seen as a guaranteed source of income for unmarried teenage mothers with grim marriage and job prospects. The president of the Alan Guttmacher Institute, an organization that studies reproductive health, commenting on a study about adolescent pregnancy and childbearing in "developed" countries, stated: "In the United States, poverty and inequity clearly are behind much of our high rates of pregnancy, birth and abortion. But lack of sensitive, confidential, lowcost contraceptive services and the denial of accurate and frank information about sex, are equally to blame."[130]

An October 2006 study by the National Campaign to Prevent Teen Pregnancy estimated that in 2004, adolescent childbearing cost U.S. taxpayers about $9 billion per year: $2.3 billion in child welfare benefits; $1.9 billion in health care expenses; $2.1 billion in spending on incarceration (for the sons of women who had children as adolescents); $6.3 billion in lost tax revenue because of lower earnings of the mothers, fathers, and children (when they were adults); and $3.6 billion in offsetting public assistance savings (younger teens receive less annually over a 15-year period than those who give birth at ages 20-2 1). Research indicates that teens who give birth are less likely to complete high school and go on to college, thereby reducing their potential for economic self-sufficiency. The research also indicates that the children of teens are more likely than children of older parents to experience problems in school and drop out of high school, and are more likely to repeat the cycle of teenage pregnancy and poverty as adults. The 2006 report contends that if the teen birth rate had not declined between 1991 and 2004, the annual costs associated with teen childbearing would have been almost $16 billion (instead of $9 billion).[131]

In recognition of the negative, long-term consequences associated with teenage pregnancy and births, the prevention of teenage and out-of-wedlock childbearing is a goal of federal social programs. Thus, there are many federal laws that address the subject of teen pregnancy prevention. The Adolescent Family Life (AFL) program, created in 1981 (Title XX of the Public Health Services Act), was the first federal program to focus on adolescents. The AFL program provides comprehensive and innovative health, education, and social services to pregnant and parenting adolescents and their infants, male partners, and families. The AFL program is authorized to provide comprehensive sex education information, including information about contraceptive methods as well as abstinence-only-focused educational information.

The Title V Abstinence Education block grant to states (Section 510 of the Social Security Act, established in 1996 by P.L. 104-193) authorized a separate state formula grant program to support abstinence-only education programs. Funds are awarded to states based on the proportion of low- income children in each state compared to the national total, and may only be used for teaching abstinence. To receive funding, a state must match every $4 in federal funds with $3 in state funds. Section 510 provided $50 million for each of the six fiscal years FY1 998-FY2003. Although the program has not been reauthorized, it received many temporary funding extensions between 2003 and 2009. Funds are administered by the Administration for Children and Families (ACF) within HHS. Prior to enactment of P.L. 111-148 (the Patient Protection and Affordable Care Act, PPACA), funding for the Title V Abstinence Education program had ended on June 30, 2009.

PPACA restored funding for the somewhat controversial abstinence-only approach to teen pregnancy prevention. PPACA appropriated $250 million for the abstinence-only block grant at $50 million per year for five years (FY2010-FY2014) . Concurrently, PPACA also established a new state formula grant program and appropriated $375 million at $75 million per year for five years (FY2010-FY2014) to enable states to operate a new Personal Responsibility Education program, which is a comprehensive approach to teen pregnancy prevention that educates adolescents on both abstinence and contraception to prevent pregnancy and sexually transmitted diseases. It also provides youth with information on several adulthood preparation subjects (e.g., healthy relationships, adolescent development, financial literacy, parent-child communication, educational and career success, and healthy life skills). The new Personal Responsibility Education program is mandated to provide programs that are evidence-based, medically accurate, and age-appropriate.

P.L. 111-117, the Consolidated Appropriations for FY20 10, included a new discretionary Teen Pregnancy Prevention (TPP) program that provides grants and contracts, on a competitive basis, to public and private entities to fund "medically accurate and age appropriate" programs that reduce teen pregnancy. Of the $110 million appropriated for the TPP program for FY20 10, $75 million is for replicating programs that are proven through rigorous evaluation to be effective in reducing teenage pregnancy, behavioral factors underlying teen pregnancy, or other related risk factors; and $25 million is for research and demonstration grants. The TPP program is administered by the new Office of Adolescent Health within HHS. P.L. 111-117 also provides a separate $4.5 million (within the Public Health Service Act program evaluation funding) to carry out evaluations of teenage pregnancy prevention approaches.

Table 3 shows that federal funding for the teen pregnancy prevention programs mentioned above amount to $256 million for FY20 10. (Note that the AFL program is required to fund only comprehensive sex education-type programs in FY20 10.)

Table 3. Federal Funding for Teen Pregnancy Prevention Programs, FY2010.

Program Name	Federal Funding for FY20 10 (in millions of dollars)
Teen Pregnancy Prevention (TPP) Program	$110.0
Evaluation Funds for TPP Program	4.5
Adolescent Family Life (AFL) Program	16.7
Personal Responsibility Education Program	75.0
Title V Abstinence Education Block Grant	50.0
Total	$256.2

Source. Table prepared by the Congressional Research Service (CRS) based on data from the Department of Health and Human Services (HHS).

In addition, there are several other federally funded programs that provide pregnancy prevention information and/or services to both teens and adults. These programs include Medicaid Family Planning, the Title X Family Planning Program, the Maternal and Child Health block grant, the TANF block grant program, the Title XX Social Services block grant, and a couple of teen pregnancy prevention programs administered by the Centers for Disease Control and Prevention (within HHS).

Select Youth Workforce Programs

Since the 1930s, federal job training and employment programs and policies have sought to connect vulnerable youth ages 14 through 24 to work and school. Generally, these young people have been defined as being vulnerable because they are low-income and have a barrier to employment, such as having dropped out of school or spent time in foster care. The Workforce Investment Act of 1998 (P.L. 105-220) is the most recent federal law to provide job training and related services to unemployed and underemployed individuals, including youth. All youth job training programs and related services are authorized under Title I of WIA and are carried out by the Department of Labor. Each of the programs has a similar purpose: to connect youth to educational and employment opportunities, and to offer similar services for doing so. As discussed previously in this report, the unemployment rate for teens is higher than for young adults and adults generally. The 2009 rate is the highest it has been during the post-World War II period, and nearly 50% of black teens were unemployed in 2009. Further, compared to their female counterparts, young men ages 16 through 24 are more likely to not be in school or working for at least one year.[132]

The WIA programs for youth include

- WIA Youth Activities, a formula grant program that includes employment and other services that are provided year-round;
- Job Corps, a program that provides job training and related services primarily at residential centers maintained by contractor organizations;
- YouthBuild, a competitive grant program that emphasizes job training and education in construction; and

- Reintegration of Ex-Offenders, a demonstration program for juvenile and adult offenders that provides job training and other services and is authorized under WIA's pilot and demonstration authority.

Together, these programs make up the federal job training system for disadvantaged young people. Youth in the programs often learn job training skills or are employed and are simultaneously working toward a high school diploma or its equivalent. However, services are carried out differently and by distinct entities. For example, local areas must provide 10 specific elements, including mentoring and follow-up services, to youth who receive services under the WIA Youth Activities formula grant program. YouthBuild program participants engage in employment and other activities primarily related to housing and other types of construction work. Job Corps is the only one of the programs that provides residential services, where youth can live onsite and receive health care services, child care, and other supports. The Reintegration of Ex-Offenders program is made up of several types of grants that provide educational services to students in schools that have been classified as "persistently dangerous," as well as employment and alternative education services to youth engaged in the juvenile justice system.

The programs generally serve vulnerable youth, but some have more targeted eligibility criteria. Participants in the Youth Activities formula grant program, YouthBuild, and Job Corps must be low-income and have specific employment barriers. The Youthful Offender component of the Reintegration of Ex-Offenders serves youth who have become involved in the juvenile justice or criminal justice system or youth at risk of becoming involved. Notably, young men are well represented in these programs, making up about half or more of the participants in each of the programs. For example, approximately 60% of the participants in Job Corps and approximately 70% of the participants in YouthBuild are males.[133]

The Youth Activities program and the Job Corps program, described in further detail directly below, highlight WIA's focus on helping at-risk young people achieve economic independence and gain skills needed for the workplace.

Youth Activities

The WIA Youth Activities formula grant program is arguably the centerpiece of the federal youth job training and employment system. As specified in the law, the program has several purposes: to provide assistance in achieving academic and employment success through activities that improve educational and skill competencies and foster effective connections to employers; to ensure ongoing adult mentoring opportunities for eligible youth; to provide opportunities for training, continued supportive services, and participation in activities related to leadership, citizenship, and community service; and to offer incentives for recognition and achievement to youth. Congress appropriated $924.1 million to Youth Activities in FY2010.

The program provides services in two ways: (1) through contracted organizations that receive WIA Youth Activities funding and collectively provide direct services to youth through what is referred to hereinafter as a local youth program; and (2) through the One-Stop System, described above. Youth Activities funds are distributed by DOL to state workforce investment boards (WIBs), which oversee workforce activities in each state, based on a formula that accounts for unemployment rates and the poverty status of youth. The state WIBs in turn distribute formula funds to programs run by local WIBs, based on similar criteria. Like state WIBs, local WIBs oversee workforce activities, but only for a designated local area. Among other activities, each local board must establish what is known as a "youth council," comprised of representatives that assist the WIB in awarding grants or contracts to youth providers that carry out youth workforce activities. Local programs must provide 10 activities or "elements" to youth that focus on education attainment, employment, follow-up services, and civic engagement.

A youth is eligible for Youth Activities if he or she is ages 14 through 21, a low-income individual, and has one or more of the following barriers: [134] deficient in basic literacy skills; a school dropout; homeless, a runaway, or a foster child; pregnant or parenting; an offender; or requires additional assistance to complete an educational program or to secure and hold employment. At least 30% of all Youth Activities funds must be used for activities for out-of-school youth, meaning youth who have dropped out *or* received a high school diploma or its equivalent but are basic skills deficient, unemployed, or underemployed. [135]

The data on participation in the program are based on the concept of program "exiters." An exiter is a participant who received a service funded by WIA or a partner program, but has not received the service for 90 consecutive calendar days and is not scheduled to receive future services. The most recent data on youth participants (i.e., exiters) is for April 1, 2008, through March 31, 2009 (i.e., PY2008). [136] Over 115,000 youth ages 14 through 21 exited the program, of whom a majority (55.6%) were female; 33% were African American and 33% were Hispanic; 14% were pregnant or parenting; and nearly all (94.5%) were low-income.

Youth Activities Coordination with TANF

In February 2009, President Obama signed into law the American Recovery and Reinvestment Act of 2009 (P.L. 111-5, ARRA, Recovery Act). One of the stated purposes of ARRA is to preserve existing jobs and create new jobs. To this end, the law appropriated $1.2 billion for the WIA Youth program. The law emphasized that funds should be spent on summer youth employment opportunities, as well as year-round employment activities for older youth. ARRA extends the age of eligibility from 21 to 24 for activities funded pursuant to the law. Funding for the act is available through PY2010, which ends June 30, 2011. The Departments of Health and Human Services and Labor issued a joint letter in January 2010 to encourage state and local TANF agencies and WIBs to consider using the TANF Emergency Contingency Fund to provide subsidized employment, as well as other benefits and services, to low-income youth. Further, the agencies encouraged co-enrollment of youth in the TANF and applicable WIA programs so that "participants in the TANF-funded subsidized employment opportunities can benefit from additional WIA services such as supportive services, occupational skills training, and other relevant services." [137] As of June 2010, 12 states and the District of Columbia have applied for and received approval to use TANF funding for summer youth employment. [138]

Job Corps [139]

Job Corps is a job training program first established in 1964 that provides services to low-income individuals ages 16 through 24, generally through contracts administered by DOL with corporations and nonprofit organizations. The purpose of Job Corps is to provide young people with the skills needed to obtain and hold a job, enter the Armed Forces, or enroll in advanced training or higher education. [140] The program provides education and training, primarily in a residential setting, to vulnerable youth. Youth also receive support services, including child care, health education, counseling, and recreation. A youth is eligible for the program if she or he is low-income and meets one or more of the following criteria: basic skills deficient; homeless, a runaway, or a foster child; a parent; or an individual who requires additional education, vocational training, or intensive counseling and related assistance in order to participate in regular schoolwork or to secure and maintain employment. Currently, there are 123 Job Corps centers in 48 states, the District of Columbia, and Puerto Rico.[141] In FY20 10, Congress appropriated $1.7 billion to Job Corps. In PY2008 (the most recent year data are available), Job Corps served 60,900 youth, of whom most (59%) were male, 52% were black, and 17% were Hispanic.[142]

Most youth enroll in Job Corps without a high school credential. According to a random assignment evaluation of the program that began in 1994 and ended in 2006, the program substantially increased the education and training services that youth receive. [143] On average, program participants received the instructional equivalent of one additional year in school, compared to about half that time for youth who were not in the program. In turn, youth improved their literacy and numeracy skills, and they were more likely to obtain a GED and vocational certificates. Further, more than 90% of Job Corps enrollees participated in an education or training program during the 48 months after random assignment, compared to 72% of the control group.[144] Participation rates were highest in GED programs (37%); high school (32%); and vocational, technical, or trade schools (29%). The program substantially increased the receipt of GEDs and vocational certificates by program participants by more than 20 percentage points each. Job Corps generated employment and earnings gains initially, but not in the long run. Except among the oldest students (those ages 20 through 24), there were no longer-term program impacts on earnings.

Select Education Programs

Finally, select education programs, carried out by the Department of Education, seek to engage disadvantaged youth in activities that will lead to a high school diploma and college degree. As shown in **Figure 4**, men's earnings are strongly associated with educational attainment. While men with advanced degrees have seen the biggest gains in inflation-adjusted wages over time, the inflation-adjusted wages of men who are high school dropouts or high school graduates have declined.

Select federal education programs, authorized under separate laws, provide support for vulnerable young adults who are at risk of dropping out or have already done so. These include the TRIO programs to encourage vulnerable high school students to go to colleges that are authorized under the Higher Education Act of 1965 (HEA), as amended; and those that fund vocational training, including the Basic State Grants program, Tech-Prep, and other smaller programs authorized under the Carl D. Perkins Career and Technical Education Improvement Act of 2006 (P.L. 109- 270, Perkins), as amended. In addition, the Department of Defense's quasi-military training program—known as Youth ChalleNGe—includes several components, including education.

Federal TRIO Programs

The Higher Education Act of 1965 (HEA, P.L. 89-329) authorizes a broad array of programs that together constitute the largest source of federal funds to support postsecondary education. HEA programs include numerous federal student aid (FSA) programs, as well as programs through which federal assistance is made available to institutions of higher education (IHEs) and other entities that support postsecondary education. The programs discussed below are intended to encourage and facilitate low-income students attending postsecondary institutions, among other similar and related goals. [145] The Higher Education Opportunity Act (HEOA, P.L. 110-315) recently amended and extended the authorization for many HEA programs through FY20 14.

The Department of Education awards five-year competitive grants to IHEs, public and private agencies and organizations, and, as appropriate, secondary schools under seven TRIO programs that are authorized under HEA. Three of these programs serve youth who are low-income, not yet enrolled in postsecondary education, and have barriers such as being a school dropout: Upward Bound (UB), Talent Search (TS), and Educational Opportunity Centers (EOC). The three programs are intended to support the educational persistence and achievement of disadvantaged students. At least two-thirds of each program's participants must be low-income and a first generation college student. Services must also be made available to foster care youth (including youth in foster care and youth who have left foster care after reaching age 13) or to homeless children and youth as defined under the McKinney-Vento Homeless Assistance Act. In FY2009, the most recent year for which data are published, the programs served over 800,000 students. [146]

Carl D. Perkins Career and Technical Education Improvement Act of 2006 (Perkins)

The purpose of the Perkins Act is to "develop more fully the academic and career and technical skills of secondary education students and postsecondary education students" who enroll in career and technical education (CTE) programs. This is to be accomplished through such activities as developing challenging academic and technical standards and assisting students in meeting these standards; promoting the development of services and activities that integrate academic and career and technical instruction and link secondary and postsecondary education; supporting partnerships among secondary schools, postsecondary institutions, local WIBs, business and industry, and intermediaries; and providing individuals with opportunities for lifelong learning to develop the knowledge and skills needed to help the United States be competitive internationally.

The Perkins Act was most recently reauthorized by the Carl D. Perkins Career and Technical Education Improvement Act of 2006 (Perkins IV, P.L. 109-270). The act contains two programs that provide federal funds to support career and technical education and relevant job experience. These programs are the Basic State Grants program (the larger program) and the Tech-Prep program. Most funding for CTE is provided at the state and local levels. As the federal share of funding for CTE represents a relatively small share of the total funding provided for CTE, it is not possible to determine which courses are fully or partially supported with federal dollars.

Basic State Grants Program

The majority of federal funding provided for CTE is delivered through basic state grants (Title I). The state allotment is based on the state's population of persons ages 15 through 65 and the state's per capita income. The law requires states to distribute at least 85% of state grant funds to the local level (i.e., to eligible recipients, such as local education agencies (LEAs) and community colleges). States have discretion in how much funding is distributed for career and technical education at the secondary level versus postsecondary CTE. That is, a state could decide to use most or all of its basic state grant funding for either secondary or postsecondary education. In practice, states generally fund both levels of education. In FY2010, funding was $1.2 billion.

While each state determines what percentage of funding will be used at the secondary and postsecondary levels, the distribution of these funds to the secondary level is determined by a formula that accounts for age distribution and poverty. At the postsecondary level, funds are distributed based on each eligible institution's number of Pell grant recipients and recipients of assistance from the Bureau of Indian Affairs.

The Perkins Act includes both required and allowable uses of these funds at the state and local levels. Several of these activities focus on both education and workforce development. In addition to the required and allowable uses of funds at the state level, the eligible agency (i.e., state) must adopt procedures it considers necessary to coordinate state level activities under Perkins with state level activities undertaken by state boards under Section 111 of WIA, which refers to the One-Stop System. The eligible agency must also adopt procedures it considers necessary to make available to the One-Stop System within the state a listing of all school dropout, postsecondary education, and adult education programs receiving assistance through the Perkins Act.

Tech-Prep Program

The Tech-Prep Program is authorized under Title II of the Perkins Act. Tech-Prep grants are awarded to consortia consisting of participants from both the secondary and postsecondary levels, such as a local education agency (LEA); a nonprofit institution of higher education offering a two-year associate's degree program, two-year certificate program, or a two-year apprenticeship program; or a proprietary institution of higher education offering a two-year associate's degree program. Consortia members may also include institutions of higher education that award a baccalaureate degree, as well as employers, business intermediaries, and labor organizations. Consortia participants develop agreements to provide at least two years of secondary school instruction prior to high school graduation and at least two years of postsecondary education instruction or an apprenticeship program of at least two years following high school graduation. In FY20 10, funding was $102.9 million.

A Tech-Prep program of study is required to build student competence in technical skills and in core academic subjects . A Tech-Prep program of study is also required to integrate academic and career and technical instruction with work-based learning experiences when possible, and to provide technical preparation in a career field. A Tech-Prep program must coordinate its activities with activities conducted under Title I of the act (Basic State Grant Program). The Perkins Act allows states to maintain a separate Tech-Prep program or combine their Tech-Prep funds with the Basic State Grant funds. If eligible agencies choose to combine program funds, funds are considered as being allotted under the Basic State Grant program and must be distributed to eligible recipients in accordance with the formulas pertaining to that program. Prior to the most recent reauthorization of the Perkins Act, states were not able to combine funds for these purposes.

Student Participation in Career and Technical Education

During PY2006-2007 (the most recent year for which data are available), states reported that about 15.6 million students were enrolled in secondary and postsecondary CTE programs. These enrollment figures represent an unduplicated count of all students reported by each state as having taken one or more CTE courses. These courses, however, *may or may not* have been funded with federal Perkins funds. Most funding for CTE is provided at the state and local levels.

Approximately 2.6 million youth (16% of total students enrolled in CTE) were enrolled in Tech- Prep in PY2006-2007.[147] Of all CTE students, the majority were secondary education students. At both the secondary and postsecondary levels, most participating students were white, followed by Hispanic and black students. In addition, about one-third of participating students at the secondary and postsecondary levels were economically disadvantaged.

Youth ChalleNGe Program

The Youth ChalleNGe Program is a quasi-military training program carried out by the Army National Guard to improve outcomes for youth who have dropped out of school or have been expelled. Education and mentoring are major components of the program. It was established as a pilot program under the National Defense Authorization Act for FY2003 (P.L. 102-484), and Congress permanently authorized it under the National Defense Authorization Act for FY1998 (P.L. 105-85). Currently, 35 programs operate in 28 states, the District of Columbia, and Puerto Rico. Congress appropriated $107 million for FY20 10. In 2009, 7,912 youth graduated from the program, of whom 79% were males, 45% were white, 28% were black, and 18% were Hispanic.[148]

Youth are eligible for the program if they are ages 16 to 18 and enroll prior to their 19th birthday, have dropped out of school or been expelled, are unemployed, are not currently on parole or probation for anything other than juvenile status offenses and not serving time or awaiting sentencing, and are drug-free. The program consists of three phases: a two-week, pre-program residential phase where applicants are assessed to determine their potential for completing the program; a 20-week residential phase; and a 12-month post-residential phase. During the residential phase, youth—known as cadets—work toward their high school diploma or GED and develop life-coping, job, and leadership skills. They also participate in activities to improve their physical well-being, and they engage in community service. Youth develop a "Post-Residential Action Plan (P-RAP)" that sets forth their goals, as well as tasks and objectives to meet those goals. The post-residential phase begins when graduates return to their communities, continue in higher education, or enter the military. The goal of this phase is for graduates to build on the gains made during the residential phase and to continue to develop and implement their P-RAP.

A core component of the post-residential phase is mentoring, during which a cadet works with a mentor to meet his or her goals as set forth in the P-RAP. This component is referred to as the "Friendly Mentor Match" process. Parents and youth are asked to nominate at least one prospective mentor prior to acceptance into the program. They are advised to identify an individual who is respected by the youth and would be a good role model.

Youth ChalleNGe was evaluated by the Manpower Development Research Corporation (MDRC), a social policy research organization, and interim findings have been released. [149]

The results of the evaluation are based on a survey administered after the youth left the program about nine months after the members of the program and control groups entered the study, when youth had just begun the program's post-residential phase, and 21 months later when youth had completed the post-residential phase. The initial evaluation found that the program group was much more likely than the control group to have obtained a GED (45.6% vs. 10.1%), to be working (51.2% vs. 42.1%) and/or attending college (10.9% vs. 2.7%), to report having good or excellent health (76.7% vs. 68.4%), to have high levels of self-efficacy (11.0% vs. 7.0%), and to be less likely to have been arrested since the start of the evaluation (14.2% vs. 20.0%). These differences are statistically significant, meaning that they can be attributed to the program's intervention. The follow-up evaluation found that the Youth ChalleNGe participants were more likely to have earned a high school diploma or GED (60.5% vs. 36.4%) and to be engaged in productive activities, including work, school or job training activities, or the military (72.1% vs. 66.4%).

FEDERAL POLICY OPTIONS

While not comprehensive, this section discusses several federal policy options that may reduce some of the economic and other barriers faced by low-income men, many of whom are fathers. This section highlights one or two policy options from each of the four policy domains discussed earlier: economic assistance, family support, human capital, and disadvantaged youth. These options include establishing an Innovation Fund that provides services to both noncustodial parents and custodial parents; examining strategies for reducing child support arrearages; changing the financing structure of child support enforcement (CSE) access and visitation programs for noncustodial parents; enhancing or expanding job training and education programs to assist low-income men and youth, which in turn can help them in providing for their (current or future) families; redefining eligibility for certain programs so that disadvantaged young adults can receive more holistic training and other services that may better prepare them for adulthood; encouraging states to serve noncustodial parents in their TANF programs; and modifying the Earned Income Tax Credit (EITC) to make noncustodial parents eligible.

Competitive Grant Funds (with an Evaluation Component) to Improve Family Well-Being

The Obama Administration's FY2011 budget includes a proposal to redirect funds from the current Healthy Marriage and Responsible Fatherhood Programs ($150 million per year through FY2010; the responsible fatherhood portion is $50 million per year) to a proposed $500 million Fatherhood, Marriage, and Families Innovation Fund. The proposed Fatherhood, Marriage, and Families Innovation Fund would be available for one year (FY2011) to provide three-year competitive grants to states.

Some commentators maintain that most low-income mothers and fathers acknowledge and accept their responsibility to their children, but also note that many of them do not have the resources to meet that responsibility. They contend that the Innovation Fund may provide the opportunities and stepping stones that many low-income parents need to benefit themselves and their children.[150] According to one budget document, "The Fatherhood, Marriage, and Families Innovation Fund will serve as a catalyst for innovative service models that integrate a variety of service streams. The results from these demonstrations could form the basis for possible future TANF and CSE program changes at the federal or state level based on a multidimensional picture of the dynamics of family functioning and material self-sufficiency and child well-being."[151]

The proposed Fatherhood, Marriage, and Families Innovation Fund would create equal funding streams to support the following two objectives: (1) supporting state-initiated comprehensive responsible fatherhood initiatives, including those with a marriage component, that rely on strong partnerships with community-based organizations; and (2) supporting state-initiated comprehensive family self-sufficiency demonstrations that seek to improve child and family outcomes by addressing the employment and self-sufficiency needs of custodial parents who face serious barriers to self sufficiency. The $500 million fund would be divided equally between the two components. Grantees would be required to participate in a rigorous evaluation as a condition of receiving funding. Grantees would be able to use the funding for program administration, monitoring, technical assistance, and research and evaluation.[152]

The core elements of the fatherhood initiatives, which focus on *noncustodial parents*, would typically include co-parenting services and conflict resolution skills development; connection to job training and other employment services; child support enforcement case management assistance; employment preparation services; training subsidies; legal services; substance abuse and mental health treatment (typically through partnerships with public agencies and community- based providers); linkages to domestic violence prevention programs; and linkages to public agencies and community-based providers offering housing assistance, benefits enrollment, and other services. Grantees would be required to demonstrate strong linkages with state CSE programs, and there would be a preference for applicants that intend to make resources available to community-based organizations to help implement components of the proposed initiatives. In addition, grantees would need to ensure that the new programs address issues related to domestic violence and have in place a plan to reduce the risk of domestic violence.[153]

Grantees of the family self-sufficiency innovation portion of the proposed fund would be required to develop promising new approaches for *custodial parents* in areas such as (1) identifying families that have serious barriers to employment, including strategies that use mechanisms of ongoing assessment or focus on families at risk of involvement in the child welfare system; (2) implementing strategies to help families address these barriers and also prepare for employment;(3) promoting child well-being in highly disadvantaged families, including child-only cases; and (4) supporting those with barriers who find jobs so they can sustain employment.[154]

Supporters of the Fatherhood, Marriage, and Families Innovation Fund contend that its implementation would "encourage and support state agencies and community-based organizations to provide holistic services to low-income families. They maintain that this funding stream could lead to a fundamental change in national policy that would provide for the delivery of more responsive TANF and non-TANF services for men and women so that they can better provide for their children and make positive contributions to their families and communities."[155]

Some supporters also point out that because programs funded by the Innovation Fund would be subject to rigorous evaluation, there would soon be evidence-based knowledge of what works and what does not work with regard to fatherhood programs for noncustodial parents and supportive services for custodial parents.

Some commentators who claim that one of the principal causes of child poverty in the United States is the absence of married fathers in the home are critical of the Innovation Fund because they say its relegates marriage promotion programs to the background, subsumed under an approach that focuses on responsible fatherhood programs and cultivating relationship skills development over encouraging marriage for low-income parents.[156] Other observers contend that although the Innovation Fund provides services and resources to both noncustodial parents and custodial parents, it continues the practice of viewing families as the mother and children with the father on the outside and not really a part of the unit. Also, some commentators opposed to using states as the grantees maintain that the use of community-based providers as the grantees rather than the states is a better model in that community-based organizations already have expertise in designing innovative programs to meet specific goals. They argue that community-based organizations do not need the state as a "go-between" or arbiter to provide a wider range of services to families.

Child Support Arrearage Reduction Strategies[157]

Large child support arrearages result in millions of children receiving less than they are owed in child support, reduced cost-effectiveness of the CSE program, and a perception that the CSE program does not consider the financial situation of low-income noncustodial parents, many of whom may be in dire economic situations. There is widespread agreement that preventing the build-up of unpaid child support through early intervention rather than traditional enforcement methods is essential to the future success of the CSE program. [158] Some commentators point out that such a proactive approach to addressing the huge accumulation of child support arrearages may help many low-income children whose parents are unemployed or underemployed. [159]

A state may have a number of objectives for reducing child support debt, including increasing the income of a custodial family and offering a noncustodial parent a "clean slate" to improve future employment and child support outcomes.[160] Research from the University of Wisconsin suggests that reduction of large child support debts may increase child support payments.[161]

The current strategic plan for the Office of Child Support Enforcement (OCSE) proposes the following procedures for reducing high child support arrearages:

- Update child support guidelines regularly and simplify child support order modification.
- Modify orders to ensure that child support obligations stay consistent with the noncustodial parents' ability to pay.

- Use automation to detect non-compliance as early as possible and contact noncustodial parents soon after a scheduled child support payment is missed.
- Update child support guidelines to recognize modern family dynamics and realities (e.g., shared custody, incomes of custodial parents, etc.).
- Consider creative ways to promote regular payment of current support, even if it means "compromising" uncollected child support arrearages, to bring the noncustodial parent back to consistently paying current child support payments. [162]

With regard to the last proposal, in an effort to reduce or eliminate child support debt some states use debt compromise, a process whereby a state forgives a portion or all of the child support debt owed to the state by the noncustodial parent in exchange for the noncustodial parent's participation in specified employment, training, or other activities. [163]

Federal law permits the use of federal TANF, including TANF Recovery Act funds or state MOE funds, to pay a benefit to a noncustodial parent to reduce or pay off child support arrearages owed to a family. Under P.L. 111-5 (the American Recovery and Reinvestment Act of 2009), a state may receive 80% federal matching funds for non-recurrent short term benefits and subsidized employment; and it could provide any of these forms of help to a needy noncustodial parent, either in conjunction with or separate from a program of arrearage reduction. [164]

It is important to note that the federal share of such debt is still owed to the federal government. In order for the federal portion of the child support debt to be compromised or eliminated, Congress would have to pass legislation to that effect.

It has also been recommended that Congress revise consumer protection limits with respect to garnishment of child support. CSE officials can garnish as much as 65% of a noncustodial parent's wages toward the payment of child support debt.[165] For low-income noncustodial parents who are unemployed or underemployed, this practice may increase the difficulty of securing and maintaining housing, transportation, and employment that are necessary for making future child support payments.[166]

Other recommendations of policymakers and observers are specifically related to incarcerated parents and include[167] (1) enabling courts to consider an individual's obligations to his or her children at the time of sentencing;[168] (2) prohibiting incarceration from being defined as "voluntary unemployment" (a term used to describe someone who has chosen not to work),[169] thereby allowing a noncustodial parent's child support order to be modified when he or she enters prison;[170] and (3) requiring states to automatically modify (or forgive) child support orders of noncustodial parents who are in prison (during the prison-intake process), only for the length of their prison sentence, unless the custodial parent objects because the inmate has income and/or assets that can be used to pay child support.[171]

Although many custodial parents agree to a certain extent that some noncustodial parents are "dead broke" rather than "deadbeats," they contend that the states and the federal government need to proceed with caution in lowering child support orders for low-income noncustodial parents. They argue that child support is a source of income that could mean the difference between poverty and self-sufficiency for some families. They emphasize that lowering the child support order is likely to result in lower income for the child. They argue that even if a noncustodial parent is in dire financial straits, he or she should not be totally released from financial responsibility for his or her children. Others agree, and argue that policymakers, when considering policies related to reducing the child support obligations of prisoners, must also consider equity issues related to the treatment of low-income noncustodial parents who may be unemployed as opposed to being in prison. They assert that it is sending the wrong message to unilaterally lower payments of persons who have broken the law and not make similar allowances for law-abiding citizens who are unemployed.[172]

It has also been suggested that it may be more expedient for Congress to mandate some of the child support arrearage remedies outlined in the OCSE FY2005-2009 Strategic Plan and elsewhere, rather than wait for states to develop individual remedies that only apply to the state that implements the policy.

Federal Matching Funds for CSE Access and Visitation Programs

The CSE Access and Visitation Grant program acknowledges and reflects the sentiment that healthy families need more than just financial support. According to OCSE, the CSE Access and Visitation Grant program, with its annual appropriation of $10 million (in aggregate to the 54 jurisdictions—the 50 states, the District of Columbia, Guam, Puerto Rico, and the Virgin Islands), has been able to provide access and visitation services to over 500,000 noncustodial parents and their families since the program became operational in FY1 998.

The CSE Access and Visitation Grant program has been a separate line item in the CSE budget account since its enactment as part of P.L. 104-193 (the 1996 welfare reform law). The Obama Administration's FY20 11 budget proposes that funding for the CSE Access and Visitation Grant program be increased by $2 million annually, from $10 million to $12 million.[173]

Some child advocates assert that the CSE Access and Visitation Grant program should be incorporated into the CSE program and receive 66% federal matching funds like other CSE program components. They contend that the existing funding structure of the program cannot meet the demand for program services. They argue that the importance of having noncustodial parents involved in their children's lives is a legitimate reason for adding an access and visitation component to the CSE program. According to one state report:

> Without increased funding support, courts and communities will continue to be limited in the number of families served, hours of service delivery will remain stagnant, expansion to accessibly located sites and facilities will be impossible, waiting lists continue to be unavoidable, providers will not have the multilingual capacity to serve the diverse populations, and low-income families and families in rural counties will continue to be underserved.[174]

They note that the establishment of the CSE Access and Visitation Grant program reflected Congress' awareness that child well-being is positively affected when noncustodial parents become more responsible and involved with their children. They maintain that the demand for access and visitation services outpaces the resources available for the program. They contend that funding limitations restrict the amount of services and the scope of available services.[175]

Other commentators note that FY2009 is the first year in the CSE program's history that child support collections have fallen (from $26.6 billion in FY2008 to $26.4 billion in

FY2009). They contend that during the current economic crisis, funding priorities for the CSE program should remain on services related to paternity establishment, and establishment and enforcement of medical and child support orders.

Job Training, Workforce Support, and Education

Current job training and workforce programs and education programs are generally not targeted to noncustodial parents, and only some focus on low-income individuals. Select job training and workforce programs for youth and other workforce models may be promising in helping noncustodial parents find work and ensuring that disadvantaged young people are adequately prepared for the financial responsibilities of a family. Further, given the association of higher educational attainment with higher wages, noncustodial parents and young people transitioning to adulthood can benefit from education programs that target disadvantaged groups.

Job Training and Workforce Programs

The adult job training and workforce programs authorized under WIA generally do not include income or barriers to employment as part of the eligibility criteria (with the exception of the Ex- Offender program). Having such criteria could concentrate resources on the most underserved adult workers. Congress could look to existing youth programs authorized under WIA as a model for targeting select populations. Nearly all of the youth served in the programs are low-income[176] and face barriers to employment, such as having dropped out of school. Half or more than half of the participants are male. These programs are also distinct from the adult programs in that many of the youth receive job training. As noted previously, the majority of participants in the WIA Adult program receive only job search assistance.

A separate approach would be to provide more-targeted workforce development services to the most disadvantaged males. The Reintegration of Ex-Offenders program has received increased funding in recent years. One option for providing additional service to men trying to re-enter the labor force is to continue funding this program and move it from a demonstration project (authorized by Section 171 of WIA) to a permanent part of WIA. A rigorous analysis of a re-entry program in New York City is being undertaken now by MDRC, a social policy research organization. Depending on the findings of that evaluation, specific program elements could be put into a permanent re-entry program under WIA, alongside permanent programs for other groups, such as Native Americans, and low-income youth. Another option is to provide funding for transitional jobs programs. The FY20 10 budget included language indicating that the Department of Labor encourages grantees to offer programs with a transitional jobs component, described further below. If transitional jobs programs are effective at reintegrating ex-offenders into the labor force, DOL could add these as an allowable activity under the formula grants for adult workers.

Overall, little is known about the effectiveness of federal job training programs in meeting the goals of WIA. The Obama Administration has proposed funding to evaluate promising approaches to serving disadvantaged populations through workforce programs. The FY20 11 Department of Labor budget request includes a new Workforce Innovation Fund (WIF). The fund would be comprised of 5% contributions each from the WIA Adult program and the WIA Dislocated Worker program, totaling $107.7 million. Grants would be awarded to states or localities to "test innovative approaches to training and reemployment services, especially for vulnerable populations, and promote rigorous evaluation of practices that already show promise."[177] The FY2011 budget request also includes funding for a similar Youth Innovation Fund, comprised of a 15% contribution from the WIA Youth program. The Innovation Fund would support testing and rigorous evaluation of innovative approaches to providing summer and year-round employment opportunities for youth, as well as interventions serving out-of-school youth ages 16 to 24.

At least one youth program authorized under WIA, Job Corps, has been rigorously evaluated and has shown impacts on family formation. Mathematica, a policy research organization, tracked the outcomes of youth in the Job Corps program from 1994 through 2006. During the first two years of the study, eligible youth were randomly assigned to the program group (permitted to enroll in Jobs Corps) or a control group (not permitted to enroll). Survey data were collected at baseline, and at 12, 30, and 40 months after the youth were randomly assigned. Mathematica issued a series of reports about youth outcomes and the benefits and costs of the program. Earlier reports found that Job Corps had several positive outcomes on youth in education and employment and was cost-effective despite its high costs. Mathematica's follow-up report in 2006 analyzed the longer-term impacts of the program based on earnings and employment rates through 2004 and updated findings from the benefit-cost analysis.[178] The study found that Job Corps increased the education and job training that participants received both inside and outside the program by about 1,000 hours (equivalent to training in a regular 10-month school). In turn, youth improved their literacy and numeracy skills, and youth were more likely to obtain a GED and vocational certificates. The program also generated employment and earnings gains initially, but not in the long run. Except among the oldest students (those ages 20 through 24), there were no longer-term program impacts on earnings. Mathematica also found that the costs to society exceed the benefits for the program. Specifically, the costs exceeded the benefits by approximately $10,300 per participant. However, the benefits exceeded costs for youth ages 20 through 24 by about $17,000 per participant.

More recently, Mathematica has examined the effects of the program on the likelihood of marriage for its participants (low-income women and men ages 20 through 28 at the time of the study).[179] The study found that Job Corps increases the likelihood of marriage for female participants. According to the study, the positive effects of marriage may reflect "the benefits of women's economic independence as well as the 'good-catch' effect in the marriage market." The study found that employment and earnings were associated with men's likelihood of marriage as well; however, researchers determined that much of this association related to unobserved individual characteristics that make men more likely to be successful in both the marriage and labor markets. In other words, Job Corps influenced the marriage outcomes of women but not men.

Subsidized Employment

Subsidized employment aims to support individuals who cannot find jobs in the labor market. These efforts may be beneficial for disadvantaged populations, including noncustodial parents. One approach to subsidized employment provides what are referred to as transitional jobs to workers with multiple barriers to employment. Transitional jobs programs are similar to other subsidized employment models, except that they focus on very hard-to-employ populations and they use subsidized work experience to prepare workers for regular unsubsidized jobs.[180] These programs also provide some form of case management and job placement services to help participants find permanent jobs, among other approaches. Participants can be placed individually in transitional jobs, often with nonprofit organizations or government; in work crews with other participants under the supervision of the transitional jobs program; or with the transitional jobs program, which may be a social enterprise that sells a product or service. Two examples of transitional jobs programs that serve TANF recipients and ex-offenders:

- The Community Jobs Program in Washington is a statewide program targeting TANF recipients, with the state TANF agency contracting with nonprofit organizations to administer the program. Participants work 20 to 30 hours per week for up to nine months, primarily at nonprofit and government agencies. They may also participate in educational activities. The contracting organizations identify work sites and provide intensive case management.
- The Center for Employment Opportunities (CEO) in New York City serves parolees by providing a four-day pre-employment class before they are placed on a work crew that is supervised by CEO staff. The crews do maintenance and repair work under contract to city and state agencies. Participants work four days per week and are paid the minimum wage. On the fifth day, participants meet with job coaches and job developers and attend supplemental activities, such as fatherhood groups. Participants work with a CEO "job developer" to find a permanent position.

The Department of Labor FY20 10 budget includes $45 million to evaluate transitional jobs strategies. Funding is authorized under WIA's Pilots and Demonstrations authority. The FY20 11 budget proposes an additional $40 million for this purpose.

Studies of transitional jobs programs, including an evaluation of CEO, show promising results on certain outcomes such as recidivism and TANF receipt, although the programs have not necessarily led to sustained increases in employment. [181] Given these limitations, some have proposed alternative models of subsidized employment, including the following: make changes to transitional jobs programs, such as providing longer subsidized positions or more opportunities for occupational skills training; adopt other subsidized employment models altogether, such as providing financial incentives for hard-to-employ workers to find and keep regular jobs; and adopt models that place participants directly into the job market, with positions that provide on- the-job training (one demonstration of an on-the-job training program for noncustodial parents whose children were on welfare had difficulty finding slots for participants and ultimately led to few gains).[182]

Work Requirements for Noncustodial Parents

As discussed previously, there is a provision of child support enforcement law that requires states to establish procedures to require non-paying noncustodial parents of children in families receiving TANF assistance to participate in mandatory work programs. [183] One policy option would be to expand this provision, establishing a mandatory work requirement for non-paying noncustodial parents, similar to work requirements for custodial parents receiving TANF assistance. Where the requirement is made mandatory for custodial parents receiving cash assistance by a cut or elimination of their welfare check, the requirement for noncustodial parents would be made mandatory through the threat of jail for noncompliance.[184]

The work requirement could be seen as eliminating the inequity in current policy that requires work for low-income custodial parents but not noncustodial parents. Work requirements for nonpaying noncustodial parents can be seen as addressing a lack of basic work discipline, just as it was seen as addressing similar issues with custodial parents on TANF assistance.

There are several issues with imposing a new work requirement on noncustodial parents. First, there is no funding source that is currently dedicated to cover the costs of enforcing such a requirement. The allowable uses of child support matching funds can be expanded to include reimbursing states for their expenditures to enforce the requirement, but that would impose a new federal budgetary cost. New funds can also be provided for this purpose through the TANF program, but if they are new funds they also entail a federal budgetary cost. Existing TANF funds can be used for this purpose; however, because of the block grant nature of TANF, using funds for new work programs for noncustodial parents would require cutting back on other TANF expenditures.

Moreover, if there was a universal work requirement for noncustodial parents, questions would be raised about what obligations the federal government or states would have if jobs were not available. A recent discussion of this proposal stated that such a requirement would probably mean that a job would have to be guaranteed, albeit on a time-limited basis.[185] Providing a job guarantee to this population also raises equity issues. Such a guarantee is not available to other men, including those who work and pay their child support. Such a guarantee is also not a part of the work requirements for custodial parents receiving TANF cash assistance.

Education Programs

Some education programs and initiatives have been particularly effective for disadvantaged groups, though none have targeted noncustodial parents. Still, some of these efforts have had beneficial impacts on family formation. In addition, they have proven to be effective at keeping young people in school, even if for the short-term. They include an education model, known as career academies, which integrate career and technical education into high school curricula, and services to community college students who are low-income. Given that evaluations of these programs show promising results, policymakers might consider expanding or replicating them.

A study by MDRC, a social policy research organization, examined the effects of the career academies model on marital status, as well as other family formation outcomes. Career academies are career and technical education programs that combine academic and technical curricula for high school students around a career theme such as health, business, or finance. Career academies are small learning communities within high schools around the country, and they have partnerships with local employers that provide work-based learning opportunities. These academies can be funded through the federal Career and Technical Education program, authorized under the Perkins Act. The study tracked the outcomes of students at careers academies in nine high schools from the time they entered high school until eight years after their scheduled graduation.[186] The students were randomly selected to participate in the career academies. The high schools are located in or near large urban school districts and have higher dropout rates and higher percentages of low-income families than other school districts nationally. More than 80% of the students in the sample were black or Hispanic.

Eight years after their expected graduation from high school, former students were surveyed about their educational outcomes, earnings and other labor market impacts, and whether they were married and had children. Alumni of the career academies were just as likely as non- academy alumni to graduate from high school or college; however, they earned more than the non-academy alumni and were more likely to live independently with children and a spouse or partner. In total, one-third of the members of the academy group were living with their children and a spouse or partner, compared to 27% of their peers. This difference represents a 23% increase in two-parent households over the rates for the non-academy group. In addition, 50.8% of the academy alumni were custodial parents, compared to 43.9% of non-academy alumni. Both of these impacts are statistically significant.

Other efforts in education have focused on students who are in community college and may be at risk of dropping out. MDRC has conducted evaluations of community college programs that provide an enhanced set of services to diverse low-income students.[187] MDRC's national demonstration, called Opening Doors, has tested interventions designed to increase persistence and raise academic achievement among these students. The students were randomly assigned to the program group or control group. One of the Opening Doors sites, Kingsborough Community College, used small learning communities in which groups of students took courses together and their instructors were expected to coordinate assignments and periodically meet to review the students' progress. Students assigned to the small learning communities were mostly 17 to 27 years old, low-income, and racially and ethnically diverse. Researchers found that they were more likely than the students in the control group to feel integrated at school, be engaged with fellow teachers and instructors, pass and earn more credits during their first semester, and to take and pass an English skills assessment test that was required for graduation. After four semesters, the young people in the communities had more credits.

Recent proposals have sought to expand efforts like Opening Doors. A bill that passed the House in the 111th Congress would have provided competitive grants to eligible states to implement the "systematic reform" of community colleges by carrying out programs and policies that were shown to be effective.[188] Priority for grants under this section would be for states focusing on serving low-income nontraditional students, dislocated workers, or students who are veterans and do not have a bachelor's degree.

Encouraging States to Serve Noncustodial Parents in TANF

Though TANF already permits states to provide both financial assistance and other benefits and services to noncustodial parents, few such parents are on the assistance rolls and there is little information on other benefits and services available to noncustodial parents. The flexibility afforded to states under TANF provides an opportunity for them to use their TANF funds in innovative and creative ways to address the needs of disadvantaged noncustodial parents.

Under the current structure of TANF, it is difficult to compel a state to use its funds for any specific benefit or service that can be theoretically provided with the block grant. This would run counter to the overall purpose of TANF of state flexibility in serving disadvantaged families with children. However, it is possible to encourage and prod states to consider using TANF for a specific benefit or service, such as aiding noncustodial parents.

Congress could require states to address whether and how it will use TANF to serve noncustodial parents as part of the TANF state plan. The state plan is a document that states must submit once every three years as a condition of receiving block grant funds. The state plan is also subject to public comment. HHS does not approve the content of the state plan; its role is to certify that the state has submitted a "complete" plan and is thus eligible to receive its block grant. Requiring that states address a plan element relating to serving noncustodial parents could put this issue on the agenda of state policymakers. Community-based organizations and other groups would also have the ability to comment on the state's plan for serving noncustodial parents under TANF.

Another potential means of prodding states to consider serving noncustodial parents is to require that they report on the number of noncustodial parents who receive various TANF benefits and services. The idea here too is that by requiring the state to address how it serves noncustodial parents, the issue becomes more visible for state policymakers. Further, information on how much a state serves noncustodial parents under TANF could aid community-based organizations and other groups in providing input to state policymakers on uses of TANF funds.

Making Work Pay for Noncustodial Parents: EITC for Noncustodial Parents

As previously discussed, many of the policies put in place in the mid-1990s and continuing to this day were aimed to "make work pay" more than welfare through supporting low-wage work. The 1993 expansion of the Earned Income Tax Credit (EITC) was the cornerstone of that policy. Research has provided evidence that the EITC expansions increased work effort, particularly among single mothers. As previously discussed, employment rates among both white and African American men without a high school diploma have declined over the past two decades. Noncustodial parents, including men living apart from their children, benefitted little from the EITC expansions of 1993.

A further expansion of wage supplements through the EITC to either all workers without children or noncustodial parents has garnered interest as a potential means of increasing work effort and financial support from noncustodial parents to their children. These proposals seek to reverse the decline in employment among men with low earnings, just as the EITC is believed to have increased the work effort of single mothers. In 2006, New York enacted a "noncustodial EITC," which provides larger earnings supplements for noncustodial parents who pay child support in at least the amount of current support they owe in a year.[189] Noncustodial parents who pay at least that much in child support receive a noncustodial EITC that is the greater of (1) twice the federal EITC they are entitled to as a childless tax filer, or (2) two-thirds of the state EITC for a filer with one child. The District of Columbia has a similar noncustodial EITC, though it is based on the District's EITC for tax filers with a child.

New York's noncustodial EITC is being evaluated by the Urban Institute.[190] The major finding from the first year of the evaluation was that the share of noncustodial parents actually receiving the credit was lower than expected. The researchers found that of 403,578 noncustodial parents with a current support order, 42,930 (11%) met all the eligibility criteria for the noncustodial EITC and only 5,280 actually received the credit in tax year 2006. More than half of all noncustodial parents did not meet the income cutoffs for the credit (income greater than $0 but less than $32,001), and about half of all noncustodial parents failed to pay all current support orders in full. Additionally, many noncustodial parents eligible for the noncustodial EITC were also eligible for the regular New York State EITC (i.e., they were also custodial parents of some children). New York does not permit simultaneous receipt of both the regular state EITC and the noncustodial EITC.

Some proposals would increase the maximum EITC for a tax filer without a qualifying child, as well as increase the income thresholds at which the credit begins to phase out and then fully phases out.[191] Other proposals have sought a different tactic for increasing the EITC earnings supplement for noncustodial parents, such as increasing the maximum EITC for all filers without children.[192] Still others have discussed various approaches to restructuring the tax credits available for families with children, including separating out the provisions to help support children (available only to families with children and potentially noncustodial parents) and those that supplement earnings to promote work among all low-wage workers, regardless of whether they support children.[193]

Increasing the Age for Youth Employment and Training Services

Another set of policy options could focus on redefining the population of youth for purposes of program eligibility. The current move from adolescence to adulthood has become longer and more complex.[194] Youth of the 1950s were more likely to follow an orderly path to adulthood. They generally completed their education and/or secured employment (for males), including military service, which was followed by marriage and parenthood in their early 20s. (This was not true for every young person; for example, African Americans and immigrants in certain parts of the country faced barriers to employment.) Unlike their postwar counterparts who had access to plentiful jobs in the industrial sector, youth today must compete in a global, information-driven economy. Many more youth now receive vocational training or enroll in colleges and universities after leaving high school. Changed expectations for women have contributed to their increased college attendance, which now exceeds that of men.[195] During the period of transition, young adults cycle between attending school, living independently, and staying with their parents. On average, parents give their children an estimated $38,000—or about $2,200 a year—between the ages of 18 and 34 to supplement wages, pay for college tuition, and help with housing costs, among other types of financial assistance.[196]

Yet disadvantaged young people often face barriers to enrolling in school or maintaining a job, and many cannot rely on financial support from their families. This, in turn, could affect their ability to provide for their own children and make meaningful contributions to society. Federal programs for disadvantaged youth recognize that adolescence is no longer a finite period ending at age 18 or even age 21. Recently, Congress temporarily extended the age of eligibility, from 21 to 24, for youth participating in the WIA Youth Activities program as part of the American Recovery and Reinvestment Act (P.L. 111-5). In the accompanying conference report for the bill (H.Rept. 111-16), Congress stated, "the age of eligibility for youth services provided with the additional funds is extended through age 24 to allow local programs to reach young adults who have become disconnected from both education and the labor market." This temporary expansion could be made permanent, as proposed by legislation that was introduced in the 111th Congress. Other youth programs authorized under WIA, Job Corps, and YouthBuild enable young people up to the age of 24 to enroll in the program.

Extending the age of youth for purposes of eligibility for federal programs can provide vulnerable young people with supports as they enter into adulthood. Several of the WIA programs discussed above, such as Job Corps and YouthBuild, include support services such as transportation, housing, and child care that can assist young people with staying in school and engaging in work. Yet not all federal programs (e.g., TANF) with a similar mission have the same emphasis on work and school or provide additional support to young people after age 21. Young people receiving TANF can count education and training toward the participation requirements, whereas those over the age of 21 must work. Despite recent efforts to coordinate TANF with the WIA Youth Activities program, youth in TANF are defined as individuals under the age of 21. And, notably, the age extension in the Youth Activities program is temporary—lasting only until June 30, 2011.

CONCLUDING REMARKS

Although social science research and analysis acknowledge the importance of the father in improving the well-being of his children, federal welfare programs have to varying degrees minimized, undervalued, or overlooked the role of fathers in the lives of children. In addition, other federal programs and/or systems that include many men on their rolls (such as employment and training programs and the criminal justice system) have not fully addressed the unique needs and circumstances of fathers, particularly those that do not have custody of their children.

According to some estimates, about half of all children who are currently under age 18 will spend or have spent a significant portion of their childhood in a home without their biological father. Currently, about one-third of all children live in families without their biological father present.

Given widespread agreement that both parents influence the well-being of their children, it may be that the next era of welfare reform will seek to alter and/or revise federal programs to reflect the importance of fathers to their children's well-being by reducing some of the program barriers faced by low-income men who are participants in the programs. Moreover, federal programs could more directly affect the status of low-income fathers by systematically targeting noncustodial fathers for employment and supportive services to enable those men to make significant positive impacts on the well-being of their own biological children and other children with whom they may interact.

End Notes

1 Congressional Research Service, *Issues in Focus—Child Well-Being*.

2 Ibid.

3 Ibid.

4 David Popenoe, "A World Without Fathers (consequences of children living without fathers)," The Wilson Quarterly, March 22, 1996. See also Wendy Sigle-Rushton and Sara McLanahan, "Father Absence and Child Well-Being: A Critical Review," Princeton University, Center for Research on Child Wellbeing (Working Paper #02-20), November 2002. (Hereinafter, Sigle-Rushton and McLanahan, "Father Absence and Child Well-Being: A Critical Review.") **Note:** Children living with a single mother is the most common living arrangement for those who live without their biological fathers. However, some children live with stepfathers or adoptive fathers, as well as with other male relatives such as grandfathers.

5 Sara McLanahan and Gary Sandefur, "Growing Up With a Single Parent: What Hurts, What Helps" (Cambridge, MA: Harvard University Press, 1994). See also L. Bumpass, "Children and Marital Disruption: A Replication and Update," Demography, vol. 21(1984), pp. 71-82.

6 In most of the studies cited in the child well-being references in this report, the presence of a stepfather did not lessen the negative effect of father absence on children.

7 Sigle-Rushton and McLanahan, "Father Absence and Child Well-Being: A Critical Review," pp. 8-9.

8 Ibid, pp. 10-12.

9 Ibid, pp. 12-13.

10 Ibid, pp. 14-15.

11 See discussion of how those who left the welfare rolls fared in U.S. Department of Health and Human Services, *Final synthesis reporting of findings of ASPE Leavers Grants*, Washington, DC, 2001.

12 Jeffrey Rosenberg and W. Bradford Wilcox, "The Importance of Fathers in the Healthy Development of Children," U.S. Department of Health and Human Services, Administration for Children and Families, Administration on Children, Youth and Families Children's Bureau, Office on Child Abuse and Neglect, 2006.

13 Ibid. See also David Popenoe, "Life Without Father: Compelling New Evidence that Fatherhood and Marriage are Indispensable for the Good of Children and Society," The Free Press (a division of Simon and Schuster), 1996.

14 This is an estimate based on HHS and Census Bureau data. See later section on The Child Support Program and Noncustodial Fathers for more details.

15 Elaine Sorenson and Chava Zibman, *Poor Dads Who Don't Pay Child Support: Deadbeat or Disadvantaged?*, The Urban Institute, Series B, No. B-30, April 2001, http://www.urban. (Hereinafter, Sorenson and Zibman, *Poor Dads Who Don't Pay Child Support: Deadbeat or Disadvantaged.*)

16 The focus of this report is on low-income noncustodial fathers. Low-income individuals are generally more disadvantaged than their higher-income counterparts in almost every realm of society.

17 Even though some of the programs discussed in this report serve persons regardless of income status, public policy is usually focused on helping the more disadvantaged persons (i.e., low-income individuals).

18 Brady E. Hamilton, Joyce A. Martin, and Stephanie J. Ventura, Births: Preliminary Data for 2008, U.S. Department of Health and Human Services, Centers for Disease Control and Prevention, National Center for Health Statistics, National Vital Statistics Report, Volume 58, Number 15, April 6, 2010.

19 U.S. Department of Education, National Center for Education Statistics, *Digest of Education Statistics 2009*, "Total fall enrollment in degree-granting institutions, by sex, age, and attendance status: Selected years, 1970 through 2018," April 2010.

20 Carmen DeNavas-Wait, Bernadette D. Proctor, and Jessica C. Smith, *Income, Poverty, and Health Insurance Coverage in the United States: 2008*, U.S. Department of Commerce, U.S. Census Bureau, Current Population Reports, P60-236(RV), September 2009, Table B2.

21 See Congressional Budget Office, *For Better or for Worse: Marriage and the Federal Income Tax*, June 1997.

22 U.S. Department of the Treasury, Internal Revenue Service, *Individual Complete Report*, Table 2.5.

23 However, standard deductions and shelter deductions used in calculating the benefit are different for Alaska, Hawaii, Guam, and the Virgin Islands than they are for the 48 contiguous states and the District of Columbia.

24 Historically, states were required to provide CSE services to Indian tribes and tribal organizations as part of the CSE caseloads. The 1996 welfare reform law (P.L. 104-193) allowed direct federal funding of tribal CSE programs at a 90% federal matching rate. In FY2008, there were 45 tribal CSE programs. For information on tribal CSE programs, see CRS Report R41204, *Child Support Enforcement: Tribal Programs*, by Carmen Solomon-Fears and Roger Walke.

25 In FY2009, the statutory maximum for federal CSE incentive payments to states (in aggregate) was $504 million.

26 The CSE program does not handle all child support payments. Some cases (40%-50%) are handled by private attorneys or collection agencies, or through mutual agreements between the parents. Thus, some of the families who received child support in 2009 probably received it without the help of the CSE program.

[27] In brief, TANF families are required to assign their child support rights to the state. As long as the child support payment collected on the TANF family's behalf is smaller than the state's TANF benefit for a family of the relevant size, the family remains on the TANF program and the child support collected for the family is divided between the state and the federal government, with the state having the authority to "pass through" some, all, or none of its share of the child support collected to the family without it affecting the family's TANF benefit and with the federal government sharing in some of the costs of giving the money to the family. The share of the child support collection that is distributed to the federal government is based on a state's Federal Medical Assistance Percentage (FMAP). The FMAP varies inversely with state per capita income (i.e., poor states have a higher federal matching rate, wealthy states have a lower federal matching rate). For more information on child support and TANF families, see CRS Report RL34 105, *The Financial Impact of Child Support on TANF Families: Simulation for Selected States*, by Carmen Solomon-Fears and Gene Falk.

[28] In FY2008, only 3.7% of CSE collections (about $978 million) were made on behalf of TANF families, about 2% of that amount (about $20 million) actually went to CSE families who received TANF benefits (pursuant to state CSE "pass through" provisions), and the rest was divided between the state and federal governments to reimburse them for TANF benefits paid to such families.

[29] Michelle Vinson and Vicki Turetsky, "State Child Support Pass-Through Policies," Center for Law and Social Policy, June 12, 2009.

[30] P.L. 109-171 gave states the option of distributing to former TANF families the full amount of child support collected on their behalf (i.e., both current support and all child support arrearages—including arrearages collected through the federal income tax refund offset program). This provision took effect on October 1, 2009, or October 1, 2008, at state option.

[31] The CSE program defines a CSE "case" as a noncustodial parent (mother, father, or putative/alleged father) who is now or eventually may be obligated under law for the support of a child or children receiving services under the CSE program. If the noncustodial parent owes support for two children by different women, that would be considered two cases; if both children have the same mother, that would be considered one case.

[32] In FY2009, 4% of CSE collections were made on behalf of TANF families, 35% were made on behalf of former TANF families, and 61% were made on behalf of families who had never been on TANF.

[33] Elaine Sorensen and Chava Zibman, "Child Support Offers Some Protection Against Poverty," Urban Institute, March 15, 2000. Also see Elaine Sorensen, "Child Support Gains Ground," Urban Institute, October 6, 2003.

[34] 34 U.S. Census Bureau, "Custodial Mothers and Fathers and Their Child Support: 2007," *Current Population Reports*, P60-237.

[35] Since, in some states, child support can be ordered by a court until a child is 21 years old or completes college, the survey data upon which this Census report is based covers parents' own children under age 21 rather than applying the U.S. Census Bureau's usual definition of children as those under age 18.

[36] U.S. Census Bureau, "Custodial Mothers and Fathers and Their Child Support: 2007," *Current Population Reports*, P60-237. For information on noncustodial parents, see Elaine Sorensen and Tess Tannehill, "Demographic Survey Results from Nine-State IV-D Programs," December 18, 2007.

[37] In most states, the child support order is initiated when parents divorce or separate or when a never-married parent seeks assistance and child support is established for the child. The child support order generally lasts until the child reaches the state's "age of majority (usually age 18)," and if the noncustodial parent owes past-due child support payments, the state can continue collecting such child support arrearages for a stipulated period beyond this age.

[38] The 2007 Census Bureau data indicate that 1.6% of custodial parents in 2007 were widowed (17,414,000 x 1.6% = 279,000; 17,414,000 – 279,000 = 17,135,000).

[39] Based on 2007 Census Bureau data, about 17% of custodial parents were fathers (17% x 17,000,000 = 2,890,000; 17,135,000 – 2,890,000 = 14,245,000).

[40] This provision is found in Section 466(a)(15) of the Social Security Act (Title 42 USC §666(a)(15)).

[41] The now defunct Welfare-to-Work (WtW) program was designed to help states and localities move hard-to-employ welfare recipients and certain low-income noncustodial parents into lasting unsubsidized jobs. The program was established in P.L. 105-3 3 (the Balanced Budget Act of 1997) to supplement TANF block grant funds. It was administered by the U.S. Department of Labor. The $3 billion grant ($1.5 billion for FY1997-1998 and $1.5 billion for FY1998-1999) consisted of two main parts: formula grants to states and competitive grants to local communities. Three-quarters of the funds were distributed by formula to states, which were required to pass on 85% of their formula funds to workforce investment boards (WIBs). The other quarter of the funds was distributed competitively based on grant applications from state and local agencies, nonprofit organizations, and public and private entities. According to evaluation information, hundreds of programs were implemented with WtW grants, through various agencies and organizations, and all were required to coordinate with TANF agencies. The WtW formula grant program was terminated by Section 105 of the Department of Labor 2004 appropriation (P.L. 108-199). Program evaluators indicated that all WtW programs had ended by the end of 2004. According to an evaluation of the WtW program by Mathematica Policy Research, Inc., and the Urban Institute: "WIA [Workforce Investment Act] administrators generally felt the WtW grants program had three positive systemic benefits: it helped to establish welfare recipients as a key

customer group for the One-Stop Career Center system; it improved the working relationship between the welfare and workforce agencies; and it made it possible to devote resources to developing and testing new strategies (e.g., employer partnerships, transitional employment, retention services) for serving the hard-to-employ" (Source: Mathematica Policy Research, Inc., and the Urban Institute, "Welfare-to-Work Grants Programs: Adjusting to Changing Circumstances," by Demetra Smith Nightingale, Carolyn Taylor O'Brien, Michael Egner, Nancy Pindus, and John Trutko, November 2003).

[42] Lawrence M. Mead, "Toward a Mandatory Work Policy for Men," The Future of Children (Princeton-Brookings), v. 17, no. 2, Fall 2007, p. 56.

[43] The Texas Noncustodial Parents (NCP) Choices Program provides enhanced child support case compliance monitoring and employment services for noncustodial parents linked to a TANF/Medicaid case who are unemployed or underemployed and are not compliant with their child support obligations. Participation in the program is mandatory as ordered by CSE associate judges in the 14 sites currently funded by the Texas Workforce Commission and the Office of Attorney General (OAG). NCP Choices launched three new sites and expanded one existing site in spring 2010. According to the Texas CSE website, noncustodial parents ordered into NCP Choices have, on average, made no payments in the eight months prior to program entry and pay an average of $176 per month in the first year after program entry. Evaluation results show this as an overall 57% increase in child support payments for noncustodial parents participating in this program as compared to a control group of similar noncustodial parents in the OAG caseload (http://www.oag.state

[44] U.S. Department of Health and Human Services, Administration for Children and Families, Office of Child Support Enforcement, "Noncustodial Parents: Summaries of Research, Grants and Practices, July 2009." See also Shane Spaulding, Jean Baldwin Grossman, and Dee Wallace, " Working Dads: Final Report on the Fathers at Work Initiative," Public/Private Ventures, 2009.

[45] U.S. Census Bureau, "Custodial Mothers and Fathers and Their Child Support: 2007," Current Population Reports, P60-237, by Timothy S. Grall, November 2009, http://www.census.gov/prod/2009pubs/p60-237.pdf. To view detailed tables, see http://www.census.gov/hhes/www/childsupport/chldsu07.pdf.

[46] Heather Koball and Desiree Principe, "Do Nonresident Fathers Who Pay Child Support Visit Their Children More?," Urban Institute, Series B, No. B-44, March 2002.

[47] Virginia Knox and Cindy Redcross, "Parenting and Providing: The Impact of Parents' Fair Share on Paternal Involvement," MDRS, October 2000.

[48] Even before the 1996 welfare reform law (P.L. 104-193), the Family Support Act of 1988 (P.L. 100-485) authorized a limited number of grants to states for demonstration projects to develop, improve, or expand activities designed to increase compliance with child access provisions of court orders.

[49] U.S. Department of Health and Human Services, Office of Child Support Enforcement, "Child Access and Visitation Grants: State/Jurisdiction Profiles for FY 2008," March 8, 2010.

[50] The following information is from CRS Report R40499, Child Support Enforcement and Ex-Offenders, by Carmen Solomon-Fears, April 7, 2009, pp. 16-17.

[51] Elaine Sorensen, Liliana Sousa, and Simon Schaner, "Assessing Child Support Arrears in Nine Large States and the Nation," The Urban Institute, July 11, 2007, pp. 19-24, http://aspe.hhs.gov/hsp/07/assessing-CS-debt/.

[52] This flexibility and discretion only applies to prospective modification of child support orders. Federal law prohibits the retroactive modification of child support orders (Section 466(a)(9) of the Social Security Act).

[53] Lauren E. Glaze and Laura M. Maruschak, "Parents in Prison and Their Minor Children," U.S. Department of Justice, Bureau of Justice Statistics Special Report, August 2008.

[54] "Every Door Closed: Facts About Parents With Criminal Records," Center for Law and Social Policy (CLASP) and Community Legal Services, Inc., 2003.

[55] "Building Knowledge About Successful Prisoner Reentry Strategies," MDRC, February 11, 2009.

[56] "Every Door Closed: Facts About Parents With Criminal Records," Center for Law and Social Policy (CLASP) and Community Legal Services, Inc., 2003.

[57] Between FY2006 and FY2009, the CSE caseload has ranged between 15.7 million and 15.8 million cases.

[58] U.S. Department of Health and Human Services, Administration for Children and Families, Office of Child Support Enforcement, "Section 1115 Demonstration Grants—Projects in Support of the Prisoner Reentry Initiative (HHS-2009- ACF-OCSE-FD-0013)," http://www.acf.hhs.gov/grants. (Hereinafter, U.S. Department of Health and Human Services, Administration for Children and Families, Office of Child Support Enforcement, "Section 1115 Demonstration Grants—Projects in Support of the Prisoner Reentry Initiative.")

[59] The Prisoner Re-entry Initiative was authorized by Section 2421 of the 21st Century Department of Justice Appropriations Authorization Act (P.L. 107-273). The 21st Century Department of Justice Appropriations Authorization Act authorized appropriations for the initiative for FY2003-FY2005. However, the initiative has received funding since FY2001. Historically, funding for the initiative has been appropriated under the Community Oriented Policing Services (COPS) appropriation, but the funds have been transferred to the Office of Justice Programs (OJP), where they are administered by the Bureau of Justice Assistance (BJA) in the Department of Justice (DOJ) (Source: CRS Report RL3 3489, An Overview and Funding History of Select Department of Justice (DOJ) Grant Programs, by Nathan James, January 16, 2008).

[60] U.S. Department of Health and Human Services, Administration for Children and Families, Office of Child Support Enforcement, "Section 1115 Demonstration Grants—Projects in Support of the Prisoner Reentry Initiative."

[61] CRS Report R40499, *Child Support Enforcement and Ex-Offenders*, by Carmen Solomon-Fears.

[62] Esther Griswold and Jessica Pearson, "Twelve Reasons for Collaboration Between Departments of Correction and Child Support Enforcement Agencies," *Corrections Today*, v. 65 Issue 3, June 2003, pp. 87-90,104.

[63] Vicki Turetsky, "Realistic Child Support Policies that Support Successful Re-entry," Center for Law and Social Policy, revised January 2007.

[64] "Report of the Re-Entry Policy Council—Charting the Safe and Successful Return of Prisoners to the Community," 2004. See also Rachel L. McLean and Michael D. Thompson, "Repaying Debts," U.S. Department of Justice, Bureau of Justice Assistance, 2007.

[65] U.S. Department of Health and Human Services, Administration for Children and Families, "Healthy Marriage Initiative, 2002-2008: An Introductory Guide," 2008, http://www.healthymarriageinfo.org/docs/acfhminitiativeguide.pdf. (Hereinafter, U.S. Department of Health and Human Services, Administration for Children and Families, "Healthy Marriage Initiative, 2002-2008: An Introductory Guide.")

[66] The other two goals are (1) providing assistance to needy families so that children may remain in their homes, or in the homes of relatives, and (2) reducing the incidence of out-of-wedlock pregnancies.

[67] These HHS agencies were the Administration for Children and Families (including the Office of Head Start, formerly known as the Head Start Bureau), the Office of Child Support Enforcement (OCSE), the Office of Refugee Resettlement, the Children's Bureau, the Office of Community Services, the Administration for Native Americans.

[68] U.S. Department of Health and Human Services, Administration for Children and Families, "Healthy Marriage Initiative, 2002-2008: An Introductory Guide."

[69] U.S. Department of Health and Human Services, Administration for Children and Families, Information Memorandum, "Fatherhood and Healthy Marriage Initiative (ACYF-CB-02-01, Attachment C)," Issuance date: March 12, 2002.

[70] The White House, "National Family Week, 2002" (George W. Bush), Proclamation 7630 of November 22, 2002.

[71] U.S. Department of Health and Human Services, "Marriage Protection Week, 2003," A Proclamation by the President of the United States of America (George W. Bush), October 3, 2003.

[72] This law also established within TANF a new categorical grant for responsible fatherhood initiatives (discussed below).

[73] U.S. Department of Health and Human Services, Administration for Children and Families, Temporary Assistance for Needy Families, *Budget Justification of Appropriations Estimates for Committee on Appropriations*, FY20 11, p. 303. According to HHS data, 60% of the grantees are nonprofit, community-based organizations. Other grantees include post-secondary institutions, state and county governments, for-profit companies, and faith-based organizations.

[74] The Department of Health and Human Services' Office of Planning, Research, and Evaluation (OPRE) has funded and continues to fund many more federally funded evaluations of healthy marriage programs. For additional information on these evaluations, see Administration for Children and Families, "Healthy Marriage Initiative, 2002- 2008: An Introductory Guide," 2008, pp. 13-15.

[75] Ibid., p. 28.

[76] U.S. Department of Health and Human Services, Administration for Children and Families, Office of Planning, Research, and Evaluation, Hispanic Healthy Marriage Initiative, http://www.acf.hhs.gov/programs/opre/strengthen/ hispanic_healthy/index.html#overview.

[77] Benjamin Scafidi et al., "The Taxpayer Costs of Divorce and Unwed Childbearing: First-Ever Estimates for the Nation and for All Fifty States," Institute for American Values, Georgia Family Council, Institute for Marriage and Public Policy, and Families Northwest, April 2008. (Hereinafter, Scafidi et al, "The Taxpayer Costs of Divorce and Unwed Childbearing: First-Ever Estimates for the Nation and for All Fifty States").

[78] The report does not separately estimate the economic costs associated with nonmarital childbearing.

[79] Scafidi et al, "The Taxpayer Costs of Divorce and Unwed Childbearing: First-Ever Estimates for the Nation and for All Fifty States."

[80] Paul R. Amato and Rebecca A. Maynard, "Decreasing Nonmarital Births and Strengthening Marriage to Reduce Poverty," *The Future of Children*, vol. 17, no. 2 (Fall 2007), p. 130.

[81] The 3.7 million figure was derived by applying the 29% reduction rate to the 12.8 million children who were in families with below poverty-level income in 2007. According to the Census Bureau, in 2007 12.8 million of the nearly 73 million related children (under age 18) living in families were in families with poverty-level income. Also, in 1970 85.2% of children lived with both parents; in 1980, 76.7%; in 1990, 72.5%; in 2000, 69.1%; and in 2007, 67.8% (see CRS Report RL34756, *Nonmarital Childbearing: Trends, Reasons, and Public Policy Interventions*, by Carmen Solomon-Fears, p. 29).

[82] Some of the "healthy marriage" literature explains that much of the debate around healthy marriage focuses on policy initiatives that may make persons more "marriageable," such as job training and employment programs, but that are distinct from the definition of "healthy marriage." (Source: Kristen Anderson Moore, Susan M.

Jekielek, Jacinta Bronte-Tinkew, Lina Guzman, Suzanne Ryan, and Zakia Redd, "What Is "Healthy Marriage"? Defining the Concept," Child Trends, Research Brief (2004-16), September 2004.)

[83] Marguerite Roulet, "Fatherhood Programs and Healthy Marriage Funding," Center for Family Policy and Practice, June 2009.

[84] Dorian Solot and Marshall Miller, "Let Them Eat Wedding Rings," Alternatives to Marriage Project, 2002.

[85] Frank F. Furstenberg, Jr., "Bringing Back the Shotgun Wedding," *National Affairs*, no. 90 (Winter 1988).

[86] Claire Hughes, "Marriage Promotion: Will It Work?," June 2004.

[87] Robert Rector, "Welfare Reform and The Healthy Marriage Initiative," The Heritage Foundation, February 10, 2005.

[88] Anne Menard and Oliver Williams, "It's Not Healthy If It's Not Safe: Responding to Domestic Violence Issues Within Healthy Marriage Programs," November 2005 (updated May 2006), p. 2.

[89] Kathryn Edin and Maria Kefalas, *Promises I Can Keep: Why Poor Women Put Motherhood Before Marriage*, University of California Press, 2005.

[90] Robert G. Wood et al., "The Building Strong Families Project—Strengthening Unmarried Parents' Relationships: The Early Impacts Of Building Strong Families," Mathematica Policy Research, Inc., May 2010, p. xii. (Hereinafter, Robert G. Wood et al., "The Building Strong Families Project—Strengthening Unmarried Parents' Relationships: The Early Impacts Of Building Strong Families.")

[91] The eight BSF programs evaluated were in (1) Atlanta, GA; (2) Baltimore, MD; (3) Baton Rouge, LA; (4) Orange and Broward counties, Florida; (5) Allen, Marion, and Lake counties, Indiana; (6) Oklahoma City, OK; (7) Houston, TX; and (8) San Angelo, TX. Note: the Oklahoma City BSF program was the only program in which, at the 15-month follow-up survey, there was a significant positive impact on couples remaining romantically involved and a significant positive impact on the quality of their relationship.

[92] Robert G. Wood et al., "The Building Strong Families Project—Strengthening Unmarried Parents' Relationships: The Early Impacts Of Building Strong Families."

[93] U.S. Department of Health and Human Services, Administration for Children and Families, "Study: Building Strong Families Evaluation Suggests Stronger Approach is Needed," May 21, 2010.

[94] The report indicated that the most distinctive characteristic of the Baltimore BSF program was that the couples in its population were less committed to each other and their relationships were more tenuous than any of the other BSF programs evaluated.

[95] Virginia Knox, Philip A. Cowan, Carolyn Pape Cowan, and Elana Bildner, "Policies That Strengthen Fatherhood and Family Relationships," MDRC, A Working Paper, 2009.

[96] Although programs that seek to help fathers initiate or maintain contact with their children and become emotionally involved in their children's lives are usually referred to as "fatherhood" programs, the programs are generally gender neutral. Their underlying goal is participation of the noncustodial parent in the lives of his or her children.

[97] U.S. Department of Health and Human Services, Administration for Children and Families, Information Memorandum, "Fatherhood and Healthy Marriage Initiative (ACYF-CB-02-01, Attachment C)," Issuance date: March 12, 2002.

[98] For information on profiles of state programs and strategies to promote parenting and responsible fatherhood, see http://www.fatherhood.gov/resources

[99] For a detailed history of responsible fatherhood programs, see Kathleen Sylvester and Kathleen Reich, "Making Fathers Count: Assessing the Progress of Responsible Fatherhood Efforts," Annie E. Casey Foundation and the Social Policy Action Network, 2002.

[100] U.S. Congress, House Ways and Means Subcommittee on Human Resources, "Hearing On Fatherhood Legislation," Statement of Chairman Nancy Johnson. 106th Congress, 1st Session (October 5, 1999), p. 4. **Note:** Much of the research underlying the aforementioned statement is based on the Urban Institute's 1997 National Survey of American Families (NSAF); see Sorenson and Zibman, "Poor Dads Who Don't Pay Child Support: Deadbeat or Disadvantaged."

[101] Other sources of federal funding for fatherhood programs include the TANF program, TANF state Maintenance-ofEffort (MOE) funding, CSE funds, and Social Services Block Grant (Title XX) funds. According to HHS, many states use TANF funds for responsible fatherhood programs. In addition, many private foundations provide financial support for responsible fatherhood programs.

[102] Under P.L. 109-171, responsible fatherhood funds can be spent on activities to promote responsible fatherhood through (1) marriage promotion (through counseling, mentoring, disseminating information about the advantages of marriage and two-parent involvement for children, etc.); (2) parenting activities (through counseling, mentoring, mediation, disseminating information about good parenting practices, etc.); (3) fostering economic stability of fathers (through work first services, job search, job training, subsidized employment, education, etc.); or (4) contracting with a nationally recognized nonprofit fatherhood promotion organization to develop, promote, or distribute a media campaign to encourage the appropriate involvement of parents in the lives of their children, focusing in particular on responsible fatherhood; and to develop a national clearinghouse to help states and communities in their efforts to promote and support marriage and responsible fatherhood.

[103] U.S. Department of Health and Human Services, Administration for Children and Families, Temporary Assistance for Needy Families, Budget Justification of Appropriations Estimates for Committee on Appropriations, FY2011, p. 303.

[104] U.S. Government Accountability Office, "Healthy Marriage and Responsible Fatherhood Initiative—Further Progress Is Needed in Developing a Risk-Based Monitoring Approach to Help HHS Improve Program Oversight," GAO-08-1002, September 2008. Also see National Responsible Fatherhood Clearinghouse, "What Works in Fatherhood Programs? Ten Lessons From Evidence-Based Practice," by Jacinta Bronte-Tinkew, Allison Horowitz, and Allison Metz, at http ://www. fatherhood. gov.

[105] Maureen Waller and Robert Plotnick, "A Failed Relationship? Low-Income Families and the Child Support Enforcement System," *Focus* (University of Wisconsin-Madison, Institute for Research on Poverty), vol. 21, no. 1 (spring 2000), pp. 12-17. See also "Family Ties: Improving Paternity Establishment Practices and Procedures for Low- Income Mothers, Fathers and Children," National Women's Law Center and Center on Fathers, Families, and Public Policy, Washington, DC, 2000, pp. 9-11.

[106] William J. Doherty, Edward F. Kouneski, and Martha Farrell Erickson, "Responsible Fathering: An Overview and Conceptual Framework—Final Report," U.S. Department of Health and Human Services, Administration for Children and Families, Center for Policy Research and Policy Studies (HHS-100-93-0012), Washington, DC, September 1996.

[107] For more information, see CRS Report RL3 1025, *Fatherhood Initiatives: Connecting Fathers to Their Children*, by Carmen Solomon-Fears. Also see http://fatherhood.hhs.gov/Research/index.shtml and http://www.fatherhood.org/ evaluation.asp.

[108] Urban Institute, "Ten Key Findings from Responsible Fatherhood Initiatives," by Karin Martinson and Demetra Nightingale, February 2008.

[109] Ibid., p. 8.

[110] Annie E. Casey Foundation, "Promoting Responsible Fatherhood," A Guide To Key Ideas, Effective Approaches, and Technical Assistance Resources for Making Connections Cities and Site Teams, 2005, http://www.aecf.org/upload/ publicationfiles/fatherhood_pages.pdf.

[111] U.S. Department of Health and Human Services, Administration for Children and Families, Children's Bureau, "The Importance of Fathers in the Healthy Development of Children," Section II, 8. Fatherhood Programs, by Jeffrey Rosenberg and Bradford W. Wilcox, 2006, http://www.childwelfare.gov/pubs/usermanuals/fatherhood/chaptereight.cfm.

[112] U.S. Department of Health and Human Services, "Father Involvement in Head Start and Early Head Start," http://fatherhood.hhs.gov/Parenting/hs.shtml.

[113] Sorenson and Zibman, *Poor Dads Who Don't Pay Child Support: Deadbeat or Disadvantaged?*

[114] Section 106 of WIA.

[115] The list of required partners, including references to the authorizing statutes for each program, is in Section 121(b)(1)(B) of WIA.

[116] For further information on the formula factors used in the state formula grant allocations, see Department of Labor, Employment and Training Administration, "Workforce Investment Act (WIA) and Wagner-Peyser Act Statutory Formulas for State Allotments," http://www.doleta.gov/budget/WIAFormDesc.pdf.

[117] Grants authorized under WIA Section 173(a)(1) are for employment and training assistance to workers affected by major economic dislocations, such as plant closures or mass layoffs.

[118] WIA Sections 132(a)(2)(A) and (a)(2)(B) require that 20% of the amount appropriated for Dislocated Worker Employment and Training Activities be reserved for national emergency grants, projects, and technical assistance. The remaining 80% is to be used for state formula grants.

[119] In FY2009, the National Reserve includes $125 million for Community-Based Job Training (CBJT) grants (see below).

[120] Thus, the date on which an individual has finished his or her participation in WIA determines the program year for which data are generated on the exiter. For example, if an individual received services throughout the entire 2008 calendar year and last received WIA services on December 15, 2008, the data for that individual are included as part of Program Year (PY) 2009. A program year runs from July 1-June 30 (e.g., PY2009 runs from July 1, 2009-June 30, 2010). Due to deadlines for submitting data for the WIASRD annual Data Book, the most recent period for which data are available is April 1, 2008-March 31, 2009. U.S. Department of Labor, *PY2008 WIASRD Data Book*, Table II-1 and Table II-12, http://www.doleta.gov/performance/results/pdf/PY_2008_WIASRD_Data_Book_FINAL_1192010.pdf.

[121] U.S. Department of Labor, *Budget Justification of Appropriations Estimates for Committee on Appropriations*, FY20 10, Volume I, Washington, DC, 2009, p. TES-74.

[122] Ibid.

[123] Sara McLanahan and Gary Sandefur, *Growing Up with a Single Parent: What Hurts, What Helps* (Cambridge, MA: Harvard University Press, 1994), pp. 3 9-56.

[124] Ib id, p. 54. These studies do not account for whether teens are cohabiting with a partner.

[125] For information on these programs, see CRS Report RL33975, *Vulnerable Youth: Background and Policies*, by Adrienne L. Fernandes-Alcantara.

[126] Brady E. Hamilton, Joyce A. Martin, and Stephanie J. Ventura, "Births: Preliminary Data for 2008," National Vital Statistics Reports, vol. 58, no. 16, April 2010.

[127] For more information, see CRS Report RS20301, *Teenage Pregnancy Prevention: Statistics and Programs*, by Carmen Solomon-Fears; and CRS Report R4061 8, *Teen Pregnancy Prevention: Background and Proposals in the 111th Congress*, by Carmen Solomon-Fears.

[128] U.S. Congress, House Ways and Means, Subcommittee on Human Resources, Testimony of Dr. Isabel V. Sawhill on Nonmarital Births and Child Poverty in the United States, June 29, 1999.

[129] General Accounting Office, Teen Pregnancy: State and Federal Efforts to Implement Prevention Programs and Measure Their Effectiveness, GAO/HEHS-99-4, November 1998.

[130] Alan Guttmacher Institute, "United States and the Russian Federation Lead the Developed World in Teenage Pregnancy Rates," News Release, February 24, 2000, p. 2.

[131] The National Campaign to Prevent Teen Pregnancy, By the Numbers: The Public Cost of Teen Childbearing, by Saul D. Hoffman. October 2006.

[132] For further information, see CRS Report R40535, *Disconnected Youth: A Look at 16- to 24-Year Olds Who Are Not Working or In School*, by Adrienne L. Fernandes-Alcantara and Thomas Gabe.

[133] U.S. Department of Labor, Office of Job Corps, *Job Corps Annual Report PY2006*, http://www.jobcorps.gov/Libraries/pdf/py06report.sflb and http://www.gao.gov/products/GAO USA, YouthBuild Program Demographics and Outcomes 2005-2009, http://www.youthbuild.org/site/c.htlRI3PIKoG/b.1418407/.

[134] Up to 5% of youth participants in a local area may be individuals who do not meet the income criteria but have at least one barrier to employment, some of which are not identical to those listed above: (1) deficient in basic literacy skills; (2) a school dropout; (3) homeless or runaway; (4) an offender; (5) one or more grade levels below the grade level appropriate to the individual's age; (6) pregnant or parenting; (7) possess one or more disabilities, including learning disabilities; or (8) face serious barriers to employment as identified by the local WIB (20 C.F.R. 664.220).

[135] Title I, Section 101(33) of the Workforce Investment Act.

[136] Youth Activities, Job Corps, and YouthBuild operate on the basis of a Program Year (PY), which runs from July 1 through June 30. For example, PY2008 is from July 1, 2008, through June 30, 2009. The incongruity between the program year and the most recent data for Youth Activities appears to be a function of the timing of data collection and the compilation of the data. That is, the most recent Data Book (PY2008) "does not use information for exiters after March 2009 because that information is incomplete." See *PY2008 Data Book*, January 19, 2010, available from DOL at http://www.doleta.gov/performance/results/pdf/PY_2008_WIASRD_Data_Book_FINAL_1192010.pdf.

[137] U. S. Department of Health and Human Services and U.S. Department of Labor, Joint ETA -A CF Letter, January 19, 2010, http://www.acf.hhs.gov/programs/ofa/policy

[138] Jamaal Abdul-Alim, "Still Waiting for Summer Jobs Bill, States Tap TANF Funds for Programs," *Youth Today*, June 14, 2010.

[139] Title I, Subtitle C of the Workforce Investment Act.

[140] 20 C.F.R. 670.110.

[141] U.S. Department of Labor, Education and Training Administration, Office of Job Corps, *Budget Justification of Appropriation Estimates for Committees on Appropriations, FY2011*, vol. III, p. OJC-17.

[142] Based on correspondence with the Department of Labor, Office of Congressional and Intergovernmental Affairs, June 2010.

[143] John Burghardt et al., *Does Job Corps Really Work? Summary of the National Job Corps Study*, Mathematica Policy Research, Inc., June 2001.

[144] Peter Z. Schochet, John Burghardt, and Sheena McConnell, *National Job Corps Study and Longer-Term Follow-Up Study: Impact and Benefit-Cost Findings Using Survey and Summary Earnings Records Data, Final Report*, Mathematica Policy Research, Inc., August 2006, pp. 16-17.

[145] For additional information on reauthorization of the HEA and background on HEA programs, see CRS Report RL34654, *The Higher Education Opportunity Act: Reauthorization of the Higher Education Act*, by David P. Smole et al.

[146] U.S. Department of Education, *FY2011 Justifications for Appropriation Estimates to the Congress, Volume II*, p. U132, http://www2.ed.gov/about/overview/budget/budget11/justifications/u-highered.pdf.

[147] It should be noted that not all states identify Tech-Prep students using the same criteria. Data on the characteristics of students participating in Tech-Prep programs were not provided. For more information, see U.S. Department of Education, Office of Vocational and Adult Education, *Carl D. Perkins Vocational and Technical Education Act of 1998: Report to Congress on State Performance Program Year 2006-07*, September 2008, available online at http://www.ed.gov/about/offices/list/ovae/resource/perkinsrpt0607.pdf.

[148] U.S. Department of Defense, National Guard, *Youth ChalleNGe Program 2009 Performance and Accountability Highlights*, 2009, https://ngcp.org/docs/uploaddocs/2009%20Annual%20Report.pdf.

[149] Dan Bloom, Alissa Gardenhire-Crooks, and Conrad Mandsager, *Reengaging High School Dropouts: Early Results of the National Guard Youth ChalleNGe Program Evaluation*, Manpower Research Development Corporation (MDRC); and Megan Millenky, Dan Bloom, and Colleen Dillon, *Making the Transition: Interim*

Results of the National Guard Youth ChalleNGe Evaluation, Manpower Research Development Corporation (MDRC), May 2010. Both publications are available at http://www.mdrc.org/project

[150] Jacquelyn Boggess, "The President's Fatherhood, Marriage, and Family Innovation Fund," Center for Family Policy and Practice, June 7, 2010.

[151] U.S. Department of Health And Human Services (ACF), "FY2011 Congressional Justification: Temporary Assistance for Needy Families (TANF)," pp. 304-305, http://www.acf.hhs.gov/programs/olab/budget/2011/TANF.pdf.

[152] Ibid, p. 305.

[153] Ibid.

[154] Ibid.

[155] Jacquelyn Boggess, "The President's Fatherhood, Marriage, and Family Innovation Fund," Center for Family Policy and Practice, June 7, 2010.

[156] The Heritage Foundation, "Married Fathers: Weapon No. 1 Against Child Poverty," June 17, 2010.

[157] Most of the information in this section was taken from CRS Report R40499, *Child Support Enforcement and Ex-Offenders*, by Carmen Solomon-Fears.

[158] U.S. Department of Health and Human Services, Administration for Children and Families, Office of Child Support Enforcement, "The National Child Support Enforcement Strategic Plan FY2005-2009," 2004, http://www.acf.hhs.gov/ programs/cse/pubs/2004/Strategic_Plan_FY2005-2009.pdf. (Hereinafter, U.S. Department of Health and Human Services, Administration for Children and Families, Office of Child Support Enforcement, "The National Child Support Enforcement Strategic Plan FY2005-2009.")

[159] Elaine Sorensen and Helen Oliver, "Policy Reforms are Needed to Increase Child Support from Poor Fathers," The Urban Institute, April 2002.

[160] U.S. Department of Health and Human Services, "State Use of Debt Compromise to Reduce Child Support Arrearages," Office of Inspector General, October 2007.

[161] Maria Cancian, Carolyn Heinrich, and Yiyoon Chung, "Does Debt Discourage Employment and Payment of Child Support? Evidence from a Natural Experiment," University of Wisconsin-Madison, Institute for Research on Poverty, Discussion Paper no. 13 66-09, July 2009.

[162] U.S. Department of Health and Human Services, Administration for Children and Families, Office of Child Support Enforcement, "The National Child Support Enforcement Strategic Plan FY2005-2009."

[163] U.S. Department of Health and Human Services, Office of Inspector General, "State Use of Debt Compromise to Reduce Child Support Arrearages," October 2007.

[164] The HHS Administration for Children and Families (ACF) cautions that as a matter of prudent use of TANF or MOE funds, it would be inadvisable, although it is technically permissible, to use such funds to pay debts unless both parties (i.e., the custodial and noncustodial parent) are needy. (Source: U.S. Department of Health and Human Services, "Questions and Answers on the American Recovery and Reinvestment Act of 2009 (Recovery Act)," Administration for Children and Families, 2009, http://www.acf.hhs.gov/programs/ofa/recovery

[165] Most child support is collected through payroll withholding. Under the Consumer Credit Protection Act (15 USC 1673(b)), 50%–65% of a parent's disposable earnings may be deducted from the noncustodial parent's paycheck. At the same time, a separate court or probation officer could require that an individual dedicate 35% of his or her income toward the combined payment of fines, fees, surcharges, and restitution. Such a situation could encourage a person to return to the behavior and illegal activities that resulted in the person's incarceration in the first place. In other words, aggressive collectors representing distinct agencies could end up contributing to a person's failure to meet his or her financial obligations and, by extension, their revocation of probation or parole.

[166] Marguerite Roulet, "Financial Literacy and Low-Income Noncustodial Parents," Center for Family Policy and Practice," June 2009.

[167] The proposed Responsible Fatherhood and Healthy Families Act of 2009 (S. 1309 and H.R. 2979) from the 111th Congress would have prohibited a state from considering a period of incarceration as voluntary unemployment in determining or modifying a noncustodial parent's child support obligation. It also would require states to temporarily suspend the child support obligation and any interest on the child support obligation during the period a noncustodial parent is incarcerated. However, it would require the state to provide the custodial parent with an opportunity to request that the child support obligation continue on the basis that the noncustodial parent has sufficient income or resources to continue to make child support payments during the noncustodial parent's period of incarceration. In addition, the bills would require states to review, and if appropriate, reduce the balance of child support arrearages permanently assigned to the state in cases where the noncustodial parent (1) does not have the ability to pay the arrearages, (2) did not seek a modification during his or her incarceration, and (3) will be more willing (because of the adjustment) to pay current child support payments consistently and on time. Finally, it must be determined that it is in the best interest of the child for the state to make such a reduction.

[168] Federal law prioritizes child support obligations above all other debts owed to the state, including restitution, and court and prison fines, fees, and surcharges. The proposed provision would allow judges, when ordering that

an individual pay fees to reimburse the state for the costs of his or her incarceration, to reduce this order by the amount of the individual's child support obligations.

[169] Some judges have ruled that incarcerated parents are responsible for their disadvantaged financial circumstances that resulted from their criminal activities because imprisonment is a foreseeable result of criminal behavior. In contrast, other judges have refused to equate incarceration with voluntary unemployment and have argued that incarcerated parents rarely have any actual job prospects or potential income and cannot alter their employment situation. (Source: Jessica Pearson, "Building Debt While Doing Time: Child Support and Incarceration," 2004.)

[170] In states that classify incarceration as "voluntary unemployment," a person's child support order may not be modified when he or she enters prison or jail.

[171] Jessica Pearson, "Building Debt While Doing Time: Child Support and Incarceration," 2004.

[172] Jennifer L. Noyes, "Review of Child Support Policies for Incarcerated Payers," Institute for Research on Poverty, University of Wisconsin-Madison, December 2006.

[173] The allotment formula is based on the ratio of the number of children in the state living with only one biological parent to the total number of such children in all states. The amount of the allotment available to a state would be this same ratio applied to $12 million.

[174] Judicial Council of California (Administrative Office of the Courts, Center for Families, Children and the Courts), "Ten Years of Access to Visitation Grant Program Services (Fiscal Years 1997–2007)," A Report to the California Legislature, March 2008, p. iv.

[175] Ibid., p. 36.

[176] Low-income individual means an individual who (1) receives, or is a member of a family that receives, cash payments through a federal, state, or local income-based public assistance program; (2) received an income, or is a member of a family that received a total family income (excluding unemployment compensation and certain other payments), for the six-month period prior to applying for youth employment and training activities, that, in relation to family size, did not exceed the higher of the poverty line, for an equivalent period, or 70% of the lower living standard income level, for an equivalent period; (3) is a member of a household that receives SNAP benefits (or has been determined to be eligible for SNAP within the six-month period prior to applying for youth employment and training activities); (4) qualifies as a homeless individual, as defined by the McKinney-Vento Homeless Assistance Act; or (5) is a foster child on behalf of whom state or local government payments are made.

[177] U.S. Department of Labor, Employment and Training Administration, *Budget Justification of Appropriation Estimates for Committees on Appropriations, FY2011*, pp. ETA-3 through ETA-5, http://www.dol.gov/dol/budget/ 201 1/PDF/CBJ-201 1-V1-03.pdf.

[178] Peter Z. Schochet, John Burghardt, and Sheena McConnell, *National Job Corps Study and Longer-Term Follow-Up Study: Impact and Benefit-Cost Findings Using Survey and Summary Earnings Records Data, Final Report*, Mathematica Policy Research, Inc., August 2006, http://wdr.doleta.gov/research/FullText_Documents/ National%20Job%20Corps%20Study%20and%20Longer%20Term%20Follow-Up%20Study%20- %20Final%20Report.pdf.

[179] Because participants were randomly assigned to the program, researchers could determine the effects of the program on employment and earnings and then look at the program's impact on the likelihood of marriage. Random assignment allows researchers to control for the possibility that family status and unobserved traits (e.g., personal abilities, temperament, responsibility, etc.) may make certain individuals more likely to be successful in the labor market.

[180] For further information, see Dan Bloom, *Transitional Jobs: Background, Program Models, and Evaluation Evidence*, MDRC, February 2010, http://www.mdrc.org/publications/553/abstract.html.

[181] Ibid.

[182] Ib id, pp. 41-45.

[183] Professor Lawrence Mead, of New York University, has written articles and testified before Congress advocating work requirements for non-paying, noncustodial parents. See Lawrence M. Mead, "Why We Need Work Programs for Fathers," *Journal of Policy Analysis and Management*, vol. 29, no. 3 (Summer 2010), pp. 610-616.

[184] All CSE jurisdictions have civil or criminal contempt-of-court procedures. Thus, if a court orders a noncustodial parent to pay his or her past-due child support and the noncustodial parent fails to do so, that parent would be in contempt-of-court and subject to jail time. Moreover, there are federal criminal penalties associated with the willful failure to pay a past-due child support obligation to a child who resides in another state and that has remained unpaid for longer than a year or is greater than $5,000. States have a lot of discretion on whether or not to use certain collection methods and when to use such methods. Generally, incarceration is the last option states use. Most states use the jail option sparingly because it "punishes" both the custodial family and the "delinquent" noncustodial parent. States realize that if a person is in jail, it is less likely that the person will be able to pay child support. Thus, it is usually the threat of jail, rather than jail per se, that results in child support payments.

[185] Ibid.

[186] James J. Kemple, *Career Academies: Long-Term Impacts on Labor Market Outcomes, Educational Attainment, and Transitions to Adulthood*, Manpower Development Research Corporation (MDRC), June 2008, http://www.mdrc.org/publications/482/overview.html.

[187] For information about these interventions and other interventions in higher education, see Thomas Brock, "Young Adults and Higher Education: Barriers and Breakthroughs to Success," *The Future of Children*, vol. 20, no. 1 (Spring 2010).

[188] The bill was H.R. 3221, the Student Aid and Fiscal Responsibility Act of 2009.

[189] For a discussion of the noncustodial EITC programs in New York and the District of Columbia, see Laura Wheaton and Elaine Sorensen, *Extending the EITC to Noncustodial Parents: Potential Impacts and Design Considerations*, Urban Institute, Washington, DC, May 23, 2009.

[190] Elaine Sorensen, *New York Noncustodial Parent EITC: Implementation and First Year Findings*, Urban Institute, Submitted to the New York State Office of Temporary and Disability Assistance, February 22, 2010.

[191] For example, S. 1309, the Responsible Fatherhood and Healthy Families Act of 2009 (111th Congress), would have doubled the EITC paid to a noncustodial parent without a qualifying child who is under a child support order enforced through the CSE program and pays at least the amount of current child support owed.

[192] This was proposed in H.R. 2979, the Julia Carson Responsible Fatherhood and Healthy Families Act (111th Congress).

[193] Stephen D. Holt and Elaine Maag, *Considerations in Efforts to Restructure Refundable Work-Based Credits*.

[194] Wayne G. Osgood et al., eds., *On Your Own Without a Net: The Transition to Adulthood for Vulnerable Populations*, (Chicago: The University of Chicago Press, 2005), pp. 4-6.

[195] Claudia Goldin, Lawrence F. Katz, and Ilyana Kuziemko, "The Homecoming of American College Women: The Reversal of the College Gender Gap," *Journal of Economic Perspectives*, vol. 20, no. 4, Fall 2006.

[196] Bob Schoeni and Karen Ross, "Material Assistance Received from Families During the Transition to Adulthood." In Richard A. Settersten, Jr., Frank F. Furstenburg, Jr., and Rubén Rumbaut, eds., *On the Frontier of Adulthood: Theory, Research, and Public Policy*, (Chicago: University of Chicago Press, 2005), pp. 404-405.

In: Child Well-Being and Nonresident Parents
Editor: Laura M. Fernandes

ISBN: 978-1-60692-382-5
© 2011 Nova Science Publishers, Inc.

Chapter 2

CHILD SUPPORT ENFORCEMENT AND EX-OFFENDERS

Carmen Solomon-Fears

SUMMARY

According to recent estimates, about 1.7 million children in the United States have parents who are currently incarcerated in state or federal prisons. Among the approximately 700,000 persons who are released from prison each year about 400,000 of them are fathers and mothers. The current economic crisis together with overcrowded prisons and state budget shortfalls are likely to result in a significant number of inmates convicted of nonviolent offenses getting early release dispensations. How these former inmates reconnect to their families impacts not only the children involved but society at large and is of great interest to Congress and the nation.

Ex-offenders re-entering communities face a host of problems, a major one being barriers to employment because of their criminal records. Most employers now conduct background checks, with the result that people are often denied employment or even fired from jobs because of their criminal records. Research indicates that employment and family support are important predictors of an ex-offender's successful re-entry into his or her community. Given that employment opportunities are scarce and may become more limited in the current economy, family support is even more important for formerly incarcerated parents.

The Child Support Enforcement (CSE) program is a federal-state program whose mission is to enhance the well-being of children by helping custodial parents and children obtain financial support from the noncustodial parents, including those in prison or who were formerly incarcerated. Child support payments enable parents who do not live with their children to fulfill their financial responsibility to their children by contributing to the payment of childrearing costs. Parents who make regular child support payments are more likely than those who do not to have better family relationships. Also, prisoner re-entry programs and responsible fatherhood programs sometimes help noncustodial parents establish positive, productive connections to their children. Research indicates that positive family relationships increase family stability and can help reduce recidivism.

Connecting children to their noncustodial parents has become a goal of federal social policy. Promoting coordination among federal and state programs may help programs optimize their resources. Some prisons and local communities are helping noncustodial parents acknowledge their child support responsibilities by offering parenting programs, informational sessions on how to deal with the CSE agency, conflict-resolution classes, and job readiness preparation. Research highlights the common ground between the prison system and the CSE system. For example, studies show that family support is one of the key factors in lowering the probability that ex- offenders will return to prison and research further indicates that being involved in the lives of one's children promotes responsible behavior, such as making regular child support payments and being productive citizens. Federally-mandated program coordination in certain areas may be one way to increase child support collections and simultaneously reduce recidivism.

This report focuses on the CSE program. It examines the CSE program within the context of large numbers of former inmates re-entering local communities. It raises several issues related to noncustodial parents who are ex-offenders (i.e., former inmates). The report also presents policy options that could help increase child support collections from low-income noncustodial parents, some of whom are former inmates. A by-product of increased child support collections could be a positive, productive relationship between ex-offenders and their children, which could result in lower recidivism rates among inmates who are noncustodial parents. This report will not be updated.

INTRODUCTION

About 1.7 million children in the United States have parents who are currently incarcerated[1] and more than 10 million U.S. children are separated from one of their parents during a portion of their childhood because of the parent's incarceration.[2]

According to the Bureau of Justice Statistics, of the 1.5 million inmates held in the nation's prisons (federal and state) in mid-2007, approximately 809,800 of them (53%) were parents of minor children. Of the estimated 700,000 persons who are released from prison each year,[3] about 400,000 of them are fathers and mothers.[4]

For the last 30 years, states have locked up more persons (many for longer periods of time) and have built more prisons to hold them. Now many states faced with reduced resources and huge prison costs are reevaluating their prison policies and practices.[5] The current economic crisis together with overcrowded prisons and state budget shortfalls may lead to thousands of parents convicted of nonviolent offenses (e.g., persons with drug offenses, burglary, check fraud, or theft convictions) getting out of prison months (in some cases, a year or more) earlier than they were sentenced. How former inmates reconnect to their families impacts not only the children involved but society at large and is of great interest to Congress and the nation.

More now than in the past, corrections institutions are acknowledging that most of their population will eventually be released, and probably sooner than the maximum time allowed by their sentence. Thus, they are moving toward a position that will allow them to effectively help inmates successfully transition back into local communities.[6] Successful re-entry means lower recidivism and thereby reduced costs for penal institutions. It also means safer communities.[7] A broad array of research indicates that the two most important factors in successful re-entry are employment and a healthy connection to one's family.[8]

The Child Support Enforcement (CSE) program is a federal-state program whose mission is to enhance the well-being of children by helping custodial parents and children obtain financial support from the noncustodial parents, including those in prison or who were formerly in prison. Child support payments enable parents who do not live with their children to fulfill their financial responsibility to their children by contributing to the payment of childrearing costs. There is a growing consensus that the CSE program is one of the financial keys to helping families remain self-sufficient. According to the most recently available data, on average, child support constitutes about 17% of family income for households who receive it. Among poor households who receive it, child support constitutes about 30% of family income.[9] Parents who make regular child support payments are more likely than those who do not to have better family relationships. Research indicates that positive family relationships increase family stability and can help reduce recidivism. The intersection of the mission of state and federal correction facilities (i.e., successful re-entry of former prisoners into local communities) and the mission of the CSE program (i.e., consistent payment of child support obligations) provides both systems with an opportunity to marshal their efforts in a way that results in positive outcomes for children. Both Congress and the Obama Administration are examining federal programs in an effort to reduce waste in the federal budget. Although programs are often evaluated in isolation, the likelihood of reduced federal and state funding may promote more innovative thinking and collaboration among agencies involved in administering the criminal justice system and CSE program.

This report examines the CSE program within the context of large numbers of former inmates reentering communities. It provides a brief review of the CSE program and data related to parents who are in state or federal prisons. Next, it analyzes several issues that relate to the payment of child support by incarcerated or formerly incarcerated parents. Then it presents policy options that address the problem of nonpayment of child support. For example, it discusses ways in which the CSE program can help ex-offenders who are parents reconnect with their children and communities. It also suggests strategies that may lead to both lower recidivism and more parents making child support payments.

BACKGROUND

This report focuses on the CSE program to explore ways to deal with nonpayment of child support by noncustodial parents who are or were in prison. As higher numbers of inmates are released, the CSE program will face more pressure to perform better in the area of increasing child support collections and reducing child support debt. If it is successful, a positive consequence may be fewer parents returning to prison. It is thought that even under current economic conditions, a positive family life will encourage formerly incarcerated noncustodial parents to keep looking for legitimate employment and to steadfastly maintain law-abiding behaviors. This section provides a brief overview of the CSE program. It also presents information and data related to noncustodial parents who are incarcerated or who were formerly incarcerated.

The Child Support Enforcement (CSE) Program

The CSE program was enacted in 1975 as a federal-state program (Title IV-D of the Social Security Act) to help strengthen families by securing financial support for children from their noncustodial parent on a consistent and continuing basis and by helping some families to remain self-sufficient and off public assistance. The CSE program provides seven major services on behalf of children: (1) parent location, (2) paternity establishment, (3) establishment of child support orders, (4) review and modification of child support orders, (5) collection of child support payments, (6) distribution of child support payments, and (7) establishment and enforcement of medical support. The CSE program serves both families that receive Temporary Assistance for Needy Families (TANF) benefits and those who do not. All 50 states and four jurisdictions (the District of Columbia, Guam, Puerto Rico, and the U.S. Virgin Islands) operate CSE programs.[10] The CSE program is administered by the federal Office of Child Support Enforcement (OCSE) which is in the Administration on Children and Families (ACF) within the Department of Health and Human Services (HHS). Most child support collections on behalf of families receiving TANF benefits are used to reimburse state and federal governments for TANF payments made to the family. Child support collected on behalf of nonwelfare families goes to the family, usually through the state disbursement unit.

The federal government and the states share program costs at the rate of 66% and 34%, respectively. The federal government also pays states an incentive payment to encourage them to operate effective CSE programs. Federal law requires states to reinvest CSE incentive payments back into the CSE program or related activities. In FY2007, the CSE program collected $24.9 billion in child support payments from noncustodial parents and served nearly 15.8 million child support cases. On average, the program collected $4.73 in child support payments for each $1 spent on the program. In that year, CSE expenditures amounted to nearly $5.6 billion.[11]

Although there is a general consensus that the CSE program is performing well,[12] in FY2007, the CSE program only made collections for about 55% of its caseload and collected only 19% of child support obligations for which it had responsibility. Part of the reason for these low performance figures is that the CSE program cannot enforce a child support obligation until one is formally established either through an administrative process (via the state CSE system), a judicial process (via the state court system), or a combination of the two (i.e., via a quasi-judicial system). Moreover, a child support order can only be established if the issue of paternity has been settled.[13] In FY2006, approximately 5 million of the 17 million children in the CSE program (i.e., 29%) had not been issued child support orders on their behalf.

Another reason for the poor performance figures is that many of those who owe child support have low incomes. A 2007 Urban Institute survey of three states—Florida, Illinois, and Pennsylvania—indicated that "Across these three states, the average monthly earnings of noncustodial parents were only $23 higher than the average monthly earnings of custodial parents. Employed non-custodial parents in Illinois had the highest monthly earnings at $2,765 per month, and those in Pennsylvania had the lowest, at $1,297 per month."[14] Although there are no recent data that provide a good estimate of how many low-income parents do not pay child support because they are financially unable to pay, most policymakers agree that the number is significant.[15]

Incarcerated Parents and Child Support Obligations

According to the Bureau of Justice Statistics, in mid-2007, about 53% of 1.5 million U.S. prisoners[16] held in the nation's prisons were parents of minor children. (See **Figure 1**.) These parents (52% of state inmates and 63% of federal inmates) reported having 1.7 million minor children.

There are no national data that differentiate inmates from other noncustodial parents in terms of percentage with child support orders, average monthly amount of child support owed, average amount paid, and amount of arrearages (i.e., past-due payments) owed, but it is widely held that inmates and former inmates pay the lowest amount of child support. Moreover, there is some anecdotal information that indicates that child support arrearages of inmates and former inmates are very high.[17]

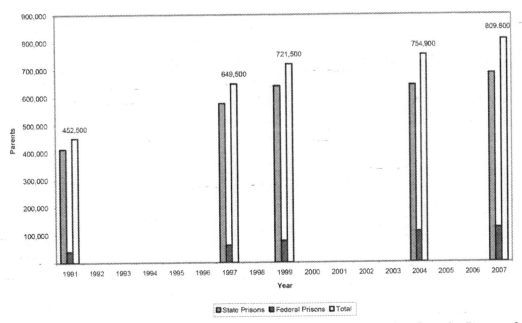

Source. Chart prepared by the Congressional Research Service, based on data from the Bureau of Justice Statistics Special Report entitled, "Parents in Prison and Their Minor Children," August 2008.

Figure 1. Estimated Number of Parents in State and Federal Prisons—Data for 1991, 1997, 1999, 2004, and 2007.

According to one study, about 25% of inmates have open child support cases. Incarcerated noncustodial parents generally owe between $225 to $313 per month in child support; and on average they enter prison owing about $10,000 in child support arrearages and leave prison owing more then $23,000 in arrearage payments.[18]

ISSUES

Given the high cost of state and federal prison systems[19] and the high recidivism rates,[20] it is not surprising that policymakers at all levels of government are interested in promoting policies and strategies that help former inmates successfully reunite with their children and families and effectively reintegrate into their communities. Research suggests that family support and employment are the two most important predictors of an ex-offender's successful re-entry into his or her community.

During this time of reduced resources at both the state and national level, policymakers and program administrators are interested in ensuring that programs are effective and efficient. The Obama Administration has stated that there will be increased scrutiny of federal programs in an effort to reduce waste in the federal budget.[21] Also, Congress, as part of its budget duties and oversight authority, will be reviewing programs for their effectiveness.

This section examines the CSE program within the analytic framework of addressing the impact of huge numbers of inmates that may be released back into local communities sooner than expected because of state and federal budget shortfalls and overcrowded prisons. It begins with a discussion of how unrealistic child support orders and high child support debt may be adversely affecting overall CSE program results and public perceptions about the program. Although most CSE data cannot be disaggregated to isolate inmates or former inmates who owe child support, many ex-offenders are low-income noncustodial parents.[22] Thus, any of the proposals that would help resolve child support issues related to the low income levels of noncustodial parents would also impact a significant percentage of inmates and former inmates who are parents. This section also discusses how the increase of mothers in prisons may impact the CSE program. Further, it looks at federal law that permits the termination of parental rights of ex-offenders.

Unrealistic Child Support Orders

A child support order legally obligates noncustodial parents to provide financial support for their children and stipulates the amount of the obligation (monthly obligation plus arrearages, if any) and how it is to be paid.

Brief History of Child Support Order Establishment

Before October 1989, the decision of how much a parent should pay for child support was left primarily to the discretion of the courts. Typically, judges examined financial statements from mothers and fathers and established awards based on children's needs. The resulting awards varied greatly. In an attempt to increase the use of objective criteria, the Child Support Enforcement Amendments of 1984 (P.L. 98-378) required each state to establish guidelines for determining child support award amounts. However, the 1984 provision did not make the guidelines binding on judges and other officials who had the authority to establish child support obligations. It was the Family Support Act of 1988 (P.L. 100-485) which required that the state- established child support award guidelines be considered the appropriate child support amount unless the court or CSE agency determined (i.e., successfully made the case) that a different amount would be in the best interest of the child.

By requiring the states to establish child support guidelines, the federal government hoped to accomplish four main goals: (1) increase the adequacy of child support awards; (2) increase the consistency and predictability of child support awards; (3) increase compliance through perceived fairness of child support awards; and (4) increase the ease of administration of child support cases.[23] States generally use one of three basic types of guidelines to determine child support award amounts: "Income shares," which is based on the combined income of both parents (37 jurisdictions);[24] "percentage of income," in which the number of eligible children is used to determine a percentage of the noncustodial parent's income to be paid in child support (13 jurisdictions);[25] and "Melson-Delaware," which provides a minimum self-support reserve for parents before the cost of rearing the children is prorated between the parents to determine the award amount (3 states).[26] One jurisdiction, Puerto Rico, did not specify which guideline it follows.[27]

Current Problems Associated with Child Support Orders

There is a lot of variation among the states with regard to the amount of the child support obligation established by the state-established child support guidelines, particularly at the lower end of the income spectrum. The variance in child support orders widens further because many states specify an income threshold below which child support orders are established differently than under the state's regular guideline rules.[28] Moreover, there are several controversial issues associated with child support awards that also increase the range in child support awards among states. These issues include whether child care costs, extraordinary medical expenses, and college costs are taken into account in determining the child support order; how the income of stepparents is treated; how the income of the noncustodial parent is allocated between first and subsequent families; whether a minimum child support award level regardless of age or circumstance of the noncustodial parent should be imposed; and the duration of the support order (i.e., does the support obligation end when the child reaches age 18; what happens to arrearages once the child reaches the age of majority).

The bottom line is that in many cases current levels of child support exceed what many middle and lower income noncustodial parents can afford to pay.[29] Also, there is much acrimony between noncustodial parents and the CSE system because noncustodial parents contend that the CSE program does not consider "affordability" as a legitimate factor in calculating child support award amounts. They point to the fact that in many states the basic living expenses of the noncustodial parent such as rent, food, and car payments are often not taken into account in determining the child support order.[30]

In addition to the guidelines, the child support obligation is dependent on the way in which the state determines the amount of income to which the guidelines should be applied. When information about actual income is not available, considered unreliable, or when a decision-maker contends that the noncustodial parent's low income is the result of voluntary unemployment or underemployment, income may be attributed to the noncustodial parent and the child support award guideline calculation is then based on that imputed income even if the imputed income is based on incorrect assumptions.

Setting child support orders at a level that exceeds a noncustodial parent's ability to pay may in some cases decrease the amount of child support received by the custodial parent because of the noncustodial parent's low income and/or because of the noncustodial parent's contention that the CSE system is unfair.[31] In contrast, CSE policies that result in realistic child support orders, especially for persons at the lower end of the income scale, may result in more child support from low-income noncustodial parents, many of whom are former inmates.

High Child Support Arrearages

Despite record collections by state CSE programs, considerable sums of child support go unpaid every year. In FY2007, $138.0 billion in child support obligations ($30.8 billion in current support and $107.2 billion in past-due support) was owed to families receiving CSE services, but only $26.1 billion was paid ($18.8 billion in current support and $7.3 billion in past-due support).[32] This meant that the CSE program only collected 19% of the child support obligations for which it had responsibility. If current collections are examined separately, the data indicate that the CSE program collected 61% of all current child support payments in FY2007. If collections on past-due support (i.e., arrearages) are examined separately, the data show that the CSE program collected less than 7% of arrearage payments in FY2007. In other words, the total amount of arrearages reported in FY2007 for all fiscal years (i.e., FY2007 and all previous years) was $107.2 billion; but only $7.3 billion was collected in FY2007.

Child Support Debt Accumulation

Child support arrearages can be accumulated in several ways, depending upon the guidelines established by the state. The first and most prevalent way is through nonpayment of child support. For each month that a noncustodial parent fails to meet the full child support obligation, the unpaid support (i.e., this is generally referred to as past-due payments or arrearages) is added to the amount the noncustodial parent owes.[33] Another way that arrearages accumulate is of special importance to ex-offenders. The arrearages mount because in most states and localities child support orders remain payable and in effect even when the noncustodial parent is unemployed or incarcerated.[34]

CSE law recognizes that a child support order, which can be in effect for 18 years or longer, may not be appropriate for the duration of the order.[35] Nevertheless, child support orders are not automatically changed when the child's or the parent's circumstances change. In order for a noncustodial parent to have his or her child support order lowered, the CSE program and the courts generally require that there be a change in the financial circumstances of the noncustodial parent. Next, the noncustodial parent must petition the CSE agency or the court to have his or her child support order modified. Although no state automatically modifies child support orders whenever there is a change in financial circumstances, CSE law now requires (pursuant to P.L. 109-171) states to review and, if necessary, adjust child support orders on behalf of children who receive TANF benefits at least once every three years. Nevertheless, in many states, being in prison is not a basis for child support modification. To the contrary, some states (courts and CSE agencies) view incarceration as voluntary unemployment. They hold that, because imprisonment is the result of an intentional criminal act, incarceration and the loss of income are voluntary acts. In some states, incarceration is just one among many factors that that are examined in determining whether or not to lower the child support order. In other states, incarcerated parents who petition the state (court or CSE agency) are usually determined eligible to have their child support order modified to a lower amount.

Unlike in earlier times (pre-1996), the CSE program has a vast array of enforcement methods that it can use to collect child support arrearages.[36] A premise of the CSE program is that having and using such enforcement tools encourages parents to meet their obligations regularly and on time and also sends the message that there are serious consequences for nonpayment of child support.

Current Problems Associated with High Child Support Arrearages

Many noncustodial parents mistakenly believe that if they fall behind in their child support payments at a time when they are legitimately unable to make the payments, the amount they owe can later be reduced or discounted by a court when an explanation for nonpayment is given. In fact, if a noncustodial parent waits to explain his or her changed financial circumstances, the court will not be able to retroactively reduce the back payments (i.e., arrearages) that the noncustodial parent owes.[37]

The large accumulation of child support arrearages is a major concern for several reasons. If these arrearages could be collected, the additional income would help the children and families who are owed this child support. Also, large balances of arrearages give the impression that state CSE programs are not performing competently. People tend to assume that if the child support debt is growing, it means that locate and enforcement tools are not working and that child support workers are not effective.[38] However, this perception may be overly simplistic because not all of the arrearage problems are within the control of the CSE program or its workers. An Urban Institute report states: "The reason we estimate that less than half of the arrears will be collected over 10 years is because so much of the arrears are owed by obligors with no or low reported income. It is very difficult to collect from obligors who have no or low reported income."[39]

The CSE program provides services to both welfare and nonwelfare families. Child support collected on behalf of nonwelfare families goes to the family (via the state disbursement unit). Collections on behalf of families receiving benefits from the TANF block grant are in part used to reimburse state and federal governments for TANF payments made to the family. The CSE strategic plan for the period FY2005-FY2009 states the following: "Child support is no longer primarily a welfare reimbursement, revenue-producing device for the federal and state governments; it is a family-first program, intended to ensure families' self-sufficiency by making child support a more reliable source of income."[40] One of the goals of the 1996 welfare reform law (P.L. 104-193, which established TANF) with regard to CSE distribution provisions was to create a distribution priority that favored families once they leave the TANF rolls. This "family first" policy was further advanced by P.L. 109-171 (the Deficit Reduction Act of 2005).[41] In 2007, 92% of child support collections went to families, nearly half of whom had previously received TANF benefits, and the remaining 8% went to reimburse the state and federal governments for TANF payments made to families.[42]

It is estimated that about 50% of the uncollected $107.2 billion in past-due payments (i.e., arrearages) is still owed to state and federal governments.

Even though the CSE program is collecting billions of dollars in arrearages each year, it does not seem to be making much progress in reducing the problem, and the overall child support debt continues to grow. In some cases, high arrearages may deter noncustodial parents from paying any child support. According to research on arrearages, when noncustodial parents perceive that the system is unfair or that the debt is too great to be overcome, the likelihood that they will pay *any* support decreases.[43]

Many noncustodial fathers maintain that the CSE system is dismissive of their financial condition and continues to pursue child support payments (current as well as arrearages) even when it knows that many of them can barely support themselves. They argue that for welfare families, the CSE program generally does not improve their child's well-being because their child support payments are used to benefit the state and federal government (i.e., welfare reimbursement) rather than their child. They contend that the CSE program causes conflicts between them and their child's mother because the women often use it as leverage by threatening to report them to CSE authorities, take them back to court, have more of their wages garnished, or have them arrested.[44]

Incarcerated Mothers

The female prison population has increased dramatically since the early 1990s. According to the Bureau of Justice Statistics, data from 2007 indicate that about 57% of the 114,420 women in a state or federal prison are mothers.[45] Between 1991 and 2007, the number of mothers in prison (state and federal) increased 122%, from 29,500 in 1991 to 65,600 in 2007. In 2007, 8.1% of the parents in prison were mothers compared to 6.5% in 1991.[46] The rising share of female inmates has been attributed to mandatory sentencing laws for drug offenses.

While there is a growing consensus that father-child bonds are just as important as mother-child bonds, many analysts contend that the short-term social impacts on children may be greater and more detrimental when mothers are imprisoned. In part, this is because mothers are still the primary caretakers of children.[47] Generally, children of incarcerated fathers continue to live with their mothers and usually do not experience a change in their living arrangements. However, children of incarcerated mothers typically have more varied and uncertain living arrangements.[48] The increase in mothers in prison is very significant because children are more likely to be removed from the home when mothers are incarcerated than they are when fathers are incarcerated.[49] Although women with children comprise only 8% of state or federal inmates who are parents (2007 data), their absence from their children as the principal caretaker greatly impacts children, many of whom have to go live with grandparents or other relatives and some of whom are placed in foster care.[50]

Data from 2004 show that 61% of female inmates of state prisons lived with their children just prior to incarceration compared to 42% of male inmates.[51] With respect to federal prisons, 78% of female inmates lived with their children just prior to incarceration compared to 51% of male inmates.[52] Some commentators have argued that it is almost impossible to punish women for their crimes without ruining their children's lives.[53]

As indicated above, most but not all mothers in prison were living with their children before they went to prison. They were the caretaker parent.[54] Although father absence is associated with a myriad of negative economic, social, and psychological outcomes for children, the stigma, trauma, and shame associated with the incarceration of their mothers may be more complex and difficult to address.[55] It has been suggested that alternatives to prison be considered for "low-risk" women who are mothers of dependent children. Such alternatives could include court diversion programs such as community-based half-way houses, community-based drug rehabilitation programs, home detention programs, or electronic monitoring programs.[56]

Termination of Parental Rights Due to Criminal Offenses

It is the intention of most incarcerated parents to reunite with their children and families after they are released from prison. However, reunification is often a difficult process and in some cases incarceration can lead to permanent severance of parental rights.[57] In some cases, dissolution of parental rights results from criminal convictions (even those unrelated to the parent's ability to care for the child). According to a report by the Children's Bureau (in the U.S. Department of Health and Human Services), a felony conviction or incarceration was grounds for termination of parental rights in 27 states.[58]

Moreover, the Adoption and Safe Families Act of 1997 (P.L. 105-89), among other things, required as a condition of receiving federal funds, that child welfare agencies file for termination of parental rights if a child had been in foster care for 15 of the last 22 months. One consequence of P.L. 105-89 is that the mandatory time limit in the law makes termination of parental rights a more likely outcome for incarcerated parents who have children in foster care. According to Bureau of Justice Statistics data, 26% of inmates in state prisons and 32% of inmates in federal prisons had already served five or more years in prison in 2004.[59]

One of the three exceptions to the mandatory time limit in the foster care rule pertains to children being cared for by a relative. If a parent is serving a long prison sentence but has relatives available to care for the child (or children), the child welfare agency may place the child with a relative of the inmate and thereby avoid the strict, adoption-oriented requirement of the federal statute.[60]

Some critics of the federal mandatory time limit in foster care provision argue that women in prison who were the primary caretaker of their children are at greater risk than imprisoned fathers of losing all legal ties to their children if the children are placed in foster care while they are serving their sentences. In other words, incarcerated fathers are less likely to be subjected to the federal provision because the children in question are already living with their mothers. In contrast, incarcerated mothers are more likely to be subjected to the federal provision because most of their children have absent fathers. Most incarcerated fathers (8 8%) report that at least one of their children is in the care of the child's other parent; whereas, only 37% of incarcerated mothers make that claim.[61]

Some observers contend that it is important for family members to become involved in the care of children with incarcerated parents as soon as they learn of the parent's arrest if they want to keep the children out of the foster care system and preserve parental ties to the children. They also maintain that it is important for child welfare agencies to recruit relatives as caregivers for children with incarcerated parents. A recently enacted law (P.L. 110-351, the Fostering Connections to Success and Increasing Adoptions Act of 2008) authorizes funding for states to locate relatives of children and to reimburse the relative caretakers of children who are placed with them. [62] However, in most cases the child welfare agencies do not have information on whether a child in their caseload has an incarcerated parent. Some analysts assert that the prisons should have a database on parents who are inmates and transmit such information to CSE agencies and child welfare agencies. [63]

A second exception to the mandatory time limit in foster care rule occurs when the state child welfare agency has documented in its state plan a compelling case that filing a termination of parental rights petition would not be in the best interest of the child. The third exception occurs when a case can be made that the parent has not been provided with the services required by the service plan for the reunification of the parent with the child. [64]

As noted previously, it is generally agreed that (1) parents in prison are less likely to recidivate if they have family support and maintain connections to their children and (2) children who have a positive relationship with their incarcerated or formerly incarcerated parent are more likely to have successful outcomes than children who are legally cut off from parents. Thus, many analysts and observers maintain that termination of parental rights because of the parent's incarceration should be a last resort that is rarely used. [65]

In addition to the emotional and psychological costs on children and parents, the termination of parental rights by definition means that the parent is no longer legally obligated to provide financial support to his or her child. In fact, the parent is legally obligated to stay away from the child and to have no contact (financial or otherwise) with the child.

POLICY OPTIONS

This section looks at ways in which some of the problems discussed above might be resolved. Continuing a historical precedent, many of the proposals or suggestions for the CSE program that are presented below originated with the states. [66] The future success of the CSE program is tied to its ability to continue to be proactive in finding and implementing services and/or approaches that resolve the many problems that the program now faces. The competition for scarce state and federal dollars makes this challenge more difficult and more imperative. This section discusses three policy options: establishment of realistic child support orders, modification of child support obligations, and program coordination.

Establishment of Realistic Child Support Orders

Many policymakers and analysts maintain that parents should share in the cost of supporting their children according to their ability to pay. They assert that the best way to do this is to set initial child support orders at appropriate levels, modify orders promptly when family circumstances change, and immediately intervene when child support is not paid. [67]

This policy option may be particularly important given the current economic downturn, and the change in many families' economic circumstances.

Although some policymakers recognize that establishing child support orders that are "too low" may deprive many children of the financial support they need, they also realize that setting child support orders "too high" may lead some noncustodial parents to seek to escape their child support obligations by opting to work in the underground economy, thereby hiding income and assets. Others caution that noncustodial parents' failure to pay onerous child support orders may increase the likelihood of incarceration, further diminishing the prospects for increasing financial support to the child and raising questions about fairness. They also note that stringent CSE efforts may also alienate noncustodial parents from their children. [68]

There is a general consensus among advocates for low-income mothers and advocates for low- income fathers that economic realities must be taken into account in the determination of child support obligations. They agree that for some low-income noncustodial parents there should be a low presumptive child support award, but not zero. They emphasize the positive difference that even small amounts of child support can add to children's well-being. They also view the establishment of some monetary obligation as an affirmation that noncustodial parents, however poor, must recognize their responsibility to provide economic support to their children. Finally, they agree that having the child support award guidelines establish presumptive minimum orders could protect the poorest noncustodial parents, if decision-makers set awards at the minimum level instead of basing them on unrealistically high levels of imputed income. [69]

In a strategy referred to as the Project to Avoid Increasing Delinquencies (PAID), the federal Office of Child Support Enforcement (OCSE) and state CSE agencies have put forth several suggestions for improving the way in which child support orders are established. They include:

- Directing state CSE agencies to use income data (e.g., quarterly wage reports from the national and state directories of new hires; state income tax data; Social Security Administration information related to retirement, survivors, and disability benefits) to help determine child support orders that more accurately reflect the noncustodial parent's true income.
- Instructing state CSE agencies and courts to presume income at a reasonable level when no income information is available (e.g., presuming state minimum wage income rather than state average earner income).
- Revising child support guidelines to account for a self-support reserve amount to accommodate the basic needs of low-income noncustodial parents.
- Limiting the use of retroactive support amounts and other add-on amounts (such as court costs and birthing costs).
- Reducing the number of default orders by encouraging noncustodial parents to participate in child support hearings.
- Allowing default orders to remain open for a specified period of time to allow for easy amendment if the noncustodial parent provides new and/or contrary information. [70]

Many of the PAID suggestions from CSE administrators could perhaps be implemented administratively. But, having the Congress pass legislation that would require all states to implement such changes might be quicker and more efficient.[71] Moreover, given the new impetus to release hundreds, if not thousands, of inmates before their prison sentences are completed, Congress may want to direct the CSE program to find ways of encouraging these ex-offenders, many of whom are noncustodial parents, to fulfill their child support responsibilities by setting child support orders at levels that might be considered more "realistic" from the perspective of noncustodial parents.

Modification of Child Support Obligations

Although only a relatively small percentage of arrearage payments were collected in FY2007, 61% of obligors continued to make payments on their child support arrearages. One interpretation of this information is that many noncustodial parents simply have too many financial obligations (e.g., food and shelter for themselves) to cover with their limited incomes; thereby, they may always be a little or a lot behind in meeting their child support obligations.

An Urban Institute study revealed the following findings: (1) high debtors were expected to pay a larger percentage of their income for current child support orders—the median child support order for high debtors was 55% of their income compared to 13% for non-debtors and 22% for those who owed less than $30,000 in child support arrearages; (2) high debtors with a current support order tended to have older orders than other obligors; (3) high debtors were more likely to have multiple current child support orders than non-debtors: (4) high debtors were less likely to pay support than non-debtors; (5) high debtors were less likely to have a known address; and (6) high debtors were twice as likely to have an interstate child support case as a non-debtor.[72]

Under the CSE program, states are given significant latitude regarding modifications and reviews of child support orders.[73] Federal law requires that states give both parents the opportunity to request a review of their child support order at least once every three years, and states are required to notify the parents of this right. In order to prevent child support arrearages, especially for noncustodial parents who are unemployed or in prison, many analysts have recommended that child support modification laws be changed so that they are more sensitive to periods of incarceration, unemployment, or injury/illness during which the noncustodial parent's ability to pay child support decreases. They note that it is virtually impossible for most incarcerated parents to stay current in meeting their monthly child support payments.

Some observers argue that if states are not inclined to waive or reduce the child support obligations of noncustodial parents who are in prison, the states could at least prohibit interest charges on overdue child support payments of these parents. They claim that interest and other charges just add to the original debt which the inmate does not have the money to pay. They argue that charging interest on uncollectible child support arrearages does not encourage noncustodial parents to make timely payments but rather alienates them and may encourage them to make no payments.[74] In contrast, others assert that charging interest is the correct approach because children need whatever support can be collected, and because paying interest on debts is something all Americans understand. They say that charging interest sends the message that if a person does not keep current with payments, he will owe more. They assert that charging interest is a fairness issue in that the custodial parent is due a child support payment at a certain time and if the money is not paid on time, the custodial parent should be further compensated.[75]

Also, as noted earlier, about 50% of the uncollected past-due child support payments (arrearages that totaled $107.2 billion in FY2007) are owed to state and federal governments.[76] Some program analysts and other interested parties contend that child support arrearages owed to state governments should be leveraged in a way that encourages the payment of current child support.

They caution that it should be done in a way that avoids sending the message that noncustodial parents can ignore child support obligations because of the possibility that the state may eventually accept less than the full amount owed. They recommend that certain groups of low- income noncustodial parents who are most likely to accumulate child support debt be targeted for interest amnesty or debt compromise programs.[77]

The current OCSE Strategic Plan proposes the following procedures for reducing high child support arrearages.

- Update child support guidelines regularly and simplify child support order modification;
- Modify orders to ensure that child support obligations stay consistent with the noncustodial parents' ability to pay;
- Use automation to detect non-compliance as early as possible and contact noncustodial parents soon after a scheduled child support payment is missed;
- Update child support guidelines to recognize modern family dynamics and realities (e.g., shared custody, incomes of custodial parents, etc.); and
- Consider creative ways to promote regular payment of current support, even if it means "compromising" uncollected child support arrearages to bring the noncustodial parent back into consistently paying current child support payments.[78]

With regard to the last proposal, in an effort to reduce or eliminate child support debt, some states use debt compromise, a process whereby a state forgives a portion or all of the child support debt owed to the state by the noncustodial parent.[79] It is important to note that the federal share of such debt is still owed to the federal government. In order for the federal portion of the child support debt to be compromised or eliminated, Congress would have to pass legislation to that effect and such legislation would have to be enacted.

It has also been recommended that Congress revise consumer protection limits with respect to garnishment of child support. CSE officials can garnish as much as 65% of a noncustodial parent's wages toward the payment of child support debt.[80] For parents released from prisons and jails, this practice may increase the difficulty of securing and maintaining housing, transportation, and employment that are necessary for making future child support payments.

Other recommendations of policymakers and observers include[81] (1) enabling courts to consider an individual's obligations to his or her children at the time of sentencing;[82] (2) prohibiting incarceration from being defined as "voluntary unemployment" (a term used to describe someone who has chosen not to work),[83] thereby allowing a noncustodial parent's child support order to be modified when he or she enters prison;[84] and (3) requiring states to automatically modify (or forgive) child support orders of noncustodial parents who are in prison (during the prison-intake process—only for the length of their prison sentence) unless the custodial parent objects because the inmate has income and/or assets that can be used to pay child support.[85]

Although many custodial parents to a certain extent agree that some noncustodial parents are "dead broke" rather than "deadbeats," they contend that the states and the federal government need to proceed with caution in lowering child support orders for low-income noncustodial parents. They argue that child support is a source of income that could mean the difference between poverty and self-sufficiency for some families. They emphasize that lowering the child support order is likely to result in lower income for the child. They argue that even if a noncustodial parent is in dire financial straits, he or she should not be totally released from financial responsibility for their children. Others agree, and argue that policymakers, when considering policies related to reducing the child support obligations of prisoners, must also consider equity issues related to the treatment of low-income noncustodial parents who may be unemployed as opposed to in prison. They assert that it is sending the wrong message to unilaterally lower payments of persons who have broken the law and not make similar allowances for law-abiding citizens who are unemployed. [86]

Large child support arrearages result in millions of children receiving less than they are owed in child support, reduced cost-effectiveness of the CSE program, and a perception that the CSE program does not consider the financial situation of low-income noncustodial parents, many of whom may be in dire economic situations. There is widespread agreement that preventing the build-up of unpaid child support through early intervention rather than traditional enforcement methods is essential to the future success of the CSE program.[87] Some commentators point out that such a proactive approach to addressing the huge accumulation of child support arrearages may help many children whose parents were former inmates. Some fathers' rights group would like Congress to pass legislation that would repeal the federal provision that prohibits the retroactive modification of child support obligations. It also has been suggested that it may be easier for Congress to mandate some of the child support arrearage remedies outlined in the CSE FY2005-2009 Strategic Plan and elsewhere, rather than wait for states to develop individual remedies that only apply to the state that implements the policy.

Program Coordination

Given the current economic crisis, states are looking to find creative ways to maximize the use of their resources. State and federal prison officials and CSE officials may find that it is mutually beneficial to work together on behalf of inmates who are parents. Some analysts have suggested that state and federal prisons can strengthen their re-entry programs by incorporating information on CSE obligations and services. Further, CSE programs can make their programs more successful by identifying parents with child support obligations while they are in prison so that parents are more able to avoid the accumulation of excessive child support arrearages and also provide information to prisoners that highlight the benefits of including child support payments in their post-release plans.[88]

Several strategies have been suggested that would involve both the criminal justice system and the CSE program to proactively address the advent of more ex-offenders being released back into local communities. They include (1) making inquiries about a prisoner's parental status and whether or not he or she is required to pay child support during the prison intake process; (2) encouraging prisoners to contact the CSE agency regarding questions about the paternity and child support order establishment rules, due process procedures, collection methods, and other concerns; (3) informing inmates about how to have their child support orders modified so that they do not incur high child support debt while in prison; (4) encouraging inmates to maintain contact with their children while they are in prison; and (5) helping former inmates develop a plan to pay their child support obligations.[89] It has also been suggested that prison intake procedures include an automated data match or weekly population list exchange among corrections and CSE agencies and that policies be implemented that assist with the child support modification process, such as providing noncustodial parents with forms, addressed envelopes, and postage.[90]

Although CSE funds may not be used to pay for criminal justice functions or employment and training activities, states are permitted to use CSE funds for child support case identification, tracking, referral, and development of payment plans. Also, Special Improvement Project (SIP) grants[91] and Section 1115 demonstration grants[92] provide funding for projects that are designed to help families achieve self-sufficiency and promote stability for children, mothers, and fathers. Both the SIP grants and the Section 1115 grants have funded projects that focus on helping incarcerated parents.[93]

In addition, federal law (pursuant to the 1996 welfare reform law—P.L. 104-193) gives CSE agencies and courts the authority to require unemployed noncustodial parents who owe child support to a child receiving TANF benefits to participate in appropriate work activities. Thus, judges can remand nonpaying noncustodial parents to a TANF work program, with the mandate to participate in the program, pay the child support owed, or be confined in jail. This obligation can be monitored, so that the noncustodial parent cannot evade it. If the parent is in fact working surreptitiously, the work program will conflict with his or her other job, forcing the parent to admit to having earnings and thereby to paying child support. If the noncustodial parent really is jobless, the program can help him or her get a job.[94] Moreover, state CSE agencies may use their federal performance incentive payments and federal parental access and visitation grants[95] to fund child-support case management services for incarcerated and formerly incarcerated parents.

Some observers contend that responsible fatherhood programs and ex-offender re-entry programs/services together with the CSE program could do more to help former inmates successfully reconnect to their children and communities if they worked in tandem, or at least formally recognized the potential contributions that they each make or could make to the ultimate well-being of children. Given that an overall goal of the aforementioned programs is to increase opportunities for families to stay connected even if a parent is or was incarcerated,[96] some observers assert that children should not be disadvantaged because they do not live in states with innovative policies that increase child support collections. They contend that some state-established policies and/or proposals may need to be mandated by Congress so that children, regardless of where they live, may benefit from the most positive CSE developments and innovative prisoner re-entry strategies. Below are brief descriptions of responsible fatherhood programs and ex-offender re-entry programs/services.

Responsible Fatherhood Programs

Responsible fatherhood programs seek to promote the financial and personal responsibility of noncustodial parents to their children and increase the participation of fathers in their children's lives.[97] Responsible fatherhood programs, in affirming the importance of fathers to their children's well-being, have to a certain extent reduced the animosity between noncustodial parents and the CSE program. It is sometimes the case that positive, constructive communication between noncustodial parents and CSE agencies leads to more child support for children.

Responsible fatherhood programs have been debated in Congress since the 106th Congress (1999), but it was not until the Deficit Reduction Act of 2005 (P.L. 109-171) that specific funding was provided for these programs.[98] P.L. 109-171 included a provision that provides up to $50 million per year (for each of the five fiscal years 2006-2010) in competitive grants to states, territories, Indian tribes and tribal organizations, and public and nonprofit community organizations (including religious organizations) for responsible fatherhood programs.[99]

Most responsible fatherhood programs include parenting education; training in responsible decision-making, conflict resolution, and coping with stress; mediation services for both parents; problem-solving skills; peer support; and job-training opportunities.[100] According to data from the Administration for Children and Families (ACF) in the U.S. Department of Health and Human Services (HHS), grantees were awarded five-year contracts to implement responsible fatherhood programs. The contracts (in aggregate) amounted to $41 million per year.

Historically, there has been tension between noncustodial parents and the CSE program. Noncustodial parents often claimed that by exclusively focusing on financial support, the CSE system devalued their role as nurturer, disciplinarian, and mentor. Most responsible fatherhood programs clearly explain the goals and duties of the CSE program and encourage noncustodial parents to interact with CSE agencies in a proactive manner.

Many responsible fatherhood programs recognize that a substantial proportion of noncustodial parents are inmates or former inmates. According to HHS data, responsible fatherhood programs in 16 states and the District of Columbia include inmates and/or former inmates as part of their target population.[101] In fact, in two states, Indiana and New Jersey, one of the responsible fatherhood program operators/grantees is the State Department of Correction. There are also a number of healthy marriage demonstration programs that support the provision of services to promote or sustain healthy relationships for couples with children, where one of the parents is incarcerated or otherwise involved with the criminal justice system (e.g., recently released from incarceration or under parole or probation).[102]

Re-entry of Former Inmates Back into Communities

It is generally agreed that programs that promote personal responsibility also are likely to promote parental responsibility which may translate into consistent payment of child support obligations. Thus, successful prisoner re-entry programs may increase the effectiveness of the CSE program along with reducing recidivism and promoting safer communities.

Most children who grow up in mother-only families, father-only families, step-parent families, or families in which the mother is cohabiting with a male partner become well-adjusted, productive adults. Nonetheless, a large body of research indicates that children who—

grow up with only one biological parent in the home are more likely to be financially worse off and have worse socioeconomic outcomes (even after income differences are taken into account) compared to children who grow up with both biological parents in the home. [103] It has been stated that nothing frays family ties like prison. According to some observers, supporting programs that help fathers, mothers, and children to maintain positive family bonds despite incarceration of one of the child's parents is likely to improve child well-being and may also help reduce recidivism. [104]

According to some data, with the exception of health care, spending on corrections has increased faster than any other item in state budgets. Supporting approaches that result in successful reentry of ex-offenders back into society means both safer communities and the improved use of tax dollars.[105] The federal government's involvement in ex-offender re-entry programs usually occurs through grant funding, which is available through a wide array of federal programs at the Departments of Justice, Labor, Education, and Health and Human Services. However, only a few of these grant programs explicitly specify funds for offender re-entry purposes. Re-entry programs vary widely in content and scope. Re-entry generally includes all the activities and programming conducted to help former inmates live as law-abiding citizens. Re-entry programs are typically divided into three phases: programs that prepare ex-offenders to reenter society while they are in prison, programs that connect ex-offenders with services immediately after they are released from prison, and programs that provide long-term support and supervision for ex- offenders as they settle into communities permanently.[106]

Some inmates use their time in prison to reflect on their lives and come to realize the importance of their children and other family relationships. They have the time and the desire to improve themselves and are thereby amenable to participating in whatever programs, classes, and activities that the prison offers. According to Bureau of Justice Statistics data for 2004, 85% of mothers and 78% of fathers in *state* prisons reported having telephone, mail, or person visits with their children while in prison. Similarly, 96% of mothers and 91% of fathers in *federal* prisons reported having some type of contact with their children while in prison. Moreover, 12% of parents in state prisons and 26% of parents in federal prisons reported that they had attended parenting or childrearing classes in the prison.[107] Both of these activities, contact with children and participation in parenting classes, are good preparation for reconnecting ex-offenders with their children and families upon their release from prison. Some observers have suggested that state and federal prisons routinely include information on responsible fatherhood and healthy marriage programs in the packets of information for persons who are soon to be released.

CONCLUDING REMARKS

Ex-offenders re-entering communities face a host of problems, a major one being barriers to employment because of their criminal records. Most employers now conduct background checks, with the result that people are often denied employment or even fired from jobs because of their criminal records. Research indicates that employment and family support are important predictors of an ex-offender's successful re-entry into his or her community. Given that employment opportunities are scarce and may become more limited in the current economy, formerly incarcerated parents may want to strengthen positive connections to their children, family, and community.

The inability of many people released from prisons and jails to meet their financial obligations can contribute to their being incarcerated again.[108] CSE policies that are receptive to noncustodial parents with a recent history of incarceration, unemployment, or low-wage jobs have been shown to increase the prospects that such individuals will maintain steady employment, regular child support payments, and contact with their children. [109] It probably would benefit both entities if the staff of CSE agencies collaborated with the staff of corrections facilities to develop policies that promote positive child support outcomes as well as successful reintegration of individuals released from prison or jail.

As noted earlier, about 53% of the 1.5 million inmates in state or federal prisons are parents with dependent children. About 57% of ex-offenders who are released from state or federal prisons each year are parents. The current economic situation is likely to increase the number of persons released from prison. According to a 2009 news report, federal judges in California ruled that California may have to reduce the number of inmates in its overcrowded prison system by up to 40%. The judges reported that the state's prison system was at about 200% of capacity. The judges suggested a two- to three-year time frame for reducing the number of inmates in the prison system. [110]

Although it is true that a child's needs for financial support do not diminish just because a parent is incarcerated, most custodial parents realize that they probably will not receive any child support while the noncustodial parent is in prison,[111] but they do expect to receive child support payments after the noncustodial parent is released from prison. However, this is not what usually happens. Instead of resuming their child support payment schedules, many newly released noncustodial parents have little or no income or assets available to them, and therefore do not make their payments. Moreover, most former inmates have difficulty finding employment after they are released from prison and they often have to rely on family members for food and shelter.

Also, when they leave prison, many parents find they have accumulated significant child support debt that they are expected to begin paying off as soon as they become employed (or sooner). Without intervention, they may face wage attachments of up to 65% of their disposable earnings to cover their child support obligations. They may also face CSE remedies such as driver's license suspension, which could limit their work options. Advocates for incarcerated parents are concerned that unrealistically high child support orders or arrearages may discourage ex- offenders from finding a regular job because regular employment allows a person's paycheck to be subject to income withholding procedures. Some advocates argue that policies and practices that allow for up to 65% of a person's disposable earnings to be garnished tempts many former inmates to find jobs in the underground economy which may lessen their chances of successfully establishing ties with their children, families, and communities and may contribute to recidivism. [112]

There are several evaluations and studies underway that will provide evidence of the effectiveness or ineffectiveness of various re-entry programs, but results from those studies are not yet available. Evaluation findings are very important because the current economic situation is causing many states to quickly reduce their prison populations, and successful re-entry of ex- offenders can reduce recidivism and thereby save both state and federal dollars.[113] Evaluations also are underway, but not yet available, with respect to healthy marriage and responsible fatherhood programs that are focusing their services on incarcerated parents or formerly incarcerated parents.[114] Evaluation findings will provide some insights about the delivery and effectiveness of marriage and family-strengthening programs for populations involved with the criminal justice system.[115]

Extreme poverty sometimes means that a person cannot take advantage of opportunities that make good financial sense. In some cases, noncustodial parents who are former inmates may be so disadvantaged that even programs that attempt to help them deal with huge child support debts (e.g., child support arrearage forgiveness or reduction programs) are of no benefit to them because they simply do not have any funds to give to their children (thus preventing them from participating in such programs). Custodial parents warn that the precarious financial situation of children must be a primary concern of policymakers in their efforts to help low-income noncustodial parents who often have only a high school education (or less), low skills, and little work experience, and may be unemployed or recently released from prison. Some policymakers contend that progress must be made in making the CSE program fair for noncustodial parents at every income level while simultaneously ensuring that children are not short-changed. It has periodically been suggested that in some cases in which the child support obligation cannot be met, in-kind assistance (such as providing child care) may be one way in which society can steadfastly adhere to the tenet that both parents are responsible for the well-being of their children while recognizing the reality of the dire financial situation in which many ex-offenders find themselves.

Connecting and/or reconnecting children to their noncustodial parents has become a goal of federal social policy.[116] Promoting coordination among federal and states programs may help programs optimize their funds and resources. Some prisons and local communities are helping noncustodial parents meet and/or acknowledge their child support responsibilities by offering parenting programs, informational sessions on how to deal with the CSE agency, conflict- resolution classes, and job readiness preparation. Research highlights the common ground between the prison system and the CSE system. For example, studies show that family support is one of the key factors in lowering the probability that ex-offenders will return to prison and research further indicates that being involved in the lives of one's children promotes responsible behavior, such as making regular child support payments and being productive citizens.[117] Federally-mandated program coordination in certain areas may be one way to increase child support collections and simultaneously reduce recidivism.

Incarceration has high costs not only for the inmate but for his or her children and family as well as society in general. Incarceration, health care, education, and other important programs, including the CSE program, are now competing with one another for state and federal funding. Given the current economic downturn state and federal agencies may start to work together to further the goals that they have in common.

End Notes

[1] Lauren E. Glaze and Laura M. Maruschak, "Parents in Prison and Their Minor Children," U.S. Department of Justice, Bureau of Justice Statistics Special Report, August 2008.

[2] "Every Door Closed: Facts About Parents With Criminal Records," Center for Law and Social Policy (CLASP) and Community Legal Services, Inc., 2003.

[3] "Building Knowledge About Successful Prisoner Reentry Strategies," MDRC, February 11, 2009.

[4] "Every Door Closed: Facts About Parents With Criminal Records," Center for Law and Social Policy (CLASP) and Community Legal Services, Inc., 2003.

[5] Jennifer Steinhauer, "To Cut Costs, States Relax Prison Policies," *The New York Times*, March 25, 2009.

[6] Amy L. Solomon, Jenny W. L. Osborne, Stefan F. LoBuglio, Jeff Mellow, and Debbie A. Mukamal, "Life After Lockup: Improving Reentry From Jail to the Community," May 2008. See also: John M. Jeffries, Suzanne Menghraj, and Creasie Finney Hairston, "Serving Incarcerated and Ex-Offender Fathers and Their Families," February 2001.

[7] Amy L. Solomon, Jenny W. L. Osborne, Stefan F. LoBuglio, Jeff Mellow, and Debbie A. Mukamal, "Life After Lockup: Improving Reentry From Jail to the Community," May 2008.

[8] Vicki Turetsky, "Realistic Child Support Policies that Support Successful Re-entry," Center for Law and Social Policy, revised January 2007. See also: Nancy La Vigne, Elizabeth Davies, Tobi Palmer, and Robin Halberstadt, "Release Planning for Successful Re-entry: A Guide for Corrections, Service Providers, and Community Groups, The Urban Institute, September 2008. [http://www.urban 1767_successful_reentry.pdf]

[9] Elaine Sorensen and Chava Zibman, "Child Support Offers Some Protection Against Poverty," Urban Institute, March 15, 2000. Also see Elaine Sorensen, "Child Support Gains Ground," Urban Institute, October 6, 2003.

[10] States were historically required to provide CSE services to Indian tribes and tribal organizations as part of the CSE caseloads. The 1996 welfare reform law (P.L. 104-193) allowed direct federal funding of tribal CSE programs at a 90% federal matching rate. In FY2007, twelve Indian Tribes or tribal organizations operated CSE programs. They are the Cherokee Nation, Chickasaw Nation, Forest County Potawatomi, Lac du Flambeau Tribe, Lummi Nation, Menominee Tribe, Navajo Nation, Osage Nation, Port Gamble S'Klallam, Puyallup Tribe, Sisseton-Wahpeton Sioux Tribe, and the Tlingit and Haida Tribe.

[11] In FY2007, the federal share of CSE total program costs was nearly $3.7 billion (66%) and the states' share was nearly $1.9 billion (34%). In FY2007, the statutory maximum for federal CSE incentive payments to states (in aggregate) was $471 million.

[12] In 2004, the CSE program was cited by the Office of Management and Budget (OMB) as being the most cost-effective program among all social services and block grant/formula programs reviewed government-wide.

[13] Every child has a biological father, but if a child's parents are not married, the law does not accept or recognize the biological father as the legal father. Unmarried parents generally establish paternity by signing a voluntary acknowledgment of paternity form or having a court determine paternity. Although the CSE program now establishes paternity for more than 95% of all newborns, it does less well in legally identifying the fathers of older children. According to the Office of Child Support Enforcement (OCSE), in FY2006 paternity was established for about 86% of the children who needed paternity established. This meant that about 2.4 million children could not receive child support payments because they did not have a legally identified father. Note that another 2.6 million children could not receive child support payments because a child support order had not been established on their behalf.

[14] "Demographic Survey Results From Nine State IV-D Programs," Courtland Consulting (MI) and the Urban Institute, December 18, 2007. (In 2006, the Census Bureau poverty threshold was $10,294 for one person, $13,167 for a two- person family, $16,079 for a three person-family, and $20,614 for a four-person family.)

[15] Based on 1997 data, it appears that about 34% of fathers with income below the poverty threshold did not pay child support because they were not able to do so. (Elaine Sorensen and Chiva Zibman, " Poor Dads Who Don't Pay Child Support: Deadbeats or Disadvantaged?, The Urban Institute, April 2002, p. 2.)

[16] According to a recent report, in June 2007, there were about 2.3 million persons in federal and state prisons and local jails. (Source: Mindy Herman-Stahl, Marni L. Kan, and Tasseli McKay, "Incarceration and the Family: A Review of Research and Promising Approaches for Serving Fathers and Families," RTI International (North Carolina), September 2008, p. 1-1.) The data in this report focus on inmates or former inmates of state or federal prisons. Thus, the 1.5 million prisoners mentioned in the body of the report does not include an additional 0.8 million persons who are in jail. Persons in jail may be awaiting trial or sentencing, waiting for transport to a state or federal prison after they have been convicted or in local prisons, or serving time on a misdemeanor sentence (usually less than one year).

[17] Pamela Caudill Ovwigho, Correne Saunders, and Catherine E. Born, "The Intersection of Incarceration & Child Support: A Snapshot of Maryland's Caseload," July 2005.

[18] "Every Door Closed: Facts About Parents With Criminal Records," Center for Law and Social Policy (CLASP) and Community Legal Services, Inc., 2003.

[19] According to a report by the Pew Charitable Trusts, total state spending on corrections—including bonds and federal contributions—totaled $49 billion in 2007 (up from $12 billion in 1987). In 2005, the average per prisoner operating cost was $23,876, ranging from a high of $44,860 in Rhode Island to a low of $13,009 in Louisiana (note that these costs do not include capital expenses). The report indicates that corrections budgets are consuming an increasing share of state general funds, leaving significantly fewer dollars for other needs. For example, Pew found that over the 20-year period 1987-2007, inflation-adjusted general fund spending on corrections rose 127% while higher education expenditures rose just 21%. Source: "One in 100: Behind Bars in America 2008," The Pew Center on the States, Public Safety Performance Project, February 2008.

[20] About 66% of persons released from prisons in the United States are rearrested within three years of their release and more than 50% are re-incarcerated. (Source: "Report of the Re-Entry Policy Council—Charting the Safe and Successful Return of Prisoners to the Community," 2004, p. xviii.)

[21] Jason Miller, "Obama offers glimpse into management reforms," Federal News Radio, February 27, 2009. http://www.federalnewsradio.com/index.php?nid=110&sid=1612040

[22] Data from the Bureau of Justice Statistics for 2004 indicate that, among parents who said they had provided primary financial support for their children, 30% of inmates in state prisons and 27% of inmates in federal prisons had income of less than $1,000 in the month before they were arrested. With respect to parents who said that they were not the one providing primary financial support for their children, 40% of inmates in state prisons and 38% of inmates in federal prisons had income of less than $1,000 in the month before they were arrested. (Source: Lauren E. Glaze and Laura M. Maruschak, "Parents in Prison and Their Minor Children," U.S. Department of Justice, Bureau of Justice Statistics Special Report, August 2008, p. 17.)

[23] Morgan, Laura W, "Child Support Guidelines: Interpretation and Application, 1996. http://www.support guidelines.com/book/chap1a.html

[24] The first step in the income shares approach is to determine the combined income of the two parents. A percentage of that combined income is used to calculate a "primary support obligation." Many states add child care costs and extraordinary medical expenses to the primary support obligation. The resulting total child support obligation is apportioned between the parents on the basis of their proportionate share of total income. The noncustodial parent's share is the child support award.

[25] The percentage of income approach is based on the noncustodial parent's gross income and the number of children to be supported (the child support obligation is not adjusted for the income of the custodial parent). The percentages vary by state. In Wisconsin, for example, child support is based on the following proportions of the noncustodial parent's gross income: one child—17%; two children—25%; three children—29%; four children—31%; and five or more children—34%.

[26] The Melson-Delaware formula starts with net income. After determining net income for each parent, a primary support allowance is subtracted from each parent's income. This reserve represents the minimum amount required for adults to meet their own subsistence requirements. The next step is to determine a primary support amount for each dependent child. Work-related child care expenses and extraordinary medical expenses are added to the child's primary support amount. The child's primary support needs are then apportioned between the parents.

[27] Laura Morgan, "Child Support Guidelines," National Conference of State Legislatures, 2009. http://www.ncsl. org/programs/cyf/models.htm

[28] "Dollars and Sense: Improving the Determination of Child Support Obligations for Low-Income Mothers, Fathers, and Children," National Women's Law Center and the Center on Fathers, Families, and Public Policy, 2002, p. 4.

[29] Ex-offenders re-entering communities face a host of problems including employment barriers stemming from their criminal records.

[30] "Issues Behind the Message of Equal Parents' Week," Children's Rights Council, 2004, http://epweek.tripod.com/ issues.html.

[31] Ingrid Rothe and Daniel R. Meyer, "Setting Child Support Orders: Historical Approaches and Ongoing Struggles," University of Wisconsin-Madison Institute for Research on Poverty, Focus, v. 21, no. 1, Spring 2000, p. 61.

[32] "Child Support Enforcement (CSE) FY 2007 Preliminary Data Report," U.S. Department of Health and Human Services, Administration for Children and Families, Office of Child Support Enforcement, April 2008.

[33] As noted earlier, child support payments are collected through a state collection and disbursement unit. CSE law requires that a State Disbursement Unit be used to collect and disburse child support payments, to keep an accurate identification of child support payments, to promptly disburse money to custodial parents or other states, and to furnish parents with a record of the current status of child support payments.

[34] Other ways in which child support arrearages accumulate include the following: (1) In all states, arrearages remain due (for various periods of time) even after the child reaches the age of majority; (2) In addition to current support, some states choose to establish retroactive support when setting new child support orders—depending on the state's policy, these retroactive arrearages may extend from two to six years prior, or they may be unlimited in their scope, extending back all the way to the time of the child's birth; (3) Child support arrearages can also be incurred for costs and fees; particularly attorney fees, court filing fees, fees for blood tests associated with the determination of paternity, and the costs associated with the child's birth; and (4) Some states charge interest on arrearages thereby increasing the amount owed. (Source: "Dollars and Sense: Improving the Determination of Child Support Obligations for Low- Income Mothers, Fathers, and Children," National Women's Law Center and Center on Fathers, Families, and Public Policy, August 19, 2002.)

[35] There are many reasons why a child support order may need to be changed. For instance, the financial circumstances of the parents may change; the necessity of child care might be eliminated; and the costs of food, clothing, medical care, school, and extracurricular activities may increase or decrease.

[36] The CSE agency can collect child support arrearages through federal and/or state income tax refund intercepts, intercept of unemployment or workers' compensation, liens against property, seizure of awards and settlements, and seizure of assets held in financial institutions. The CSE agency also has the authority to

withhold or suspend the use of driver's licenses, professional licenses, and recreational and sporting licenses of persons who owe past-due child support payments.

[37] The Omnibus Budget Reconciliation Act of 1986 (P.L. 99-509), among other things, in effect, prohibited the retroactive modification of child support obligations thereby making it very difficult for courts and administrative entities to forgive or reduce child support arrearages.

[38] "Office of Child Support Enforcement FY 2006 Annual Report to Congress," U.S. Department of Health and Human Services, Administration for Children and Families, Office of Child Support Enforcement, March 2009. Also see Elaine Sorensen, Liliana Sousa, and Simon Schaner, "Assessing Child Support Arrears in Nine Large States and the Nation," The Urban Institute, July 11, 2007. [http://aspe.hhs.gov/hsp/07/assessing-CS-debt/]

[39] Elaine Sorensen, Liliana Sousa, and Simon Schaner, "Assessing Child Support Arrears in Nine Large States and the Nation," The Urban Institute, July 11, 2007, p. 7. http://aspe.hhs.gov/hsp/07/assessing-CS-debt/

[40] "The National Child Support Enforcement Strategic Plan FY2005-2009," U.S. Department of Health and Human Services, Administration for Children and Families, Office of Child Support Enforcement, 2004. See http://www.acf.hhs.gov/programs/cse/pubs/2004/Strategic_Plan_FY2005-2009.pdf.

[41] P.L. 109-17 1 simplifies CSE distribution rules and extends the "families first" policy by providing incentives to states to encourage them to allow more child support to go to both former welfare families and families still on welfare.

[42] TANF recipients now make up just 14% of the CSE caseload. The largest group in the CSE caseload, representing about 46% of the cases, are families who formerly received TANF benefits. Families who never received TANF assistance comprise 41% of the CSE caseload. (The figures are based on preliminary FY2007 data from the federal Office of Child Support Enforcement.)

[43] "Dollars and Sense: Improving the Determination of Child Support Obligations for Low-Income Mothers, Fathers, and Children," National Women's Law Center and the Center on Fathers, Families, and Public Policy, 2002, p. 2.

[44] "Family Ties: Improving Paternity Establishment Practices and Procedures for Low-Income Mothers, Fathers and Children," National Women's Law Center and the Center on Fathers, Families, and Public Policy, 2000, p. 9-11.

[45] Heather C. West and William J. Sabol, "Prisoners in 2007," U.S. Department of Justice, Bureau of Justice Statistics Bulletin 224280, December 2008.

[46] Lauren E. Glaze and Laura M. Maruschak, "Parents in Prison and Their Minor Children," U.S. Department of Justice, Bureau of Justice Statistics Special Report, August 2008, Appendix Table 1, p. 13. Also see Ross D. Parke and K. Allison Clarke-Stewart, "Effects of Parental Incarceration on Young Children," working paper prepared for the National Policy Conference (The Urban Institute)—From Prison to Home: The Effect of Incarceration and Reentry on Children, Families and Communities, January 30-31, 2002.

[47] Ross D. Parke and K. Alison Clarke-Stewart, "Effects of Parental Incarceration on Young Children," working paper prepared for the National Policy Conference (The Urban Institute)—From Prison to Home: The Effect of Incarceration and Reentry on Children, Families and Communities, January 30-31, 2002.

[48] Nancy G. LaVigne, Elizabeth Davies, and Diana Brazzell, "Broken Bonds: Understanding and Addressing the Needs of Children with Incarcerated Parents," The Urban Institute, February 2008, p. 3.

[49] Christopher A. Swann and Michelle Sheran Sylvester, "The Foster Care Crisis: What Caused Caseloads to Grow?," Demography, v. 43, no. 2, May 2006, p. 309-335.

[50] Bureau of Justice Statistics data from 2004 indicates that inmates who were mothers (11%) were five times more likely than inmates who were fathers (2%) to report that their children were in the care of a foster home, agency, or institution. Source: Lauren E. Glaze and Laura M. Maruschak, "Parents in Prison and Their Minor Children," U.S. Department of Justice, Bureau of Justice Statistics Special Report, August 2008.

[51] Lauren E. Glaze and Laura M. Maruschak, "Parents in Prison and Their Minor Children," U.S. Department of Justice, Bureau of Justice Statistics Special Report, August 2008, p. 16.

[52] Ibid, p. 16.

[53] Tammerlin Drummond, "Mothers in Prison," Time, October 29, 2000.

[54] For statistical information on custodial fathers, see "Custodial Mothers and Fathers and Their Child Support: 2005— Supporting Detailed Tables," U.S. Census Bureau, P60-234, August 2007. http://www.census.gov/hhes/www/ childsupport/cs05.html

[55] Nancy G. LaVigne, Elizabeth Davies, and Diana Brazzell, "Broken Bonds: Understanding and Addressing the Needs of Children with Incarcerated Parents," The Urban Institute, February 2008.

[56] "Supporting Families with Incarcerated Parents," National Human Services Assembly, Family Strengthening Policy Center, Policy Brief No. 8, September 2005.

[57] Creasie Finney Hairston, "Children with Parents in Prison: Child Welfare Matters," Child Welfare (CW) 360°, Spring 2008, p. 4.

[58] "Grounds for Involuntary Termination of Parental Rights: Summary of State Laws," U.S. Department of Health and Human Services, Administration for Children and Families, Children's Bureau, Child Welfare Information

Gateway, data current through June 2007. (Note that the 27 states were tabulated by the Congressional Research Service.)

[59] Lauren E. Glaze and Laura M. Maruschak, "Parents in Prison and Their Minor Children," U.S. Department of Justice, Bureau of Justice Statistics Special Report, August 2008, p. 20. Note that the published breakouts for "length of time in prison" were only for large time spans such as 12 months to 59 months.

[60] Philip M. Genty, "The Inflexibility of the Adoption and Safe Families Act and its Unintended Impact upon the Children of Incarcerated Parents and Their Families," Child Welfare (CW) 360⁰, Spring 2008, p. 10.

[61] Figures based on data from 2004 for inmates of state prisons. Source: Lauren E. Glaze and Laura M. Maruschak, "Parents in Prison and Their Minor Children," U.S. Department of Justice, Bureau of Justice Statistics Special Report, August 2008, p. 5.

[62] For more information, see CRS Report RL34704, *Child Welfare: The Fostering Connections to Success and Increasing Adoptions Act of 2008*, by Emilie Stoltzfus.

[63] Philip M. Genty, "The Inflexibility of the Adoption and Safe Families Act and its Unintended Impact upon the Children of Incarcerated Parents and Their Families," Child Welfare (CW) 360⁰, Spring 2008, p. 11.

[64] "Grounds for Involuntary Termination of Parental Rights: Summary of State Laws," U.S. Department of Health and Human Services, Administration for Children and Families, Children's Bureau, Child Welfare Information Gateway, data current through June 2007.

[65] Nancy G. LaVigne, Elizabeth Davies, and Diana Brazzell, "Broken Bonds: Understanding and Addressing the Needs of Children with Incarcerated Parents," The Urban Institute, February 2008.

[66] States have always been at the forefront with respect to incorporating innovative ideas/strategies into the CSE program. In 2004, the CSE program was cited by the Office of Management and Budget (OMB) as being the most cost- effective program among all social services and block grant/formula programs reviewed government-wide.

[67] "Office of Child Support Enforcement FY 2006 Annual Report to Congress," U.S. Department of Health and Human Services, Administration for Children and Families, Office of Child Support Enforcement, March 2009.

[68] Ingrid Rothe and Daniel R. Meyer, "Setting Child Support Orders: Historical Approaches and Ongoing Struggles," University of Wisconsin-Madison Institute for Research on Poverty, *Focus*, v. 21, no. 1, Spring 2000, p. 61.

[69] "Dollars and Sense: Improving the Determination of Child Support Obligations for Low-Income Mothers, Fathers, and Children," National Women's Law Center and the Center on Fathers, Families, and Public Policy, 2002, p. 11.

[70] "PAID—Project to Avoid Increasing Delinquencies (Practices Guide, version 2.0)," Federal Office of Child Support Enforcement, Administration for Children and Families, July 2008.

[71] The CSE program is a federal-state program in which the federal government inserted itself into an arena that had historically been considered family or domestic relations law which was under the purview of a state's court system. The federal nexus was the billions of federal dollars used to fund programs that assisted low-income single-parent families in which one parent was deceased, incapacitated, unemployed, or absent from the home. Traditionally, it has been the practice of the Congress to impose its child support enforcement mandates on the states by requiring the states to enact state laws that implement certain policies in exchange for federal matching funds for the CSE program.

[72] Elaine Sorensen, Liliana Sousa, and Simon Schaner, "Assessing Child Support Arrears in Nine Large States and the Nation," The Urban Institute, July 11, 2007, p. 19-24. http://aspe.hhs.gov/hsp/07/assessing-CS-debt/

[73] This flexibility and discretion only applies to prospective modification of child support orders. As discussed earlier, federal law prohibits the retroactive modification of child support orders.

[74] Jennifer L. Noyes, "Review of Child Support Policies for Incarcerated Payers," Institute for Research on Poverty, University of Wisconsin-Madison, December 2006.

[75] "Colorado Multiple Initiative Grant, A Study of Interest Usage on Child Support Arrears, State of Colorado," PSI, Achieving Excellence in Child Support Program Operations, June 1, 2000.

[76] Elaine Sorensen, Liliana Sousa, and Simon Schaner (The Urban Institute), "Assessing Child Support Arrears in Nine Large States and the Nation," July 11, 2007. http://aspe.hhs.gov/hsp/07/assessing-CS-debt/

[77] "The Story Behind the Numbers: Who Owes the Child Support Debt?," U.S. Department of Health and Human Services, Administration for Children and Families, Office of Child Support Enforcement, July 2004.

[78] "The National Child Support Enforcement Strategic Plan FY2005-2009," U.S. Department of Health and Human Services, Administration for Children and Families, Office of Child Support Enforcement, 2004. See http://www.acf.hhs.gov/programs/cse/pubs/2004/Strategic_Plan_FY2005-2009.pdf

[79] "State Use of Debt Compromise to Reduce Child Support Arrearages," U.S. Department of Health and Human Services, Office of Inspector General, October 2007. Most child support is collected through payroll withholding. Under the Consumer Credit Protection Act [15 USC 1673(b)], 50%–65% of a parent's disposable earnings may be deducted from the noncustodial parent's paycheck.

[80] At the same time, a separate court or probation officer could require that an individual dedicate 35% of his or her income toward the combined payment of fines, fees, surcharges, and restitution. Such a situation could

encourage a person to return to the behavior and illegal activities that resulted in the person's incarceration in the first place. In other words, aggressive collectors representing distinct agencies could end up contributing to a person's failure to meet his or her financial obligations and, by extension, their revocation of probation or parole.

[81] The *proposed* Responsible Fatherhood and Healthy Families Act of 2007 (S. 1626 was introduced by Senators Bayh and Obama and H.R. 3395 was introduced by Representative Danny Davis et al.) which was introduced in the 110th Congress would have prohibited a state from considering a period of incarceration as voluntary unemployment in determining or modifying a noncustodial parent's child support obligation. It also would have required states to temporarily suspend the child support obligation and any interest on the child support obligation during the period a noncustodial parent is incarcerated. However, it would have required the state to provide the custodial parent with an opportunity to request that the child support obligation continue on the basis that the noncustodial parent has sufficient income or resources to continue to make child support payments during the noncustodial parent's period of incarceration. In addition, the bills would have required states to review, and if appropriate, reduce the balance of child support arrearages permanently assigned to the state in cases where the noncustodial parent (1) does not have the ability to pay the arrearages, (2) did not seek a modification during his or her incarceration, (3) will be more willing (because of the adjustment) to pay current child support payments consistently and on time, and (4) it is in the best interest of the child for the state to make such a reduction.

[82] Federal law prioritizes child support obligations above all other debts owed to the state, including restitution, and court and prison fines, fees, and surcharges. The proposed provision would allow judges, when ordering that an individual pay fees to reimburse the state for the costs of his or her incarceration, to reduce this order by the amount of the individual's child support obligations.

[83] Some judges have ruled that incarcerated parents are responsible for their disadvantaged financial circumstances which resulted from their criminal activities because imprisonment is a foreseeable result of criminal behavior. In contrast, other judges have refused to equate incarceration with voluntary unemployment and have argued that incarcerated parents rarely have any actual job prospects or potential income and cannot alter their employment situation. Source: Jessica Pearson, "Building Debt While Doing Time: Child Support and Incarceration," 2004.

[84] In states that classify incarceration as "voluntary unemployment," a person's child support order may not be modified when he or she enters prison or jail.

[85] Jessica Pearson, "Building Debt While Doing Time: Child Support and Incarceration," 2004.

[86] Jennifer L. Noyes, "Review of Child Support Policies for Incarcerated Payers," Institute for Research on Poverty, University of Wisconsin-Madison, December 2006.

[87] "The National Child Support Enforcement Strategic Plan FY2005-2009," U.S. Department of Health and Human Services, Administration for Children and Families, Office of Child Support Enforcement, 2004. See http://www.acf.hhs.gov/programs/cse/pubs/2004/Strategic_Plan_FY2005-2009.pdf.

[88] Esther Griswold and Jessica Pearson, "Twelve Reasons for Collaboration Between Departments of Correction and Child Support Enforcement Agencies," Corrections Today, v. 65 Issue 3, June 2003, pp. 87-90,104.

[89] Vicki Turetsky, "Realistic Child Support Policies that Support Successful Re-entry," Center for Law and Social Policy, revised January 2007.

[90] "Report of the Re-Entry Policy Council—Charting the Safe and Successful Return of Prisoners to the Community, "2004. See also: Rachel L. McLean and Michael D. Thompson, "Repaying Debts," U.S. Department of Justice, Bureau of Justice Assistance, 2007.

[91] The Special Improvement Project (SIP) grant program provides federal funding for projects that further the national child support mission and goals and help improve program performance. Under the authority of Section 452(j) of the Social Security Act, SIP grants provide federal funds for research and demonstration programs and special projects of regional or national significance. Eligible grant applicants include state and local public agencies, nonprofit agencies (including faith-based organizations), and Tribal organizations.

[92] Section 1115 of the Social Security Act authorizes OCSE to fund demonstration project grants.

[93] In FY2006, a SIP grant was awarded to a faith-based organization in Louisiana to partner with the local CSE agency and a district court to help non-custodial parents find employment and increase their understanding of the court process and their knowledge of child support so they are better able to meet their parental obligations. Also, in FY2006, Maryland and the District of Columbia received section 1115 demonstration funds to develop court and other business practices for quick review and adjustment of child support orders associated with incarcerated parents. (Source: "Office of Child Support Enforcement FY 2006 Annual Report to Congress," U.S. Department of Health and Human Services, Administration for Children and Families, Office of Child Support Enforcement, March 2009.)

[94] Lawrence M. Mead, "Toward a Mandatory Work Policy for Men," *The Future of Children* (Princeton-Brookings), v. 17, no. 2, Fall 2007, p. 56.

[95] In order to promote visitation with children and better relations between custodial and noncustodial parents, the 1996 welfare reform law (P.L. 104-193) provided $10 million per year for grants to states for access and visitation programs, including mediation, counseling, education, and supervised visitation.

96 "Incarceration, Reentry and Child Support Issues: National and State Research Overview," Center for Policy Research, Policy Studies, Inc., March 2006.

97 Although programs that seek to help fathers initiate or maintain contact with their children and become emotionally involved in their children's lives are usually referred to as "fatherhood" programs, the programs generally are gender- neutral. Their underlying goal is participation of the noncustodial parent in the lives of his or her children.

98 Other sources of federal funding for fatherhood programs include the TANF program, TANF state Maintenance-ofEffort (MOE) funding, CSE funds, and Social Services Block Grant (Title XX) funds. According to HHS, many states use TANF funds for responsible fatherhood programs. In addition, many private foundations provide financial support for responsible fatherhood programs.

99 Under P.L. 109-171, responsible fatherhood funds can be spent on activities to promote responsible fatherhood through (1) marriage promotion (through counseling, mentoring, disseminating information about the advantages of marriage and two-parent involvement for children, etc.), (2) parenting activities (through counseling, mentoring, mediation, disseminating information about good parenting practices, etc.), (3) fostering economic stability of fathers (through work first services, job search, job training, subsidized employment, education, etc.), or (4) contracting with a nationally recognized nonprofit fatherhood promotion organization to develop, promote, or distribute a media campaign to encourage the appropriate involvement of parents in the lives of their children, particularly focusing on responsible fatherhood; and to develop a national clearinghouse to help states and communities in their efforts to promote and support marriage and responsible fatherhood.

100 For more information on responsible fatherhood programs, see CRS Report RL3 1025, *Fatherhood Initiatives: Connecting Fathers to Their Children*.

101 Information on the responsible fatherhood grants in each of the 10 HHS regions is available at http://www.acf.hhs.gov/programs/ofa/hmabstracts/index.htm.

102 Pursuant to the Deficit Reduction Act (P.L. 109-17 1), the Healthy Marriage Promotion program is funded at approximately $100 million per year to support research and demonstration projects by public or private entities.

103 Sara McLanahan and Gary Sandefur, "Growing Up With a Single Parent: What Hurts, What Helps" (Cambridge, MA: Harvard University Press, 1994); see also L. Bumpass, "Children and Marital Disruption: A Replication and Update," *Demography*, vol. 2 1(1984), pp. 7 1-82.

104 Wade F. Horn, "Responsible Fatherhood and the Role of the Family," Remarks at the Serious and Violent Offender Reentry Initiative Grantee Conference in Washington, D.C., September 30, 2002.

105 "Report of the Re-Entry Policy Council—Charting the Safe and Successful Return of Prisoners to the Community," 2004.

106 CRS Report RL34287, *Offender Reentry: Correctional Statistics, Reintegration into the Community, and Recidivism*, by Nathan James.

107 Lauren E. Glaze and Laura M. Maruschak, "Parents in Prison and Their Minor Children," U.S. Department of Justice, Bureau of Justice Statistics Special Report, August 2008, p. 18 and p. 20.

108 Katherine A. Beckett, Alexes M. Harris, Heather Evans, "The Assessment and Consequences of Legal Financial Obligations in Washington State," Washington State Minority and Justice Commission, August 2008.

109 "Report of the Re-Entry Policy Council—Charting the Safe and Successful Return of Prisoners to the Community," 2004, p. 327.

110 "California may have to cut prison population by 40 percent," CNN, February 10, 2009. http://www.cnn.com/2009/CRIME/02/10/california.prisons

111 In most cases, past-due support accumulates while the noncustodial parent is in prison. But, unless he or she has assets, such as property, bank accounts, or any income such as wages from a prison job, it is unlikely that child support can be collected while the noncustodial parent is in prison.

112 Rachel L. McLean and Michael D. Thompson, "Repaying Debts," U.S. Department of Justice, Bureau of Justice Assistance, 2007, p. 22.

113 "Building Knowledge About Successful Prisoner Reentry Strategies," MDRC, Issue Focus, February 11, 2009. Also see Mindy Herman-Stahl, Marni L. Kan, and Tasseli McKay, "Incarceration and the Family: A Review of Research and Promising Approaches for Serving Fathers and Families," RTI International (NC), September 2008. See also "The National Evaluation of the Responsible Fatherhood, Marriage and Family Strengthening Grants For Incarcerated and Re-entering Fathers and Their Partners," U.S. Department of Health and Human Services, Office of the Assistant Secretary for Planning and Evaluation, ASPE Research Brief, December 2008.

114 Tasseli McKay and Christine Lindquist (RTI International),"The National Evaluation of the Responsible Fatherhood, Marriage and Family Strengthening Grants for Incarcerated and Re-entering Fathers and Their Partners," ASPE Research Brief, December 2008.

115 Ibid, p. 2.

[116] Such is the case for the following federal programs: CSE visitation programs, responsible fatherhood programs, healthy marriage programs, and the Temporary Assistance for Needy Families (TANF) statute (see purpose language of Title IV-A of the Social Security Act).

[117] Esther Griswold and Jessica Pearson, "Twelve Reasons for Collaboration Between Departments of Correction and Child Support Enforcement Agencies," Corrections Today, June 2003.

In: Child Well-Being and Nonresident Parents
Editor: Laura M. Fernandes

ISBN: 978-1-60692-382-5
© 2011 Nova Science Publishers, Inc.

Chapter 3

PARENTS IN PRISON AND THEIR MINOR CHILDREN

Lauren E. Glaze and Laura M. Maruschak

An estimated 809,800 prisoners of the 1,518,535 held in the nation's prisons at midyear 2007 were parents of minor children, or children under age 18. Parents held in the nation's prisons—52% of state inmates and 63% of federal inmates—reported having an estimated 1,706,600 minor children, accounting for 2.3% of the U.S. resident population under age 18. Unless otherwise specified in this report, the word *parent* refers to state and federal prisoners who reported having minor children. The word *children* refers to youth under age 18.

Between 1991 and midyear 2007, parents held in state and federal prisons increased by 79% (357,300 parents). Children of incarcerated parents increased by 80% (761,000 children), during this period (figure 1). The most rapid growth in the number of parents held in the nation's prisons and their children occurred between 1991 and 1997 (both up 44%). From 1997 to midyear 2007, the number of parents and children continued to grow, but at a slower pace (both up 25%).

The findings in this report are based on the latest data collected through personal interviews with prisoners participating in the Bureau of Justice Statistics' (BJS) 2004 Survey of Inmates in State and Federal Correctional Facilities (SISFCF), which is comprised of two separate surveys. One survey is conducted in state adult correctional facilities and the other is conducted in federal correctional facilities. Estimates presented in this report may not be comparable to previously published reports. See *Incarcerated Parents and Their Minor Children* at <http://www.ojp.usdoj.gov/bjs/ abstract/i ptc. htm>.

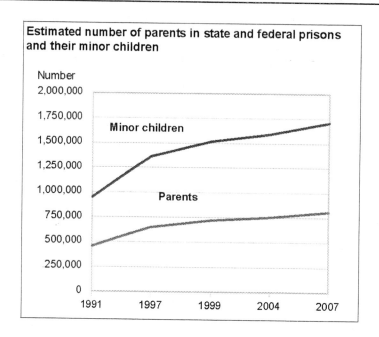

Figure 1.

Parents of Minor Children Held in the Nation's Prisons Increased By 79% Between 1991 and Midyear 2007

Growth in the number of parents held in state and federal prisons was outpaced by the growth in the nation's prison population between 1991 and midyear 2007. Parents incarcerated in state and federal prisons increased by 79% during this period while the custody population grew by 92%.

Detailed information is available in appendix tables in the online version of this report on the BJS Website at <http://www.ojp.usdoj.gov/bjs/pub/ pdf/pptmc.pdf>.

Parents held in state prison increased from 413,100 in 1991 to 686,000 at midyear 2007 (table 1). Children of parents in state prison increased from 860,300 to 1,427,500 during this period. The largest growth in the number of parents (up 40%) held in state prison and their children (up 42%) occurred between 1991 and 1997, compared to a 19% increase for parents and a 17% increase for their children between 1997 and midyear 2007.

The Number of Children Under Age 18 with a Mother in Prison More Than Doubled since 1991

The nation's prisons held approximately 744,200 fathers and 65,600 mothers at midyear 2007 (appendix table 1). Fathers in prison reported having 1,559,200 children; mothers reported 147,400.

Since 1991, the number of children with a mother in prison has more than doubled, up 131%. The number of children with a father in prison has grown by 77%. This finding reflects a faster rate of growth in the number of mothers held in state and federal prisons (up 122%), compared to the number of fathers (up 76%) between 1991 and midyear 2007.

Table 1. Estimated number of parents in state and federal prisons and their minor children.

Total		State	Federal[a]
Number of parents			
2007[b]	809,800	686,000	123,800
2004[c]	754,900	644,100	110,800
1999	721,500	642,300	79,200
1997	649,500	578,100	62,500
1991	452,500	413,100	39,400
Number of children			
2007[b]	1,706,600	1,427,500	279,100
2004[c]	1,590,100	1,340,300	249,800
1999[d]	1,515,200	1,338,900	176,300
1997[d]	1,362,900	1,223,800	139,100
1991[d]	945,600	860,300	85,100

Note. See *Methodology* for details about estimation methods. See appendix table 1 for estimates by gender.

[a] Estimates were based on the prisoner custody population in each year. The total custody population included inmates held in privately operated facilities and community corrections centers (30,379 in 2007; 24,768 in 2004; and 3,828 inmates in privately operated facili-ties in 1999). In 1991 and 1997, the number of inmates in these facil-ities was not known.

[b] The 2007 estimates were based on the distribution of parents from the 2004 SISFCF.

[c] Numbers were estimated based on the custody population in state (1,241,034) and federal (176,156) prisons on June 30, 2004.

[d] Estimates may not be comparable to previously published BJS reports.

Of the estimated 74 million children in the U.S. resident population who were under age 18 on July 1, 2007, 2.3% had a parent in prison (table 2). Black children (6.7%) were seven and a half times more likely than white children (0.9%) to have a parent in prison. Hispanic children (2.4%) were more than two and a half times more likely than white children to have a parent in prison.

More than 4 in 10 fathers in state or federal prisons were black; almost 5 in 10 mothers were white

Similar to men in the general prison population (93%), parents held in the nation's prisons at midyear 2007 were mostly male (92%) (not shown in table). More than 4 in 10 fathers were black, about 3 in 10 were white, and about 2 in 10 were Hispanic (appendix table 2). An estimated 1,559,200 children had a father in prison at midyear 2007; nearly half (46%) were children of black fathers.

Almost half (48%) of all mothers held in the nation's prisons at midyear 2007 were white, 28% were black, and 17% were Hispanic. Of the estimated 147,400 children with a mother in prison, about 45% had a white mother. A smaller percentage of the children had a black (30%) or Hispanic (19%) mother.

**Table 2. Minor children in the U.S. resident population with a
parent in state or federal prison, by race and Hispanic origin, 2007.**

	Estimated number of minor children with a parent in prison	Percent of all minor children in the U.S. resident population
U.S. total*	1,706,600	2.3%
White, non-Hispanic	484,100	0.9%
Black, non-Hispanic	767,400	6.7
Hispanic	362,800	2.4

Note. Children were assumed to have the same race/ethnicity as the incarcerated parent. Percentages were calculated based on the U.S. resident population under age 18 as of July 1, 2007.

*Includes children of other races. Other races include American Indians, Alaska Natives, Asians, Native Hawaiians, other Pacific Islanders, and persons identifying two or more races.

The majority of prisoners reported having a minor child, a quarter of which were age 4 or younger

When interviewed during the 2004 survey, the majority of state (52%) and federal (63%) inmates reported having at least one child under age 18 (appendix table 3). Women in state prison (62%) were more likely than men (51%) to report being a parent. Among federal inmates, 63% of male inmates and 56% of female inmates reported being a parent.

Nearly 1 in 4 state (23%) and federal (24%) inmates reported having one child. Federal inmates (39%) were more likely than state inmates (29%) to report having multiple children. Women (41%) in state prison were more likely than men (29%) to report having more than one child. Similar percentages of women (36%) and men (39%) held in federal prison reported having multiple children. Parents in state and federal prisons reported having two children, on average (not shown in table).

Twenty-two percent of the children of state inmates and 16% of the children of federal inmates were age 4 or younger (table 3). For both state (53%) and federal (50%) inmates, about half their children were age 9 or younger. Children of female state inmates were slightly older than children reported by male state inmates. More than half (53%) of the children reported by women were between age 10 and 17, compared to 47% of the children reported by men.

More than a third of minor children will reach age 18 while their parent is incarcerated

Based on the number of adult children reported during the 2004 survey, the total number of children affected by an incarcerated parent can be calculated by subtracting the amount of time served by the parent from their adult child's age. Using this method, parents in prison had nearly 1.9 million children at the time of admission (table 4). Of those children, an estimated 715,600 will reach age 18 while their parent is incarcerated.

Incarcerated parents of minor children most likely to be age 25 to 34

State inmates age 25 to 34 (64%) interviewed during the 2004 survey were most likely to be parents of minor children, followed by inmates age 35 to 44 and inmates age 24 or younger (table 5). Thirty-one percent of inmates age 45 to 54 reported being a parent. The likelihood of being a parent in state prison was lowest among inmates age 55 or older (13%). Among state prisoners in all age categories except age 45 to 54, women were more likely than men to report being a parent. There was no difference in the prevalence of being a parent between men and women age 45 to 54.

Federal inmates age 25 to 34 (74%) and age 35 to 44 (72%) were more likely to report being a parent, compared to inmates in all other age categories. Forty-seven percent of inmates age 45 to 54 and 46% of inmates age 24 or younger reported being a parent. Federal inmates age 55 or older were least likely to report that they had minor children.

Table 3. Percent of minor children of parents in state and federal prisons at time of interview, by gender, 2004.

Age of minor child	Percent of minor children among parents in state prison			Percent of minor children among parents in federal prison		
	Total	Male	Female	Total	Male	Female
Total	100.0%	100.0%	100.0%	100.0%	100.0%	100.0%
Less than 1 year	2.4%	2.5%	1.6%	0.7%	0.7%	1.1%
1-4 years	20.0	20.3	16.7	15.1	15.3	12.6
5-9 years	30.2	30.3	29.1	33.8	34.0	30.1
10-14 years	31.6	31.4	33.8	35.1	35.0	35.8
15-17 years	15.8	15.5	18.8	15.3	15.0	20.4

Table 4. Estimated number of minor children of state and federal inmates at time of admission, at interview, and at expected release, by gender, 2004.

	Estimated number of minor children of parents in state prison			Estimated number of minor children of parents in federal prison		
	Total	Male	Female	Total	Male	Female
At admission*	1,596,100	1,463,400	132,700	282,600	265,900	16,700
At interview	1,340,300	1,223,700	116,600	249,800	235,200	14,600
At expected release*	1,000,500	905,600	94,900	162,600	151,000	11,600

*Does not include children of parents in prison who did not report time served or time expected to be served.

**Table 5. Percent of state and federal inmates who were
parents of minor children, by age and gender, 2004.**

Age of inmates who were parents of minor children	Percent of parents in state prison			Percent of parents in federal prison		
	Total	Male	Female	Total	Male	Female
All inmates	51.9%	51.2%	61.7%	62.9%	63.4%	55.9%
24 or younger	44.1%	43.5%	55.4%	45.8%	45.7%	47.5%
25-34	64.4	63.3	80.7	74.1	74.1	74.5
35-44	58.9	58.3	65.7	71.9	72.1	68.2
45-54	31.0	31.4	25.8	47.0	48.3	31.2
55 or older	12.6	12.9	^	23.8	25.3	^

Note: See appendix table 16 for estimated total counts.
^Estimate not reported. Sample size too small (10 or fewer) to provide reliable data.

For men held in state prison, the likelihood of being a parent varied across racial categories (appendix table 4). Hispanic (57%) and black (54%) men were more likely than white (45%) men to report being a parent. Findings were similar for men held in federal prison. White men (48%) in federal prison were the least likely of all male inmates to report having children. Black (70%) and Hispanic (69%) men were equally likely to be parents. The likelihood of being a parent for white, black, and Hispanic women held in state prison did not vary by race. In federal prison, Hispanic women (63%) were more likely than white women (47%) to report being a parent.

In state prison, the likelihood of being a parent was most common among married inmates (71%), compared to inmates who were separated (64%), divorced (55%), never married (45%), or widowed (36%). Among federal inmates, married inmates were more likely to report being a parent than inmates in all marital statuses except those inmates who were separated from their spouse. There was no difference in the prevalence of being a parent between married federal inmates and separated federal inmates. The likelihood of being a parent varied little by education for both state and federal inmates.

Drug and public-order offenders in state and federal prisons were more likely than violent offenders to have children

Among male state prisoners, violent (47%) and property (48%) offenders were less likely to report having children than public-order (60%) and drug (59%) offenders (table 6). For women held in state prison, violent (57%) offenders were less likely than drug (63%), property (65%), and public-order (65%) offenders to be a mother.

The prevalence of being a parent differed by gender and offense for inmates held in state and federal prisons. For state inmates, female (65%) property offenders were more likely to be a parent than male (48%) property offenders. In federal prison, male (69%) drug offenders were more likely than female (55%) drug offenders to report having children.

Among men held in federal prison, drug offenders (69%) were more likely than property (54%) and violent (50%) offenders to report having children (appendix table 5). Public-order offenders (62%) were also more likely than violent offenders to report having children. For women in federal prison, the likelihood of being a mother did not differ by offense.

Inmates in state and federal prisons with a criminal history were more likely to be parents of minor children than those with no criminal history

The likelihood of being a parent in prison varied slightly based on criminal history, including prior probation, parole, and incarceration sentences. Prisoners with a criminal history were more likely to report being a parent than prisoners with no criminal history. In state prison, 53% of inmates with a criminal history reported having children, compared to 48% with no criminal history. Sixty-six percent of parents held in federal prison reported having a criminal history, compared to 57% of parents with no criminal history.

In state prison, drug recidivists (62%)—offenders with a prior drug offense—had a higher likelihood of being a parent than violent (52%) and other (54%) recidivists. For women in state prison, and both men and women in federal prison, the likelihood of being a parent did not vary by type of recidivist (appendix table 6).

Male (50%) and female (61%) inmates in state prison who reported no prior incarceration sentences were equally likely to be a parent as male (53%) and female (65%) inmates with 10 or more prior incarcerations. In federal prison, findings were similar for men while women with no prior incarceration sentences (54%) were less likely to be a mother than women who reported they had 10 or more prior incarcerations (81 %).

Fewer than half of parents in state prison lived with their minor children either in the month before arrest or just prior to incarceration

Thirty-seven percent of parents held in state prison reported living with at least one of their children in the month before arrest, 44% reported just prior to incarceration, and 48% reported at either time (table 7). Mothers were more likely than fathers to report living with at least one child. More than half of mothers held in state prison reported living with at least one of their children in the month before arrest, compared to 36% of fathers. More than 6 in 10 mothers reported living with their children just prior to incarceration or at either time, compared to less than half of fathers.

Table 6. Percent of state inmates who were parents of minor children, by current offense and gender, 2004.

Offense	Total	Male	Female
All inmates	51.9%	51.2%	61.7%
Violent	47.5%	47.1%	57.3%
Property	49.9	48.2	64.7
Drug	59.6	59.3	62.5
Public-order	59.9	59.6	65.0

Note. See appendix table 17 for estimated total counts.

Table 7. Parents in state prison who reported living with their minor children in the month before arrest or just prior to incarceration, by gender, 2004.

Lived with their minor children	Total	Male	Female
In month before arrest	37.1%	35.5%	55.3%
In two-parent household	17.9	18.3	13.6
In single-parent household	19.2	17.2	41.7
Prior to incarceration	43.8%	42.4%	60.6%
Either in the month before arrest or just prior to incarceration	47.9%	46.5%	64.2%
Estimated number of parents in state prison	636,300	585,200	51,100

Parents held in federal prison were more likely than those held in state prison to report living with a child in the month before arrest, just prior to incarceration, or at either time (appendix table 7). Mothers in federal prison were more likely than fathers to report living with a child.

More than 4 in 10 mothers in state prison who had minor children were living in single-parent households in the month before arrest

Parents held in state prison were equally likely to report living with their children in a single-parent household (19%) as they were to report living with their children in a two-parent household (18%) in the month before arrest. Mothers were three times more likely to report living in a single- parent household (42%) than in a two-parent household (14%). Fathers reported similar percentages of living in single or two-parent households in the month before their arrest.

Parents held in federal prison were more likely overall to report having lived in two-parent versus single-parent households in the month before arrest. Mothers (52%) were more than two and a half times more likely than fathers (19%) to have lived in single-parent households.

Fathers living with their minor child relied heavily on someone to provide daily care

Mothers and fathers in state prison responded differently when asked who provided most of the daily care for their minor children. Among parents in state prison who had lived with their minor children just prior to incarceration, mothers (77%) were almost three times more likely than fathers (26%) to report that they had provided most of the daily care for their children (appendix table 8). Sixty-three percent of fathers reported sharing the daily care, compared to 18% of mothers. About 1 in 10 fathers relied on someone to provide daily care for their children, compared to 1 in 20 mothers. Similar results were found for mothers and fathers in federal prison.

Fathers most commonly reported the child's mother as current caregiver of their children, while mothers most commonly reported the child's grandparents

The other parent (84%) was the most commonly reported caregiver for children of parents in state prison, followed by grandparents (15%), and other relatives (6%) (table 8). Three percent reported that their children were in the care of a foster home, agency, or institution.

Mothers and fathers in state prison provided different responses about their children's current caregivers. Eighty- eight percent of fathers reported that at least one of their children was in the care of the child's mother, compared to 37% of mothers who reported the father as the child's current caregiver.

Mothers in state prison most commonly identified the child's grandmother (42%) as the current caregiver. Nearly a quarter (23%) identified other relatives as the current caregivers of their children. The percentage of fathers in prison who reported that their children were in the care of a grandmother (12%) or other relative (5%) was much smaller. Mothers (11%) were 5 times more likely than fathers (2%) to report that their children were in the care of a foster home, agency, or institution.

About half of parents in state prison provided the primary financial support for their minor children

Mothers (52%) and fathers (54%) in state prison were equally likely to report that they provided primary financial support for their minor children prior to their incarceration (appendix table 9). Three-quarters (75%) reported employment in the month prior to their arrest. Parents who supported their children financially were more likely to have been employed (80%) in the month prior to arrest and to report wages or salary (76%) as income.

Of parents with minor children who did not provide primary financial support, 68% reported employment in the month before their arrest and 64% reported wages or salary as income. More than a third (36%) of mothers in state prison reported government transfers such as welfare, Social Security, or compensation payment as income. Mothers were more likely than fathers to report receiving government transfers regardless of who provided the primary financial support for their children. The findings were similar for parents held in federal prison.

Table 8. Current caregiver of minor children of parents in state prison, by gender, 2004.

Children's current caregiver[a]	Total	Male	Female
Other parent	84.2%	88.4%	37.0%
Grandparent	15.1%	12.5%	44.9%
Grandmother	14.0	11.6	42.1
Grandfather	4.3	3.6	12.0
Other relatives	6.2%	4.7%	22.8%
Foster home or agency	2.9%	2.2%	10.9%
Friends, others[b]	2.9%	2.4%	7.8%
Estimated number of parents in state prison	636,300	585,200	51,100

[a] Includes all parents with minor children. Detail may sum to more than 100% because some prisoners had multiple minor children living with multiple caregivers.

[b] Includes inmate's friends, friends of the inmate's children, cases where the parent reported that the child now lived alone, and others.

Parents in state prison who provided primary financial support were more likely to report that they lived with their children in the month before arrest or just prior to incarceration (table 9). Among parents in state prison who provided the primary financial support to their children, mothers (89%) were more likely than fathers (67%) to report that they had lived with their children.

More than three-quarters of state prison inmates who were parents of minor children reported that they had some contact with their children since admission

Seventy percent of parents in state prison reported exchanging letters with their children, 53% had spoken with their children over the telephone, and 42% had a personal visit since admission (appendix table 10).[1] Mothers were more likely than fathers to report having had any contact with their children. Mothers and fathers were equally likely to report having had personal visits with their children. A higher percentage of parents in federal prison reported contact with their children. In federal prison, 85% reported telephone contact, 84% had exchanged letters, and 55% reported having had personal visits.

More than three-quarters of state prison inmates who were parents of minor children reported that they had some contact with their children since admission (table 10). Thirty-nine percent of fathers and 56% of mothers in state prison had at least weekly contact with their children since admission. Parents (86%) in state prison who reported living with their minor children in the month before arrest or just before incarceration were more likely to report having contact with their children than parents (72%) who had not lived with their children. Mothers (62%) and fathers (49%) who had lived with their children were more likely to report they had at least weekly contact with their children than mothers (44%) and fathers (30%) who had not lived with their children.

Table 9. Financial support of minor children provided by parents in state prison prior to their incarceration, by gender, 2004.

	Total	Male	Female
Provided primary financial support	54.0%	54.1%	51.9%
Lived with minor child in the month before arrest or prior to incarceration	68.6%	66.9%	88.6%
Did not provide primary financial support	46.0%	45.9%	48.1%
Lived with minor child in the month before arrest or prior to incarceration	23.3%	22.0%	37.6%
Estimated number of parents in state prison	636,300	585,200	51,100

Table 10. Frequency of contact with adult or minor children among state inmates who were parents of minor children, by gender, 2004.

	Any contact			Weekly or more			Weekly or more		
	Total	Male	Female	Total	Male	Female	Total	Male	Female
All parents in state prison	78.6%	78.1%	85.0%	39.9%	38.5%	55.7%	38.8%	39.6%	29.3%
Lived with minor children*									
Yes	86.0%	85.5%	89.7%	50.1%	48.6%	62.3%	35.9%	36.9%	27.4%
No	72.1	71.9	76.5	30.9	30.2	44.2	41.2	41.7	32.3
Time expected to serve until release									
Less than 6 months	78.5%	77.7%	84.8%	47.3%	45.9%	56.9%	31.2%	31.7%	27.9%
6-11 months	79.1	78.4	84.8	42.8	41.3	55.9	36.2	37.1	28.9
12-59 months	79.0	78.5	86.7	39.4	38.4	54.9	39.6	40.1	31.8
60 or more months	78.6	78.5	80.6	32.3	31.7	47.9	46.3	46.8	32.8
No release expected	74.0	74.0	74.8	22.4	21.3	^	51.6	52.7	^

Note. See appendix table 18 for estimated total counts. The contact question included in the 2004 SISFCF asked about contact with any child, which could include children age 18 or older.

*Inmate lived with minor children in the month before arrest or just prior to incarceration.

^Estimate not reported. Sample size too small (10 or fewer) to provide reliable data.

While the percent of parents in state prison who reported contact with their children varied little by expected release date, those having less time to serve reported more frequent contact with their children. About half (47%) of parents who expected to be released within six months reported at least weekly contact with their children, compared to 39% who expected to be released in 12 to 59 months, and 32% in 60 or more months. Among parents who did not expect to be released, 22% reported at least weekly contact with their children.

Half of parents in state prison reported that they had a family member who had been incarcerated

Mothers in state prison (58%) were more likely than fathers (49%) to report having a family member who had also been incarcerated (table 11). Parents in state prison most commonly reported a brother (34%), followed by a father (19%). Among mothers in state prison, 13% reported a sister and 8% reported a spouse. Six percent of fathers reported having a sister who had also been incarcerated; 2%, a spouse.

While growing up, 40% of parents in state prison reported living in a household that received public assistance, 14% reported living in a foster home, agency, or institution at some time during their youth, and 43% reported living with both parents most of the time (appendix table 11). Mothers (17%) held in state prison were more likely than fathers (14%) to report living in a foster home, agency, or institution at some time during their youth. Parents in federal prison reported lower percentages of growing up in a household that received public assistance (31%) or living in a foster home, agency, or institution (7%). These characteristics varied little by gender for parents held in federal prison.

Table 11. Family incarceration of state inmates who were parents of minor children, by gender, 2004.

	Total	Male	Female
Family member ever incarcerated	49.6%	48.9%	58.4%
Mother	6.4	6.1	10.4
Father	18.8	18.6	20.7
Brother	34.4	34.2	36.8
Sister	6.5	6.0	13.0
Child	2.0	1.7	5.2
Spouse	1.9	1.5	7.5
Estimated number of parentsin state prison	636,300	585,200	51,100

Table 12. Homelessness, physical/sexual abuse, medical/mental health problems, or substance dependence/abuse problems among state inmates who were parents of minor children, by living arrangement and gender, 2004.

	All parents in state prison	Lived with minor children*		Did not live with minor children*	
		Male	Female	Male	Female
Homelessness in year before arrest	8.9%	4.0%	8.5%	12.0%	28.7%
Ever physical/sexual abuse	19.9	16.1	59.7	15.7	72.4
Current medical problem	40.6	39.7	50.0	39.6	57.6
Any mental health problem	56.5	54.5	72.8	55.2	75.3
Any substance dependence/abuse	67.4	65.0	63.6	68.8	81.5
Estimated number of parents in state prison	636,300	272,200	32,800	313,000	18,300

Note. Measures of substance dependence or abuse and mental health problems were based on criteria specified in the "Diagnostic and Statistical Manual of Mental Disorders," fourth edition (DSM-IV). For details, see Drug Use and Dependence, State and Federal Prisoners, 2004, <http://www.ojp.usdoj.gov/bjs/abstract/dudsfp04.htm> and *Mental Health Problems of Prison and Jail Inmates*, <http://www.ojp.usdoj.gov/bjs/abstract/mhp-pji.htm>.
*Inmate lived with minor children in the month before arrest or just prior to incarceration.

More than a third (34%) of parents in state prison reported that during their youth, their parents or guardians had abused alcohol or drugs. Mothers in state prison (43%) were more likely than fathers (33%) to have had this experience. Fewer parents (27%) in federal prison reported having a parent or a guardian who had abused alcohol or drugs.

Mothers in state prison more likely than fathers to report homelessness, past physical or sexual abuse, and medical and mental health problems

Among parents in state prison, 9% reported homeless- ness in the year before arrest, 20% had a history of physical or sexual abuse, and 41% reported a current medical problem. Fifty-seven percent of parents in state prison met the criteria for a mental health problem and 67% met the criteria for substance dependence or abuse (appendix table 12).[2] In comparison, parents in federal prison reported lower percentages of homelessness (4%) in the year before arrest, past physical or sexual abuse (11%), current medical problems (36%), mental health problems (43%), and substance dependence or abuse (56%).

Mothers in state prison were two times more likely than fathers to report homelessness in the year before arrest, four times more likely to report past physical or sexual abuse, and almost one and half times more likely to have either a current medical or mental health problem. The comparison by gender among parents held in federal prison was similar to those held in state prison, with the exception of homelessness in the year before arrest. Both male and female parents held in federal prison had similar rates (4.0%) of homelessness in the year before arrest.

Reports from fathers in state prison that showed past physical or sexual abuse, current medical problems, mental health problems, and substance dependence or abuse did- not vary overall by living arrangement (table 12). However, fathers who had not lived with their children were three times more likely than those who had lived with their children to report homelessness in the year prior to arrest.

Mothers held in state prison who had not lived with their children were three times more likely to report homelessness (29%) than those who had lived with their children (9%). Mothers who had not lived with their children were also more likely to report past physical and sexual abuse, current medical problems, and substance dependence or abuse than those who had lived with their children.

Table 12. Homelessness, physical/sexual abuse, medical/mental health problems, or substance dependence/abuse problems among state inmates who were parents of minor children, by living arrangement and gender, 2004.

	All parents in state prison	Lived with minor children*		Did not live with minor children*	
		Male	Female	Male	Female
Homelessness in year before arrest	8.9%	4.0%	8.5%	12.0%	28.7%
Ever physical/sexual abuse	19.9	16.1	59.7	15.7	72.4
Current medical problem	40.6	39.7	50.0	39.6	57.6
Any mental health problem	56.5	54.5	72.8	55.2	75.3
Any substance dependence/abuse	67.4	65.0	63.6	68.8	81.5
Estimated number of parents in state prison	636,300	272,200	32,800	313,000	18,300

Note. Measures of substance dependence or abuse and mental health problems were based on criteria specified in the "Diagnostic and Statistical Manual of Mental Disorders," fourth edition (DSM-IV). For details, see Drug Use and Dependence, State and Federal Prisoners, 2004, <http://www.ojp.usdoj.gov/bjs/abstract/dudsfp04.htm> and Mental Health Problems of Prison and Jail Inmates, <http://www.ojp.usdoj.gov/bjs/abstract/mhppji.htm>.

*Inmate lived with minor children in the month before arrest or just prior to incarceration.

More than 4 in 10 parents in the nation's prisons who met the criteria for substance dependence or abuse had received treatment since admission

About 4 in 10 parents in state prison who met the criteria for substance dependence or abuse reported ever receiving treatment for drug or alcohol abuse; 56% reported participating in other drug or alcohol abuse programs (appendix table 13). Forty-three percent of parents who met the criteria reported treatment since admission. For fathers (10%) and mothers (14%), placement in a residential facility or unit for drug or alcohol abuse was the most common treatment since admission. Parents held in federal prison who met the criteria for substance dependence or abuse reported similar percentages of alcohol or drug treatment and program participation.

Of parents in state prison who had a mental health problem, 46% reported ever receiving treatment. About a third (31%) had been treated since admission. Prescription medication was the most common treatment for both those who had reported ever having treatment (38%) and for those who had received treatment since admission (25%).

About a third (33%) of parents in state prison with a mental health problem reported that they had ever received therapy and 18% reported they had ever had an overnight hospital stay. A fifth (21%) of parents with a mental health problem reported that they had received therapy since admission; 5% had an overnight hospital stay.

Mothers were more likely than fathers to report treatment for mental health problems either before or after admission to a state prison. In state prison, prescribed medication was the most common treatment for parents with a mental health problem.

While parents in federal prison were less likely than those in state prison to report mental health treatment, the patterns by gender were similar for both. Participation in alcohol, drug, or mental health treatment did not vary by whether parents had lived with their children in the month before arrest or just prior to incarceration (table 13).

Table 13. Alcohol or drug and mental health treatment history of inmates in state prison who were parents of minor children and who had an alcohol or drug or mental health problem, by living arrangement and gender, 2004.

	All parents in state prison	Lived with minor childrena		Did not live with minor childrena	
		Male	Female	Male	Female
Alcohol or drug treatmentb					
Ever any treatment or programs	69.8%	68.9%	74.3%	69.6%	77.2%
Received treatment since admission	42.9	41.7	46.4	43.0	49.8
Estimated number of parents who had an alcohol or drug problem	428,600	177,900	20,900	215,000	14,800
Mental health treatmentc					
Ever any treatment	46.4%	42.2%	70.4%	44.1%	77.3%
Received treatment since admission	30.9	25.6	52.4	29.7	57.8
Estimated number of parents who had a mental health problem	359,200	148,700	23,900	172,900	13,700

[a] Inmate lived with minor children in the month before arrest or just prior to incarceration.
[b] Based on parents in state prison who had an alcohol or drug problem.
[c] Based on parents in state prison who had a mental health problem.

Among parents in state prison, two-thirds reported they had a work assignment; over half had attended self-help or improvement classes since admissions

In state prison, about 7 in 10 mothers (70%) and fathers (67%) reported participating in work assignments since admission (appendix table 14). About two-thirds (65%) of mothers and more than half (57%) of fathers had attended self-help or improvement classes. While mothers and fathers were equally likely to report participating in employment and educational programming, mothers (27%) were about two and a half times more likely than fathers (11%) to attend parenting or childrearing classes. Mothers and fathers (both 62%) were equally likely to report having a high school diploma or GED at admission.

Parents held in federal prison reported participating in work assignments and self-help programs and having a high school diploma or GED more frequently than parents in state prison. More than 9 in 10 parents in federal prison reported participating in a work assignment. Since admission, more than 7 in 10 had attended self-help or improvement classes. About 7 in 10 reported having a high school diploma or GED upon admission.

Similar percentages of participation in self-help or improvement classes were found between mothers and fathers in state prison who had lived with their children and those who had not lived with their children prior to arrest or incarceration (table 14). Mothers who had lived with their children prior to arrest or incarceration (72%) were more likely than mothers who had not lived with their children (67%) to participate in work assignments.

Table 14. Work assignments, program participation, and education among state inmates who were parents of minor children, by living arrangement and gender, 2004.

	All parents in state prison	Lived with minor children[a]		Did not live with minor children[a]	
		Male	Female	Male	Female
Work assignments[b]	66.8%	67.9%	72.2%	65.7%	66.6%
Self-help or improvement classes since admission	57.2%	57.4%	65.4%	55.8%	63.4%
Parenting or childrearing classes	11.9	12.1	29.7	9.3	22.5
Employment programs	30.4	30.6	33.2	30.1	26.9
Vocational or job-training program	26.5	26.2	27.0	26.8	22.2
Employment counseling	9.4	9.6	12.4	8.8	11.3
Education programs[c]	30.3	29.4	33.2	30.8	31.5
Other pre-release programs[d]	31.2	32.0	39.3	29.3	39.4
Had GED or high school diploma upon admission	62.4%	63.0%	65.5%	62.2%	56.4%
Estimated number of parents in state prison	636,300	272,200	32,800	313,000	18,300

[a] Inmate lived with their minor children in the month before arrest or just prior to incarceration.

[b] Includes work assignments both inside and outside the prison.

[c] Excludes vocational training. Includes basic classes up to 9th grade, high school diploma or GED classes, college level classes, or English as a second language.

[d] Includes inmate assistance/counseling groups, inmate self-help/personal improvement groups, including parent awareness groups, life skills/community adjustment classes, and other pre-release programs.

Mothers in prison had served less time at time of interview and expected to be released in a shorter amount of time than fathers

Over half (52%) of parents in state prison had served between 12 and 59 months at the time of their interview (appendix table 15). A quarter (26%) had been in prison 60 months or more. Mothers and fathers were equally likely to have been in prison for 12 to 59 months. For longer lengths of stay, mothers (13%) were less likely than fathers (27%) to have been in prison for 60 or more months.

About 4 in 10 mothers in state prison expected to be released within 6 months. An additional 21% expected to be released in 6 to 11 months. Among fathers in state prison, a quarter expected to be released in less than 6 months and 15% percent expected to be released in 6 to 11 months. Compared to mothers in federal prison, fathers had served more of their sentence at the time of their interviews and expected to have a longer time remaining until their release.

Time served and time expected until release varied little for fathers by whether they had lived with their children in the month before arrest or just prior to incarceration while differences were found among women (table 15). Compared to mothers who had not lived with their children in the month before arrest or just prior incarceration (46%), mothers who had lived with their children (39%) were less likely to expect to be released in less than 6 months.

Table 15. Time served since admission and time to be served until expected release among state inmates who were parents of minor children, by gender, 2004.

	All parents in state prison	Lived with minor children[a]		Did not live with minor children[a]	
		Male	Female	Male	Female
Time served since admission[b]					
Less than 6 months	9.4%	8.4%	17.9%	8.8%	17.8%
6-11 months	13.1	11.7	19.9	13.3	19.4
12-59 months	51.9	52.5	47.8	51.8	53.8
60+ months	25.5	27.4	14.5	26.1	9.0
Time left to be served on current sentence[c]					
Less than 6 months	26.7%	25.4%	39.0%	25.4%	46.0%
6-11 months	15.4	15.0	20.5	14.8	20.3
12-59 months	37.9	37.6	30.2	39.8	26.4
60+ months	17.8	19.6	9.1	17.7	6.4
No release expected	2.3	2.4	1.2	2.3	^
Estimated number of parents in state prison	636,300	272,200	32,800	313,000	18,300

^Estimate not reported. Sample size too small (10 or fewer) to provide reliable data.
[a] Inmate lived with minor children in the month before arrest or just prior to incarceration.
[b] Based on time served from admission until time of interview.
[c] Based on time from interview to expected date of release.

Methodology

Survey of Inmates in State and Federal Correctional Facilities

The Survey of Inmates in State and Federal Correctional Facilities (SISFCF), 2004, is comprised of two separate surveys. One survey is conducted in state adult correctional facilities and the other is conducted in federal correctional facilities. The surveys provide nationally representative data on state prison inmates and sentenced federal inmates. Both surveys use the same questionnaire and a stratified two-stage sample design where facilities are selected in the first stage and inmates to be interviewed in the second stage.

The state prison sample was selected from a universe of 1,585 facilities that were either enumerated in the 2000 Census of State and Federal Correctional Facilities (CSFCF), or had opened between the completion of the Census and April 1, 2003. A total of 287 state prisons participated in the survey; 2 state prisons refused, 11 were closed or had no inmates to survey, and 1 was erroneously included in the universe.

The federal prison sample was selected from 148 prisons and satellite facilities holding inmates on January 4, 2003. Thirty-nine of the 40 federal prisons selected participated in the survey.

A total of 14,499 inmates in the state facilities were interviewed; 1,653 inmates refused to participate, resulting in a second-stage nonresponse rate of 10.2%. A total of 3,686 inmates in federal facilities were interviewed and 567 refused to participate, for a second-stage nonresponse rate of 13.3%. After the initial sample of inmates, a secondary sample of 1 in 3 drug offenders was selected for participation in the federal survey.

Accuracy of the estimates

The accuracy of the 2004 SISFCF depends on sampling and measurement errors. Sampling errors occur by chance because a sample rather than a complete enumeration of the population was conducted. Measurement error can be attributed to many sources, such as nonresponse, recall difficulties, differences in the interpretation of questions among inmates, and processing errors.

The sampling error, as measured by an estimated standard error, varies by the size of the estimate and the size of the base population. These standard errors may be used to construct confidence intervals around percentages. For example, the 95-percent confidence interval around the percentage of state inmates who reported being a parent is approximately 51.9% plus or minus 1.96 times 1.41% (or 49.1% to 54.7%).

These standard errors may also be used to test the statistical significance of the difference between two sample statistics by pooling the standard errors of the two sample estimates. For example, the standard error of the difference between male and female state inmate parents who lived with their children in the month before arrest or just prior to incarceration would be 3.69% (or the square root of the sum of the squared standard errors for each group). The 95% confidence interval around the difference would be 1.96% times 3.69% (or 7.23%). Since the difference of 17.7% (64.2% minus 46.5%) is greater than 7.2%, the difference would be considered statistically significant. Differences discussed in this report were significant at the 95% confidence level.

Number of parents in prison who had minor children

To estimate the number of parents by gender in the 1991, 1997, and 2004 SISFCF survey years, the distribution of parents from each of the survey years was applied to the prisoner custody population by gender for that specific year. In 1999 and 2007, the surveys were not conducted. To estimate the number of parents by gender in 1999, the distribution of parents from the 1997 SISFCF was applied to the prisoner custody population by gender in 1999. The distribution of parents by gender from the 2004 SISFCF was used to estimate the number of parents in prison at midyear 2007, by applying the distribution to the midyear 2007 prisoner custody population by gender.

In 2007, 2004, and 1999, the total federal custody population included inmates held in privately operated facilities and community corrections centers (30,379 in 2007; 24,768 in 2004; and 3,828 in privately operated facilities in 1999). In 1991 and 1997 the number of inmates in these facilities was not known.

The 2007 estimates of the number of parents by race and gender were calculated based on the 2004 SISFCF distribution of parents, which was then applied to the midyear 2007 custody population, by race and gender. The 2004 estimates of the number of parents in prison by race and gender were calculated using the same method except the 2004 SISFCF distribution was applied to the midyear 2004 custody population, by race and gender.

Number of minor children of parents in prison

For this report, published estimates for 1991, 1997, and 1999 were re-estimated to ensure comparability for the period covered. The 2004 SISFCF allowed prisoners to report a maximum of ten children. The 1997 SISFCF only allowed prisoners to report a maximum of six children and the 1991 SISFCF only allowed prisoners to report a maximum of five children. The 1997 distribution for six children was used to estimate the number of prisoners with six children in 1991. The 2004 distribution for seven through ten children was used to estimate the number of prisoners with seven through ten children in both 1991 and 1997.

Washington, DC 20531
Official Business
Penalty for Private Use $300
Revised 1/8/09

For each year, the estimated number of parents by gender was multiplied by the number of minor children reported by male and by female inmates. The estimates were then summed by gender for each year and reported as the totals. Because this estimation method was used, estimates presented in this report may not be comparable to previously published BJS reports. See *Incarcerated Parents and Their Children* at <http://www.ojp.usdoj.gov/bjs/ abstract/i ptc. htm>.

The 2007 estimates by race and gender for the number of minor children of parents in prison were calculated based on the 2004 SISFCF distribution of parents and the number of minor children they reported. This distribution was then applied to the midyear 2007 custody population by race and gender. The estimated number of parents by race and gender was multiplied by the number of minor children they reported. The estimates were summed by race and gender for each year and reported as the totals. The 2004 race and gender estimates for the number of minor children of parents in prison were calculated using this same method except the 2004 SISFCF distribution was applied to the midyear 2004 custody population, by race and gender.

The Bureau of Justice Statistics is the statistical agency of the U.S. Department of Justice. Jeffrey L. Sedgwick is director.

This Special Report was written by Lauren E. Glaze and Laura M. Maruschak. William J. Sabol, Ph.D. and Christopher J. Mumola provided statistical review. Lara E. Allen and Margaret E. Noonan verified the report.

Georgette Walsh edited the report, Tina Dorsey produced the report, and Jayne Robinson prepared the report for final printing, under the supervision of Doris J. James.

August 2008, NCJ 222984

This report in portable document format and in ASCII and its related statistical data and tables (includes 20 appendix tables) are available at the BJS World Wide Web Internet site: <http:// www.ojp.usdoj.gov/bjs/abstract/pptmc.htm>.

Office of Justice Programs
Innovation • Partnerships • Safer Neighborhoods <http://www.ojp. usdoj.gov>.

Appendix Table 1. Estimated number of parents in state and federal prisons and their minor children, by inmate's gender.

	Total	Parents in state prison			Parents in federal prison[a]		
		Total	Male	Female	Total	Male	Female
Number of parents							
2007	809,800	686,000	627,800	58,200	123,800	116,400	7,400
2004[b]	754,900	644,100	592,300	51,800	110,800	104,200	6,600
1999	721,500	642,300	593,800	48,500	79,200	74,100	5,100
1997	649,500	587,000	544,100	42,900	62,500	58,500	4,000
1991	452,500	413,100	386,500	26,600	39,400	36,500	2,900
Number of minor children							
2007	1,706,600	1,427,500	1,296,500	131,000	279,100	262,700	16,400
2004[b]	1,590,100	1,340,300	1,223,700	116,600	249,800	235,200	14,600
1999[c]	1,515,200	1,338,900	1,223,400	115,500	176,300	165,700	10,600
1997[c]	1,362,900	1,223,800	1,121,400	102,400	139,100	130,800	8,300
1991[c]	945,600	860,300	802,300	58,000	85,100	79,200	5,900

Note. See *Methodology* for details about estimation methods.

[a] Estimates were based on the prisoner custody population in each year. The total custody population included inmates held in privately operated facilities and community corrections centers (30,379 in 2007; 24,768 in 2004; and 3,828 inmates in privately operated facilities in 1999). In 1991 and 1997, the number of inmates in these facilities was not known.

[b] Numbers were estimated based on the June 30, 2004, custody population in state (1,241,034) and federal (176,156) prisons.

[c] Estimates may not be comparable to previously published BJS reports. See Methodology for more detail.

Appendix Table 2. Estimated number of parents in state and federal prisons and their minor children, by inmate's gender, race, and Hispanic origin, 2004 and 2007.

| | Male | | | | Female | | | |
	Total[a]	White[b]	Black[b]	Hispanic	Total[a]	White[b]	Black[b]	Hispanic
State inmates								
Number of parents								
2007	627,800	197,800	262,400	127,600	58,200	29,000	16,100	8,800
2004[c]	592,300	189,800	279,500	113,100	51,800	23,300	19,000	8,200
Number of children 2007	1,296,500	373,400	577,900	263,500	131,000	60,000	39,600	22,900
2004[c]	1,223,700	358,000	611,600	233,000	116,600	47,900	45,700	21,000
Federal inmates								
Number of parents 2007	116,400	25,900	57,000	32,500	7,400	2,700	2,200	2,300
2004[c]	104,200	20,900	49,300	31,000	6,600	2,000	2,100	2,200
Number of children 2007	262,700	45,100	144,800	71,200	16,400	5,600	5,100	5,200
2004[c]	235,200	36,300	125,400	67,800	14,600	4,200	4,900	4,900

Note. See *Methodology* for estimation methods.

[a] Includes other races. Other races include American Indians, Alaska Natives, Asians, Native Hawaiians, other Pacific Islanders, and persons identifying two or more races.

[b] Excludes persons of Hispanic or Latino origin.

[c] Numbers were estimated based on the June 30, 2004 custody population in state (1,241,034) and federal (176,156) prisons.

Appendix Table 3. State and federal inmates who reported having minor children, by gender, race, and Hispanic origin, 2004.

| | | Number of minor children | | | |
	Percent of inmates with minor children	1	2	3	4 or more
State inmates	51.9%	22.5	14.8	8.1	6.5
Male*	51.2%	22.7	14.4	7.8	6.3
White, non-Hispanic	44.8%	21.6	12.9	6.5	3.8
Black, non-Hispanic	54.0%	23.3	14.4	7.9	8.4
Hispanic	57.0%	23.4	17.6	9.7	6.3
Female*	61.7%	20.7	19.3	12.4	9.3
White, non-Hispanic	61.8%	23.0	21.7	10.6	6.4
Black, non-Hispanic	61.0%	18.1	17.8	14.1	11.1
Hispanic	64.1%	18.3	15.9	14.1	15.8
Federal inmates	62.9%	24.4	17.8	10.9	9.8
Male*	63.4%	24.8	17.9	10.9	9.9
White, non-Hispanic	47.8%	26.2	12.7	6.3	2.5
Black, non-Hispanic	70.0%	24.2	18.1	12.9	14.8
Hispanic	68.5%	23.4	23.7	12.5	8.9
Female*	55.9%	19.5	17.0	10.7	8.7
White, non-Hispanic	47.4%	17.9	14.6	8.5	6.5
Black, non-Hispanic	55.2%	18.1	16.3	10.2	10.6
Hispanic	63.4%	21.6	18.2	13.9	9.6

Note. See appendix table 16 for estimated total counts.

*Includes inmates of other races. Other races include American Indians, Alaska Natives, Asians, Native Hawaiians, other Pacific Islanders, and persons identifying two or more races.

Appendix Table 4. Percent of state and federal inmates who were parents of minor children, by selected characteristics and gender, 2004.

	Parents in state prison			Parents in federal prison		
	Total	Male	Female	Total	Male	Female
All inmates	51.9%	51.2%	61.7%	62.9%	63.4%	55.9%
Race						
White, non-Hispanic	46.3%	44.8%	61.8%	47.8%	47.8%	47.4%
Black, non-Hispanic	54.4	54.0	61.0	69.2	70.0	55.2
Hispanic	57.4	57.0	64.1	68.1	68.5	63.4
Other race*	51.5	50.8	59.6	61.8	61.9	60.7
Marital status						
Married	71.3%	71.3%	71.0%	75.7%	76.9%	60.2%
Widowed	36.2	35.3	40.9	36.9	38.2	33.2
Divorced	55.0	54.7	59.0	58.8	59.0	56.1
Separated	64.2	63.9	66.4	68.9	68.8	69.7
Never married	44.6	43.7	60.6	57.7	58.1	52.4
Education completed						
8th grade or less	49.5%	48.6%	61.8%	65.6%	66.2%	57.6%
Some high school	55.2	54.6	63.8	70.5	71.0	64.3
GED	51.3	50.6	64.1	62.4	62.8	56.6
High school graduate	52.1	51.6	58.7	63.9	64.6	54.8
Some college or more	48.5	47.3	59.2	54.6	55.1	49.8
U.S. citizenship						
Citizen	51.6%	50.8%	61.8%	62.2%	62.7%	54.8%
Non-citizen	56.7	56.6	64.7	67.5	67.7	64.2

Note. See appendix table 16 for estimated total counts.
*Other race includes American Indians, Alaska Natives, Asians, Native Hawaiians, other Pacific Islanders, and persons identifying two or more races.

Appendix Table 5. Percent of state and federal inmates who were parents of minor children, by current offense and gender, 2004.

	Parents in state prison			Parents in federal prison		
Current offense	Total	Male	Female	Total	Male	Female
All inmates	51.9%	51.2%	61.7%	62.9%	63.4%	55.9%
Violent	47.5%	47.1%	57.3%	49.9%	49.8%	52.4%
Homicide[a]	40.3	39.9	46.6	51.6	51.7	^
Sexual assault[b]	45.4	45.3	61.9	30.7	30.1	^
Robbery	47.0	46.5	59.6	49.5	49.5	49.2
Assault	56.9	56.5	64.2	56.2	56.5	^
Property	49.9%	48.2%	64.7%	53.8%	53.5%	55.5%
Burglary	44.4	43.8	61.4	29.0	^	^

Appendix Table 5. (Continued).

Current offense	Parents in state prison			Parents in federal prison		
	Total	Male	Female	Total	Male	Female
Larceny	49.9	47.8	61.8	40.9	^	^
Motor vehicle theft	52.0	51.2	67.6	43.8	^	^
Fraud	60.2	56.8	68.1	58.7	59.2	56.5
Drug	59.6%	59.3%	62.5%	67.6%	68.7%	54.5%
Possession	56.9	55.9	64.3	63.0	64.5	^
Trafficking	61.3	61.3	61.7	67.9	68.9	55.9
Public-order	59.9%	59.6%	65.0%	62.4%	62.3%	64.7%
Weapons	64.9	64.9	66.4	63.8	63.8	65.6
DWI	52.9	52.6	59.3	38.7	^	^

Note. See appendix table 17 for estimated total counts.

^Estimate not reported. Sample size too small (10 or fewer) to provide reliable data.

[a] Includes murder and manslaughter.

[b] Includes rape and other sexual assault.

Appendix Table 6. Percent of state and federal inmates who were parents of minor children, by criminal history and gender, 2004.

	Parents in state prison			Parents in federal prison		
	Total	Male	Female	Total	Male	Female
All inmates	51.9%	51.2%	61.7%	62.9%	63.4%	55.9%
Status at time of current arrest						
None	50.4%	49.9%	58.3%	63.3%	64.1%	53.8%
Status	54.0	53.0	65.5	61.8	61.7	63.8
On parole	50.0	49.6	59.6	59.5	60.0	46.1
On probation	57.2	56.1	67.3	64.5	64.1	69.7
Escaped from custody	43.6	40.9	66.5	^	^	^
Criminal history[a]						
None	48.0%	47.0%	57.9%	57.4%	58.0%	53.0%
Priors	53.2	52.5	63.5	66.0	66.3	59.9
Violent recidivists[b]	52.3	51.9	63.6	62.6	62.7	59.1
Drug recidivists only	61.9	62.4	58.7	70.3	71.3	54.5
Other recidivists[c]	53.5	52.4	64.2	67.7	68.1	61.6
Number of prior incarcerations						
0	50.8%	49.8%	61.4%	62.0%	62.8%	53.9%
1	53.2	52.5	63.9	60.8	61.0	56.4
2-4	53.1	52.7	60.6	68.8	69.0	61.0
5-9	50.6	50.2	60.5	62.0	61.6	76.2
10 or more	53.9	53.2	65.2	61.7	60.3	80.5

Note. See appendix table 17 for estimated total counts.

^Estimate not reported. Sample size too small (10 or fewer) to provide reliable data.

[a] Includes prior probation, parole, and incarceration sentences.

[b] Recidivists with at least one current or past violent offense.

[c] Includes recidivists with unknown offense types.

Appendix Table 7. Parents in federal prison who reported living with their minor children in the month before arrest or just prior to incarceration, by gender, 2004.

Lived with their minor children	Parents in federal prison		
	Total	Male	Female
In month before arrest	48.1%	46.4%	72.8%
In two-parent household	27.2	27.6	20.7
In single-parent household	20.9	18.8	52.1
Prior to incarceration	52.2%	50.5%	78.3%
Either in the month before arrest or just prior to incarceration	56.4%	54.7%	80.9%
Estimated number of parents in federal prison	81,300	76,200	5,100

Appendix Table 8. Daily care and living status of minor children of parents in state and federal prisons, by gender, 2004.

	Parents in state prison			Parents in federal prison		
	Total	Male	Female	Total	Male	Female
Inmate lived with children just prior to incarceration	43.8%	42.4%	60.6%	52.2%	50.5%	78.3%
Estimated number of parents	636,300	585,200	51,100	81,300	76,200	5,100
Most of daily care of children provided by[a]—						
Inmate who lived with children	31.8%	26.1%	77.1%	36.1%	31.3%	82.8%
Inmate shared care with someone else	58.3	63.3	18.1	54.9	59.0–	14.5
Care was provided mostly by someone else	9.9	10.5	4.7	9.0	9.7	2.7
Estimated number of parents	278,900	248,100	30,800	42,500	38,600	3,900
Children currently living together[b]	61.9%	62.3%	59.0%	60.7%	61.0%	57.9%
Estimated number of parents	188,300	167,400	20,900	29,400	26,800	2,600

[a]Includes parents who lived with their minor children just prior to incarceration.
[b]Includes parents who had multiple minor children and lived with their minors just prior to incarceration.

Appendix Table 9. Financial support of minor children, employment, and income among parents in state and federal prisons, by gender, 2004.

	Parents in state prison			Parents in federal prison		
	Total	Male	Female	Total	Male	Female
Parents who provided primary financial support	54.0%	54.1%	51.9%	67.2%	67.1%	68.5%
Employed in month before arrest	80.3%	81.5%	66.4%	77.0%	77.6%	67.7%
Sources of income						
Wages or salary	75.9%	77.1%	60.7%	73.0%	73.4%	67.5%
Transfer payments	11.7	9.6	36.1	8.4	7.4	23.7
Family/friends	10.1	9.1	21.0	8.5	8.0	15.4
Child support/alimony payments	1.0	^	9.3	0.6	^	7.5
Illegal sources	24.1	24.3	21.2	35.7	36.3	26.8
Other	2.9	2.9	3.3	3.6	3.7	^
Personal income in the month before current arrest						
No income	1.2%	1.1%	2.5%	1.0%	^%	^%

Appendix Table 9. (Continued).

	Parents in state prison			Parents in federal prison		
	Total	Male	Female	Total	Male	Female
Less than $200	2.1	2.1	3.3	2.2	2.2	^
$200-599	13.1	12.3	23.8	11.1	10.5	19.4
$600-999	13.8	13.3	19.8	12.2	11.9	16.9
$1,000-1,999	33.0	33.4	28.3	27.5	27.5	27.3
$2,000-4,999	23.6	24.4	14.0	22.5	22.8	17.0
$5,000 or more	13.1	13.5	8.3	23.5	24.1	14.8
Current caregiver of child receiving financial assistance	34.7%	34.3%	39.2%	29.1%	28.6%	35.4%
Parents who did not provide primary financial support	46.0%	45.9%	48.1%	32.8%	32.9%	31.5%
Employed in month before arrest	68.1%	70.1%	47.3%	66.4%	67.5%	49.1%
Sources of income						
Wages or salary	63.5%	65.5%	42.7%	60.4%	61.0%	50.8%
Transfer payments	10.0	9.0	20.9	8.0	7.5	15.4
Family/friends	12.7	12.0	20.6	10.4	10.1	14.4
Child support/alimony payments	0.4	^	4.8	^	^	^
Illegal sources	30.0	30.0	30.4	37.6	38.1	29.9
Other	2.0	2.1	^	3.9	3.8	^
Personal income in the month before current arrest						
No income	2.7%	2.4%	6.9%	2.0%	^%	11.5%
Less than $200	3.7	3.4	7.2	4.8	4.8	^
$200-599	17.4	16.7	25.0	17.4	17.3	18.7
$600-999	16.3	16.2	18.2	13.4	13.6	11.1
$1,000-1,999	29.5	30.1	22.6	25.9	26.0	24.7
$2,000-4,999	19.4	20.0	12.1	15.7	16.0	12.4
$5,000 or more	11.0	11.2	8.0	20.7	20.9	17.4
Current caregiver of child receiving financial assistance	29.2%	29.1%	30.6%	22.1%	22.0%	23.7%
Estimated number of parents	636,300	585,200	51,100	81,300	76,200	5,100

^Estimate not reported. Sample size too small (10 or fewer) to provide reliable data.

Appendix Table 10. Frequency of telephone, mail, and personal contacts with adult or minor children among state and federal inmates who were parents of minor children, by gender, 2004.

Frequency and type of contact with minor children	Parents in state prison			Parents in federal prison		
	Total	Male	Female	Total	Male	Female
Any type of contact						
Daily or almost daily	9.1%	8.7%	14.1%	18.8%	18.3%	26.9%
At least once a week	30.8	29.8	41.6	46.1	45.9	48.2
At least once a month	22.3	22.7	18.1	17.0	17.1	14.7
Less than once a month	16.5	16.9	11.2	9.4	9.6	6.2
Never	21.4	21.9	15.0	8.8	9.1	3.9
Telephone						
Daily or almost daily	5.3%	5.0%	8.6%	16.9%	16.5%	23.4%

Frequency and type of contact with minor children	Parents in state prison			Parents in federal prison		
	Total	Male	Female	Total	Male	Female
At least once a week	17.5	17.1	22.4	40.9	40.7	43.7
At least once a month	15.6	15.6	15.7	17.2	17.2	16.9
Less than once a month	15.0	15.3	12.4	10.1	10.2	7.4
Never	46.6	47.1	40.9	14.9	15.4	8.5
Mail						
Daily or almost daily	4.5%	4.3%	6.9%	4.2%	4.0%	7.7%
At least once a week	24.0	23.0	35.3	29.0	28.3	40.4
At least once a month	23.2	23.3	22.5	31.0	31.2	28.2
Less than once a month	17.9	18.3	13.0	19.8	20.2	12.9
Never	30.4	31.1	22.3	16.0	16.3	10.7
Personal visits						
Daily or almost daily	0.6%	0.6%	^%	^%	^%	^%
At least once a week	5.9	5.7	7.7	4.6	4.4	7.6
At least once a month	12.5	12.3	14.6	14.7	14.7	15.5
Less than once a month	22.5	22.7	19.7	35.6	35.9	31.5
Never	58.5	58.6	57.7	44.7	44.7	44.6
Estimated number of parents	636,300	585,200	51,100	81,300	76,200	5,100

Note. The contact question included in the 2004 SISFCF asked about contact with any child, which could include children age 18 or older.

^Estimate not reported. Sample size too small (10 or fewer) to provide reliable data.

Appendix Table 11. Family background of state and federal inmates who were parents of minor children, by gender, 2004.

	Parents in state prison			Parents in federal prison		
	Total	Male	Female	Total	Male	Female
While growing up, parent—						
Ever received public assistance	39.9%	39.8%	41.3%	31.2%	31.2%	31.7%
Ever lived in foster home, agency, or institution	14.0%	13.7%	17.3%	7.0	6.9	7.6
Lived most of the time with—						
Both parents	43.1%	43.2%	41.1%	45.5%	45.2%	50.6%
One parent	43.5	43.7	42.0	41.2	41.6	34.3
Someone else*	11.5	11.2	14.0	12.6	12.5	14.1
Foster home, agency, or institution	1.9	1.8	3.0	0.7	0.7	^
Parents or guardians of inmate ever abused alcohol or drugs—	33.7%	32.9%	43.0%	27.2%	27.0%	31.4%
Alcohol only	19.6	19.3	23.6	19.2	19.4	17.3
Drugs only	3.1	3.0	3.7	2.2	2.0	5.3
Both alcohol and drugs	11.0	10.6	15.7	5.8	5.6	8.8
None	66.3	67.1	57.0	72.8	73.0	68.6
Estimated number of parents	636,300	585,200	51,100	81,300	76,200	5,100

^Estimate not reported. Sample size too small (10 or fewer) to provide reliable data.

*Includes grandparents, other relatives, friends, and others.

Appendix Table 12. Homelessness, physical/sexual abuse, medical/mental health problems, or substance dependence/ abuse problems among state and federal inmates who were parents of minor children, by gender, 2004.

	Parents in state prison			Parents in federal prison		
	Total	Male	Female	Total	Male	Female
Homelessness in year before arrest	8.9%	8.3%	15.9%	3.9%	3.9%	4.4%
Ever physical/sexual abuse	19.9%	16.0%	64.4%	10.8%	8.0%	53.6%
Physically abused	16.6	13.4	52.8	9.1	6.6	46.8
Sexually abused	8.7	5.7	43.3	3.7	2.0	29.0
Current medical problem	40.6%	39.6%	52.8%	35.6%	35.0%	44.8%
Mental health problem						
Any mental health problem	56.5%	55.0%	73.8%	42.6%	41.3%	62.1%
Recent history of mental health problem	22.6	20.4	48.8	11.9	10.3	35.1
Symptoms of mental health disorders	50.1	49.0	63.2	38.6	37.7	52.6
Substance dependence/abuse						
Any alcohol or drugs	67.4%	67.1%	70.1%	56.4%	56.7%	51.3%
Alcohol only	44.4	45.0	37.6	36.7	37.0	32.5
Drugs only	55.4	54.8	62.8	45.7	45.9	43.4
Estimated number of parents	636,300	585,200	51,100	81,300	76,200	5,100

Note. Measures of substance dependence or abuse and mental health problems were based on criteria specified in the "Diagnostic and Statistical Manual of Mental Disorders," fourth edition (DSM-IV). For details, see Drug Use and Dependence, State and Federal Prisoners, 2004, <http://www.ojp.usdoj.gov/bjs/abstract/dudsfp04.htm> and Mental Health Problems of Prison and Jail Inmates, <http:// www.ojp.usdoj.gov/bjs/abstract/mhppji.htm>.

Appendix Table 13. Alcohol or drug and mental health treatment history of inmates in state and federal prisons who were parents of minor children and who had an alcohol or drug or mental health problem, by gender, 2004.

	Parents in state prison			Parents in federal prison		
	Total	Male	Female	Total	Male	Female
Alcohol or drug treatment[a]						
Ever any treatment or programs	69.8%	69.3%	75.6%	69.1%	68.7%	75.9%
Any treatment	41.1	39.8	55.5%	36.9	36.2	49.5
Other alcohol/drug programs	56.3	56.2	58.0	54.4	53.9	61.7
Received treatment since admission	42.9%	42.4%	48.0%	45.9%	45.4%	54.1%
Any treatment	15.2	14.5	22.1	15.8	15.5	21.0
Residential facility or unit	10.1	9.7	14.3	8.9	8.5	16.8
Counseling by a professional	6.4	6.1	9.5	7.2	7.2	7.4
Detoxification unit	0.8	0.7	2.1	^	^	^
Maintenance drug	0.2	^	0.8	^	^	^

	Parents in state prison			Parents in federal prison		
	Total	Male	Female	Total	Male	Female
Estimated number of parents who had an alcohol or drug problem	428,600	392,800	35,800	45,900	43,300	2,600
Mental health treatment[b]						
Ever any treatment	46.4%	43.5%	71.0%	31.5%	29.0%	57.0%
Had overnight hospital stay	18.0	16.7	28.7	8.5	7.7	15.6
Used prescribed medications	37.8	34.8	63.0	24.3	21.6	50.2
Had professional mental health therapy	33.0	30.5	54.3	22.8	20.7	44.4
Received treatment since admission	30.9%	28.3%	52.9%	21.2%	19.0%	43.3%
Had overnight hospital stay	4.7	4.7	4.4	2.1	1.9	4.0
Used prescribed medications	24.5	22.3	43.6	17.0	15.3	34.0
Had professional mental health therapy	20.5	18.7	36.2	13.3	11.8	27.7
Estimated number of parents who had a mental health problem	359,200	321,600	37,600	34,700	31,500	3,200

^Estimate not reported. Sample size too small (10 or fewer) to provide reliable data.

[a] Based on inmate parents who had an alcohol or drug problem.

[b]Based on inmate parents who had a mental health problem.

Appendix Table 14. Work assignments, program participation, and education among state and federal inmates who were parents of minor children, by gender, 2004.

	Parents in state prison			Parents in federal prison		
	Total	Male	Female	Total	Male	Female
Work assignments[a]	66.8%	66.5%	70.2%	93.0%	93.0%	93.6%
Self-help or improvement classes since admission	57.2%	56.5%	64.9%	72.8%	72.2%	81.0%
Parenting or childrearing classes	11.9	10.6	27.0	25.9	24.8	42.1
Employment programs	30.4	30.4	31.1	37.4	37.0	43.9
Vocational or job-training program	26.5	26.6	25.5	32.6	32.4	35.4
Employment counseling	9.4	9.1	12.1	11.8	11.4	18.3
Education programs[b]	30.3	30.0	32.7	46.9	47.0	45.4
Other pre-release programs[c]	31.2	30.5	39.7	38.1	37.3	48.6
Had GED or high school diploma upon admission Percent	62.4%	62.4%	62.2%	70.7%	70.9%	68.6%
Estimated number	636,300	585,200	51,100	81,300	76,200	5,100
Completed GED since admission[d] Percent	2.0%	2.0%	^	^	^	^
Estimated number	81,000	73,700	^	^	^	^

^Estimate not reported. Sample size too small (10 or fewer) to provide reliable data.

[a] Includes work assignments both inside and outside the prison.

[b] Excludes vocational training. Includes basic classes up to 9th grade, high school classes to get a diploma, or GED, college level classes, or English as a second language.

[c] Includes inmate assistance/counseling groups, inmate self-help/personal improvement groups, including parent awareness groups, life skills/community adjustment classes, and other pre-release programs.

[d] Based on inmate parents who at the time of admission on their current sentence had not completed high school or did not have a GED.

Appendix Table 15. Time served since admission and time to be served until expected release among state and federal inmates who were parents of minor children, by gender, 2004.

	Parents in state prison			Parents in federal prison		
	Total	Male	Female	Total	Male	Female
Time served since admission[a]						
Less than 6 months	9.4%	8.7%	17.7%	4.6%	4.5%	7.0%
6-11 months	13.1	12.5	19.8	7.5	7.1	14.1
12-59 months	51.9	52.1	49.9	56.2	55.9	60.5
60+ months	25.5	26.7	12.6	31.6	32.6	18.4
Time left to be served on current sentence[b]						
Less than 6 months	26.7%	25.4%	41.1%	14.2%	13.3%	28.1%
6-11 months	15.4	14.9	20.4	9.9	9.3	17.2
12-59 months	37.9	38.7	28.9	40.3	40.3	40.8
60+ months	17.8	18.6	8.2	34.1	35.5	13.6
No release expected	2.3	2.4	1.1	1.5	1.6	^
Estimated number of parents	636,300	585,200	51,100	81,300	76,200	5,100

^Estimate not reported. Sample size too small (10 or fewer) to provide reliable data.
[a] Based on time served from admission until time of interview.
[b] Based on time from interview to expected date of release.

Appendix Table 16. Estimated number of inmates, by selected characteristics and gender, 2004.

	Estimated number of state inmates			Estimated number of federal inmates		
	Total	Male	Female	Total	Male	Female
Total	1,226,200	1,143,400	82,800	129,300	120,200	9,100
Race/Hispanic origin						
White, non-Hispanic	431,500	394,000	37,500	33,600	30,900	2,700
Black, non-Hispanic	496,900	469,200	27,700	56,000	53,200	2,900
Hispanic	222,700	211,100	11,600	32,400	29,700	2,700
Other race*	75,100	69,100	5,900	7,200	6,400	800
Age						
24 or younger	212,400	200,900	11,400	11,600	10,800	800
25-34	405,500	379,800	25,700	49,700	46,700	2,900
35-44	373,700	341,800	31,900	37,300	34,500	2,800
45-54	172,700	161,100	11,600	22,200	20,600	1,700
55 or older	61,900	59,700	2,200	8,500	7,600	900
Marital status						
Married	201,600	186,600	15,100	33,600	31,200	2,400
Widowed	24,100	20,100	4,000	1,500	1,100	400
Divorced	241,600	222,400	19,200	26,200	24,200	2,000
Separated	62,600	55,100	7,500	6,600	5,900	700
Never married	696,200	659,200	37,000	61,400	57,900	3,500

	Estimated number of state inmates			Estimated number of federal inmates		
	Total	Male	Female	Total	Male	Female
Education completed						
8th grade or less	150,800	141,100	9,700	14,000	13,000	1,000
Some high school	298,100	277,300	20,800	20,700	19,100	1,600
GED	367,000	347,000	20,000	37,200	35,300	1,900
High school graduate	265,400	247,100	18,300	31,200	29,000	2,100
Some college or more	144,900	130,900	14,000	26,200	23,800	2,500
U.S. Citizenship						
Citizen	1,163,000	1,081,600	81,400	108,100	100,400	7,700
Non-citizen	63,200	61,800	1,400	21,200	19,800	1,300

Note. Estimates may not sum to totals due to rounding.

*Includes American Indians, Alaska Natives, Asians, Native Hawaiians, other Pacific Islanders, and persons identifying two or more races.

Appendix Table 17. Estimated number of inmates, by offense, criminal history, and gender, 2004.

	Estimated number of state inmates			Estimated number of federal inmates		
	Total	Male	Female	Total	Male	Female
Total	**1,226,200**	**1,143,400**	**82,800**	**129,300**	**120,200**	**9,100**
Offense						
Violent	587,200	562,700	24,500	18,900	18,200	700
Homicide[a]	148,800	139,400	9,300	3,100	3,000	100
Sexual assault[b]	131,400	130,200	1,300	1,100	1,100	^
Robbery	155,100	149,800	5,400	11,000	10,600	400
Assault	124,500	118,100	6,400	2,600	2,500	100
Property	229,900	206,200	23,700	8,400	7,100	1,400
Burglary	100,200	97,000	3,200	600	600	^
Larceny	47,600	40,800	6,900	600	500	100
Motor vehicle theft	20,800	19,800	1,000	400	400	^
Fraud	35,100	24,700	10,400	6,000	4,900	1,200
Drug	261,500	235,900	25,500	71,400	66,000	5,500
Possession	73,000	64,300	8,700	3,800	3,600	200
Trafficking	181,400	166,100	15,300	65,200	60,300	5,000
Public-order	145,500	136,700	8,800	26,500	25,400	1,000
Weapons	30,500	29,900	600	14,200	14,000	200
DWI	32,300	30,600	1,700	300	300	^
Status at time of arrest						
None	698,400	654,200	44,200	94,600	87,400	7,200
Status	527,800	489,200	38,600	34,700	32,800	1,900

Appendix Table 17. (Continued).

	Estimated number of state inmates			Estimated number of federal inmates		
	Total	Male	Female	Total	Male	Female
On parole	229,100	220,000	9,100	16,000	15,500	500
On probation	293,800	264,800	29,000	18,200	16,800	1,300
Escaped from custody	4,900	4,400	500	500	500	^
Criminal history						
None	288,700	261,300	27,400	45,600	40,500	5,100
Priors	937,500	882,000	55,400	83,700	79,700	4,000
Violent recidivists[c]	536,700	518,200	18,500	32,800	32,000	800
Drug recidivists only	42,200	37,400	4,800	10,900	10,200	700
Other recidivist[d]	358,600	326,500	32,100	40,000	37,500	2,500
Number of prior incarcerations						
0	561,400	512,900	48,500	71,800	64,900	6,900
1	267,900	252,100	15,800	27,300	26,100	1,200
2-4	250,500	238,600	11,800	21,700	21,100	600
5-9	101,600	97,400	4,100	6,200	6,000	200
10 or more	44,800	42,300	2,500	2,300	2,100	200

Note. Estimates may not sum to totals due to rounding.
^Based on a number of cases which rounded to less than 100.
[a] Includes murder and manslaughter.
[b] Includes rape and other sexual assault.
[c] Recidivists with at least one current or past violent offense.
[d] Includes recidivists with unknown offense types.

Appendix Table 18. Estimated number of parents in state prison, by selected characteristics and gender, 2004.

	Parents in state prison		
	Total	Male	Female
All parents in state prison	636,300	585,200	51,100
Lived with minor children*			
Yes	305,000	272,200	32,800
No	331,300	313,000	18,300
Time expected until release			
Less than 6 months	169,800	148,700	21,200
6-11 months	97,800	87,400	10,400
12-59 months	241,200	226,300	14,800
60 or more months	113,000	108,800	4,200
No release expected	14,500	14,000	500

Note. Estimates may not sum to totals due to rounding.
*Inmate lived with minor children in the month before arrest or just prior to incarceration.

Appendix Table 19. Standard errors of the estimated percentages, state inmates, by gender, 2004.

Base of the estimate and gender	Estimated percentages					
	98 or 2	90 or 10	80 or 20	70 or 30	60 or 40	50
1,500						
All inmates	5.83	12.50	16.67	19.09	20.41	20.83
Male	5.53	11.85	15.80	18.10	19.35	19.75
Female	2.45	5.25	6.99	8.01	8.57	8.74
2,000						
All inmates	5.05	10.83	14.43	16.54	17.68	18.04
Male	4.79	10.26	13.69	15.68	16.76	17.11
Female	2.12	4.54	6.06	6.94	7.42	7.57
2,500						
All inmates	4.52	9.68	12.91	14.79	15.81	16.14
Male	4.28	9.18	12.24	14.02	14.99	15.30
Female	1.90	4.06	5.42	6.21	6.64	6.77
5,000						
All inmates	3.20	6.85	9.13	10.46	11.18	11.41
Male	3.03	6.49	8.66	9.92	10.60	10.82
Female	1.34	2.87	3.83	4.39	4.69	4.79
10,000						
All inmates	2.26	4.84	6.46	7.40	7.91	8.07
Male	2.14	4.59	6.12	7.01	7.50	7.65
Female	0.95	2.03	2.71	3.10	3.32	3.39
20,000						
All inmates	1.60	3.42	4.56	5.23	5.59	5.71
Male	1.51	3.25	4.33	4.96	5.30	5.41
Female	0.67	1.44	1.92	2.19	2.35	2.39
30,000						
All inmates	1.30	2.80	3.73	4.27	4.56	4.66
Male	1.24	2.65	3.53	4.05	4.33	4.42
Female	0.55	1.17	1.56	1.79	1.92	1.96
50,000						
All inmates	1.01	2.17	2.89	3.31	3.54	3.61
Male	0.96	2.05	2.74	3.14	3.35	3.42
Female	0.42	0.91	1.21	1.39	1.48	1.51
82,794						
All inmates	0.79	1.68	2.24	2.57	2.75	2.80
Male	0.74	1.60	2.13	2.44	2.61	2.66
Female*	0.33	0.71	0.94	1.08	1.15	1.18
100,000						
All inmates	0.71	1.53	2.04	2.34	2.50	2.55

Appendix 19. (Continued).

Base of the estimate and gender	Estimated percentages					
	98 or 2	90 or 10	80 or 20	70 or 30	60 or 40	50
Male	0.68	1.45	1.94	2.22	2.37	2.42
200,000						
All inmates	0.51	1.08	1.44	1.65	1.77	1.80
Male	0.48	1.03	1.37	1.57	1.68	1.71
400,000						
All inmates	0.36	0.77	1.02	1.17	1.25	1.28
Male	0.34	0.73	0.97	1.11	1.19	1.21
600,000						
All inmates	0.29	0.63	0.83	0.95	1.02	1.04
Male	0.28	0.59	0.79	0.91	0.97	0.99
800,000						
All inmates	0.25	0.54	0.72	0.83	0.88	0.90
Male	0.24	0.51	0.68	0.78	0.84	0.86
1,143,377						
All inmates	0.21	0.45	0.60	0.69	0.74	0.75
Male*	0.20	0.43	0.57	0.66	0.70	0.72
1,226,171						
All inmates*	0.20	0.44	0.58	0.67	0.71	0.73

Note. The reliability of an estimated percentage depends on the size and its base. Each standard error when multiplied by 1.96 provides a 95-percent confidence interval around an estimated percentage. To calculate the difference between two estimated percentages, take the square root of the sum of each squared standard error for the percentages being compared.
* The total number of male, female, and all state prisoners in 2004.

Appendix Table 20. Standard errors of the estimated percentages, federal inmates, by gender, 2004.

Base of the estimate and gender	Estimated percentages					
	98 or 2	90 or 10	80 or 20	70 or 30	60 or 40	50
500						
All inmates	6.33	13.56	18.08	20.71	22.14	22.60
Male	6.01	12.89	17.19	19.69	21.05	21.48
Female	2.78	5.96	7.94	9.10	9.73	9.93
1,000						
All inmates	4.47	9.59	12.79	14.65	15.66	15.98
Male	4.25	9.11	12.15	13.92	14.88	15.19
Female	1.97	4.21	5.62	6.43	6.88	7.02
2,000						
All inmates	3.16	6.78	9.04	10.36	11.07	11.30
Male	3.01	6.44	8.59	9.84	10.52	10.74
Female	1.39	2.98	3.97	4.55	4.86	4.96

Base of the estimate and gender	Estimated percentages					
	98 or 2	90 or 10	80 or 20	70 or 30	60 or 40	50
5,000						
All inmates	2.00	4.29	5.72	6.55	7.00	7.15
Male	1.90	4.08	5.43	6.23	6.66	6.79
Female	0.88	1.88	2.51	2.88	3.08	3.14
7,500						
All inmates	1.63	3.50	4.67	5.35	5.72	5.84
Male	1.55	3.33	4.44	5.08	5.43	5.55
Female	0.72	1.54	2.05	2.35	2.51	2.56
9,063						
All inmates	1.49	3.19	4.25	4.87	5.20	5.31
Male	1.41	3.03	4.04	4.62	4.94	5.05
Female*	0.65	1.40	1.87	2.14	2.28	2.33
12,500						
All inmates	1.27	2.71	3.62	4.14	4.43	4.52
Male	1.20	2.58	3.44	3.94	4.21	4.30
15,000						
All inmates	1.16	2.48	3.30	3.78	4.04	4.13
Male	1.10	2.35	3.14	3.59	3.84	3.92
25,000						
All inmates	0.89	1.92	2.56	2.93	3.13	3.20
Male	0.85	1.82	2.43	2.78	2.98	3.04
40,000						
All inmates	0.71	1.52	2.02	2.32	2.48	2.53
Male	0.67	1.44	1.92	2.20	2.35	2.40
50,000						
All inmates	0.63	1.36	1.81	2.07	2.21	2.26
Male	0.60	1.29	1.72	1.97	2.10	2.15
75,000						
All inmates	0.52	1.11	1.48	1.69	1.81	1.85
Male	0.49	1.05	1.40	1.61	1.72	1.75
100,000						
All inmates	0.45	0.96	1.28	1.46	1.57	1.60
Male	0.43	0.91	1.22	1.39	1.49	1.52
120,237						
All inmates	0.41	0.87	1.17	1.34	1.43	1.46
Male*	0.39	0.83	1.11	1.27	1.36	1.39
129,300						
All inmates*	0.39	0.84	1.12	1.29	1.38	1.41

Note. The reliability of an estimated percentage depends on the size and its base. Each standard error when multiplied by 1.96 provides a 95-percent confidence interval around an estimated percentage. To calculate the difference between two estimated percentages, take the square root of the sum of each squared standard error for the percentages being compared.

* The total number of male, female, and all federal prisoners in 2004.

End Notes

[1] Question was asked about contact with any child, which could include children 18 years of age or older.

[2] Inmates met the criteria for a mental health problem if they had a recent history of a mental health problem in the year before arrest or since admission, or if they experienced, in the 12 months prior to the interview, symptoms of mental health disorders. See *Mental Health Problems of Prison and Jail Inmates*, <http://www.ojp.usdoj. gov/bjs/abstract/mhppji.htm>.

In: Child Well-Being and Nonresident Parents
Editor: Laura M. Fernandes

Chapter 4

WHAT ABOUT THE DADS?: CHILD WELFARE AGENCIES' EFFORTS TO IDENTIFY, LOCATE AND INVOLVE NONRESIDENT FATHERS

U.S. Department of Health and Human Services

ACKNOWLEDGMENTS

The authors would like to acknowledge the assistance of many individuals. First, we wish to thank state child welfare and child support officials for their support and cooperation throughout the study—Janice Mickens, Dave Graham, Bill Aldrich, Nick Espadas, and Teresa Coffman in Arizona; Mia Alvarado, Mary Kennedy, Kathleen McCarthy, and Mary Cummings in Massachusetts; Dorothy Renstrom, Erin Sullivan-Sutton, Alexandra Beutel, and Mary Arveson in Minnesota; and Paul Montebello, John Brown, Deborah Vines, and Jason Johnson in Tennessee. Most importantly, we wish to thank the hundreds of front-line caseworkers in the four states as well as the local child welfare administrators who provided their time and input to this study.

Our subcontractor, the National Opinion Research Center (NORC), had overall responsibility for the study's caseworker data collection. NORC staff members, Dennis Dew and Lauren Doerr, provided exceptional direction and management of the caseworker telephone interviews.

In addition to the authors, several current and former Urban Institute staff contributed to the study. Dr. Freya Sonenstein contributed to the overall study design and early direction of the study. Henry Chen was invaluable in conducting the many statistical analyses throughout the study. Drs. Matthew Stagner, Elaine Sorensen, and Marla McDaniel provided substantive and editorial contributions.

We also wish to express our thanks to our Federal Project Officers, Laura Feig Radel and Linda Mellgren, for their invaluable oversight and input throughout the course of the study.

EXECUTIVE SUMMARY

Over the past decade an interest in fathers and their contributions to family stability and children's healthy development has heightened the attention paid within the child welfare field to identifying, locating, and involving fathers. Many of the children served by child welfare agencies have nonresident fathers. In addition, the Adoption and Safe Families Act of 1997 renewed focus on expediting permanency for children in out-of-home placement. Engaging fathers of foster children can be important not only for the potential benefit of a child-father relationship (when such a relationship does not pose a risk to the child's safety or well-being), but also for making placement decisions and gaining access to resources for the child. Permanency may be expedited by placing children with their nonresident fathers or paternal kin, or through early relinquishment or termination of the father's parental rights. Through engaging fathers, agencies may learn important medical information and/or that the child is the recipient of certain benefits, such as health insurance, survivor benefits, or child support. Apart from the father's potential as a caregiver, such resources might support a reunification goal or a relative guardianship and therefore enhance permanency options for the child.

While research is lacking on whether engaging fathers enhances the well-being or case outcomes of foster children, lack of father involvement means that caseworkers may never know whether a father can help his child. Few studies have examined nonresident fathers as placement resources for their children and there is no research about child-father visitation or research on the effects of involving nonresident fathers in the lives of children being served by child welfare agencies (Sonenstein, Malm, and Billing 2002).

The Urban Institute, with the National Opinion Research Center (NORC) at the University of Chicago, conducted the *Study of Fathers' Involvement in Permanency Planning and Child Welfare Casework* to provide the Administration for Children and Families and the Assistant Secretary for Planning and Evaluation, both components within the U.S. Department of Health and Human Services, with a description of the extent to which child welfare agencies identify, locate, and involve nonresident fathers in case decision making and permanency planning. The study was designed to:

- examine the extent to which child welfare agencies, through policies and practices, involve nonresident fathers of foster children in casework and permanency planning;
- describe the various methods used by local agencies to identify fathers of children in foster care, establish paternity, and locate nonresident fathers;
- identify challenges to involvement, including characteristics and circumstances that may be constraints and worker opinions of nonresident fathers;
- identify practices and initiatives that may increase father involvement; and
- explore how child support agencies' information resources may assist child welfare agencies to identify and locate nonresident fathers.

The results of this study provide empirical evidence on the steps that child welfare agencies currently take to identify, locate, and involve nonresident fathers in case planning; the barriers encountered; and the policies and practices that affect involvement.

Methodology

The study was conducted in four states, Arizona, Massachusetts, Minnesota, and Tennessee, using three methods of data collection—interviews with child welfare administrators, case-level data collection through interviews with caseworkers, and data linkage between child welfare and child support systems. We interviewed local agency caseworkers about particular cases between October 2004 and February 2005 to examine front-line practices related to nonresident fathers. Cases were selected from among children who had been in foster care for at least 3 months but no more than 36 months. Children in the sample were all in foster care for the first time (first placement episode), and the child welfare agency's records indicated that each of the children's biological fathers were alive but not living in the home from which the child was removed. Additionally, only one child per mother was eligible for the study.

Description of Nonresident Fathers of Foster Children

Data on 1,958 eligible cases (83% response rate) were collected through telephone interviews with 1,222 caseworkers. The nonresident fathers of the children sampled represent a varied group. While most caseworkers, at the time of the interview, knew the identity of the fathers of children in the study's sample (88%), paternity had not yet been established for over one-third of the total sample's children (3 7%). A comparison with mothers found that demographic characteristics of identified nonresident fathers are similar to those of the resident mothers though fathers are slightly older (36 vs. 32 years old, on average) and more likely to have been married at some point. As expected, caseworkers appear to know less about nonresident fathers. The percent of "don't know" responses is much higher for nonresident fathers than for similar questions about resident mothers.

Findings on Identifying Nonresident Fathers

Caseworkers provided detailed information on practices used to identify nonresident fathers of children in foster care. Below are findings from both the administrator and caseworker interviews include the following:

- *Most nonresident fathers are identified early in a case.* Caseworkers indicate that over two-thirds of nonresident fathers (68%) are identified at case opening. Many administrators reported that caseworkers begin trying to identify a child's father during the child protection investigation. Many administrators thought efforts were stronger and more successful early in a case but after the investigation had ended. Case-level findings suggest that nonresident fathers not identified early on are less likely to have contact with the agency.
- *Caseworkers ask a number of individuals for help in identifying the father but many do not provide information.* For cases with fathers not identified at the time of case opening, the caseworker typically reported asking a number of different

individuals—the child's mother, mother's relatives, other workers—for assistance in identifying the father. Only one-third of the mothers who were asked to provide information on an unidentified father did so, and other sources were not very successful either.

Findings on Locating and Contacting Nonresident Fathers

Workers also reported on how they located nonresident fathers who had been identified and circumstances that may make contacting the father difficult. Findings include the following:

- *Caseworkers ask a number of individuals for help in locating nonresident fathers.* Caseworkers reported asking for help from the mother, the mother's relatives, the child, siblings, and other workers as well as the father's relatives to help locate the nonresident father. Workers also consulted a number of other sources including law enforcement, public assistance and department of motor vehicles records, and telephone books.
- *Few caseworkers sought the assistance of the state's child support agency in locating the nonresident father.* While over 60 percent of workers noted that their agency encouraged referrals to child support for help locating the father, in only 20 percent of the cases in which the father had not been located did the worker make such a referral. In 33 percent of the cases workers noted the state parent locator service was used.
- *In slightly over half of all cases (55%), the nonresident father had been contacted by the agency or worker.* Contact was broadly defined to include in-person contact, telephone calls, or through written or voicemail communication.
- *Several circumstances make it hard to contact fathers.* The most frequently reported circumstance that affected contact with the father was the father being unreachable by phone (60%); 31 percent of fathers were reported to have been incarcerated at some point in the case, although it was noted as causing difficulty with contact in only about half of these cases; and other circumstances—such as unreliable transportation, homelessness or unstable housing, and being out of the country— while cited less frequently caused greater difficulty with agency-father contact.

Findings on Father Involvement

When local child welfare administrators were asked about potential benefits and drawbacks to father involvement in child welfare cases they reported that involving fathers may benefit both the child and the father. However, administrators were quick to caution that this was true only when such involvement poses no safety risk to the child or mother. Almost three-quarters (72%) of caseworkers noted that father involvement enhances child well-being and in over 90 percent of cases in which the father was contacted the caseworkers reported sharing the case plan with the father and telling him about his child's out-of-home placement.

However, only a little over half of caseworkers of children in the study sample (53%) believed nonresident fathers want to be a part of the decision-making process about their children and most reported that nonresident fathers need help with their parenting skills. Other findings include the following:

- *Half of the contacted nonresident fathers expressed interest in having their children live with them (50% of contacted fathers or 28% of the entire sample.)*
- *While 45 percent of the contacted fathers were considered as a placement resource, this represents only a quarter of all sampled cases.* Caseworkers report a wide range of circumstances and problems that are likely to complicate any efforts to place the child in the home of his or her father, and some administrators seemed to favor paternal kin as a placement resource. However, administrators mentioned that even if a father cannot be a placement resource they could offer tangible benefits such as financial support or critical knowledge of the birth family's medical history.
- *Over half of the contacted fathers (56%) had visited their child while he or she was in foster care.* However, this represents less than one third (3 0%) of all fathers in the sample.

Issues Preventing Placement with Nonresident Fathers

For cases involving fathers with whom the agency had made contact, workers were asked to identify problems or issues that prevented the child from being placed with his or her father. Findings include the following:

- *Many fathers are either substance abusers or involved in the criminal justice system.* In over half the contacted cases (58%), workers noted fathers with drug or alcohol abuse problems and half of the fathers were involved with the criminal justice system in some way (i.e., incarcerated, on parole, or awaiting trial).
- *Fathers are often non-compliant with services.* Caseworkers reported offering services to fathers in over half of the cases (5 9%) but reported only 23 percent of the fathers had complied with the services offered.
- *Many nonresident fathers have multiple problems.* Workers reported that over forty percent of the contacted fathers (42%) had 4 or more of the 8 problems listed in the survey.

However, it should be noted that these are the same kinds of problems and issues that face mothers of children in foster care.

Caseworker Training on Father Involvement

While previous studies have noted a lack of training on father involvement, a significant portion of the study's caseworker respondents (70%) reported having received training on engaging fathers. At least for the four states studied here, training on fathers appears to be fairly widespread. And while few significant differences were found between male and female caseworkers or among groups of workers with differing opinions on working with fathers, several differences were found between trained and untrained caseworkers. Findings include the following:

- *Caseworkers who received training were more likely than workers who did not receive training to report having located fathers of children in the study's sample.*
- *Significant differences were found in some of the methods used to locate fathers.*Workers who received training were more likely to seek help from the father's relatives, another worker, search public aid records, and phone books.
- *Significant differences were also found between the two groups of workers with regard to a number of father engagement type activities.* Workers reporting training were more likely than other workers to report sharing the case plan with the father and seeking financial assistance from him as part of the case plan. These workers were also more likely to report the agency considered placement with the father and that the father had expressed interest in the child living with him.

Results of Child Support Data Linkage

The linkage of cases between the child welfare and child support systems explored the potential for more extensive use of child support information by child welfare caseworkers. The results indicate that in many cases, child welfare workers do have information on paternity, location, and support that coincides with child support agency records. There were instances, however, in which child support records had information that was missing or conflicted with that recorded by child welfare workers. Given the importance of paternity establishment and the accuracy of this determination it seems prudent that child welfare workers utilize child support agencies as a means of obtaining this information and for confirming the accuracy of their own information.

Even if a child's mother or other sources provide information about a father's location, such information may be out of date or inaccurate simply because of the mobility of families and fathers. In many cases, child support administrative data systems may have more current information through either state or Federal Parent Locator Services. Recent advances in data sharing across states and on a federal level have allowed state child support systems to be a good source of information on nonresident fathers involved in child welfare cases. The data matching performed in this study indicated that on child welfare cases in which locate information through state or federal parent locator services was sought (about two-thirds of all cases in the matching sample, with some variation across states), these methods were successful in providing location information in 96 percent of cases. Information on official child support orders and collection on orders would also be beneficial to child welfare caseworkers as part of an overall assessment of the nonresident father as a placement resource for his child.

Implications for Practice and Future Research

This study is an exploratory look at nonresident fathers of children in the child welfare system. The findings provide a description of nonresident fathers of children in foster care from the perspective of caseworkers and administrators, what nonresident fathers can or cannot provide to their children, and where they fit within families served by child welfare agencies is the foundation of casework practice.

While the study findings do not define best practices, they can inform practice. Some practice areas that agencies should examine include the following:

- *Search for nonresident fathers early in the case.* Gathering information about a nonresident father's identity as part of case investigation or other assessment activities appears to be effective since a majority of the fathers had been identified early in the case. Agencies should consider whether information about fathers is being sought consistently at (or before) the time a child is first placed in foster care.

- *Provide guidance and training to caseworkers on identifying, locating, and involving fathers.* Caseworker practice related to nonresident fathers appears case specific and variable. Agencies should make clear what steps caseworkers should consider when mothers do not know or share information about the child's father. Caseworker training appears to help caseworkers understand the importance of father involvement and facilitates consideration of a father placement option. Specialization of work with fathers may be worth exploring. A number of administrators reported that specialization proved helpful to their agencies, particularly with regard to seeking the location of missing fathers.

- *Agencies may need to examine whether services offered to fathers are designed to engage fathers.* The study found a small percent of nonresident fathers, when offered services, complied with all the services offered. Further attention may need to be focused on how caseworkers present service options to nonresident fathers and how societal expectations play a role in these interactions.

- *Address domestic violence and worker safety concerns.* Caseworkers and administrators expressed a reluctance to involve some fathers because doing so might reintroduce potential abusers into volatile family situations. Administrators also raised concerns regarding worker safety when contacting the fathers of children on the caseload. Unless safety concerns are effectively addressed, both those related to worker safety as well as those related to the safety of the child and mother, efforts to involve fathers are likely to stall. Safety concerns need to be acknowledged and assessed at a case level and, as previously noted, through training. However, that nearly half of the fathers were never contacted by the agency suggests that little assessment of the actual risk presented is occurring.

- *Use child support data more consistently.* Child support information, including father location, paternity, and financial support, can be a helpful tool in considering placements with fathers or other ways in which fathers can play a constructive role in their children's lives.

- *Develop models for involving fathers constructively.* Unless the child has a case plan goal of placement with his/her father or his kin, caseworkers often are not sure what, if anything, they should be doing beyond sharing the child's case plan or offering visitation. There is considerable room for programming that engages nonresident fathers on behalf of their children in ways that could extend beyond the child's stay in foster care and supports the child's best interests.

This study also serves as a starting point for further research. For example, using the same dataset, more detailed state-specific analyses would be helpful in examining how different policies affect casework practice toward nonresident fathers. State and local characteristics (e.g., rural/urban, poverty measures) could be added to the dataset and used in a variety of analyses to examine state and local practice differences. The regression models could be modified to include a different set of independent variables. While not a large sample, children who have a goal of placement with their father could be examined. Case outcomes could be examined for children reunified with mother and children placed with fathers.

Additionally, other research could include efforts to collect qualitative data to examine the relationship between permanency goals and casework, specifically casework involving fathers. Qualitative research could also examine specific methods of identifying, locating and involving fathers. Further examination of training opportunities for caseworkers and the impact on practice directed at nonresident fathers is also suggested.

1. BACKGROUND

Introduction

Recent interest in fathers and their contributions to family stability and children's healthy development has increased the attention of child welfare agencies on the tasks of locating biological fathers and involving them in case planning. Many, if not most, of the children served by child welfare agencies have nonresident fathers. Adoption and Foster Care Analysis and Reporting System (AFCARS) 2002 data on foster children reveal that a majority—between 50 percent and 80 percent—of the foster children in each state were removed from single-mother or unmarried couple families.[1] However, the child welfare field lacks information about current policies and practices, and efforts made to identify, locate, and engage fathers vary considerably from locality to locality. Few studies have examined nonresident fathers as placement resources for their children and there is no research about child-father visitation or the effects of involving fathers in the lives of children being served by child welfare agencies (Sonenstein, Malm, and Billing 2002).

Engaging fathers of foster children is likely to be important not only for the potential benefit of a child-father relationship (not possible or preferred in some cases), but also for making placement decisions and gaining access to resources. Permanency may be expedited by placing children with their nonresident fathers or paternal kin, or through early relinquishment or termination of the father's parental rights. Through engaging fathers, agencies may learn important medical information and/or that the child is the recipient of certain benefits (e.g., health insurance, survivor benefits, child support). While it is too soon to tell whether engaging fathers enhances the well-being or case outcomes of foster children, lack of father involvement means that caseworkers may never know whether a father can help his child.

The Urban Institute, with the National Opinion Research Center (NORC) at the University of Chicago, conducted the *Study of Fathers' Involvement in Permanency Planning and Child Welfare Casework* to provide the federal government[2] with a description of the extent to which child welfare agencies identify, locate, and involve nonresident fathers in case decision making and permanency planning. For the purposes of this study, nonresident fathers include biological fathers who do not reside with their children, usually because of divorce, separation, or a nonmarital birth.[3] The results of this study provide empirical evidence on the steps that child welfare agencies currently take to identify, locate, and involve nonresident fathers in case planning; the barriers workers encounter; and the policies and practices that appear to facilitate involvement. Because little information is available on whether child welfare agencies are using the Federal Parent Locator Service as provided under new legislative authority, the study is also designed to examine the use of child support resources to identify and locate fathers.

Recent child welfare policies and practices appear to have increased the focus on fathers. The Adoption and Safe Families Act of 1997 (ASFA) significantly reduced the time child welfare agencies have to make permanency decisions for children in foster care, which may affect how agencies identify, locate, and involve the biological fathers of foster children. For example, ASFA encourages child welfare agencies to use the Federal Parent Locator Service employed by child support enforcement programs to help locate fathers and other relatives. Concurrent planning,[4] also encouraged under ASFA, may prompt earlier efforts to locate fathers because the father, or his relatives, may be identified as a placement resource even while the caseworker seeks to reunify the child with his or her mother. Moreover, if adoption becomes the case goal, a diligent search for the father must be undertaken. While judicial guidelines have long sought early identification of fathers, the implementation of ASFA may increase the likelihood that this is occurring more consistently.

ASFA also reemphasized that kin should be sought whenever possible when identifying placements for foster children. Paternity establishment becomes vital to identifying a father and any of his relatives as potential caregivers. Family group conferencing or family meetings are increasingly being used by child welfare agencies to involve these extended family members in the case decision-making process. Using these techniques puts agencies in a better position to identify, locate, and involve nonresident fathers in case planning.

Literature Review

Over the past two decades many studies have examined the role of noncustodial fathers in the lives of their children. The literature review conducted in Sonenstein et al. (2002) cited numerous studies that focused on father involvement as it relates to child well-being and the degree to which a variety of factors affect involvement. Studies examined paternity, marital status, race and ethnicity, and payment of child support to determine nonresident father involvement. Research studies have examined fathers in both the general and the low-income populations. Child well-being was measured by examining outcomes such as academic performance, behavioral problems, and self-esteem.

For the most part, however, the literature review revealed the dearth of research specific to the topic of nonresident father involvement in the child welfare system. While we found a few studies that focused attention on fathers as potential placement resources for their children (Greif and Zuravin 1989; Rasheed 1999), there was no research about child-father visitation or the effects of involving fathers in the lives of children being served by child welfare agencies. A number of studies examined gender bias in general social work practice (Greif and Bailey 1990; Kahkonen 1997; Lazar, Sagi, and Fraser 1991; O'Hagan 1997). Only one study explored practices further by examining whether fathers were being ignored as a resource for discharge planning (Franck 2001).

We found some research on efforts to promote collaboration between child welfare and child support enforcement agencies. The results of a diligent search project in South Carolina appear promising; missing parents were located in over 75 percent of the cases referred by child welfare staff, and more than half of these cases were located in less than a month. However, the focus of the effort was on identifying and locating fathers primarily for the purposes of expediting the termination of parental rights, to hasten adoption proceedings (South Carolina Department of Social Services 2000). Research describes other collaborative efforts focused on increasing child support collections. Few programs, with the exception of a parental involvement project in Illinois, focus attention on finding noncustodial fathers as placement resources (Roy 2000).

In the last several years, literature continued to examine the impact of family structure on child well-being and the nature of paternal involvement. One study found that father involvement, even if a child did not grow up in an intact family, was positively associated with educational outcomes (Flouri and Buchanan 2004). Research using the 1999 National Survey of America's Families (NSAF) indicated that the well-being of children raised in cohabiting biological or nonbiological families and single-mother families did not differ (Brown 2004). This research expands upon the ongoing discussion of comparisons of child outcomes in married versus non-married families.

Current research also delves deeper into factors that may affect paternal involvement, such as race, ethnicity, religion, age of a child, and gender ideologies held by fathers (Bulanda 2004; Hofferth 2003; Hofferth and Anderson 2003; Wilcox 2002). One study in particular examined the effects of race and ethnicity on noncustodial father involvement, determining that Hispanic children had the lowest levels of contact with their nonresident fathers (King, Harris, and Heard 2004). The study also found that when minority fathers do stay involved with their children, they are more likely than white fathers to engage in behaviors that most favor their children's well-being, such as talking about problems or attending religious services.

Attention continues to focus on the particular perspectives and circumstances of low-income fathers (see Nelson 2004 for a review of the literature on low-income fathers). In a series of interviews with low-income men receiving General Assistance, researchers interviewed men about their own fathers and their children. Of the interviewees with children, many said that the mothers of their children had limited their (father) contact, often as a result of unpaid child support (Kost 2001). Another set of researchers interviewed low-income men whose children were enrolled in the Early Head Start program and found that most of the men were either living with or married to their children's mothers and said they had someone to talk to about being a father (Vogel et al. 2003).

Researchers have shown continued interest in the issues surrounding payment of child support. An Urban Institute study indicated that the proportion of children in low-income families receiving child support had significantly increased between 1996 and 2001, growing from 31 to 36 percent (Sorensen 2003). Still, recent research has underscored challenges to child support receipt, such as low male earnings and incarceration (Bloomer, Sipe, and Ruedt 2002; Cancian and Meyer 2004; Pearson and Hardaway 2000).

Since the 2002 literature review prepared for this study, the amount of research pertaining to fathers in the child welfare system has grown considerably, although the body of research is still relatively small. The Annie E. Casey Foundation funded a study to determine practitioners' perceptions of the state of child welfare practice on fathers (National Family Preservation Network 2001). Workers in child welfare systems and community organizations indicated unanimously that there was a need for more outreach to fathers with children involved in the child welfare system. Many said that fathers were hesitant to come forward and often assumed they were only sought for child support payments. Caseworkers indicated that they had had little to no training on father engagement. Some fatherhood program staff involved in the groups said that fathers need other men to talk to, leading to recommendations for more men as caseworkers in the child welfare system (National Family Preservation Network 2001).

More recent research examines specific child welfare practices on father engagement. Family meetings and conferences were designed to encourage family input. Recent studies examined two such practices—family group conferences and family group decision-making—for the extent to which fathers and paternal relatives were contacted or present for the conference as well as how many children were subsequently placed with their fathers or paternal relatives (Shore et al. 2002; Thoennes 2003). While the rates of contact with fathers and paternal relatives were still lower than for mothers, the results reveal a willingness to reach out to fathers by agencies implementing a family meeting–type approach.

An early review of 22 states' Child and Family Service Reviews (CFSRs) noted a lack of father and paternal relative involvement in the case planning process.[5] A more recent review of the 2001–2004 CFSRs noted concern about an overall lack of contact with fathers by caseworkers, even when fathers were involved with the family (National Resource Center for Family-Centered Practice and Permanency Planning 2005). Analysis of National Survey of Child and Adolescent Well-Being data found that almost three-quarters (72 percent) of children in foster care reported seeing their biological fathers twice per month or less, and 41 percent had never visited with their fathers (U.S. Department of Health and Human Services, 2003).

O'Donnell and colleagues (2005) examined front-line practices on fathers through focus groups with caseworkers. According to the caseworkers, fathers are generally peripheral to the child welfare system and often view the agency with distrust, especially if they have a criminal record. Workers also noted that they were less likely to initiate father involvement with families involving multiple fathers. Some young female caseworkers said they felt like fathers resented them or challenged their authority. Male caseworkers were less likely to voice frustration with involving fathers and more likely to support more gender-sensitive services to engage fathers. However, workers in four of the five focus groups generally said that fathers should not get child welfare services that are different from those for mothers. Caseworkers also indicated that they thought mothers hinder fathers' involvement in child welfare. Mothers may restrict information they give to caseworkers out of anger, fear (perhaps of violence by children's fathers), mistrust of workers, or a preference that the father not know about the child welfare involvement.

Caseworkers also felt that many fathers have little commitment to their children. Participants in one group identified this issue as the primary reason for low paternal involvement, while the other four groups said it was a significant but not determining factor in involvement levels. Authors of the study said that caseworker responses indicated they did not have a unified way of thinking about fathers or their needs, signaling a need for more professional development on how to engage and involve fathers in casework practice.

Other recent studies have examined the location and involvement of nonresident or absent parents in child welfare services. In Washington, an evaluation of state policy and local practices on both custodial and noncustodial fathers identified reasons why fathers showed low levels of involvement or were not considered appropriate placement resources by the agency (English 2002). Reasons included an unwillingness to work with the agency, incarceration, a history of child or sex abuse, or unknown whereabouts. While most fathers in the study were identified, one-fifth to one-third in each study site were never located. Another study found that caseworkers in kinship foster care services had no contact with a majority of the fathers of children participating in the research. Caseworkers had more contact with fathers in cases in which all children in a family had the same father as opposed to multiple fathers (O'Donnell 2001).

Project Goals and Objectives

This study sought to examine how child welfare agencies identify, locate, and involve nonresident fathers of children in foster care in casework and permanency planning. The study also sought to determine the feasibility of using child support resources to aid in identifying and locating fathers of children in care. Specifically, the study was designed to:

- examine the extent to which child welfare agencies, through policies and practices, involve nonresident fathers of foster children in casework and permanency planning;
- describe the various methods used by local agencies to identify fathers of children in foster care, establish paternity, and locate nonresident fathers;
- identify challenges to involvement, including father characteristics that may be constraints and worker opinions;
- identify practices and initiatives that may increase father involvement; and
- explore how child support resources may assist child welfare agencies in identifying and locating nonresident fathers through case linkage.

Early on during the design phase, a conceptual framework was developed (figure 1-1). The framework outlined four broad domains that could affect nonresident father involvement. Illustrated in the top rows of Figure 1-1, the domains are as follows:

- *Policies.* Explicit statements about how nonresident fathers should be involved in case decisions. Usually they take a written form and can be found in policy statements, caseworker manuals, etc. Policies can vary by how recently they have been issued and how completely they have been implemented.

- *Practices.* What caseworkers do most commonly with cases. Practices may conform or diverge from official policy and can be a function of leadership (or lack thereof), the local office, the training and supervision of the workers, and the individual beliefs and opinions of the caseworkers.

- *Administrative/organizational resources and linkages.* The way programs, particularly child welfare and child support programs, are organized and linked together through communication and supervisory channels can facilitate or hinder the availability of resources and mechanisms for identifying and locating fathers. Relations between the child welfare agency and the court are also fundamentally important in determining how quickly and comprehensively fathers are identified and located.

- *Characteristics of program participants.* The involvement of fathers in child welfare cases can be helped or hindered by the characteristics of the population served. Whether the father was ever married to the mother, whether he was the perpetrator of abuse or neglect of the child or mother, and whether he is geographically close to the child will all affect his level of involvement. When cases involve mothers who are reluctant to identify or contact the father or who fear abuse, negotiation of father involvement may be especially problematic.

A caseworker's ability to involve a particular father in the casework process depends on whether or not the father of the child is identified and whether or not he is located and is geographically available. The likelihood that a child's father is identified and located is influenced by factors in the four domains listed above. Starting with the characteristics of the child and mother, we assume, for example, that the father will be identified, although not necessarily located, if the child was born within a marriage. The father is more likely to be identified, and perhaps located, if the child has been on welfare and the local child support enforcement program has worked the case. Policies and practices within the child welfare agency and the courts will affect how much effort caseworkers make to identify fathers and to locate them when this information is not readily available. If the policies and practices reflect minimal commitment to father involvement, then there is little likelihood that efforts will be made to locate and identify them. If policies and practices reflect more than minimal commitment, the ease or difficulty of identifying and locating the father could mean the difference between involvement and noninvolvement.

Even when a father is identified and located, the extent of his involvement in the case can vary substantially. The length of time the child was in foster care and the length of time the caseworker worked the case are likely to influence father involvement. Types of involvement are many and include sharing the case plan with both parents, identifying paternal and kinship placement resources, obtaining health insurance and/or financial support resources, child-father visitation and providing services to both mothers and fathers. The bottom row of our conceptual figure illustrates the potential positive outcomes that are expected for the child, the father, and the agency.

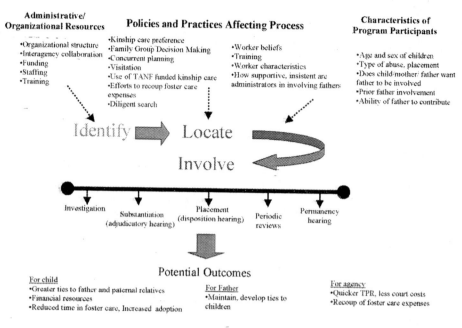

Figure 1-1.

Methodology

Our study of father involvement consisted of three methods of data collection—interviews with child welfare administrators, case-level data collection through interviews with caseworkers, and data linkage between child welfare and child support systems in four states. The interviews with local child welfare administrators were designed to collect information on policies and resources for fathers of children served by child welfare agencies. Caseworkers were interviewed about their opinions and front-line practice with nonresident fathers. In the sections below we describe state selection and the methodology we used to implement the administrator and caseworker interviews and data linkage components.

State Selection

Because state policy and local convention are believed to influence caseworker efforts with regard to nonresident fathers, the study was designed to assess how child welfare agencies are performing regarding father involvement. We decided against a nationally representative sample because we are particularly interested in the difference in performance among jurisdictions, differences that would be lost within a national sample. While budget constraints dictated the exact number of states chosen, we based our decision to examine only a select number of states primarily on the following:

- The study is exploratory in that many of these issues have not been previously researched. A study of this scale will allow the federal government to determine whether the proposed methods and questions are feasible before committing larger resources to the topic.

- Without being generalizable to the nation, results from four states will provide a sense of whether there is a range of practice in father involvement. Furthermore, the results will be generalizable to these four states and will provide practical information to inform state policies.
- The study will provide sufficient information upon which to generate hypotheses for further research should that prove warranted and will provide an indication of whether certain issues, practices, and populations merit more extensive focus.

In selecting our study states, we excluded a number from consideration because of limitations in their information systems or small foster care caseloads that would make the burden of this study greater than we could feasibly ask the states to agree to. We also eliminated some states due to the timing of their federal CFSRs. When the CFSR coincided with the preliminary stages of this study, we chose not to overburden state and local child welfare officials with involvement in a study demanding both their own and caseworker time.

Remaining states were stratified by size (under or over 5,000 foster care cases with a 3–36 month duration), by type of agency administration (state or county-administered child welfare system)[6], and by whether the state had a known fathers initiative. Arizona, Massachusetts, Minnesota, and Tennessee were selected as our study states. With regard to size, the four states represent two small (Minnesota and Arizona) and two large (Massachusetts and Tennessee) states. Minnesota has the only county-administered child welfare system and Tennessee was the only state in which a fathers' initiative was not identified during the study's preliminary stages.

Administrator Interviews

We interviewed 53 local child welfare administrators between July 2004 and January 2005 (a 98 percent response rate). Administrators were selected slightly differently in each of the four states to accommodate differences in the structure of the child welfare agency. However, each administrator interviewed represented a local office included in the case-level data collection. In Minnesota, which has a county-administered child welfare system, state officials selected 10 local administrators to participate in the interviews based on size of the county office and the state's knowledge of the variability in casework practices. In Tennessee, all 13 regional administrators were asked to participate. In Massachusetts, administrators of the 15 local area offices in which case-level data collection took place were asked to participate. In Arizona, all six district-level managers were included and state officials identified 10 assistant district managers to participate in the interviews.

We designed the administrative interviews to collect information about

- policies and practices in effect in the office;
- administrative and organizational resources available to the office and caseworkers;
- general characteristics of the birth parents of foster children; and
- administrators' opinions and attitudes toward engaging fathers in the casework process and the likely outcomes of this involvement for the agency, the caseworkers, and the children.

We used a protocol for each interview that provided flexibility so differences between states and localities could be identified and examined.[7] The length of the interviews ranged from 30 to 45 minutes.

Information obtained during each administrator interview was organized and summarized into individual Microsoft Office Word documents. The content of these documents was then coded and entered into a qualitative content analysis database (Nud*ist software). Findings from the administrative interviews are presented in chapter 2.

Case-Level Data Collection

Sample selection and design

We interviewed local agency caseworkers about particular cases in each of the four study states between October 2004 and February 2005 to examine front-line practices on nonresident fathers. We selected cases that met the following criteria:

- Children had been in foster care for at least 3 months but no more than 36 months.
- Children were in foster care for the first time (first placement episode).
- Only one child per mother was eligible for the study.[8]
- Biological fathers were alive but not living in the home from which the child was removed.

State child welfare information technology (IT) staff performed the initial task of extracting cases from their State Automated Child Welfare Information Systems that met the above criteria. States were able to extract cases meeting the first three criteria without difficulty; however, identifying children removed from homes in which their father did not reside proved more difficult. The data structure requested by the federal AFCARS process for "caretaker family structure" was helpful, though in most states additional programming was necessary using "relationships" data fields. Because of the variability of how states determined case eligibility on the last criterion, we built screening criteria into the caseworker questionnaire so cases that did not meet the study criteria could be eliminated at the time of the interview. These cases constitute "ineligible" cases.

The fathers in the study are referred to as nonresident fathers. We feel this term best describes the group of fathers about whom information was provided through caseworker interviews. Central to our study was that children sampled were removed from homes in which their biological fathers did not reside. Thus, by definition, the fathers of the foster children in our study were "nonresidents" of the child's home. Within the broad category, the sample includes fathers who are unmarried, married (either to the birth mother or someone else), divorced and widowed. The sample also contains children for whom paternity has and has not yet been established. The fathers of many children in the sample retain their parental rights, but in some cases parental rights have been terminated or relinquished.

Once the state extracted the universe of cases that met the above criteria, the study statistician developed the state sampling designs.[9] In each state a two-stage design was developed. In the first stage, caseworkers managing at least two cases meeting the criteria were identified. Caseworkers managing only one case meeting the criteria were eliminated. [10] All the children managed by the first-stage caseworkers constituted the second-stage sampling frame. Two children were selected randomly from each sampled caseworker. The design called for selection of 300 caseworkers per state, for a total of 2,400 cases.

Caseworker engagement and response rates

The survey contractor, NORC, mailed advance letters to selected caseworkers that identified the purpose of the study and the selected cases workers would be asked to discuss. In most of the localities, the NORC advance letters were mailed after correspondence about the study had been sent by the agency itself. The caseworker questionnaire contains separate sections designed to collect demographic and case-related information on the following individuals: caseworkers, foster children, nonresident fathers, and birth mothers.[11] We conducted a pretest in Baltimore, Maryland, and Fairfax County, Virginia, and incorporated recommendations into the final questionnaire. The final version was programmed into the Computer-Assisted Telephone Instrument (CATI) system used by NORC to administer complex telephone interviews. Telephone interviews with caseworkers averaged one hour.

Response rates for caseworker interviews in each of the four states are provided in table 1-1. The response rates included in the table include only eligible, completed cases. As discussed earlier, because of the difficulty states had in identifying households in which birth fathers did not reside, we included a series of screening questions. In total, 408 cases were determined to be ineligible due to the child having lived with the father at the time of removal (not considered a nonresident father), ineligible due to the father of the child having died prior to or within six months of case opening, or ineligible due to the child was in an adoptive home. [12] The majority (62 percent) of these cases were ineligible due to the child having lived with the father. Thus, while child welfare automated information systems have made considerable gains in accuracy and completeness, information on a child's household of origin, specifically, adults in the household, remains difficult to capture.

NORC provided case-level data and caseworker respondent information to the Urban Institute in both SAS and ASCII formats. Urban Institute staff members removed ineligible cases, conducted cleaning and edit checks, and then ran frequencies and cross-tabulations using all the data fields. Descriptive findings from the case-level data collection are presented in chapter 3, and results of additional analyses are presented in chapter 4 of this report.

Table 1-1. Caseworker Interview Response Rates.

State	Total cases, n	Total cases minus ineligible completed cases, n	Total completed cases, n[a]	Total eligible, completed cases, n[b]	Response rate, % [c]
AZ	750	671	640	561	84
MA	756	617	662	523	85
MN	509	442	411	344	78
TN	758	635	653	530	83
All	2,773	2,365	2,366	1,958	83

[a] Includes both eligible and ineligible cases.

[b] Ineligible cases included cases in which the child's father had been residing in the home at the time of removal, cases in which the child's father died prior to or shortly after case opening, and adoptive homes.

[c] Response rates were calculated using eligible cases (second column of numbers) only.

Child Support Data Linkage

In each study state, we sought to determine the feasibility of using child support enforcement data systems to assist child welfare agencies in identifying and locating fathers. We compared data collected from the caseworker survey on a variety of child support related issues—paternity, use of locating resources, collections—with similar data provided by child support data systems. In addition, state and local policies and practices for referring foster care cases to child support for reimbursement of foster care costs were examined during administrator and caseworker interviews.[13]

We did not begin the data linkage process until caseworker interviews were complete. The caseworker interview has several questions that allow a caseworker to exclude a case from the data linkage component of the study. While we purposefully inserted questions designed to eliminate cases in which a referral to child support might bring harm to either the foster child or caregiver, workers were provided latitude in that no specific reason had to be given for asking that a case be excluded. [14] A significant portion (30 percent) of the cases was excluded from the linkage based on caseworker responses. Caseworkers were more likely to have noted domestic violence as a problem for the father and more likely to have reported a bad relationship between the mother and nonresident father in the excluded cases than the cases included in the linkage component.[15]

Researchers constructed a separate file for each state that contained only the list of case identification numbers provided earlier for sampling purposes for the survey. Researchers then sent this file to each state's child welfare IT specialist to merge identifying information (child's name, Social Security Number, mother's and father's names, Social Security numbers, and employer information). State officials then transferred the completed file directly to the state's child support agency.

Child support IT staff added any child support information available in their automated system—paternity, child support order (attempted, established, collections), noncustodial parent located, state locator resources used/successful, and federal locator resources used/successful. Child support IT staff then removed identifying information from the file and transferred the file back to the Urban Institute for analysis.

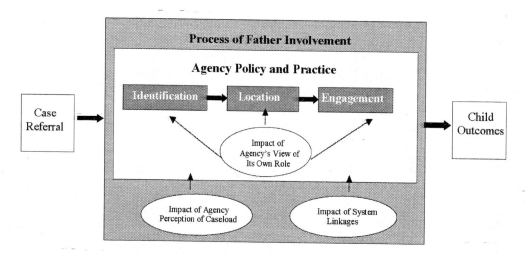

Figure 2-1. Flowchart of Father Involvement.

The chapters that follow present findings from the administrator interviews, case-level data collection through caseworker interviews, and data linkage between child welfare and child support. Results from the administrator interviews are provided first in chapter 2 to provide policy and agency context for the case-level data collection. Descriptive analyses of the case- level data are then presented in chapter 3. Results of more extensive analyses using the case-level data and the child support case linkage, and a summary and conclusions are presented in chapter 4.

2. RESULTS OF ADMINISTRATOR INTERVIEWS

The sections that follow present findings from the interviews with local child welfare administrators. The findings are organized around three central themes that arose in our examination of both policy and practice on fathers' involvement: an agency's perception of nonresident fathers and the impact on casework, an agency's view of its own role in father involvement, and an agency's description of other systems that involve fathers. We interpret these three themes as general agency philosophies that have an impact on both policy and practice on father involvement (figure 2-1). Throughout this chapter, we also contrast policies and practices among and within the study states when doing so helps illustrate important points.

Agency Perception of Fathers and Their Involvement

How child welfare agencies approach involving nonresident fathers in casework practice is influenced by how they perceive the potential impact of fathers on children. In general, most administrators with whom we spoke thought the potential for father involvement in child welfare casework and permanency planning was a positive thing. They often cited a general trend over time toward increased focus on fathers (particularly with special populations such as incarcerated fathers) or family-centered practice in their agencies. On the other hand, administrators often tempered their positive perception of the potential for father involvement with grounded examples of barriers to fathers' participation in a case. These factors may affect a caseworker's level of effort as well.

Caseload Information

Agency perception of who nonresident fathers are and what they can offer their children likely influences any efforts to involve nonresident fathers in casework. To illuminate this perception, we asked administrators about the size and composition of the nonresident father population. Administrators generally estimated that between 30 and 80 percent of the children in their care have nonresident fathers, a wide range that was consistent across all four states in the study.

The wide variety of special populations (e.g., incarcerated fathers, immigrants) mentioned by administrators, while changing from site to site, illustrated that administrators perceived the nonresident father population as having a diverse set of needs and experiences. They have a complex view of "father involvement" that incorporates flexibility for the specifics of each unique case. While administrators in all states said their caseloads included incarcerated fathers, estimates of the size of this group ranged from "a handful" to nearly half of the caseload. Some offices made a caveat that the number of unidentified fathers might conceal higher incarceration rates. Consistently, administrators cited drug charges, particularly methamphetamine usage in rural areas, and violent offenses as reasons for nonresident father incarceration. Many administrators, and nearly all of those in Massachusetts, mentioned serving birth parents with a history of domestic violence. Some administrators, particularly those in areas along the U.S-Mexico border in Arizona, said their offices regularly deal with nonresident immigrant fathers. In Tennessee, a state that has seen striking growth in its immigrant population in recent years,[16] administrators confirmed that immigrant fathers were a small but growing part of child welfare cases.

Perceived Benefits of Father Involvement

While recognizing the differing situations of nonresident fathers, administrators identified potential benefits of father involvement. First and foremost, administrators said that father involvement, provided it poses no safety risk, is beneficial to a child's well-being. Fathers can offer emotional, financial, and social support to their children. Even if a father cannot be the caretaker for his child, a child's knowledge of his or her father may help the child sort through abandonment or other emotional issues. Father involvement may have other, more tangible benefits for a child, such as critical knowledge of medical or genetic information or financial benefits, such as consistent child support payments or benefits for children of veterans.

Administrators said father involvement could be beneficial for the child welfare agency, birth mothers, and fathers themselves. Father involvement can allow some children to avoid outof-home care altogether or can lead to quicker permanency when a child can be placed with his or her father or his kin.[17] Administrators noted that quicker permanency saves child welfare agency resources, allowing agencies to use resources for other cases in need. Agencies could benefit from father involvement by reduced overall caseloads in the long run, even if more intensive efforts increased time spent on cases in the short term. Administrators also said that father involvement could lead to a more positive work environment; if fathers are meaningfully involved in cases, administrators said work could be more fulfilling to a case manager with a social work background. Finally, a minority of administrators mentioned that birth mothers might feel less isolated or stressed if children's fathers were involved. A small number also mentioned that father involvement might lead to fathers feeling more empowered and responsible for their children.

In addition to the benefits they see from father involvement, most agency administrators said they had noticed an increase in agency and court focus on fathers in the past several years. Agencies have introduced new initiatives, such as family-group conferencing, that seek parent and kin involvement, and they have undertaken renewed efforts to search for fathers more diligently. Some administrators also said that there is increased emphasis on involving fathers earlier in a case. Some administrators in all states mentioned an increase in their agency or state's focus on serving fathers, particularly incarcerated ones. They noted that judges were more open to awarding custody to nonresident fathers than they were in the past. Many administrators said that child support enforcement agencies had become more aggressive in searching for fathers, too.

Administrators cited a number of reasons for an increased focus on fathers. Administrators often mentioned that judges and legal departments place pressure on agencies to abide by legal requirements for parental involvement, perhaps leading to earlier father identification or more diligent searches. In some cases, lawsuits against the child welfare agency prompted an increased focus on fathers. Administrators sometimes referred to state or local leadership as an impetus for involving fathers, indicating that leadership tone has affected worker or agency efforts. Some administrators also pointed to federal legislation as a motivating force to improve father involvement. For example, some administrators in Massachusetts and Arizona mentioned that since the Adoption and Safe Families Act of 1997, the agency has focused on quicker permanency and consequently on fathers and paternal kin who could act as placement resources. Other administrators depicted budget shortfalls, both in child welfare and child support, as reasons for an increased focus on recouping foster care expenses from birth parents (both mothers and fathers).

Drawbacks to or Costs of Father Involvement

In addition to the benefits of father involvement, the administrators with whom we spoke identified a variety of potential drawbacks or costs. One of the two most common concerns of administrators was that father involvement could reintroduce an abuser into a family or renew parental conflict. Administrators in all states repeatedly mentioned a danger of involving fathers with a history of domestic violence or violence to a child. A few administrators mentioned that some women involved with the child welfare agency had intentionally moved to their districts to escape abusive partners. In the words of one administrator, father involvement could "destabilize women who are already unable to care for their children." One administrator also mentioned that female caseworkers might feel threatened by fathers with a history of domestic violence, thereby creating a difficult working environment. Even if birth parents merely argue, increasing a father's involvement may require a worker to invest more time in a case to strike compromises between birth parents. Because of these drawbacks, administrators in all states routinely mentioned parental conflict or a mother's safety as reasons for excluding nonresident fathers from the case process or at least approaching their involvement with caution.

An equally common concern voiced by administrators was that increasing father involvement would create more work for caseworkers, already described as overburdened by high caseloads. Involving a father and his kin in a case introduces more people with whom workers must consult. In addition, involving fathers, especially those out-of-state, may increase agency costs of providing services or transportation for visits. Some administrators stressed that the term "father involvement" evokes an image of a single father per case, whereas the reality is that a sibling group with the same mother may have multiple fathers. Involving each child's father in a case of this sort could overwhelm a caseworker, making his or her attempts to engage fathers less likely. If a nonresident father is not the best placement for a child, involving him in a case may create barriers to other permanency options, such as an adoptive or guardianship placement with the mother's kin, if the father decides to fight for custodial rights. Some administrators qualified their concern over burdens on worker time by saying that the increased workload that would occur in the short-term would likely be outweighed in the long-term by overall caseload reductions if children could be placed with fathers or paternal relatives or if fathers were to be located more quickly to expedite adoption proceedings, leading to more efficient uses of resources.

There are certain other situations that make working with fathers more difficult for child welfare agencies. Although several administrators noted that they find many fathers by working with the corrections agencies, once found, incarcerated fathers present unique challenges. Many administrators noted that involvement with the criminal justice system may make caseworkers less likely to engage a father. Some administrators noted an internal conflict between wanting to put an incarcerated father in a child's case plan yet recognizing that an unrealistic service expectation would then follow (e.g., one Massachusetts administrator remarked that if a worker enters a father serving a life sentence into a case plan, the worker would then have to visit him once a month). Arranging for children to visit incarcerated fathers can be time-consuming if extensive travel is involved or prisons have complex protocols for admitting visitors. Some administrators also said that the process of visitation might be traumatic for children and intimidating to caseworkers.

Involving nonresident fathers with substance abuse issues may also present drawbacks for the agency and children. Quite a few administrators said that a history of substance of abuse would make workers less likely to involve a father in case planning. Attempts to engage fathers who are suffering from a drug addiction may be fruitless or require intensive services.

Administrators depicted some specific drawbacks or costs to involving immigrant nonresident fathers in a child welfare case. Certain characteristics of this population, such as potential language barriers or frequent migration, may cost the agency money and time in efforts to locate and engage fathers. A birth mother and other family members may be hesitant to provide any information about an undocumented father for fear that he will be deported. It may also be difficult to engage nonresident immigrant fathers in child welfare casework. Administrators, particularly those in Tennessee, noted that a scarcity of local translation services made connecting with this population more difficult. Finally, agencies may be wary of placing children with undocumented fathers because of the lack of information available to the agency. Some administrators noted that it is difficult to do criminal background checks or prove that the men have steady income if they are paid "under the table." Others expressed concern over placing a child with an immigrant father who could take the child and return to his native country, where U.S. courts would have no jurisdiction.

Each agency's perception of the nonresident father population involved in its cases can affect policy and practice in a number of ways. It can influence the types of efforts made to identify fathers and the supports agencies offer to fathers. Characteristics of this population may also influence the approach that the agency uses toward father engagement. In the end, the balancing act that agencies do to weigh the potential benefits of father involvement with the challenges that may exist for each father influences agency efforts to involve nonresident fathers. In the following section, we turn our attention to this dynamic: the way that an agency's view of its own role in facilitating or guarding father involvement affects policy and practice. We also highlight differences between states on key factors to provide a more in-depth look at each state's policies and practices on father involvement (table 2-1).

Table 2-1. Key Factors on Nonresident Father Involvement by State.

State	Timing of Father Identification	Case Plans and Nonresident Fathers	Father-specific Programming[a]	Legal Representation	Information Sharing with Child Support and TANF to Identify and Locate Fathers
Arizona	Begins during investigation or petition phase; policy requires searches for missing parents at least once every 6 months	Case plans should include nonresident fathers but do not always do so in practice; administrators say it is difficult to create case plan for each parent	Administrators report little activity	Fathers receive court-appointed representation in child welfare proceedings	Administrators say sharing varies with child support enforcement and TANF, part of the Department of Economic Security, which includes the child welfare agency
Massachusetts	Begins during investigation but most thorough during assessment period (45 day period after case has been assigned for assessment)	Case plans do not always include fathers in practice; not difficult to create case plan for each parent, which is routine for cases with a history of domestic violence	Over half of administrators mention agency/CBO partnerships to provide programming	Fathers receive court-appointed representation in child welfare proceedings	Administrators say sharing with TANF varies by office, and some child welfare agencies have Memoranda of Understanding with TANF; sharing information with child support enforcement is fairly rare, though answering questions for child support is more common
Minnesota	Begins at intake, the point at which placement looks likely, or during the assessment	Nonresident father inclusion depends on variety of characteristics of father; reports of creation of separate plans varies widely across districts	Administrators mention father programming by TANF, child support, local organizations, and the agency itself	Fathers do not receive court-appointed representation in child welfare proceedings	Administrators rarely mention sharing information with TANF; relationship with child support enforcement is close and information-sharing common
Tennessee	Searches for fathers vary in timing; workers often ask about fathers at a meeting 7 days after child comes into care	Frequent reports of inclusion of fathers in case plans among study states, regardless of father characteristics; creation of separate plans depends on the region	Administrators report little activity	Fathers do not receive court-appointed representation in child welfare proceedings	Administrators say since the split of the department that contained TANF and child welfare, information sharing has become more difficult, although child welfare benefits workers still have some access to TANF data systems

Notes: TANF = Temporary Assistance for Needy Families; CBO = community-based organization.

a We define father-specific programming to include any services targeted to fathers or non-custodial parents (who are likely to be fathers), some of whom may have children involved with the child welfare agency. For example, these services could include support groups, nurturing classes, batterers' intervention programs, or seminars on the rights of noncustodial parents.

Agency Role in Father Involvement

Our administrator interviews reflect differences in how agencies view their role in affecting father involvement. Two separate factors appear to be at work—the balance between strict legal requirements and flexible social work practices, and the applied definition of client (e.g., a single child, an entire family including nonresident fathers and other kin, or the dyad of the child and the custodial parent from whom the child was removed).

In this section we discuss both of these factors and the potential impact on policy and practice. We divide father involvement into three distinct stages: identification, location, and engagement.

Father Involvement through a Legal or Social Work Lens

Administrators identified two philosophical influences on involving fathers: one that focused on the legal requirements of father involvement enforced by the courts and carried out by agency legal departments and one that focused on the social work framework of the agency's mission, with an emphasis on practice that engaged fathers apart from legal requirements. For example, when probed about father involvement, some administrators emphasized their agency's compliance with state law or district requirements to search for fathers within a given time frame. They referred often to agency legal departments and the pressures of the court system to find fathers. Through their descriptions of father involvement, these administrators revealed the influence of the legal aspects of child welfare casework. Other administrators tended to focus on the flexibility of the agency's approach to fathers, emphasizing family-based practice and meeting the needs of each individual father, particularly after identification and location had occurred. Some had a wide knowledge of father-specific programming available in their communities, or they had hired particular staff to serve fathers. These administrators revealed the influence of a social work philosophy on their policy and practice.

This is not to imply that administrators held only one of these philosophies. On the contrary, our interviews indicated that most administrators balanced these two philosophies given the context of the child welfare population and dynamics affecting the local agency.

Nonetheless, it is important to remember these influences as we explore the practical aspects of father involvement throughout this section.

The View of the "Client": Who Do Agencies Serve?

Administrators differed in the way that they identified their clients. Some administrators emphasized that agencies work for each child rather than the parents and child. Of these administrators, some emphasized that this stance was particularly useful when trying to engage fathers, who may at first feel suspicious of a caseworker and the worker's relationship with the child's mother. Other administrators said their agencies focused on each child and those adults living with the child at the time of placement. Placing a premium on reunification, these administrators viewed nonresident fathers as outside the family unit and therefore less of a priority, particularly early in a case. Finally, some administrators stressed that their agencies approached families, defined broadly to include nonresident fathers, as the client, thereby making sure that father involvement was a priority with caseworkers. One administrator described this philosophy as a "the more the merrier" attitude toward father involvement. This view appeared to be the most prevalent of the three among administrators in our interviews. Administrators with this view often noted a bias in the system against nonresident fathers, seen even in small ways, such as organizing case records by a mother's last name instead of a child's. Again, it is important to remember the role that this philosophical orientation may have on practical efforts of agencies to identify, locate, and engage nonresident fathers.

The Agency's Role in Policy and Practice

The varying approaches cited above could affect policy and practice throughout all phases of father involvement: identification, location, and engagement (including receipt of services). In this section, we make extensive use of state examples to illustrate both the breadth of practice and the range of policies that agencies employ when involving nonresident fathers.

Identifying nonresident fathers

The point at which agencies attempt to identify nonresident fathers varies by state and, to a lesser extent, by local agency. (See table 2-1 for a description of each state's practices) While many administrators said workers begin trying to identify a child's father during the investigation phase, most seemed to think that efforts were stronger and more successful early in a case but after investigation. Arizona was unique in its widespread mention of a policy to look for absent parents at least every six months. Some offices in the state opt to do the search more frequently, an effort they call a best practice rather than district policy, while others said their offices searched for fathers less frequently in practice than policy dictated. Administrators in all states said court and legal pressure to identify fathers usually occurred toward the end of a case, although there is a trend in some courts and among agency attorneys to press for identification earlier.

States also vary in the ways they establish paternity, both for purposes of involving a father in a case and for the purposes of placement opportunities or relinquishment or termination of parental rights. The methods used to establish paternity varied more with the specifics of a case than by state or local office. Generally, agency administrators said that workers relied on birth certificates, voluntary recognition of parentage, and a mother's word to establish paternity.

Workers typically request birth certificates at the time that a placement looks likely, although in some cases, birth certificates may take a long time to reach local offices, particularly if a child was born out of state or outside the United States. A mother may identify a father in writing, and then the agency can pursue DNA testing if the alleged father denies paternity.

Most administrators said their offices rarely used DNA testing, although there were some (particularly in Tennessee) who said that it was used routinely to establish paternity. The person or agency financially responsible for paternity testing may differ by state or local office. Administrators said that the child welfare agency, its legal department, or local court could be responsible for financing paternity testing; in Tennessee, some administrators said alleged fathers could be responsible for the cost of DNA testing in certain circumstances. Sometimes paternity establishment is listed as a task for the agency in a child's case plan when a father has not been identified by the time the case plan is created. Administrators in all states reported that agencies had encountered problems when men believed to be fathers of children served by the agency later turned out not to be; these problems typically arose when the children in question were placed with kin of the alleged fathers. In these cases, the agency originally relied on a mother's word (perhaps while an alleged father was missing) or birth certificates, and later DNA testing revealed that the men were not birth fathers.

Reliance on a child's mother for information about a nonresident father was a common refrain among agency administrators. Whether due to simple proximity or the likelihood of knowledge, agencies primarily rely on birth mothers for information about the identity of a child's father and his whereabouts. Several administrators noted that judges ask women about their children's fathers under oath; administrators said this approach placed more pressure on birth mothers who might not be as cooperative with a caseworker. In Tennessee, some administrators mentioned that the agency's court liaisons often ask mothers about a child's birth father during the initial proceedings. Since the passage of the Personal Responsibility and Work Opportunity Reconciliation Act of 1996, which linked father identification more closely with a family's eligibility for welfare benefits, some Temporary Assistance for Needy Families (TANF) agencies have assisted child welfare in identifying birth fathers.

Locating nonresident fathers

States vary widely in their use of staff to locate fathers. Overall, administrators said caseworkers were responsible for doing the first search for absent fathers. Some check a variety of sources, such as phone books, last known employers, and a diverse set of agencies. Most administrators noted that search efforts are dependent on the characteristics of a case and the individual caseworker.

After workers do an initial search, they may consult others within the child welfare or other agencies for assistance if they have not located the parent. In Arizona, which had a consistent process and timeframe for searching for fathers, workers rely on legal departments or clerical staff in the local office who are good at searches to find fathers. Arizona offices also have uniform access to the State Parent Locator service for a fee when local searches yield no results. In contrast, most Massachusetts administrators said there are no designated staff to search for fathers, although some administrators mentioned that kinship workers could take on this responsibility. In some Massachusetts offices without specific search workers, administrators said they wished they had kinship workers to do searches or thought that such staff would be more efficient for the agency.

Minnesota did not seem to have a specific process or pattern for staffing father searches. County directors mentioned a variety of staff positions that would aid in searches: case aides, workers particularly adept at searches, workers specializing in working with unmarried parents, legal staff, child support enforcement workers, and workers hired through a contracted community-based organization.

Most administrators in Tennessee said that no designated staff members search for fathers, although some directors mentioned agency legal staff assistance or a staff member hired by a contracted community-based organization for searches. Tennessee's child welfare benefits workers, who are part of the child welfare agency but are particularly adept in the family assistance (welfare) system, have access to some TANF information that might include information on fathers, so they can assist caseworkers in searches. One Tennessee agency recently received permission to create a diligent search staff position, and another area has considered creating a similar position.

Engaging nonresident fathers

Administrators focused less frequently on efforts to engage nonresident fathers than on efforts to identify or locate them. When they did mention father engagement, they often talked about policies requiring the agency to serve (e.g., by providing parenting classes) and visit incarcerated fathers. Worker training rarely focused on ways to engage fathers specifically, emphasizing engagement of kin more generally. An administrator in one state said training does not include very much father engagement material because engagement is not a legal matter. However, some administrators mentioned a trend toward greater father engagement. Others suggested the best approaches to engaging fathers include assuring fathers that the agency does not work for the mother, offering services to fathers early in a case, and asking fathers about their own families as placement resources.

- *Including fathers in case plans.* One of the ways administrators noted to engage a father was to include him in the child welfare case plan. While some states appear to include fathers more frequently than others, administrators in all states acknowledged that fathers are not always included in case plans. (See table 2-1 for a description of each state's practices.) Reasons for fathers' exclusion could include incarceration, domestic violence, lack of paternal interest in the child, inability to identify or locate a birth father, and a father's proximity to the agency. Among the study states, Tennessee seemed most committed to including fathers, even those who were absent or alleged, in case plans.[18] If fathers are unknown, workers are often expected to create tasks for the agency, such as a diligent search or paternity testing.
  One potential concern noted about including nonresident fathers in case plans is that inclusion may compromise each parent's confidentiality or renew conflict in parents' relationships. All administrators, when probed, said it would be possible to create separate plans, but most often agencies create only one plan for each child. Arizona administrators said it was very difficult to create separate plans for each parent because of the state's data system, while Massachusetts seemed to do it easily and routinely. Administrators in Massachusetts repeatedly and without prompting mentioned a history of domestic violence as a reason to create separate case plans for parents. In Minnesota, some counties do not create separate plans for each parent (in some cases saying domestic violence and confidentiality have not been problems); others seemed to create separate plans any time a nonresident father was involved, regardless of his relationship with the child's mother. In Tennessee, some agencies noted using only one plan, while others use two for separated parents or end up creating two if parents will not meet together.
- *Serving fathers.* Some administrators indicated a trend toward providing services to nonresident fathers more frequently. Some mentioned legal necessity, child well-being, or federal or agency reviews of their own deficiencies as motivating factors for increasing services. Services mentioned included parenting classes, batterers' intervention programs, therapy, and fatherhood programs. Particularly in Arizona, administrators expressed concern over serving undocumented immigrant fathers and remarked that state law[19] may limit access to services such as housing subsidies and health insurance. Factors like substance abuse or fathers' aggression toward workers may also act as barriers to serving fathers. In Massachusetts, one administrator mentioned that fathers react more positively to services provided by community-

based organizations than to agency programs. In Minnesota, several administrators mentioned ongoing efforts, sometimes in relationship to child support enforcement, to inform fathers of their legal rights and direct them to legal aid. Hennepin County, Minnesota (Minneapolis), has a pilot project that targets nonresident father engagement. Administrators in Tennessee mentioned community- based fatherhood programs (although administrators tended not to know much about them) and personalized services that fathers can receive (e.g., batterers' intervention classes). Some Tennessee administrators mentioned transportation or availability of services in rural areas as barriers to serving fathers.

In addition to more general services, many agencies either offer or refer fathers to father-specific programming. (See table 2-1 for a description of each state's practices.) These referrals may go to a community-based organization that works independently or in partnership with the child welfare agency or to other government agencies, such as TANF or child support. Among the states participating in our study, Massachusetts and Minnesota seemed to have the most organized systems of programming targeted to fathers. More than half of the Massachusetts administrators mentioned ongoing partnerships between local agencies and community organizations to provide father- specific programming. Often, the agency helped fund and organize a program, but providers were actually located in community organizations or split their time between the child welfare agency and the community provider. Some Massachusetts administrators mentioned having workers who were designated to serve fathers. Services include batterers' intervention classes or anger management programs, fatherhood classes, parenting lessons for fathers, reentry programs for incarcerated fathers, and programs targeting teenage fathers. Similarly, some Minnesota administrators mentioned father-specific services in the community, including efforts to reach fathers by child support and TANF. Several administrators mentioned legal aid services for fathers, and one county has a specialized worker to work with fathers. Ramsey County, Minnesota (St. Paul), refers some fathers to a fatherhood program for African-American men with children in the child welfare system.

Administrators in Tennessee and Arizona appeared to be less knowledgeable of services available to fathers in the community, potentially because many of them oversaw larger districts than the administrators in Massachusetts and Minnesota. However, one district in Arizona was in the process of working with a behavioral health group to serve fathers with children involved in child welfare. In Tennessee, while some administrators knew of father-specific programs, most did not know whether the agency had referred fathers to the programs. None of the four states stood out as having widespread or strong father initiatives.

- *Placing children with fathers.* When a nonresident father is considered appropriate to care for his child, perhaps with the aid of available services, the agency may place a child with him. Administrators varied in the terminology they used for this process: Some considered it a placement as any other kin placement, while others were adamant that a child living with a nonresident father should not be called a placement at all. Policies also differed across and within states (except in Massachusetts, where responses were more consistent). In Massachusetts, where administrators commonly said a child living with a nonresident father is not a placement, agencies have fewer institutional barriers for the process. Fathers receive a home assessment to determine risk to a child, while other kin placements would receive a full home study. Fathers' criminal records are reviewed within the local agency, while criminal records of other potential kin require regional or area approval before a placement can occur. In contrast, while administrators in Minnesota said that fathers are given preference as placement resources, most said that the standards and assessment procedures for fathers are the same as those for other kin.

- *Representing fathers in court.* States also differed in their policy on legal representation in court for nonresident fathers. (See table 2-1 for a description of each state's practices.) In Arizona, fathers often receive court-appointed representation in child welfare proceedings, though this may vary by judge or the point in a case at which a father expresses interest in becoming involved. One administrator mentioned that some appointed attorneys may search for missing fathers on their own. In Massachusetts, there is a state policy to appoint attorneys for fathers in child welfare cases, assuming the fathers are financially eligible for legal assistance. Two Minnesota administrators mentioned community programs they direct fathers to for legal assistance. No administrators in Tennessee mentioned court-appointed attorneys.

- *Recouping foster care expenses.* Some administrators indicated their states had placed new emphasis on recouping foster care expenses from nonresident fathers in recent years. In some cases, administrators said child support agencies initiated increased focus on recouping expenses, while child welfare agencies may have led the effort in others. States have different processes and criteria to determine whether or not a nonresident father will be responsible for the costs. Across states, administrators noted judicial discretion to waive the payment and a lack of an enforcement mechanism as reasons that the agency cannot recoup money. Additionally, some administrators who said that there was a process to recoup foster care expenses indicated that there was a lack of incentive on the part of the agency to adhere closely with the policy, given that recovered money frequently goes directly back to the state rather than to the local agency.

In Massachusetts, administrators overwhelmingly had a negative view of the efficacy of the contracted agency to recoup foster care expenses, saying that little money was recovered. In Arizona, when a child comes into care, the caseworker is responsible for completing a parental assessment and determining how much each parent can pay. The worker then submits the assessment in the court report, leaving it up to each judge to actually order the repayment. Some judges (and workers) may see the process as unfair and not order the payments. Others may order the payments, but many administrators said the lack of an enforcement mechanism leaves the policy without much "bite." In practice, most administrators said that the agency collects little money through this policy. Administrators in Minnesota said that the child support office does try to recoup foster care expenses from both parents and for both title IV-E and non-IV-E eligible children. While some administrators said efforts have remained the same in recent years, others said child support has stepped up its efforts due to budget pressures. Tennessee administrators said that caseworkers typically ask judges to order child support payments through the enforcement agency. Judges vary in how often they actually make the orders, and at least one administrator said the enforcement process is weak. (See table 2-1 for a visual depiction of state practices.)

Description of Service System Linkages

Interviews with child welfare administrators also focused on the service system linkages that child welfare agencies use to involve nonresident fathers. The way an agency perceives its partners may affect how or whether that agency connects with other systems to engage fathers. In this section we address child welfare agency relationships with child support and TANF agencies and the court system. (See table 2-1 for brief overviews on sharing information with TANF and child support.) We also address other relationships that local administrators identified as important in their efforts to involve nonresident fathers in child welfare casework.

Child Support Enforcement

Minnesota and Tennessee highlighted descriptions of particularly active relationships with child support agencies. These two states consistently reported sharing information to identify and locate fathers. Administrators in Minnesota often referred to good relationships with child support, and most referred to some process that would allow them to get fathers' information from this agency. In fact, administrators often indicated that child support enforcement was a primary resource in agencies' efforts to identify fathers. A few administrators referred to an automatic information-sharing system in which child welfare contacts child support when a IV-E eligible child comes into care. One county administrator in Minnesota said that child support now sends one worker to all child protective services hearings to ensure child support is discussed at the hearing.

Administrators in Tennessee also reported established relationships with child support and widespread information sharing. The sharing may be informal, formal but direct (meaning that there is an established process or form to use to share information, but workers still do it themselves), or through the courts or agency attorneys. Child welfare benefit workers in Tennessee are privy to some child support data. The state also automatically refers cases to child support when a child comes into care. In addition, the child welfare agency has court liaison staff attend child support hearings.

The relationship between child welfare agencies and their local child support agencies for sharing information about fathers appeared more tentative in Arizona and Massachusetts. In Arizona, the child support and child welfare agencies are both part of the Department of Economic Security. Administrators noted a decline in concern over information sharing with child support since child welfare became part of the same state department a couple of years ago. Provided that workers ask for child support information in their official capacity, all workers should theoretically be able to access information about fathers through child support. On the ground, though, while some Arizona administrators said their offices regularly worked with child support to identify fathers, others said they could not access this information but wished they could. Child welfare workers in some districts can ask district-level parent locator staff to access some available child support records, so the two agencies have at least some capacity to link data. Generally, though, Arizona administrators spoke of increasing collaboration with child support, including joint meetings or collocation.

Most administrators in Massachusetts reported obtaining some information from child support about fathers, although the practice appeared infrequent in some offices. One administrator noted that workers in the local office would have no idea how to get information from child support. In contrast, some administrators reported that child support asks the child welfare agency for information on fathers with relative frequency. Caseworkers who do obtain information on fathers from child support have a form they must complete and give to the child support agency. Child protective services appears to have no computer access to any child support records.

Temporary Assistance for Needy Families (TANF)

Some child welfare agencies also indicated sharing information about fathers with local welfare (TANF) agencies. This practice seemed most common in Arizona and least frequent in Minnesota. Some administrators in Arizona indicated, unlike in the case of the tentative relationship with child support, the child welfare agency could access some TANF information freely, particularly through shared data systems (even though all three are part of the same agency). Massachusetts and Tennessee both reported wide variation in the degree of collaboration between TANF and the child welfare agency. Some administrators mentioned that TANF sometimes pushed mothers to identify fathers. In Massachusetts, most administrators said they got information from TANF (or could do so in theory), but the formality of the process varied from established memoranda of understanding to informal caseworker interactions. Minnesota administrators did not mention working with TANF often. Those who did said the relationship to share information about fathers was mainly informal through caseworkers.

The relationship in Tennessee between child welfare agencies and TANF illuminates changes over time and factors influencing data sharing in a couple of ways. Previously part of the Department of Human Services, the Department of Children's Services was created in 1996. Administrators mentioned the fact that the two programs are now administered by separate agencies as a barrier to getting information to identify fathers. Second, Tennessee has specialized staff, the child welfare benefits workers, who have access to some TANF computer systems. Some administrators said that they use the benefits workers to search for fathers, while others either said benefits workers were no longer allowed to share information or appeared to have never shared information. Some administrators also reported that caseworkers foster informal relationships with TANF workers that allow them to access information about fathers.

Courts

Administrators with whom we spoke seemed to view the courts more as a source of oversight rather than a partner in father involvement. Respondents highlighted a variety of ways in which courts could influence father involvement: judicial pressure on or assistance to agencies searching for fathers, court involvement in efforts to recoup foster care expenses, court pressure to evaluate all potential child placement resources, the role of courts in establishing paternity, and the permission of the court to share information across agencies that might help locate fathers. Administrators varied in their assessments of judges–some judges ask early and often about a child's birth father, while others rarely do or only do so late in a case. Administrators who noticed variation across judges sometimes mentioned the backgrounds of particularly aggressive judges (e.g., a father himself, a former child welfare agency attorney, etc.) as an explanation for their practice.

Some administrators depicted changes in judicial practice over time. A few expressed disappointment that the relationship with the court had become more litigious or that there were more "legal hoops" for the agency now than in the past. Administrators who said they noticed a difference in the aggressiveness of courts on father involvement said attention to fathers had increased or that fathers were more likely to receive custody now than in the past. Agency attorneys may also push workers to do more thorough searches. Some administrators mentioned pending lawsuits or judicial "scolding" as reasons for more diligent searches.

In general, we did not discover any court initiatives in the study states that were specifically seeking to improve nonresident father involvement in child welfare casework. However, in some states, court initiatives have improved father involvement indirectly. Three Minnesota administrators mentioned the Juvenile Justice Initiative, which placed an emphasis on quicker permanency. As a result of this initiative, administrators said judges look more closely at fathers as placement resources now. In Arizona, the state passed legislation that provided parents, including noncustodial fathers, the right to a jury trial in decisions of termination of parental rights. On the other hand, the absence of court initiatives directed at fathers (and the preliminary evidence that judges can impact agency practice on fathers) may indicate that fostering court innovation and partnerships with child welfare agencies on father involvement could be an area of future growth.

Other Community Partners

In addition to child support, TANF, and the courts, agencies identified other community partners with which they worked or would like to work to involve fathers. Multi-agency collaboration varied widely within and across states. Some of the collaborative efforts to locate fathers mentioned included searches with the Department of Motor Vehicles, Department of Corrections or local law enforcement agencies, mental health agencies, or local school systems. Some Arizona respondents mentioned that they had contacts with the Mexican consulate or the Mexican agency dealing with child welfare to identify or locate fathers of immigrant children. Massachusetts is notable for its collaboration with local community-based organizations to create or support father-specific programming or services.

Administrator Perceptions of Facilitators and Barriers to Partnerships

Many administrators talked about confidentiality concerns as a major barrier when attempting to get information from other agencies (e.g., TANF, child support enforcement, schools) about nonresident fathers. Some administrators mentioned limited data access to child support or TANF information, even if the departments were part of the same umbrella agency. Since some state administrators indicated that information sharing should not be a problem, local administrators' identification of confidentiality as an issue may reveal a misunderstanding of what is legally permitted.

Administrators mentioned that data sharing was more common in rural areas or in instances where child welfare workers had a good relationship with workers in other agencies. Administrators in rural areas said that child welfare workers may literally work alongside TANF or child support workers or may know them personally, due to the small size of their offices. This phenomenon may exist in some urban areas too, where some administrators said states have created multipurpose service centers for clients that include many agencies.

One additional barrier to agency collaboration that is of note is the impact of agencies' different missions. This issue was particularly important when child welfare administrators talked about the relationship with child support. In recent years, with state budget cuts and more federal and state emphasis on enforcing child support orders, administrators often depicted child support agencies as more aggressive with nonresident fathers. Some administrators noted that recouping money was not in the mission of child welfare agencies, where a parent's lack of income or resources such as housing is often a barrier to reunification or permanency for a child.

Implications for Analyses of Case-level Data and Future Research

The results of the administrator interviews provide a rich context upon which to interpret findings from the caseworker interviews and case linkage to child support information. During telephone interviews, caseworkers were asked about two children on their caseload—how the worker identified and located their fathers. Workers provided information on different agencies they may have contacted such as child support and TANF, as well as different individuals they may have asked (e.g., mothers, relatives) for information. We examined a variety of father characteristics, many of them specifically mentioned by administrators. For example, workers were asked whether the child's father was involved with the criminal justice system, whether or not he was out-of-state or out of the country, and whether or not he was the perpetrator of child abuse or family violence. These data provide a more detailed description of fathers and potential challenges to father involvement. Of particular interest to administrators will be information on worker opinions on the benefits and drawbacks to involving fathers.

The results of our administrator interviews also provide context for our case-level data linkage to child support information. Each child case was linked to child support data to determine whether information exists on paternity establishment, the location of the nonresident parent, utilization of state or federal locating resources and whether the locating resources were successful. Information on whether a child support order was attempted, established, and collected upon was also sought. Results of these analyses provide case-level information on the feasibility and utility of using child support resources to increase father involvement.

Local agency practices on fathers differ across the four study states, as well as within states, on many levels. As our interviews with administrators show, some of the difference may be the overarching philosophy of the agency and courts. Differing practices may also reflect individual case differences, such as father characteristics and relationships between fathers and the mothers of children served. Case-level analyses provide a clearer picture of these factors since we asked caseworkers to provide information on both father and mother characteristics (including problems or issues that make it difficult to place the child in their home) as well as reasons why the parent is difficult to locate and involve (e.g., out-of-state, no transportation, no phone). The results from the caseworker interviews and child support data linkage are presented in the following chapters.

3. DESCRIPTIVE ANALYSES OF CASEWORKER INTERVIEWS

This chapter presents descriptive findings from the case-level data obtained through telephone interviews with caseworkers in the four study states. Caseworkers were asked about children on their caseload, the child's birth parents, and their own opinions about working with fathers. Descriptive analyses are presented in this chapter with additional analyses, both descriptive and multivariate presented in chapter 4.

Introduction

Description of Subgroups

As discussed in chapter 1, a total of 1,222 caseworkers were interviewed. Data were compiled on a total of 2,366 foster children; 1,958 were eligible for analysis.[20] As shown in figure 3-1, in 1,721 (88%) of the eligible cases, caseworkers reported that the father had been *identified*[21], and in 1,071 (55%) of the eligible cases the father had been *contacted*[22] by the worker or agency at least once.[23] The results presented in this chapter reflect findings based on different groups of cases, depending upon the topic. For example, questions pertaining to child-father visitation were only asked of caseworkers that had made contact with the father at some point during the case.[24]

Caseworkers who cited no contact with the father would have no (or unreliable) information on recent visitation.

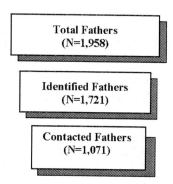

Figure 3-1. Total Numbers of Fathers in Analysis Subgroups.

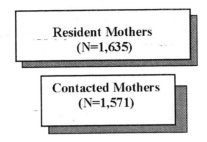

Figure 3-2. Total Numbers of Mothers in Analysis Subgroups.

In this discussion of findings, percentages of the overall sample are provided in certain sections for context. For example, while contacted fathers comprise 62 percent of identified fathers, they represent 55 percent of all fathers in the sample.

A box at the beginning of each section informs the reader of the universe of case responses reported on in the section. Tables present unweighted Ns with percentages weighted to be representative of all foster care cases with nonresident fathers in each of the four states analyzed in the survey.[25]

Study states were asked to identify children in out-of-home placement who had been removed from homes in which their biological fathers did not reside. The primary method states used to identify these cases in their state automated child welfare information systems (SACWIS) was a household composition data field. Single, female-headed households constituted the great majority of the cases. However, after conducting the pretest a subgroup of cases was identified—cases in which both the biological father and birth mother were not in the home from which the child was removed.

Thus, a new group of "nonresident" mother cases was identified. The entire population of mothers included 1,635 resident and 323 nonresident mothers.[26] As shown in figure 3-2, caseworkers reported that 1,571 of the 1,635 resident mothers (96%) had been contacted by the worker or agency. Unlike fathers, resident mothers were assumed to be identified and located at the time of interview (given the child had been removed from her household). Findings from descriptive analyses of resident mothers are presented in this chapter to provide context to the findings on nonresident fathers. For example, understanding what percentage of mothers had problems or issues similar to nonresident fathers is helpful. Because nonresident mothers are the group of mothers presumably most comparable to nonresident fathers, caseworkers with cases involving nonresident mothers were asked the same series of identification questions. Analyses involving nonresident mothers are presented in chapter 4. These analyses are of particular interest because comparisons between nonresident fathers and nonresident mothers can be made on agency identification, location, and engagement.

Timing of Father Identification and Contact

The study's goal was to examine fathers' involvement in permanency planning and child welfare casework. The timing of events such as identifying, locating and contacting the father is important to this chapter's discussion. An assumption is made that timing can directly impact the level of effort demanded of the child's caseworker. For example, some identified fathers may have presented themselves to the agency or worker at the time of placement or earlier in the case. Presumably, the child's foster care worker (the study's interview respondent) would expend little effort identifying or locating this type of identified father. And thus, caseworkers with cases in which the father was identified at the time of placement were not asked to respond to questions about whom they asked for assistance (See table 3-15). On the other hand, if the father had not yet been identified at the time of placement, what is the likelihood of that father ever having contact with the agency? How difficult might it be for a worker to identify a father later in the case? The contacted fathers (5 5%) can either be the result of casework practices that emphasize identifying and contacting all fathers or it could also be that the 55 percent of fathers contacted were those that made contact easy (i.e., identified themselves to the agency upon learning of the agency's involvement).

To examine this issue in more detail, we divided fathers into three categories depending upon the timing of their identification, location, and contact. Categories include (1) fathers identified and located at time of case opening, (2) fathers identified but not located at time of case opening and fathers not identified at time of case opening but identified within 30 days, and (3) fathers not identified until after 30 days of case opening.[27] Figure 3-3 provides information on the likelihood of contact for fathers in each of the categories.

As shown, fathers most likely to be contacted by a worker are fathers who were identified and located when the case opened. Only 22 percent of these fathers have not yet had contact with the agency.[28] When identification occurred more than 30 days after case opening, contact was unlikely. Almost 90 percent (87%) of these fathers had not yet been contacted or the caseworker did not know whether contact had occurred. Later in this chapter we discuss the methods used by workers to identify and locate fathers and present circumstances of nonresident fathers that may make these tasks difficult.

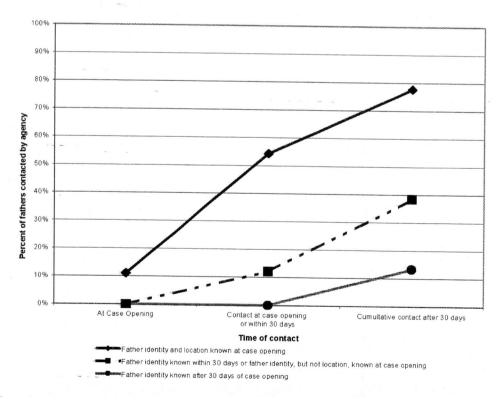

Figure 3-3. Likelihood of Contact for Fathers Identified at Different Points.

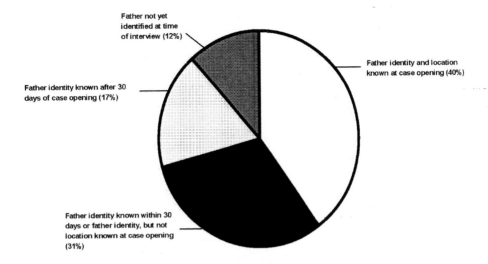

Figure 3-4. Breakdown Cases by Timing of Father Identification.

The majority of fathers are identified at case opening or shortly thereafter—40 and 31 percent, respectively, in the first two categories. Cases with fathers whose identity was not known until sometime after 30 days from case opening represent 17 percent, and unidentified fathers comprise the remaining 12 percent (See figure 3-4).

When reviewing the findings on fathers in this chapter, it is important to keep in mind the heterogeneity of each subgroup of analysis. For example, *identified* fathers (N=1,721) include both fathers who have had contact with the agency as well as fathers who have not had contact. Likewise, *contacted* fathers (N=1,071) include fathers who, according to caseworkers, visited with their children since case opening as well as fathers who have not visited with their children.

Organization of Chapter

The descriptive findings from the case-level data provide information on a wide range of topics. Information on the caseworker respondents, child demographic and case information, and resident mothers is presented first to provide context and is contained in the following three sections. Descriptive information about resident mothers is provided in this chapter for context for interpreting the information on fathers. State-by-state data are not presented in the tables but variation is discussed in the text.

The final section presents study findings on fathers. Many of the findings presented will be examined in more depth in the next chapter. For example, whether the type of father (alleged or legal[29]) affects agency interactions and father-child visitation will be examined in the next chapter. Also, in the next chapter, direct comparisons between nonresident fathers and nonresident mothers are examined.

Description of Caseworker Respondents

The sample of caseworker respondents is similar to child welfare workers nationwide. Survey respondents were slightly more likely to be female (81% vs. 72%) than workers overall. Our respondents had one more year of experience than the general population of social workers in public child welfare agencies (8 years vs. 7 years).[30] The racial breakdown of caseworkers is somewhat diverse with a fairly large group of African American caseworkers (20%). However, ethnicity is less diverse, only 8 percent of workers noted they were of Hispanic origin.

While a sizable majority of caseworker respondents reported having received training on identifying, locating and involving nonresident fathers, fewer had received specific training on referring cases to child support for locate assistance. Overall, the sampled caseworkers feel strongly that father involvement is good for children but many also feel that fathers need help with parenting skills. Perhaps intuition tells these workers that children need their fathers, but the reality of working cases means they have experience with fathers who are unable to successfully parent their children.

Characteristics

Table 3-1 presents a description of the caseworker respondents. As shown, most respondents were female (8 1%). Relatively little variation in caseworkers' gender was found among the study states—Massachusetts had the most male respondents (22%) versus a low of 16 percent in Minnesota. White workers made up the largest racial group (69%) while African-American workers comprised almost 20 percent. However, the race of caseworkers varied greatly among the study states—Tennessee had the largest percentage of African-American workers (42%) while Minnesota had the lowest percentage (8%). Similarly, 8 percent of caseworkers were Hispanic, but this varied from a low of 1 percent in Tennessee to a high of 16 percent in Arizona. The majority of workers had bachelor's degrees (73%), 17 percent of which were bachelors of social work. Workers had an average of 8 years of experience in child welfare. Minnesota's workers were most experienced (12.6 years) and Tennessee workers least experienced (5.2 years). Minnesota also had more workers with master's degrees (44%).

Table 3-1. Caseworker Respondent Characteristics.

N=1,222	%
Gender, % female	81.2
Race (*N*=1 ,222)	
White	69.3
African American	18.4
American Indian or Alaskan Native	1.4
Mixed	1.8
Other	6.2
Missing	2.9
Spanish, Hispanic, or Latino origin (*N*=1 ,222)	7.6
Highest Level of Education (*N*=1 ,222)	
Bachelor's	73.4
Master's	22.7
Doctoral	0.5
Other	3.3
Years in child welfare (mean)	8.1

Training and Opinions

Caseworkers were asked questions about whether they had received training on identifying or locating fathers. A series of questions were also asked to elicit each worker's opinions about involving fathers in casework. Table 3-2 presents the findings related to workers' training and opinions.

Overall, 70 percent of workers said they had received training on how to identify, locate, or engage fathers. Far fewer caseworkers (3 2%) noted having received training on how to refer cases to child support for assistance locating the father. Caseworkers in Minnesota and Tennessee were more likely to report having received training on father engagement or child support. Massachusetts had the lowest proportion of caseworkers that received training in each area. Massachusetts also had a notably lower proportion of caseworkers that indicated their agency encourages referrals to the child support agency for locating services (46%, compared to 76% in Minnesota).

Overall, most caseworkers thought that father involvement enhances child well-being (72%), though only about half (53%) reported that nonresident fathers want to be part of the decision-making process with regard to their children. Workers in Minnesota were the most likely to report that father involvement enhances children's well-being and that nonresident fathers want to be involved in decisions regarding their children.

Many workers noted that working with fathers can be difficult. The vast majority of caseworkers agreed that fathers need assistance with their parenting skills (82%) and 44 percent noted that working with nonresident fathers makes a case more complicated. However, only 6 percent of caseworkers reported that working with nonresident fathers is more trouble than it's worth.

Table 3-2. Caseworker Training and Opinions.

N=1,215	%
Training on. . .	
How to identify, locate, or engage fathers	69.9
Procedures for referring to child support for locate services	32.3
Opinions	*% agree or strongly agree*
Nonresident fathers need help with their parenting skills	81.7
Involvement of nonresident fathers enhances a child's well-being	72.2
Nonresident fathers want to be part of decision-making process with regard to their children	53.3
Dealing with nonresident fathers makes a case more complicated	43.6
Working with nonresident fathers is more trouble than it's worth	6.2

Note. Seven caseworkers did not respond to the training and opinion section of the questionnaire.

Description of Children

The following tables (tables 3-3 through 3-6) provide a description of the children about whom caseworkers were interviewed.[31] Compared to 2003 national Adoption and Foster Care Analysis and Reporting System (AFCARS) data, the sampled children are somewhat younger (8.6 vs. 10.2). However, this is likely due to the sample selection criteria regarding children's length of time in care (children were to have been in care 3-36 months) and that all were in foster care for the first time. The gender breakdown was similar (52% male vs. 48% female) but race/ethnicity varied considerably from AFCARS data. Our sample is more white (60% vs. 39%) and less African American (21% vs. 3 5%). The survey instrument disaggregated Hispanic origin from race that may account for some of these differences as well as the less diverse populations in the four study states. The placements settings for sampled children did not differ much from AFCARS data. Permanency goals varied slightly with sample children somewhat less likely to have a goal of reunification with birth parents (39% vs. 48%).

The reasons for placement differ only slightly from national data with more caseworkers noting higher levels of neglect (82% vs. 60%). However, the study definition of neglect included emotional abuse and while AFCARS breaks this type of abuse out from the others. Much like the national data, mothers represent the largest group of perpetrators. Biological fathers were not in the household, thus, the cases sampled do not reflect similar rates of fathers as perpetrators and likely to be higher rates of other male perpetrators (i.e., mother's boyfriends, stepfathers).

Demographic information is presented in Table 3-3. The remaining tables provide case information including whether paternity was established, the reason for the placement, current placement, and permanency goals.

The average age of the children was almost nine years old (8.6), with Massachusetts's children the oldest on average of the study states (9.6 years) and children in Arizona the youngest (7.1 years). Gender distribution was relatively equal in all states, with Massachusetts having the most extreme split of 54 percent female to 46 percent male. Children with siblings made up the vast majority (83% or above) in all four states.[32]

There was considerable variability in the race/ethnicity of the foster children in the study within the four states. Arizona caseworkers reported that 40 percent of the study children in their state were Hispanic, compared to 25 percent in Massachusetts, 13 percent in Minnesota, and 3 percent in Tennessee. White children comprised the largest proportion in all four states, followed by African-American children. The state with the highest proportion of African-American children was Tennessee at 36 percent and the lowest proportion was 11 percent in Arizona.

Children were in care for almost two years, on average. The amount of time caseworkers reported being responsible for the case averaged just less than one year (11 months), but varied from six months in Arizona to 14 months in Tennessee. Table 3-4 provides details on the placements in which the sampled children were living at the time of the caseworker interview. Across states, 65 percent of children were eligible for Title IV-E. The proportion of eligible children varied greatly from 42 percent in Massachusetts to 69 percent in Tennessee, with Minnesota and Arizona both over 74 percent.

Table 3-3. Child Characteristics.

N=1,958	
Age (mean)	8.6
Gender, % female	51.6
Race	%
White	60.2
African American	21.3
American Indian or Alaskan Native	2.8
Asian	.7
Mixed	8.6
Other	1.1
Missing	5.3
U.S. citizenship	98.3
Spanish, Hispanic, or Latino origin	23.1
Have at least one sibling	85.4

Table 3-4. Child Placement Details.

N=1,958	%
Title IV-E eligible	64.8
Current Placement	%
Non-kin foster home	38.0
Kin foster home	28.1
Other	17.7
Group home or residential treatment	11.1
Adoptive placement[a]	4.8
Don't know	.4

[a] Adoptive placements are pre-adopt placements, not post- finalization.

Traditional, non-kin foster care was the placement setting of 38 percent of the children in the study. Non-kin foster care placements varied from 34 percent of children in Arizona to 45 percent in Tennessee. Over a quarter of children were placed with kin ranging from 20 percent in Massachusetts to 38 percent in Arizona. Of the children placed with kin, 21 percent were placed with paternal relatives (ranging from 17% in Minnesota to 24% in Arizona). Other placements comprised 34 percent of children in this study. These placements included runaways, children who had been reunified[33], and children placed in residential care, group homes, or independent living.

Caseworkers reported on why children came into care (Table 3-5). The large majority of children were placed because of neglect (82%), physical abuse (16%) or sexual abuse (9%). Twenty percent were placed for other reasons including (in order of descending frequency), parental substance abuse, emotional or verbal abuse, medical neglect, domestic violence, educational neglect, abandonment, parental mental illness, and abuse of the child's siblings. Children may have suffered more than one type of maltreatment. There was only slight variation between the states in the type of abuse/neglect. The most variation was seen in the "other abuse" category, ranging from 18 percent in Massachusetts to 27 percent in Minnesota.

Perpetrators of physical abuse were most often the mother (57%), followed by her boyfriend or husband (35%), then "other" perpetrators (15%), which included other relatives, caregivers, or acquaintances through parents or other family members. "Other" and "stepfather or mother's boyfriend" (38% each) were the most frequent perpetrator category for sexual abuse. The mother was the overwhelming perpetrator of neglect (95%), followed to a much lesser degree by fathers (11%), her boyfriend or husband (8%), and "other" adults or caretakers (6%). State variation for perpetrator type for specific types of abuse/neglect is difficult to examine due to small numbers.

Because the study criteria defined sample fathers as not residing in the home from which the child was removed, it is not surprising that these fathers are less likely to physically or sexually abuse their children than are other men in relationships with the child's mother. This was not the case with neglect with more similar percentages of caseworkers noting the nonresident father as the perpetrator of the neglect (11%) than the child's stepfather or mother's boyfriend (8%). Some state differences did exist. Caseworkers indicated the father was the perpetrator of sexual abuse in 26 percent of cases in Arizona, while the other three states were 19 percent or less, but overall levels of abuse by fathers were low.

Table 3-5. Reasons for Placement and Perpetrator Type.

N=1,958	%
Neglect (all that apply, N= 1,580)	*82.1*
Types of perpetrators	
Mother	95.0
Father	11.4
Stepfather or mother's boyfriend	7.7
Other	6.3
No perpetrator identified	0.2
Physical Abuse (all that apply, N=311)	*15.6*
Types of perpetrators	
Mother	57.2
Stepfather or mother's boyfriend	34.7
Other	14.7
Father	8.1
No perpetrator identified	3.2
Sexual Abuse (all that apply, N= 179)	*9.4*
Types of perpetrators	
Other	37.9
Stepfather or mother's boyfriend	37.7
Father	14.2
Mother	5.3
No perpetrator identified	10.6

Table 3-6. Case Permanency Goals.

N=1958	%
Reunify with mom	35.3
Non-relative adoption	18.8
Relative adoption	10.5
Independent living	6.2
Relative guardianship	7.9
Reunify with dad	4.2
Non-relative foster care	2.8
Relative foster care	1.1
Non-relative guardianship	1.1
Other	11.3
Don't know	0.8

Caseworkers were asked about the child's permanency goal and the responses were coded to several categories (table 3-6). The most frequent permanency goal was reunification with the mother (35%) followed by non-relative adoption (19%). Only 4 percent of cases with nonresident fathers were aiming to reunify the child with the father. Permanency goals varied slightly among states. Reunifying the child with his or her mother ranged from 23 percent in Minnesota to 44 percent in Tennessee while non-relative adoption varied from 16 percent in Arizona to 28 percent in Minnesota.

Description of Resident Mothers

As noted in the introduction to this chapter, because mothers most likely had custody of their children (that is, they lived in the household from which the child was removed), it is unlikely that caseworkers have to spend time identifying or locating these mothers; caseworkers were not asked about these activities. Contacting the mother would have most likely occurred during the initial investigation phase. As discussed earlier, nonresident mothers will be compared with nonresident fathers in analyses presented in chapter 4.

The findings in this section further describe the cases we sampled. Resident mothers are the birth parents from whom the child was removed given our criteria that the biological father not live in the household. Much of the data that follows was expected. For example, according to caseworkers, almost half (4 8%) of the mothers were never married. Other findings such as the percent of mothers who had been incarcerated at some point during the case process (29%) may come as a surprise to some policymakers in the field. The majority (60%) of mothers faced four or more problems.

While they face many barriers, it seems clear that many mothers still have strong connections to their children in care. Almost three-quarters (74%) still had parental rights to the child. The vast majority of the mothers had visited with their children (only 4 percent had no visits at the time of the worker interview) at some point during the case process. And while only 20 percent of mothers provided financial support at some point since the child was in care, nearly half the mothers had provided non-financial support during the out-of-home placement.

Characteristics

**Resident
Mothers**

Tables 3-7 and 3-8 provide information on characteristics of the study children's mothers. Table 3-7 includes a range of information including demographic characteristics, the mother's current living situation, and marital status. Table 3-8 provides information on the status of their parental rights.

Mothers were an average of 32 years old, ranging from 15 to 64. Most mothers were white (67%), 20 percent were African-American. Almost 20 percent of the mothers were of Hispanic origin (18%). Over 90 percent of all resident mothers were U.S. citizens, either through birth or naturalization. Most mothers had a high school education or less, if the mothers educational attainment was known to workers. Caseworkers reported that they did not know the mother's education in over a quarter of the cases.

Never-married mothers comprised the largest group (47%) of resident mothers. Almost 20 percent were married. Six percent of these mothers were married to the child's biological father. Another 18 percent of mothers were divorced, ranging from 12 percent in Arizona to 23 percent in Minnesota.

Almost 20 percent of mothers lived alone. A few mothers lived with the child's father.[34] Overall, almost a quarter of the resident mothers (23%) lived with a man other than the child's father, ranging from 18 percent in Minnesota to 28 percent in Massachusetts. Nearly half the mothers (49%) of the mothers living with another man also lived with others, usually her other children or his children, friends, or relatives.

Almost one third (31%) of caseworkers reported that mothers lived in some other living situation including being incarcerated; living with family members, friends, or female partners; living in a shelter or other group care environment; or being homeless.

Table 3-8 provides information on whether the resident mothers had parental rights to their child in foster care at the time of our interviews. As shown, the majority of resident mothers (74%) still have parental rights to the study child, ranging from 50 percent in Minnesota to 79 percent in Tennessee. Most mothers also have parental rights to their other children (64%).

Barriers to Contacting Mothers

Table 3-9 presents findings on circumstances that made contacting mothers difficult for the agency or worker. Overall, workers noted a quarter (26%) of the resident mothers faced none of the circumstances, 21 percent of mothers faced only one barrier, 41 percent of mothers faced two or three circumstances, and 12 percent of mothers had four or more circumstances apply. The most frequently cited circumstances were mothers who had transportation difficulties (5 2%) and were unreachable by phone (50%). A third of mothers were homeless and 29 percent had been incarcerated at some point during the case process. States varied considerably on the percent of resident mothers who had been incarcerated during the case process (from a low of 16% in Massachusetts to 37% in Tennessee). Caseworkers reported having great difficulty in contacting mothers when they were unreachable by phone, homeless, or lived out of state.

Table 3-7. Resident Mother Characteristics.

N=1 635	
Age (mean)	32.4
Race	%
White	66.7
African American	20.2
American Indian or Alaskan Native	3.6
Asian	.5
Mixed	2.3
Other	1.1
Don't know	5.6
Spanish, Hispanic, or Latino origin	17.8
U.S. citizenship	%
Yes	95.0
No	2.4
Don't know	2.6
Highest level of education	%
Less than 12 years	37.0
High school diploma or GED	28.7
Some college, vocational school	6.8
College degree/graduate school	1.2
Don't know	26.3
Marital status	%
Never married	47.4
Married to someone other than child's father	12.8
Married to, but separated from, child's father	5.8
Divorced from child's father	9.7
Divorced from someone other than child's father	7.9
Separated	3.6
Widowed	0.4
Don't know	12.4
Living situation	%
Living alone	18.5
Living with father of child[a]	2.6
Living with another male	23.3
Other	21.4
Don't know	34.2

[a] Sampled cases were selected because the child's father was not living in the home. However, during the interim between sample pull and interview, the living arrangement could have changed.

Table 3-8. Status of Resident Mothers' Parental Rights.

N=1,635	
Parental rights to **this** *child*	%
Still has parental rights	73.5
Mother's rights were terminated	18.4
Mother relinquished her rights	5.9
Don't know	2.2
Rights of mother to her **other** *children*	%
Still has rights to other children	64.2
Relinquished or terminated	24.8
N/A mother has no other children	5.3
N/A not known if mother has other children	1.3
Don't know	4.4

Table 3-9. Barriers to Contacting Resident Mothers.

N=1,635		
Type of circumstance (all that apply)	%	*% caused difficulty*
Transportation difficulties	51.6	61.8
Unreachable by phone	50.2	94.2
Homeless/unstable address	33.5	83.2
Incarceration[a]	28.9	45.4
Out of state	15.8	75.0
Out of country	2.0	44.8
Language barrier	1.6	44.0

[a] Twenty-one percent of those "incarcerated at some point during the case process" were incarcerated at the time of the survey.

Child-Mother Visitation

Contacted
Mothers

Table 3-10 provides information on children's visitation with their mothers.[35] Caseworkers reported that the majority of mothers had visited their children since case opening (88%). Eighty-two percent of mothers who had visited their child since case opening maintained monthly contact over the prior six months, and 45 percent had at least weekly contact. Almost all (96%) of the mothers with phone contact had visited with their child.

Caseworkers reported that half (51%) the mothers who had visits with their children over the past six months always or almost always attended planned visitation. Mothers in Massachusetts always or almost always attended visitation more frequently than the other states (59% versus a low of 43% in Minnesota).

Table 3-10. Resident Mother Visitation.

N=1,571	%
Percent of mothers who have visited with child (since case opening)	87.5
Visitation (w/in past 6 months) (N= 1,370)	%
Always or almost always attends planned visits	50.8
Sometimes attends	13.3
Rarely attends	9.9
Never attends or has no planned visits	22.2
Don't know	3.8
Frequency of visitation (w/in past 6 months)(N= 1,020)	%
No visits	4.8
One visit	11.9
Monthly	20.1
Twice a month	17.6
Weekly	29.6
More than once a week	15.0
Don't know	1.1

Note. All workers who had been in contact with mothers were asked whether the mother has ever visited the child (N=1,571). If the mother had ever visited, workers were asked about her attendance for planned visitations (N=1,370). If mothers rarely, sometimes, almost always, or always attend planned visitation (N=1,020), workers were asked the frequency of visitation.

Table 3-11. Resident Mother Support.

N=1,571	
Ever provided financial support	%
Yes	20.1
No	75.7
Don't know	4.2
Type of financial support (N= 321)	%
Regular (weekly or monthly)	21.9
Some, not regular	19.5
Occasional, sporadic	44.1
None of these options	10.9
Don't know	3.6
Ever provided non-financial support (diapers, etc.)	%
Yes	46.7
No	51.3
Don't know	2.0

Financial Support by Mothers

Based on several assumptions, caseworkers carrying cases involving resident mothers were asked slightly different questions concerning agency engagement. Caseworkers were asked questions pertaining to financial assistance from the mother (Table 3-11) under the assumption that since the child had been removed from her home, the mother, in addition to the father, would be looked to as a source of financial support.[36]

As shown, about 20 percent of mothers provided financial support at any point since the child was in care. However, nearly half provided non-financial support at some point during the child's stay in placement. Of those providing financial support, 22 percent provided weekly or monthly support. There were few state variations on mother's financial assistance with the exception of Arizona, which reported fewer mothers providing both financial and non-financial support (11% vs. 16-22% for the other states).

Mother Problems

As shown in Table 3-12, mothers had a range of problems or issue areas that caseworkers felt were reasons why the child was not currently placed with the mother. A prior finding of abuse/neglect and substance abuse were the most frequent problems cited by caseworkers. Almost 40 percent of mothers were noted as having criminal justice involvement. Inadequate housing, unemployment, and mental or physical health concerns were cited in over half of the cases.

Casework practice likely becomes more difficult when parents have multiple problems. The range of services that must be coordinated and provided is more complicated for the mother to navigate and the agency to manage. Workers noted 24 percent of the mothers had two or three of the problems and 60 percent reported mothers with four or more problems.

Description of Nonresident Fathers

The nonresident fathers of the children sampled represent a varied group. While most workers, at the time of the interview, knew the identity of the fathers (8 8%), over one-third of the total sample (37%) had not yet established paternity. Like the resident mothers, most nonresident fathers still retained their parental rights (6 6%). Demographic characteristics of identified nonresident fathers are similar to those of the resident mothers though fathers are slightly older (36 vs. 32 years old) and less likely to have never married (30% vs. 48%). As expected, caseworkers appear to know less about nonresident fathers, as the percent of "don't know" responses is much higher than for similar questions for resident mothers.

Cases involving unidentified or not located fathers means the caseworker may have to perform tasks to identify and locate the father. A variety of individuals and resources were noted by caseworkers as methods they used to obtain information on fathers. As previously discussed, the likelihood of a worker having contact with a nonresident father diminished greatly if the identity and location of the father was not known at, or shortly after, case opening.

While the vast majority of caseworkers noted sharing the case plan with contacted fathers and telling fathers about their child's placement (94% and 96%), they noted only half of contacted fathers expressed an interest in the child living with him. Caseworkers noted a number of barriers to contacting fathers. The most frequent barrier, father unreachable by telephone, was also the barrier that workers reported as causing the most difficulty. Given the saturation of cell phone use within the general population, this barrier might seem outdated. Perhaps this new technology that allows for caller identification and frequent changes in numbers has affected caseworker expectations. Caseworkers themselves are likely to be more accessible by cell phone making them doubly frustrated by clients who are not equally accessible.

Like mothers, nonresident fathers face numerous challenges to having their children live with them but far fewer fathers are visiting their children. For cases in which fathers had been contacted, over 40 percent (42%) of caseworkers noted fathers with four or more problems—the most frequently cited problem was alcohol and drug use (58%). Not surprisingly, nonresident fathers were less likely to have visited their child at least once than resident mothers. Still, over half (55%) of the contacted fathers had done so. And of the fathers who had visited, almost a third (31%) visit at least weekly. While most of the contacted fathers were not providing financial or non-financial support, some were doing so. Almost thirty percent (29%) had provided financial support at some point since case opening and almost a third (3 2%) had provided non-financial support.

The sections that follow provide detailed tables and discussion of these issues.

Paternity Establishment

Total Fathers

Table 3-13 provides information on whether the fathers in our study were only alleged to be the fathers or had paternity established (which we refer to as legal birth fathers). Caseworkers were asked whether paternity had been established for the child and if so, by what method.[37] Likewise, if the caseworker responded that paternity had not yet been established, a series of questions were asked to examine why this had not yet occurred. These data reveal that the majority of nonresident fathers had established paternity and were known to workers at the time of placement. Sixty-three percent of nonresident fathers were fathers with established paternity; the balance remained alleged. In only a small minority of cases (3%), did mothers claim exemption from identifying the father based on a threat to herself or her child. Multiple possible fathers were identified in 25 percent of the cases, with considerable variation among states (17% in Tennessee to 32% in Arizona).

Of cases with paternity established, 42 percent of workers cited paternity had been established through the father's name on the birth certificate and 24 percent noted genetic testing. Determination of paternity through having the father's name on the birth certificate varied from 26 percent in Minnesota to 49 percent in Tennessee. Genetic testing as the method ranged from 14 percent in Tennessee to 39 percent in Arizona. For children whose paternity had not been established (37% of the overall sample), caseworkers most frequently cited "other" reasons (58%) than those offered in the question posed to them. "Other" reasons why paternity was not established included not knowing who the father was, alleged fathers failing paternity tests, not having the father's name on the birth certificate, the alleged father abandoning the child, or the mother or father refusing to cooperate. Inability to locate the alleged father (35%), and the alleged father being unaware of the child (19%) or his denial of the child (21%) were also frequently cited reasons for not establishing paternity. A relatively small proportion of cases had a paternity action in progress (7%).[38]

Table 3-12. Resident Mother Problems.

N=1,571		%
Type of Problem	Yes	Don't know
Alcohol/drugs	65.4	1.5
Prior finding of abuse/neglect	58.6	1.4
Unemployment	58.1	3.0
Inadequate housing/homelessness	57.4	2.6
Mental/physical health	54.1	3.1
Domestic violence	39.7	6.8
Criminal justice involvement	37.5	4.4
No child care	26.2	4.8
Agency offered services for all problems	83.7	1.6
Mother complied with all services offered	40.3	1.3

Table 3-13. Paternity Establishment.

N=1,958	
Type	%
Legal	62.8
Alleged	37.2
More than one potential father identified	24.8
Mother claim exemption from identifying father	2.9
How was paternity established? (N= 1239)	%
Father's name on birth certificate	42.0
Genetic/DNA testing	24.4
Voluntary paternity document	16.1
Father states he is the father and/or signed non-legal documents	5.8
Established by default order	0.6
Other	8.2
Don't know	3.0
Why paternity not established (all that apply, N= 718)	%
Other	57.8
Unable to locate alleged father	35.1
Alleged father denies paternity	21.3
Alleged father unaware of child	18.9
Action in progress	7.3
DNA excluded alleged father	8.5

Status of Fathers' Parental Rights

Important to the discussion of nonresident fathers is whether or not the father has parental rights to his child in foster care. Analyses were conducted on all cases because parental rights can be terminated when diligent search efforts fail to identify a father. Findings from more detailed analyses of this issue are presented in chapter 4. As shown in table 3-14, most of the cases in this study involved nonresident fathers (66%) with parental rights to their children still intact. All states have relatively low levels of nonresident fathers relinquishing their rights, ranging from 3 percent in Arizona to 9 percent in Minnesota. Termination of rights is more prevalent than relinquishment in each of the states, and highest in Minnesota at 37 percent.

Identifying Nonresident Fathers

Table 3-15 presents information provided by caseworkers on efforts to identify the study children's fathers. That is, for cases in which the father's identity was not known at case opening (a minority of the cases), workers were asked whom they contacted in an attempt to identify him.[39] As one would expect, the birth mother is likely to be the first person the worker asks about an unidentified father. Indeed, caseworkers reported asking the birth mother to identify the father in the vast majority of cases (84%). However, when asked, a little less than one third (31%) of the mothers provided information that could identify the father (e.g., name, S SN). Practices aimed at asking other individuals to identify the father appear to be less consistent and vary across states. In 44 percent of the cases, workers asked maternal relatives (ranging from 29% in Massachusetts to 50% in Arizona). In 40 percent of cases the worker asked another worker about the identity of the father. Children were consulted in 38 percent of cases, leading to a positive identification almost a quarter (23%) of the time. States varied in the degree to which they sought information from the child's siblings (84% had at least one sibling, although not all were old enough to have assisted in identifying the father). Tennessee asked siblings in 20 percent of cases, Minnesota asked siblings in about 10 percent of cases, and workers in Massachusetts and Arizona asked siblings in less than 6 percent of cases.[40]

The most effective method of identifying the father was asking paternal relatives, though caseworkers are unlikely to use this method because the father is unidentified.[41] However, when asked, 38 percent of paternal relatives provided identifying information. Other sources child welfare workers used to identify fathers (19%) included friends of the mother, fathers of other children and ex-husbands or boyfriends. Other methods lead to identification information in about 23 percent of cases that used them.

Table 3-14. Status of Fathers' Parental Rights.

N=1955	
*Parental rights to **this** child*	%
Still has parental rights	65.9
Father's rights were terminated	20.3
Father relinquished his rights	4.8
Don't know	9.0
*Rights of father to his **other** children*	%
Still has rights to other children	41.9
Relinquished or terminated	8.7
N/A father has no other children	3.6
N/A not known if father has other children	19.1
Don't know	26.7

Note. N does not equal 1958 due to 3 fathers who died since the case was opened.

Table 3-15. Identifying Nonresident Fathers.

N=446		
Who was asked to identify father?	**%asked**	**%provided information (of those who were asked)**
Child's mother	83.7	30.9
Mother's relatives	44.4	20.9
Another worker	39.7	30.4
Child (only asked on children over 6)	37.9	23.4
Child's sibling	10.8	21.1
Father's relatives[a]	9.6	38.2
Other	18.5	23.2

Note. These questions were only asked for cases in which the fathers had not been identified at the time of case opening. See Figure 3-3 for the cumulative percentage of identified fathers over time.

[a] Caseworkers who responded to this question may be referring to paternal relatives of the study child's siblings. While the father of the study child was not identified, it could be that the caseworker believes the child has the same father as one or more of the child's siblings and asks these relatives for help in identifying the study child's father.

Characteristics

Identified
Fathers

Table 3-16 provides demographic characteristics of the identified fathers (that is, the 1,721 fathers who were identified at some point prior to the caseworker interview). These fathers were an average of 36 years old, with a range of 14 to 78. Just over half were white, 21 percent were Hispanic, and 23 percent were African- American. Arizona had the largest proportion of Hispanic fathers (37%) while Tennessee had the smallest (3%). Tennessee had the largest proportion of African-American fathers (37%) while Arizona had the smallest (13%). Minnesota had the smallest proportion of white fathers (45%) while Arizona had the largest (60%).

The vast majority of nonresident fathers were U.S. citizens, either by birth or naturalization. However it should be noted that workers did not know the father's immigration status in 22 percent of the cases in which they knew the father's identity. Only 4 percent were known to be non-citizens. Most caseworkers knew the educational attainment of few nonresident fathers in our study (30%). The vast majority of those with known education levels were at or below high school equivalency.

Table 3-16. Nonresident Father Characteristics.

N=1,721	
Age (mean)	36.3
Race (N = 1,720)	%
White	53.9
African American	23.0
American Indian or Alaskan Native	2.2
Asian	.6
Mixed	1.0
Other	2.1
Don't know	17.2
Spanish, Hispanic, or Latino origin	20.9
U.S. citizenship	%
Yes	74.1
No	4.0
Don't know	21.9
Highest level of education	%
Less than 12 years	13.1
High school diploma or GED	15.0
Some college, vocational school	2.2
Don't know	69.7
Marital status	%
Never married	29.9
Married to, but separated from, birth mother	10.9
Married to someone other than birth mother	11.7
Divorced from birth mother	11.6
Divorced from someone other than birth mother	4.7
Separated	1.3
Don't know	29.9
Living situation (N= 1,056) [a]	%
Living alone	13.9
Living with birth mom of child[b]	4.0
Living with woman other than birth mom (romantic)	22.4
Other	24.1
Don't know	35.6

[a] These questions were only asked for cases in which the fathers had been identified and the agency or worker had made contact with the father in the past 6 months.

[b] Length of time between sample selection and interview means living arrangements may have changed.

Caseworkers reported almost a third of the cases (30%) involved fathers who were never married. Almost a quarter (23%) were married, 11 percent still married to the birth mother. Another 12 percent were divorced from the birth mother. The proportion of married fathers was largest in Tennessee (2 8%) compared to a low of 15 percent in Minnesota. Tennessee had the largest percentage of divorced fathers (24%) and Arizona had the lowest (13%).

Table 3-17. Locating Nonresident Fathers.

N=802		
Who was asked about father's location? (all that apply)	**% asked**	**% provided information (of those who were asked)**
Child's mother	86.0	39.8
Another worker	40.0	40.3
Mother's relatives	33.4	28.6
Child (only asked if child is 7 or older)	34.3	27.6
Father's relatives	20.4	60.3
Child's sibling (only asked if child had siblings)	9.6	22.8
Other	29.8	49.1
What records were searched? (all that apply)		
Law enforcement records	44.4	30.7
Public aid (TANF, Food stamps, Medicaid)	34.4	14.2
Telephone books	30.7	10.2
DMV records	22.1	18.4
Utility company records	11.0	7.8
Other	21.6	23.2

Note. Only cases in which fathers were not located at time of case opening were included in these analyses.

Caseworkers reported not knowing the living situation of 36 percent of the identified nonresident fathers in the study. Twenty-two percent of fathers were reported to live with a woman who was not the child's mother, 14 percent lived alone, and 4 percent lived with the birth mother. As noted with resident mothers' living situations, while cases were eligible only if the biological father was not living in the home from which the child was removed, due to the length of time between sample pull and interview date, living arrangements may have changed. Almost one-quarter (24%) of the fathers did not live in any of the previously mentioned living situations. Other arrangements include incarceration, living with adult family members, and military deployment.

Locating Fathers

Earlier we noted the methods caseworkers used to identify nonresident fathers. This section describes methods used to locate fathers. The base population for these analyses is the 1,721 fathers (88%) identified at any point before the interview with the caseworker. Slightly over half of the identified fathers (52%) were located at case opening and thus, the worker did not have to locate the father.

For cases involving identified fathers not located at the time the case opened, caseworkers were asked questions about methods used to locate fathers who had been identified. Similar to findings on identifying methods, almost all caseworkers (86%) reported asking the child's mother how to locate nonresident fathers (table 3-17). Caseworkers reported less than half of the mothers (40%) who were asked, provided information on the father's location and there was considerable state variation (from 34% in Arizona to 51% in Minnesota) in this practice. Workers also asked other workers (40%), mother's relatives

(33%), and the child (34%). Minnesota workers were most likely to ask other workers (53%) and Massachusetts' workers were least likely to ask other workers (2 8%). While the states were similar on the percent of workers asking children, the percent of success with this method varied greatly, from only 10 percent in Arizona to 38 percent in Tennessee. The most successful resources were paternal relatives, giving location information 60 percent of the time, although these relatives were only utilized by 20 percent of caseworkers.

There was considerable variation across states in other resources searched to find fathers. Arizona consistently utilized resources from other departments in a greater proportion of cases when compared to the three other states. Law enforcement records were most frequently searched (22% in Massachusetts to 57% in Arizona), followed by public aid files (10% in Massachusetts to 56% in Arizona).

Child welfare workers also found means of locating fathers that were not originally included in the survey responses. These resources included newspaper ads, bankruptcy records and credit bureaus, other benefits workers, "calling every surname in town," family and friends, Internet searches, and putative father registries.[42]

Table 3-18 provides information on locating resources. Overall, caseworkers contacted the state child support offices in 20 percent of cases. Interestingly, when asked whether the agency encouraged them to make referrals to child support, 63 percent of all caseworkers responded "yes." Minnesota (3 9%) and Tennessee (3 3%) were more likely to refer cases to child support than Arizona (18%) and Massachusetts (3%). Caseworkers who heard back from child support offices at the time of the interview averaged 43 percent across the states, ranging from 35 percent in Arizona to 78 percent in Minnesota.

Thirty-three percent of caseworkers reported that the state parent locator services had been used to locate the father in the case.[43] There was considerable variability among states in the use of both the state and federal parent locator services. Use of the state locator services was reported in 79 percent of Arizona's cases while use of the state locator services was only reported in 3 percent of Massachusetts' cases. Caseworkers reported not knowing whether state locator services were used in a substantial portion of cases including 32 percent in Minnesota and 23 and 21 percent in Tennessee and Massachusetts, respectively. Federal parent locator services (FPLS) were also most frequently used in Arizona cases.[44] In 18 percent of Arizona's cases, workers reported use of the FPLS while the other states ranged from 0 to 2 percent. The proportion of "don't know" responses was substantial averaging 31 percent across the four states.

Table 3-18. Locate Resources.

N=802	%
State child support office contacted	20.1
State parent locator service	33.4
Federal parent locator service	7.5
Other locating resource	7.6

Note. Only cases in which fathers were not located when the case opened were included in these analyses.

Table 3-19. Nonresident Father Information in Case Record.

N=1,721	%
Full name	87.3
Birth date [a]	77.2
Social security number	43.6
Address	38.1
Paternal relatives	35.1
Phone number	33.9
Employer information	11.8
Alias	9.7
Other information	18.0

[a] Caseworkers were asked the father's age. When a father's age was provided either through preload data or through asking the worker respondent it was considered having date of birth in the case record.

Table 3-20. Barriers to Contacting Nonresident Fathers.

N=1,721		
Type of circumstance (all that apply)	%	% caused difficulty
Unreachable by phone	59.9	94.0
Out of state	31.4	80.5
Incarceration [a]	30.5	53.1
Problem transportation	21.5	70.0
Homeless/unstable address	10.6	84.5
Out of country	5.1	93.9
Language barrier	3.1	78.3

[a] Of the "ever incarcerated," 43 percent were incarcerated at the time of the survey. All other incarcerated fathers had been incarcerated at some point since the case opening.

Caseworkers were asked what types of identifying and locating information on fathers were located in the case record (table 3-19). Most caseworkers reported having the full name (87%)[45] and date of birth (77%) of the child's identified father in the case file. The presence of other information was less frequent, but included social security number (44% total, ranging from 27% in Massachusetts to 58% in Arizona), address (38% total, ranging from 30% in Massachusetts to 43% in Tennessee), names of paternal relatives (35%), phone number (34%), and other information (1 8%).[46] Relatively few caseworkers had information about the father's employment (12% total, ranging from 6% in Massachusetts to 17% in Tennessee).

Agency Contact with Fathers and Barriers to Contact

Table 3-20 provides information on worker and agency contact with identified fathers. Barriers to contact were asked of all cases whether or not the agency had made contact with the father. Caseworkers were asked which circumstances posed a barrier to contacting nonresident fathers. Caseworkers were also asked to report on the type of relationship between the mother and nonresident father.

If caseworkers indicated fathers were affected by any circumstance, they were asked if the circumstances made contact difficult. Sixty percent reported that fathers were unreachable by phone, which caused difficulty in almost all (94%) cases. Thirty-one percent of fathers were out of state, which caused difficulty in 81 percent of cases. This finding argues for making more extensive use of the Federal Parent Locator Service, since state locator services cannot locate out-of-state parents. Thirty-one percent of fathers had been incarcerated at some point since case opening, and 43 percent of those were currently incarcerated. The proportion of currently incarcerated fathers ranged from 32 percent of total incarcerated (since case opening) in Minnesota to 48 percent of total incarcerated in Tennessee. Incarceration caused difficulty in 53 percent of cases.

Language barriers, being out of the country, and being homeless were circumstances that affected relatively small proportions of fathers, although they made contact difficult. Of the circumstances listed, incarceration and transportation issues created the least difficulty for caseworkers.

Though some workers reported that some fathers experienced no circumstances that affected contact (14%), many workers reported multiple circumstances that may cause barriers to contact. In 42 percent of the cases, workers reported two or three barriers and in 7 percent of the cases, four or more barriers.

Another barrier to contact with the nonresident father is the relationship between the birth mother and nonresident father. Almost two-thirds of the cases were reported to involve relationships in which parents are hostile with one another, hardly ever or never talk to one another.[47] Workers did not know the type of relationship between the parents in 9 percent of the cases. The type of relationship does appear to affect agency-father contact. Fathers in relationships reported to be friendly or romantic were more likely to have contact with the agency than fathers in relationships reported to be less positive (92%** vs. 65%).

Child-Father Visitation

> **Contacted Fathers**

Caseworkers were asked to describe visitation between the nonresident father and his child in foster care (table 3-21). Before presenting the findings it is important to note that a nonresident father's visitation with his child in foster care is not unrestrained. Custody and visitation orders often dictate visitation for separated and divorced fathers. Fathers may also be restrained due to protection orders established to prohibit contact with the child's mother. Kinship arrangements with maternal kin may also create some restraints for fathers in visiting their children. Even non- kin foster care arrangements can set up constraints to father-child visitation. Over fifty (5 6%) percent of nonresident fathers who had been identified and had at least one contact with the agency had visited their child at least once since the child had been in foster care. This represents only 30 percent of the total sample of nonresident father cases. The analyses in this section included cases in which the father had been contacted at least once during the case (at the time of the interview). Forty percent of these fathers always or almost always attend planned visits while almost a third (29%) never attend planned visits or have no planned visits. While this figure seems somewhat promising in terms of fathers engaging with their children while the children are in foster care, the 40 percent who always or almost always visit are only 13 percent of the total sample of nonresident fathers. Most fathers had at least one visit with clusters of responses at one visit (21%), monthly (23%) or weekly (19%) visitation. Twelve percent of caseworkers reported nonresident fathers see their children more than once a week. Similar to resident mothers, the vast majority (84%) of the fathers who had phone contact also visited with their children.

Father Engagement

Tables 3-22 and 3-23 provide findings on engaging nonresident fathers in casework. Again, workers were only asked to respond to these questions if the father of the case in question had had contact with the worker or agency; thus, the questions were asked in 1,071 cases. Important to remember is that the contacted fathers represent just over half (55%) of the total sample.

Caseworkers with cases involving fathers whom the agency had not yet contacted were not asked questions about father engagement. For cases in which fathers had been contacted, a range of issues representing possible engagement both between the worker and the father as well as between the father and his child were examined. Types of agency engagement include whether the agency shared the case plan with the father and whether or not the agency considered placing the child with his or her father or paternal relatives. Father engagement includes whether a father had expressed an interest in having his child live with him and whether he provided the child with financial or non-financial support.

Table 3-21. Nonresident Father Visitation.

N=1 ,071	
Percent of fathers who have visited with child (since case opening)	55.5
Visitation (w/in past 6 months)(N= 608)	%
Always or almost always attends planned visits	40.3
Sometimes attends	14.3
Rarely attends	13.5
Never attends or has no planned visits	28.5
Don't know	3.5
Frequency of visitation (w/in past 6 months)(N= 400)	%
No visits	6.4
One visit	20.9
Monthly	23.1
Twice a month	15.5
Weekly	19.2
More than once a week	12.1
Don't know	2.9

Note: All workers who had been in contact with fathers were asked whether he ever visited the child. If the father had ever visited, workers were asked about his attendance for planned visitations (N=608). If fathers rarely, sometimes, almost always, or always attend planned visitation (N=400), workers were asked the frequency of visitation.

Table 3-22. Nonresident Father Engagement.

N=1,071	%
Father told of child's out-of-home placement	95.9
Agency shared plan with fathers	93.5
Father expressed interest in child living with him	50.3
Agency considered placing child with father	45.1
Agency considered placing child with paternal relatives (N=791)[a]	53.9
Agency sought health care coverage from father as part of the case plan	14.3
Agency sought financial assistance from father as part of the case plan	36.6

[a] Only asked of cases in which the child was not in paternal kin placement.

Caseworkers report telling almost all contacted fathers about the child's out-of-home placement (96%) and sharing the case plan with them (94%). Half of the contacted fathers expressed an interest in having the child live with them. Caseworkers reported considering placement with 45 percent of contacted fathers, ranging from 34 percent in Massachusetts to 51 percent in Minnesota. Workers initiated an assessment for 87 percent of fathers the agency considered as potential placement resources, and performed a child protective services (CPS) clearance on 83 percent of them. The proportion of cases in which a CPS clearance check was conducted varied by state—from 71 percent in Massachusetts to 89 percent in Tennessee. Consideration of paternal relatives as placement options varied from 44 percent of cases with contacted fathers in Massachusetts to 67 percent in Minnesota, with an average of 54 percent across the study states.[48]

There was considerable variation between states in whether or not caseworkers sought health care coverage or financial assistance from nonresident fathers. Seeking health insurance coverage was part of the case plan in 9 percent of the contacted father cases in Massachusetts, but 21 percent in Minnesota. In Massachusetts, 11 percent of case plans included obtaining financial assistance from the father, compared to 38 percent in Minnesota, 41 percent in Arizona, and 55 percent in Tennessee.

The proportion of cases with contacted fathers who ever provided financial support (table 3-23) was largest in Tennessee (35%) and smallest in Arizona (21%). In most cases where the father had provided financial support, the support came regularly (43%) or occasionally (33%). Almost one-third of contacted fathers (32%) had provided non-financial support such as clothes, diapers, child care, food, or health insurance. Almost a quarter (23%) of the fathers provided both financial and non-financial support; 9 percent only financial, and 12 percent only nonfinancial. States varied somewhat with Arizona having only 18 percent of fathers providing both financial and non-financial support while in Massachusetts and Tennessee, a quarter of fathers (25%) provided both. Arizona workers reported only 5 percent of fathers providing only financial support while 14 percent of Minnesota workers reported fathers providing only financial support.

Table 3-23. Nonresident Father Support.

N=1,071	
Ever provided financial support	%
Yes	29.0
No	58.9
Don't know	12.1
Type of financial support (N= 349)[a]	%
Regular (weekly or monthly)	43.2
Some, not regular	12.4
Occasional, sporadic	32.8
None of these options	8.0
Don't know	3.7
Ever provided non-financial support	%
Yes	31.5
No	56.4
Don't know	12.2

a Only cases in which the father had ever provided financial support were asked about the type of support.

Table 3-24. Nonresident Father Problems.

N=1,071		%
Type of Problem (all that apply)	Yes	Don't know
Alcohol/drugs	58.2	15.2
Criminal justice involvement	52.5	13.3
Inadequate housing/homelessness	41.7	12.4
Unemployment	40.7	15.1
Domestic violence	33.3	17.9
Prior finding of abuse/neglect	29.6	8.5
Mental/physical health	22.9	15.4
No child care	21.2	15.1
Agency offered services for all problems	*58.6*	*5.1*
Father complied with all services offered	*22.5*	*3.5*

Note. Caseworkers were asked about the problem areas of fathers with whom they had been in contact (N=1,071). If a father had a problem in one or more areas, workers were asked whether or not services were offered to him (N=929). If services were offered, workers were asked whether or not he complied with provided services (N=522).

Father Problems

Caseworkers were asked questions regarding the problems or issues of concern that affect whether or not a child can be placed with the father. As shown (table 3-24), the most frequently cited problem for fathers was alcohol/drug abuse (58%). Slightly over half the contacted fathers were reported to have problems associated with criminal justice involvement.[49] States varied slightly in the problems noted for fathers. Unemployment was reported less in Massachusetts' cases (32% vs. 39-46% in the other states) and a prior finding of abuse/neglect was cited more frequently as a problem in Massachusetts' cases (40% vs. 25-27% in the other states). Arizona reported more cases in which fathers had alcohol or drug problems (64%) while Massachusetts and Tennessee had the least with 54%.

Multiple problems almost certainly impact fathers' ability to care for and visit their children. In 14 percent of the cases, workers noted fathers with no problems but in over 40 percent (42%) workers report fathers with four or more of the problems listed. There was some variation in the proportion of fathers with multiple problems. Tennessee reported slightly less fathers (3 5%) with four or more problems than the other states (42-46%).

Caseworkers were asked whether services were provided to nonresident fathers to assist them in overcoming the problems identified and whether or not fathers had complied with services. In almost 60 percent (5 9%) of the contacted father cases caseworkers reported offering services to fathers but workers reported only 23 percent of fathers had complied with all the services offered.

Summary of Descriptive Analyses

This chapter presented findings on the case-level data collection effort conducted in four states— Arizona, Massachusetts, Minnesota, and Tennessee. Data on 1,958 eligible cases were collected through telephone interviews with 1,222 caseworkers. Workers provided detailed information on casework practices regarding nonresident fathers of children in foster care and the characteristics and potential limitations of these fathers.

Nonresident fathers had been identified by local child welfare agencies in almost 90 percent (8 8%) of the cases by the time of the interview (see figure 3-5) and most were identified early on in the case process. As the case unfolds it becomes less likely that an unidentified father will be identified even though workers are making efforts. For cases with fathers not identified at the time of case opening, the caseworker reported asking a number of different individuals—the child's mother, mother's relatives, other workers—for assistance in identifying the father. Less than a third of the mothers (31%) who were asked provided identifying information on the father, and other sources were not very successful either. We examined whether practices differed by whether or not the child's mother provided information under the assumption that if the mother did not provide information, the caseworker would have more incentive to ask for assistance from other individuals. The assumption held true for some categories—for example, caseworkers reported seeking help from a mother's relatives in only about a third of cases (3 1%) in which mothers provided identifying information and in over half the cases (55%) in which mothers did not provide identifying information ($p < .0 1$). Caseworkers were also more likely to report seeking help from the child and siblings in cases in which the mother did not provide information on the father. However, workers were not more likely to seek help from another worker in these cases. It appears as if casework practice regarding identifying fathers is case specific and variable.

Workers also reported on how they located fathers who had been identified. Similar to the questions related to identifying fathers, caseworkers reported asking for help from the mother, the mother's relatives, the child, siblings, and other workers as well as the father's relatives. Workers also consulted a number of other sources including law enforcement, public assistance and department of motor vehicles records, and telephone books. Caseworkers were more likely to report seeking help from a variety of sources including mother's relatives, siblings, DMV records, public assistance records, telephone books and utilities, when the mother did not provide locate information on the father than when the mother did provide such information. However, the percent of cases in which workers asked these sources is low. And, while over 60 percent of workers noted that their agency encouraged referrals to child support for locating the father, in only 20 percent of the cases in which the father had not been located did the worker refer the case to child support. In the next chapter, findings from the child support data linkage are presented and a more detailed discussion is provided.

Workers were asked to report on circumstances that may make contact with the nonresident father difficult. The most frequently reported circumstances were fathers who were unreachable by phone (60%). While incarceration was cited as a circumstance in almost a third of cases (31%), it was noted as causing difficulty with contact in only about half of these cases (53%). [50] Other circumstances—such as unreliable transportation, homelessness or unstable housing, and being out of the country—while cited less frequently caused greater difficulty with agency-father contact. The type of relationship between the mother and nonresident father also affects agency-father contact. Fathers in relationships perceived as hostile by the caseworker or fathers who hardly ever or never talk to the mother were less likely to have had contact with the agency.

Slightly over half of all cases had fathers who had been contacted by the worker (55%) (See figure 3-5). Workers were asked specific questions related to agency-father engagement and father-child visitation for the contacted fathers. Over 90 percent of caseworkers reported sharing the case plan with these contacted fathers and telling him about his child's out-of-home placement, though this represents only about half of the entire sample. Far fewer of the contacted fathers had visited their child (56%) representing only 30 percent of all fathers in the sample.

Caseworkers reported half of the contacted fathers expressed an interest in having the child live with them (28% of entire sample). For cases involving fathers with whom the agency had made contact, workers were asked to identify problems or issues that prevented the child from being placed with his or her father. In over half the contacted cases (5 8%), workers noted fathers with drug or alcohol abuse problems and half of the fathers were involved with the criminal justice system in some way (i.e., incarcerated, on parole, awaiting trial). Caseworkers reported offering services to fathers in over half of the cases (5 9%) but reported only 23 percent of the fathers had complied with the services offered.

Many nonresident fathers have multiple problems. Workers reported over forty percent (42%) of the contacted fathers had four or more of the problems listed. It is important to emphasize that these data represent only the fathers with whom the agency or worker had contact. Fathers who have not been identified, located, or contacted by the agency may have more or fewer problems than the contacted fathers. However, it is interesting to note that caseworkers reported a similar frequency of problems for resident mothers. Comparisons between nonresident mothers and nonresident fathers are presented in chapter 4.

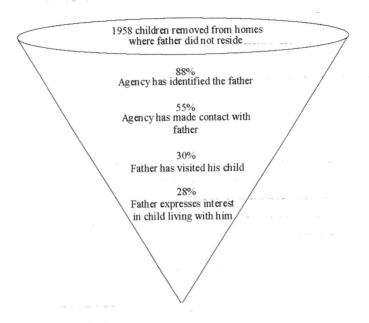

Figure 3-5. Father Engagement.

Overall the caseworkers interviewed appear to have conflicting opinions about father involvement. Most reported that father involvement enhances child well-being (72%) but only about half (53%) reported that nonresident fathers want to be part of the decision making about their children. In the next chapter, we examine whether worker bias may affect whether nonresident fathers are identified and contacted.

Engaging and involving nonresident fathers of foster children in permanency planning and casework is important and challenging for child welfare agencies. The findings presented in this chapter provide a first step in understanding this issue. While it may be tempting to use these data to paint a picture of casework practice and fathers that is not flattering (e.g., agencies must not be doing their best to engage nonresident fathers if only 55 percent of fathers have been contacted, and nonresident fathers must not care about their children because only 30 percent of fathers have visited their child), it would be premature. Findings from this exploratory study provide a first sketch, yet further analyses are needed in order to examine specific questions about casework practices. The analyses presented in chapter 4 provide some preliminary results for the next step in the process.

4. ADDITIONAL ANALYSES AND CONCLUSIONS

Overview

In chapter 3 we presented descriptive information about the study children's nonresident fathers—the fathers' characteristics, contact with the child welfare agency, and involvement with their children. This chapter presents findings from analyses conducted on subgroups of nonresident fathers to determine if differences exist. We also compare and contrast nonresident fathers and nonresident mothers for context.[51] Comparisons across groups of cases with differing child, case, and caseworker characteristics are also examined. Finally, multivariate analyses were conducted to examine factors associated with identified and involved fathers.[52]

This chapter also presents findings from the study's child support linkage component. This component, described in more detail in chapter 1, was implemented to examine the feasibility of using child support information to assist in identifying and locating nonresident fathers of children in foster care. Lastly, a summary of all study findings is provided.

Research and Practice as Guides

Examining nonresident parent and caseworker characteristics through comparative analyses of certain subgroups will help us understand factors that might influence caseworker activities (i.e., casework practices). Gaining a more complete understanding of how caseworkers identify, locate, and involve nonresident fathers will move the field closer to effectively utilizing all available resources, both maternal and paternal, to ensure the best outcomes for children in out-of-home placement. In part because there is so little research to guide these analyses, we relied more heavily on our knowledge of practice to guide the analyses presented in this chapter. Where research findings do exist, we attempted to incorporate such findings into our analysis plan.

First we tried to compare groups that, for casework purposes, might present differently. Nonresident fathers were grouped by whether they were reported to be the child's alleged or legal birth father. A legal father of a child in foster care might have more interest in and involvement with the child welfare agency. A caseworker may be required to (by policy or protocol) or feel more obligated to provide case information to a legal, rather than an alleged, father. Administrators noted problems occurring when children were placed with kin of men believed to be their fathers but later discovered not to be. Clearly, casework practices directed at nonresident fathers may differ by whether or not paternity is established.

Casework practices toward nonresident mothers and nonresident fathers and characteristics of the two groups were also examined. Child welfare policies and practices are often described as being maternally focused.[53] While resident mothers were described in chapter 3, comparing mothers and fathers in similar situations (i.e., not living in the home from which their child was removed), provides a more unbiased examination of casework practices. For example, caseworkers in a recent study on fathers in child welfare cases noted that a father's incarceration might be cause for less engagement (O'Donnell 2005). The analyses presented in this chapter will examine whether incarceration is reported by caseworkers as a barrier to contact for both nonresident mothers and nonresident fathers.

Caseworkers were asked whether or not the father was ever considered as a placement resource. These responses led to the creation of two subgroups of fathers—those who were considered as a placement option and those who were never considered or dismissed early in the case.[54] And while it would seem likely that the fathers' characteristics would affect whether they were considered as a placement resource, local agency policies and protocols are also likely to impact this determination. In fact, child welfare agencies routinely identify and assess nonresident parents as potential placement resources, and some states' policies explicitly give them preference. (Sonenstein et al. 2002).

Case characteristics including type of placement, permanency goal, length of placement, and child's age were also examined through comparative analyses. For example, we wanted to know whether nonresident fathers are more likely to visit their children if the children are placed with kin versus with non-kin. Past research has shown children visit with parents more frequently when placed with kin (Geen 2003). However, given the majority of kin placements are with maternal family, visits with fathers could be less affected or even negatively affected if the relationship between the father and mother's kin is poor. We also examined whether identifying and locating methods differ if the child was living with kin. If a child is placed with kin, do caseworkers make fewer efforts to identify and locate the father?

Casework practice is premised on the case plan or permanency goal for the foster child. That is, if the case goal is to reunify the child with his or her mother, then services and practices are directed at that goal. Would a case plan goal of adoption translate into more aggressive efforts to identify and locate nonresident fathers to meet diligent search requirements for adoption? Would visits between the child and his or her father be less frequent?

Given the passage of the Adoption and Safe Families Act and the renewed focus on expedited permanency for children in placement it seems likely that the length of placement could affect caseworkers' actions, particularly as they attempt to identify and locate fathers. And while focusing on permanency would appear to increase attention on nonresident fathers (due to the father being a potential placement resource and the caseworker needing access to paternal kin) caseworkers might react differently. Clearly, many caseworkers (44% of respondents) feel that involving nonresident fathers makes a case more complicated (See chapter 3, page 57). Perhaps the expedited nature of today's casework means workers have less time to devote to father inclusion.

Similar to other casework practices, a father's involvement is likely to be influenced by his child's age. Fathers may be more or less likely to visit their child depending upon the age of the child. Older children may have weaker ties to their nonresident fathers or, conversely, older children may be more emotionally ready to initiate or continue a relationship with a nonresident father. Older children may also be less likely to have a goal of adoption and, thus, the caseworker may make fewer efforts to identify the father to terminate his parental rights.

Caseworker characteristics may also influence practice with nonresident fathers. A recent study noted in the literature review in chapter 1 examined differences in practices related to fathers by caseworkers' gender. Male caseworkers were less likely to voice frustration with involving fathers (O'Donnell et al. 2005). Responses to our training and worker opinion questions provide additional ways to group caseworkers for analysis. Caseworkers who received training on how to identify, locate, and involve nonresident fathers would likely do so more competently. Caseworkers reporting more positive opinions of nonresident fathers may also be more likely to engage fathers. We categorized workers according to their responses to two opinion questions: caseworkers who "agreed" or "strongly agreed" that (1) nonresident fathers want to be part of the decision-making process with regard to their children, and (2) involvement of nonresident fathers enhances a child's well-being. Workers who responded "neither agreed or disagreed," "disagreed," or "strongly disagreed" with both of the statements were grouped together. Caseworkers were also grouped according to whether they had received training on how to identify, locate, or engage nonresident fathers.

The comparison group analyses were conducted to identify certain factors we could further examine through multivariate analyses. With the logistic regression, factors that might be associated with the identified and involved nonresident fathers of children in foster care could be examined. Involved fathers were defined in two ways—through visiting with the child and through support provided to the child. Previous studies on nonresident fathers have examined their involvement by similar means (Lerman and Sorensen 2000).

Limitations

There are several limitations to the data presented in this chapter. Unlike the descriptive analyses presented in chapter 3, the comparison group and multivariate analyses required constructs be developed. Results of prior research studies would usually guide such construct development. However, little research has been conducted on this study's population of nonresident fathers (i.e., fathers of children in foster care who were not residing in the home from which the child was removed). Some studies noted in the literature review section of chapter 1 and in this chapter's overview section guide our analyses. For example, caseworkers in a recent study on fathers in child welfare cases noted that a father's incarceration might be cause for less engagement (O'Donnell et al. 2005). Criminal justice involvement is examined as it relates to barriers to contact for the worker and as one of the reasons why the child cannot be placed with his or her father. We also obtained data on whether the nonresident father perpetrated the abuse or neglect. Both these factors may be associated with fathers' involvement and are included in the logistic regression. When we were unable to base the specific analyses on past research we examined the data from a general knowledge of casework practice.

Much of the general father involvement research is premised on the belief that father involvement affects child well-being, either positively or negatively. Our study is different in many ways. First, the population of nonresident fathers includes only fathers of children served by child protection agencies. Father involvement is defined differently for a family being served by a child welfare agency than it would be for a family not involved with child welfare. Visitation may be quite different—it is planned and often supervised by agency staff.[55] Visitation may only be allowed for fathers with whom the child has an established relationship or for legal fathers. A permanency goal of adoption by a non-relative may preclude visitation between the father and child. Caseworkers' efforts to contact a nonresident father may be directed at terminating his parental rights, not fostering the father-child relationship.

In addition to the different context in which we are examining father involvement, all our data is obtained through the lens of the child welfare caseworker. Some caseworkers responded "don't know" to certain questions. Caseworker responses to questions about practices (e.g., Did you share the case plan with the father?) were less likely to be "don't know" responses than questions about the father's characteristics and the problems that affected whether the child could be placed with him.

Some prior research findings could not be examined with our data. For example, some research suggests that a father's marital status is a factor in whether he gains custody of his children when they are removed from the mother's custody due to abuse or neglect (Greif and Zuravin 1989). However, caseworkers were unable to provide marital status for 30 percent of all nonresident fathers in the study sample. The percent of missing data is substantially higher for alleged fathers and fathers who were not considered as a placement resource.

Another important limitation to this chapter's findings is the structure of the caseworker questionnaire. To obtain the most accurate and updated information, we limited certain questions to caseworkers who had been in "contact" with the nonresident father. We did not want caseworkers who had never been in contact with a nonresident father to respond to questions such as his marital or housing status, whether he had ever expressed interest in his child living with him, and the like. We were certain that responses to these types of questions—without actual contact with the father—would likely be secondhand from the child's mother or guesswork on the part of the caseworker. Contact was defined broadly. The frequency of contact may have varied considerably but these data were not collected. For our study, the distinction is whether contact had ever been made.

The "contact" determination is likely to bias findings because of differential contact rates for certain subgroups. For example, while 73 percent of legal fathers had contact with the worker or agency, only 35 percent of alleged fathers did. Every nonresident mother had been contacted versus only 55 percent of all nonresident fathers. It is important to note that the "contact" differential only affects the analyses conducted on questions about "contacted father" cases (see discussion in chapter 3, page 49). Comparisons between fathers considered for placement and those not similarly considered, are not affected by the "contact" differential. The question on whether placement had been considered was only asked of cases involving contacted fathers; however, our inability to determine the frequency and duration of contact does affect the interpretation of the findings. It could well be that fathers whom the worker considered as a placement for the child were fathers with whom the worker had fairly frequent contact while fathers not considered for placement had only minimal contact with the worker. As discussed later in this chapter, large percentages of "don't know" responses on problem areas of fathers the agency did not consider for placement preclude a comparison of problems across the two groups of fathers.

Comparison Groups

In the following sections, findings from analyses on efforts to identify, locate, and involve nonresident fathers are presented. Comparisons across subgroups are presented first. First alleged and legal father subgroups are examined. Then nonresident fathers are examined in relation to nonresident mothers and finally, cases are examined by whether the father was ever considered as a placement resource.

Alleged vs. Legal fathers

As noted in chapter 3, all fathers for whom paternity was established were considered to be the study child's legal birth father. [56] Fathers for whom paternity had not yet been established or for whom caseworkers did not know whether paternity had been established were considered alleged fathers.

Demographic characteristics

Some differences were found between alleged and legal fathers (table 4-1). Significant differences were found in age. Legal birth fathers were on average slightly older than alleged fathers. Legal fathers were also more likely to be white and not Hispanic. Differences in level of education, marital status, and living situation cannot be examined due to high levels of "don't know" responses for cases with alleged fathers.[57]

Table 4-1. Nonresident Father Characteristics—Legal and Alleged Fathers.

	Legal fathers (N= 1,240) %	Alleged fathers (N=481) %
Age (mean)	37.0**	34.0
Race		
White	60.3**	38.3
African American	21.7	26.2
American Indian or Alaskan Native	2.4	1.5
Asian	.7	.3
Mixed	.9	1.1
Other	1.7	3.1
Don't know	12.2**	29.5
Spanish, Hispanic, or Latino origin	17.5**	29.2
U.S. citizenship		
Yes	81.9	55.0
No	3.4	5.4
Don't know	14.7	39.6
Highest level of education (% don't know)	62.7	87.0

Based on t-tests, statistically significant differences between the alleged and legal father groups are denoted as * = $p < .05$ and ** = $p < .01$.

Locating methods

Overall, caseworkers reported that fewer alleged fathers than legal fathers had been located at case opening: over half (62%) of legal fathers compared to 29 percent of alleged fathers.[58] Methods used to locate nonresident fathers are shown in table 4-2. As shown, caseworkers reported asking mothers for help locating the child's father in the vast majority of both groups of fathers (85% and 87%). The same holds true for asking children for help locating their fathers. In similar portions of both groups of fathers, workers asked children for help (34%).

Workers did report searching public aid records (30%** vs. 41%, $p < .01$), DMV records (19%** vs. 26%, $p < .05$), and use of the state parent locator (27%** vs. 42%, $p < .01$), more frequently in alleged father cases than legal fathers.

Not shown in table 4-2 is the percentage of sources that provided location information. As one might expect, caseworkers reported that mothers, mother's relatives, other workers, children, and siblings were all more likely to provide locate information for legal fathers than for alleged fathers. And, while use of some sources was more prevalent among cases involving alleged fathers, law enforcement records and public aid records were more likely to provide locate information for legal fathers than alleged fathers.

Table 4-2. Locating Methods—Legal and Alleged Nonresident Fathers.

	Legal fathers (N=465) %	Alleged fathers (N=337) %
Who was asked about father's location? (all that apply)		
Child's mother	84.9	87.4
Another worker	37.8	42.8
Mother's relatives	27.4	41.4
Child (only asked if child is age 7 or older)	34.0	34.7
Father's relatives	26.7**	12.2
Child's sibling (only asked if child had siblings)	9.1	10.4
Other	28.0	32.1
What records were searched? (all that apply)		
Law enforcement records	45.3	43.3
Birth certificate, vital stats	39.8	44.9
Public aid (TANF, Food stamps, Medicaid)	29.7**	40.7
Telephone books	27.6	34.8
DMV records	18.9*	26.3
Utility company records	9.0	13.7
Other	21.2	22.2
Locating resources utilized (all that apply)		
State parent locator	26.6**	42.4
Federal parent locator	5.7	9.9
Other locating resource	6.4	9.2

Based on t-tests, statistically significant differences between the alleged and legal father groups are denoted as * = $p < .05$ and ** = $p < .01$.

Barriers to contact

Barriers to contact with the worker were also examined for the alleged and legal fathers; however, "don't know" responses accounted for the majority of responses for alleged fathers. This is predictable if caseworkers have not yet determined if the alleged father is the child's legal father, the worker is likely to know less about the father. The percent of "don't know" responses for alleged fathers ranged from a low of 14 percent for "unreachable by phone" to a high of 71 percent for "problem transportation."

One noteworthy finding was that incarceration made contact difficult more frequently in cases involving alleged versus legal fathers (66%** vs. 50%, $p < .0 1$). This is likely the result of limitations on staff visits and contact with fathers who have not established paternity. Policies and procedures for prison visitation by caseworkers and by children are variable across states, communities, and individual jail or prison facilities.[59]

Problems

Large numbers of "don't know" responses also made examining differences in problem areas and in services offered to legal and alleged fathers difficult to interpret. Due to frequent "don't know" responses for alleged fathers, legal fathers (for whom more caseworkers answered the questions) were reported as being more likely to have each of the problems. As noted earlier, both groups represent "contacted" fathers; however, alleged fathers were less likely to have been contacted and thus are disproportionately represented.

Engagement

We conducted analyses to examine agency engagement with both groups of fathers. As shown in table 4-3, the overwhelming majority of both groups of nonresident fathers was told of the outof-home placement and shared the case plan. [60] However, significant differences exist between the two groups of fathers in the father's interest in the child living with him and the agency considering placing the child with him. [61] Both of these questions had similar, low percentages of "don't know" responses for both groups. Not shown in table 4-3 is the percentage of fathers assessed by the agency. If considered as a placement resource, legal fathers were more likely to be assessed by the agency than alleged fathers (89%* vs. 73%, $p < .05$). Caseworkers also reported legal fathers were far more likely to have provided financial or non-financial support since the case opened. [62]

We asked caseworkers about the status of the relationship between the father and mother for a number of reasons (table 4-4). For many nonresident fathers, the mothers of their children have considerable control over when and if he visits the child. While the children in the study sample are in out-of-home placement, the relationship between the father and mother may still impact the father's engagement with his child. Though caseworkers noted a greater percent of alleged fathers never talk to the mother of their child (43%** vs. 32%, $p < .01$), a small, but statistically significant percentage of legal fathers were reported to be in a "hostile" relationship with the mother of their child (1 4%* * vs. 3%, $p < .01$). A similar percentage of legal fathers were reported by caseworkers to be "just friends" with the mother of their child (1 0%* * vs. 1%, $p < .01$).

Table 4-3. Nonresident Father Engagement—Legal and Alleged Fathers.

	Legal fathers (N=902) %	Alleged fathers (N= 168) %
Father told of child's out-of-home placement	96.2	94.1
Agency shared plan with fathers	93.4	93.8
Father expressed interest in child living with him	54.2**	31.0
Agency considered placing child with father	47.5**	32.5
Agency considered placing child with paternal relatives[a]	55.9*	43.2
Agency sought health care coverage from father as part of case plan	16.1 * *	5.1
Agency sought financial assistance as part of case plan	38.1 *	28.8
Father ever provided financial support	33.6**	5.5
Father ever provided non-financial support	35.8**	9.6

Based on t-tests, statistically significant differences between the alleged and legal father groups are denoted as * = $p < .05$ and ** = $p < .01$.

[a] Only asked of cases in which the child was not in paternal kin placement.

Table 4-4. Mother-Father Relationship—Legal and Alleged Fathers.

	Legal fathers (N=1,005) %	Alleged fathers (N=292) %
Never talk to each other	32.1**	42.7
Hardly ever talk to each other	19.6	17.7
Hostile toward each other	13.6**	3.4
Just friends	9.3**	1.2
On-again/off-again relationship	6.0	7.0
Steady relationship	4.1 *	1.8
Other	8.2	13.1
Don't know	7.2	13.7

Based on t-tests, statistically significant differences between the alleged and legal father groups are denoted as * = p < .05 and ** = p < .01.

Table 4-5. Status of Parental Rights—Legal and Alleged Nonresident Fathers.

	Legal fathers (N= 1,239)%	Alleged fathers (N= 716) %
Still has parental rights	71.1 **	57.2
Father's rights were terminated	17.0**	25.8
Father relinquished his rights	6.1	2.4
Don't know	5.8	14.4

Based on t-tests, statistically significant differences between the alleged and legal father groups are denoted as * = p < .05 and ** = p < .01.

Termination of parental rights

Even when paternity has not been established (i.e., the child's father is "alleged") or in cases where the father is unknown, a father's parental rights can be terminated. However, as expected, legal fathers retained their parental rights more often than alleged fathers (71%** vs. 57%, p < .01) (See table 4-5). Caseworkers reported that parental rights had been terminated for one- quarter of alleged fathers.

Nonresident fathers vs. nonresident mothers

As noted in chapter 3, cases involving "nonresident" mothers were identified during interviews with caseworkers.[63] Because these cases involved both mothers and fathers who were not living in the same household as the child prior to the child's removal from the home, agency and worker practices toward these two groups of parents may be similar.

Nonresident mothers differ slightly from resident mothers (see tables 3-7 through 3-12 for a complete description of resident mothers). Nonresident mothers were slightly older (34 vs. 32) and more likely to be African American (26% vs. 20%) and Hispanic origin (23% vs. 18%). As one would expect, the percent of "don't know" responses are greater in some categories for cases with nonresident mothers. Caseworkers did not know the nonresident mother's level of education for more than half (52%) of cases compared to 26 percent for resident mothers. The percentage of "don't know" responses was also greater for living situation and marital status of nonresident mothers compared to resident mothers.

Identifying and locating methods

Only 5 of the 323 (1.5%) nonresident mothers were unidentified at case opening compared to 446 of the 1,958 (23%) nonresident fathers. Comparative analyses on identification methods between unidentified nonresident mothers and fathers cannot be conducted because of the very small number of nonresident mothers unidentified at case opening. Nonresident mothers were more likely to have been located at case opening compared to nonresident fathers (78%** vs. 52%, $p < .01$).[64] While caseworkers asked the same types of individuals and used similar resources in trying to locate both nonresident fathers and nonresident mothers, though they asked more frequently for nonresident mothers. For example, workers reported searching public aid records for both nonresident mothers and nonresident fathers but more frequently for nonresident mothers (51 %* vs. 34%, $p < .05$). Children were more likely to be asked to help locate their nonresident mother than nonresident father (62%** vs. 34%, $p < .01$). Siblings were also more likely to be asked to help locate nonresident mothers (26%* vs. 10%, $p < .05$).

Barriers to contact

Among parents identified by caseworkers, nonresident mothers appear to share circumstances with nonresident fathers that might pose barriers to contact by caseworkers (see table 4-6). For both, workers most frequently noted that the nonresident parent was unreachable by telephone, which caused the most difficulty (94% and 95% respectively) for contact. It is important to note that in all the categories caseworkers responded "don't know" more often for nonresident fathers than for nonresident mothers.[65] Overall, nonresident fathers were more likely to be out of state. Among parents for whom caseworkers had some information, nonresident mothers were more likely to be incarcerated (40%* vs. 31%, $p < .05$) and have transportation and housing issues.

Table 4-6. Barriers to Contact—Nonresident Fathers and Nonresident Mothers.

Type of circumstance (all that apply)	Nonresident mother (N=281) %	Nonresident father (N= 1,719) %
Unreachable by phone	66.3	59.9
Out of state	23.9*	31.4
Incarceration	39.2*	30.5
Problem transportation	50.1 **	21.5
Homeless/unstable address	39.2**	10.6
Out of country	3.4	5.1
Language barrier	1.8	3.1

Based on t-tests, statistically significant differences between the alleged and legal father groups are denoted as * = $p < .05$ and ** = $p < .01$.

Problems and services

Caseworkers reported more problems for nonresident mothers than nonresident fathers on all problems except criminal justice involvement (table 4-7). The percent of "don't know" responses was greater for nonresident father cases than for nonresident mothers. The percentage of "don't know" responses for nonresident fathers ranged from 9 to 18 percent for the types of problems.[66] While caseworkers reported a lower percentage of "don't know" responses for nonresident mothers, the same categories elicited the least (prior finding of abuse) and the greatest (domestic violence) number of "don't knows." It is also important to note that the phrasing of the question may have impacted caseworker response. Caseworkers were asked about problems of each parent that made the child's placement with them difficult.[67]

Engagement

For those with contact, caseworkers were as likely to tell a nonresident mother as a nonresident father that her child is in out-of-home care (98% vs. 96%, respectively, see table 4-8). Workers also share the case plan with an equally large percentage of nonresident mothers as nonresident fathers. There is, however, a large difference in the percent of workers noting that the nonresident mother has expressed an interest in having the child live with her, compared to the nonresident fathers (68%** vs. 50%., $p < .01$). Similar percentages of nonresident mothers and nonresident fathers were considered as a placement resource by caseworkers (52% vs. 45%).

While caseworkers noted more nonresident fathers had provided financial support since the case opened, nonresident mothers were somewhat more likely to have provided non-financial support to the child.

Table 4-7. Problems—Nonresident Mothers and Nonresident Fathers.

Type of problem (all that apply)	Nonresident mothers (N=251) %	Nonresident fathers (N=1,071) %
Alcohol/drugs	79.0**	58.2
Criminal justice involvement	50.5	52.5
Inadequate housing/homelessness	66. 8**	41.7
Unemployment	68.5**	40.1
Domestic violence	37.4	33.3
Prior finding of abuse/neglect	59.7**	29.6
Mental/physical health	53.3**	22.9
No child care	33.1**	21.2
Agency offered services for all problems	*80.5***	*58.6*
Father/mother complied with all services offered	*31.7*	*22.5*

Note. Caseworkers were asked about the problem areas of fathers/mothers with whom they had been in contact (N=1,071 fathers, 251 mothers). If a father had a problem in one or more areas, workers were asked whether or not services were offered to him/her (N=929 fathers, 241 mothers). If services were offered, workers were asked whether or not he/she complied with provided services (N=522 fathers, 187 mothers).

Based on t-tests, statistically significant differences between the alleged and legal father groups are denoted as * = p < .05 and ** = p < .01.

Table 4-8. Engagement—Nonresident Mothers and Nonresident Fathers.

	Nonresident mothers (N=251) %	Nonresident fathers (N= 1,071) %
Father (mother) told of child's out-of-home placement	97.7	95.9
Agency shared plan with fathers (mothers)	96.0	93.5
Father (mother) expressed interest in child living with him (her)	68.4**	50.3
Agency considered placing child with father (mother)	51.6	45.1
Agency considered placing child with paternal (maternal) relatives[a]	54.1	53.9
Agency sought health care coverage from father (mother) as part of the case plan	12.4	14.3
Agency sought financial assistance from father (mother) as part of the case plan	35.5	36.6
Father (mother) ever provided financial support	23.6	29.0
Father (mother) ever provided non-financial support	36.1	31.5

[a] Only asked of cases in which the child was not in paternal (maternal) kin placement.

Based on t-tests, statistically significant differences between the alleged and legal father groups are denoted as * = p < .05 and ** = p < .01.

Table 4-9. Status of Parental Rights—Nonresident Mothers and Nonresident Fathers.

	Nonresident mother (N=283) %	Nonresident father (N= 1,955) %
Still has parental rights	73.4*	65.9
Parental rights were terminated	18.3	20.3
Father (mother) relinquished his (her) rights	6.7	4.8
Don't know	1.7**	9.0

Based on t-tests, statistically significant differences between the alleged and legal father groups are denoted as * = p < .05 and ** = p < .01.

Termination of parental rights

An examination of termination of parental rights (table 4-9) found that while there was a slight difference in percentages of nonresident mothers and nonresident fathers who retained rights to their child in foster care, a greater percentage of "don't know" responses for nonresident father cases could mediate this finding.

Visitation

Overall, a greater percentage of nonresident mothers had visited with the child at least once since case opening (77%** vs. 56%, $p < .01$).[68] Caseworkers report that nonresident mothers have similar attendance at planned visits to nonresident fathers (i.e., always, sometimes, or rarely attends planned visits). Nonresident mothers are more likely than nonresident fathers to have phone contact with their children (49%** vs. 28%, $p < .01$).

Fathers as Placement Resources

Caseworkers were asked whether the agency had ever considered placing the child with his or her father. Cases in which the agency had considered placing the child with his or her father were grouped as "placement father" cases. Cases in which the caseworker responded "no" were assigned to the "non-placement father" group.[69] Analyses were conducted to examine differences between the two groups of fathers.

Demographic characteristics

Few differences were found in the demographic characteristics of placement and non-placement fathers.[70] We examined marital status to determine whether there were any differences between the two groups. Previous research has noted the presence of a female partner to be a factor in whether fathers gain custody of their children (Greif and Zuravin, 1989). Significant differences were found in the nonresident fathers in our study sample. Nonresident fathers considered for placement were more likely to be living with another woman (27%** vs. 17%, $p < .01$). Fathers considered for placement were also more likely to be divorced from the child's mother (1 6%** vs. 8%, $p < .01$).

Barriers to contact

Caseworkers noted circumstances that might pose barriers for contact with nonresident fathers of children in foster care. Table 4-10 provides the results from comparative analysis of placement and non-placement groups of cases. Significant differences were found in frequency of incarceration and being unreachable by phone. Fathers considered for placement were less likely to be incarcerated at some point during the case (27%** vs. 47%, $p < .01$) and less likely to be unreachable by phone (47%* vs. 57%, $p < .01$).

Table 4-10. Barriers to Contact—Fathers Considered as Placement Resources.

Type of circumstance (all that apply)	Father was considered for placement (N=493)%	Father was not considered for placement (N=557) %
Unreachable by phone	47.1 **	57.1
Out of state	27.5	26.2
Incarceration	26.8**	46.8
Problem transportation	29.9	29.3
Homeless/unstable address	14.4	15.4
Out of country	2.2	3.6
Language barrier	2.7	4.3

Note. Caseworkers responded "don't know" to the question regarding whether the agency had considered the father as a placement resource in 21 identified and contacted father cases.

Based on t-tests, statistically significant differences between the alleged and legal father groups are denoted as * = p < .05 and ** = p < .01.

Table 4-11. Engagement—Placement and Non-placement Father Cases.

	Father considered for placement (N= 493) %	Father not considered for placement (N=557) %
Father told of child's out-of-home placement	98.0**	94.1
Agency shared plan with fathers	99.0**	89.1
Father expressed interest in child living with him	77.2**	28.6
Agency considered placing child with paternal relatives [a]	61.1 **	47.4
Agency sought health care coverage from father as part of the case plan	19.1**	9.9
Agency sought financial assistance from father as part of the case plan	48.2**	26.7
Father ever provided financial support	39.0**	20.5
Father ever provided non-financial support	45.5**	20.4

Note. Caseworkers responded "don't know" to the question regarding whether the agency had considered the father as a placement resource in 21 identified and contacted father cases.

[a] Only asked of cases in which the child was not in paternal or maternal kin placement.

Based on t-tests, statistically significant differences between the alleged and legal father groups are denoted as * = $p < .05$ and ** = $p < .01$.

Problems and services

Due to the large percent of "don't know" responses for non-placement father cases, examining data on problem areas across the two groups of cases is difficult. Overall, the data suggest that workers reported more problems for fathers with whom the agency considered placing the child. As discussed in the overview section of this chapter, caseworkers are likely to have less contact with fathers with whom the agency did not consider placing the child and thus, less likely to know of the father's problems. In only one category—mental/physical health problems—did caseworkers report a higher percentage for fathers not considered for placement.[71] Workers reported mental/physical health issues for 22 percent of fathers considered for placement and 35 percent of fathers not considered for placement.

Engagement

As shown in table 4-11, fathers with whom the agency considered placing the child were significantly more likely to have been told about the child's placement even though both groups were told in over 90 percent of the cases. Caseworkers noted sharing the case plan more often with these fathers as well. Perhaps not surprising is that a greater percent of fathers considered for placement expressed an interest in the child living with them, according to caseworkers (77%** vs. 29%, $p < .01$). Fathers considered for placement were more likely to provide financial support (39%** vs. 21%, $p < .01$) and non-financial support (46%** vs. 20%, $p < .01$).

Case Characteristics

Kin vs. Non-kin Placement

We examined cases where children were placed in kin and non-kin placements to determine whether differences exist. First, we examined methods of identifying and locating nonresident fathers by type of placement. We also examined father-child visitation by whether the child was in a kinship or non-kinship placement. In addition, we examined problems or issues for nonresident fathers of children in the two types of foster care placements.

Identifying and locating fathers

Methods of identifying nonresident fathers did not differ greatly by whether or not the child was placed with kin. Not surprisingly, workers did seek help from the mother's relatives to identify the father in cases in which the child was living with kin (54%* vs. 41%, $p < .05$). There were more significant differences found in locating methods. As with identifying, caseworkers noted seeking the help of the mother's relatives more often in cases in which the child was living with kin (51%** vs. 27%, $p < .01$). They also more frequently noted seeking help with locating from the father's relatives (27%* vs. 18%, $p < .05$).

Workers also were more likely to search law enforcement (54%* * vs. 41%, p < .01), DMV (31%** vs. 19%, $p < .01$) and public aid (48%** vs. 30%, $p < .01$) records for nonresident fathers of children placed with kin. State and federal parent locator services were used more often for locating nonresident fathers of children placed with kin (state: 49%** vs. 28%, $p < .01$ and federal: 13%* vs. 5%, $p < .05$).

Visitation

As shown in table 4-12, caseworkers noted only a slightly greater percentage of cases in which the father is visiting the child if the child is in a kinship placement. Nonresident fathers with children in kinship placements were also more likely than their counterparts with children in non-kin placements to have always or almost always attended visits. Caseworkers reported that children living with kin were almost twice as likely than children living in a non-kin placement to visit with their father weekly or more frequently (45%** vs. 24%, $p < .01$). Telephone contact between child and father was only slightly more likely when the child was in a kinship placement (31% vs. 27%).

Fathers' problems

Overall, caseworkers' reports of fathers' problems did not differ greatly by whether or not the child was living with kin. However, a greater percentage of fathers of children placed in kinship care were reported to have problems with alcohol/drug use compared to fathers of children in non-kin care but the difference is not significant.[72]

Table 4-12. Father-Child Visitation—Children in Kin and Non-kin Placements.

	Child in kinship placement (N= 512) %	Child in non-kinship placement (N=1,432) %
Percent of fathers who have visited with child (since case opening)	60.0	53.8
Visitation (w/in past 6 months)		
Always or almost always attends planned visits	46.9	37.1
Sometimes attends	16.5	13.3
Rarely attends	11.8	14.3
Never attends or has no planned visits	22.3	31.6
Don't know	2.6	3.7
Frequency of visitation (w/in past 6 months)		
No visits	3.6	7.3
One visit	16.2	23.4
Monthly	21.4	24.2
Twice a month	10.6	18.3
Weekly	25.5*	15.8
More than once a week	19.0*	8.5
Don't know	3.7	2.5

Note. Of the 1,958 nonresident father cases, caseworkers responded "don't know" for the type of placement the child is currently residing in 14 cases.

Based on t-tests, statistically significant differences between the alleged and legal father groups are denoted as * = $p < .05$ and ** = $p < .01$.

Case Plan Goal

As discussed in chapter 3, the most common permanency goal for children in the study was reunification with the mother (35%); the second most common was a non-relative adoptive placement (19%). We examined locate methods for both groups of cases and found few differences between the two groups.

Cases with a goal of reunification with the mother were more likely than cases with a goal of adoption by a non-relative to have a father located at case opening (55%** vs. 45%, $p < .01$). While few differences were found in the types of resources contacted (e.g., law enforcement or DMV records) and use of state and federal parent locator services, a significant difference was found with regard to asking the child. Cases with a goal of reunification with the mother were more likely than cases with a goal of non-relative adoption to seek help from the child in locating the father (38%** vs. 15%, $p < .01$).

Length of Placement

We categorized cases according to whether, at the time of sampling, the child had been in foster care more or less than one year.[73] We thought that identifying and locating methods might be different based on length of placement. While there were few differences in the methods used to identify nonresident fathers between the two groups of cases there were several differences found in locating methods. The only significant difference found in identifying methods was that cases in which the child had been in care for more than one year were more likely to have sought help identifying the father from another worker (47%* vs. 34%, $p < .05$).

Children in care less than one year were more likely to have had a father located at case opening than children in care for more than one year (56%* vs. 48%, $p < .05$). We also found differences in locating methods. Caseworkers reporting on children in placement more than one year were more likely to search all types of locating resources including law enforcement records (51%** vs. 39%, $p < .01$), public aid records (43%** vs. 26%, $p < .01$), phone book (36%* vs. 26%, $p < .05$), DMV records (29%** vs. 16%, $p < .01$), and utility records (16%** vs. 6%, $p < .01$). State and federal parent locator resources were also more likely to be used with cases in out-of-home placement for longer periods of time. Caseworkers noted that state and federal parent locator resources were used more frequently for cases of children in placement more than one year (state: 40%** vs. 26%, $p < .01$, federal: 10%* vs. 5%, $p < .05$).[74]

Age of Child

We examined possible differences in how workers seek out and involve fathers of younger and older children by categorizing children into two age groups—0 to 5 years and 6 years and older—to determine whether differences could be detected on a number of casework dimensions. The two groups of children had similar case lengths—children 5 and younger had an average case length of 1.8 years while children 6 and older had an average case length of 2.2 years.

The two groups of children did not differ in terms of visits with the father. Caseworkers reported 54 percent of fathers of children 0 to 5 had visited their child since case opening and 56 percent of fathers of children over 5 years of age had visited. As expected, workers reported a larger percent of fathers had had phone contact with older children (32%** vs. 9%, $p < .01$). Identifying and locating methods were similar for the two groups of cases except where differences were expected because of younger children's developmental limitations (e.g., workers reported asking siblings for help identifying fathers more often in older child cases). Other slight differences were likely the result of a somewhat longer case length for older children. For example, for cases involving older children, more caseworkers reported not knowing when in the case process the father was identified. Caseworkers were also more likely to respond "don't know" to a number of the questions about methods used to locate the father on cases involving older children (e.g., Were father's relatives sought for assistance in locating the father?). The number and frequency of fathers' problems did not appear to differ much between the two groups of child cases.

Caseworker Characteristics

Results of analyses of the worker subgroups are presented below. Findings of analyses by caseworkers' gender are presented first. Then caseworkers were grouped by whether or not they received training in involving fathers and their opinions about working with nonresident fathers.[75]

Gender

Overall, there were only slight differences between male and female caseworkers on most casework dimensions. [76] Similar percentages of cases for both male and female caseworkers involved sharing the case plan with the father, telling the father his child was in out-of-home placement, and fathers expressing interest in having his child live with him. The one significant difference was with regard to the agency considering placing the child with the father. Cases with male caseworkers were more likely to have fathers considered as a placement resource (55%** vs. 43%, $p < .01$). Cases with male and female caseworkers had similar percentages of fathers who had contact with the agency and fathers who visited with their children since case opening.

More specific analyses of different identifying and locating methods (e.g., Did the worker ask the mother for help identifying/locating the father?) revealed only one significant difference. The one difference noted was that cases with male caseworkers were less likely to have obtained identifying information from the child (6%** vs. 28%, $p < .01$).

Worker Training

Worker training did appear to impact some casework practices. [77] Differences were found between cases with workers who had received training on identifying, locating, and engaging nonresident fathers and cases in which the worker did not receive training. Workers were more likely to seek assistance with locating the father from other workers, the mother's relatives and father's relatives in cases in which the worker reported having received training. Workers were also more likely to report having used telephone books to locate the father in cases involving trained workers. The case plan was more likely to be shared in cases involving a worker who reported receiving training than in cases in which the worker did not receive training (95%** vs. 89%, $p < .01$). These workers were also more likely to report that the agency had considered placing the child with the father (48%** vs. 37%, $p < .01$), the father had expressed in interest in having the child live with him (53%* vs. 43%, $p < .05$), and the agency sought financial assistance from the father as part of the plan (40%** vs. 27%, $p < .01$). A significant difference was also found between the two groups of cases with regard to whether a CPS clearance check was performed on the nonresident father for whom placement was considered (86%* vs. 74%, $p < .05$).

While cases with workers who received training were somewhat more likely than other cases to have fathers who had visited with their child (58% vs. 51%), the difference was not significant. A greater percentage of cases with trained workers had a nonresident father whose location was known at case opening (54%* vs. 48%, $p < .05$). Methods used to identify fathers were similar across the two groups of workers. However, significant differences were found with methods used for locating fathers—seeking help from father's relatives (25%** vs. 10%, $p < .01$), seeking help from another worker (43%* vs. 34%, $p < .05$), and searching public aid records (38%** vs. 26%, $p < .01$), and telephone books (38%** vs. 26%, $p < .01$).

Caseworker Opinions

Caseworker opinions about father involvement do not appear to have a large impact on casework practices identifying and locating nonresident fathers. As noted previously, workers were grouped according to their responses to a series of opinion questions. [78] The two groups of caseworkers reported similar percentages of fathers being told about the child's out-of-home placement and sharing the case plan with the father. The first group of workers was more likely to report the agency considered placing the child with the father (49%** vs. 34%, $p < .01$).

Slight differences, though not significant, were found with fathers expressing interest in having his child live with him. Fifty-three percent of cases with workers who reported positive opinions had fathers who had expressed an interest in his child living with him while only 47 percent of the cases with workers who reported less positive opinions did.

Very few differences were noted in how workers identified and located nonresident fathers. The one significant difference found between the two groups of workers involved locating methods. Workers with more positive opinions reported searching public aid records more often than other workers (39%**, 23%, $p < .01$).

Multivariate Analyses

In this section we present findings from multivariate analyses examining factors associated with identified father cases, cases in which the nonresident father is reported to be visiting with his child, and cases in which the nonresident father is reported to be supporting his child. Three logistic regression models are presented.

Sample

As discussed in detail in chapter 1, the sample consists of data on 1,958 cases obtained during telephone interviews with caseworkers in each of the four study states—Arizona, Massachusetts, Minnesota, and Tennessee.[79] Sampled cases met a variety of criteria. The one criterion unique to this sample of foster care children is that in each case the biological father was a nonresident, i.e., not living in the home from which the child was removed. Chapter 3 presents findings from detailed descriptive analyses of the sample.

The three models presented use samples of different sizes due to the way in which the caseworker questionnaire was structured. In all 1,958 cases, caseworkers were asked questions about whether or not the nonresident father was identified. However, questions on father-child visitation and father support were only asked if cases involved identified fathers and fathers with whom the agency or worker had contact. [80] Thus, while the samples are smaller, the number of independent variables is greater for the models on visitation and support. The father identification model, while using a larger sample, contains fewer independent variables.[81]

Measures

The analyses focused on three dependent measures: fathers who were identified; fathers who were reported to be visiting their children twice a month or more; and fathers who were reported to be providing financial or non-financial support[82] to their children. Because of the exploratory nature of this study, we chose to incorporate a large number of independent variables in the logistic regression models. Categories of independent variables include case characteristics and characteristics of the children, fathers, and caseworkers.

Case characteristics include state, case length, the type of maltreatment, perpetrator, current placement type, permanency goal, and whether the case had a resident mother (the mother was in the home from which the child was removed).[83] Child characteristics include gender, age, and race. Caseworker characteristics include gender, race, years of experience in the child welfare field, and whether the worker received training on how to identify, locate, and involve nonresident fathers. Father characteristics include age, type of father (alleged or legal), whether he still maintains parental rights to the child[84], whether he was ever married to the mother of the child, whether he ever expressed interest in his child living with him, and whether or not the agency ever considered placing the child with his or her father.[85] We also recoded variables on circumstances that could be barriers to contact between the father and agency (see chapter 3 page 83) to create a multi-circumstance variable. Three or more circumstances, regardless of whether the caseworker reported it as a barrier, were considered to be multi- circumstance cases. Caseworkers reported on fathers' problems that were reasons why the child could not be placed with him (see chapter 3 page 88). Three or more problem areas were recoded as a multi-problem father case. [86] We also include a relationship variable. This variable was coded from caseworker responses to a question about the relationship between the nonresident father and birth mother of the child.[87]

Lastly, father support and father visitation variables were included. As mentioned earlier, the father support variable was defined to include fathers providing financial support or non-financial support. Father visitation was defined in two different ways. For the dependent variable used in the father visiting model, visitation was defined as cases in which caseworkers reported fathers visiting their child twice a month or more. However, for the independent variable used in the family support model, a more generic definition was used. Using the frequency of visits definition of father visitation made the number of usable observations extremely low so the definition used in the family support model was broadened to include cases in which the caseworker reported the father had ever visited the child since case opening.

Analyses

We conducted logistic regression analysis to examine which factors were associated with our three dependent measures. We ran three separate models to measure the relative odds that a father would be identified, visiting, or supporting his child. It is important to note that the cross- sectional dataset does not allow examination of the timing of events. Without knowledge of the timing of caseworker decisions and other events such as termination of parental rights, causality cannot be determined for associated factors.

Results

Results from a logistic regression model examining factors associated with father identification are shown in table 4-13. Several independent variables were found to be significant. Two child characteristics—age and race—were significant. Case characteristics found to be significant include current placement type and whether the case had a resident mother. Caseworker characteristics found to be significant include gender and race.

The child's age was positively associated with an identified father. Older children had an increased likelihood of having an identified father. Cases involving African American and Hispanic children were associated with decreased odds of having an identified father. Cases in which the child was in a non-relative foster placement, adoption or guardianship placement, or other placement[88] were also associated with decreased odds of having an identified father compared to children in relative foster care. Cases in which there was a resident mother (child was removed from a home in which the child's mother resides) were associated with increased odds of having an identified father than cases involving nonresident mothers. Cases involving male caseworkers and African American caseworkers (compared to white caseworkers) were associated with decreased odds of having an identified father.

Table 4-14 presents results from a logistic regression model identifying factors associated with father visitation. Multiple factors were found to be associated with whether or not a nonresident father is visiting his child. [89] Several factors were associated with increased odds of the father visiting using the reference variables presented. Compared to cases in Massachusetts, Arizona cases were more likely to have a father visiting his child. Cases with a goal of reunifying with the father or placement/guardianship with a relative were also associated with increased odds of having a father visiting. Cases with fathers who were older, who had expressed an interest in the child living with him, or who had provided support to the child were all more likely to have a visiting father. Cases involving fathers with multiple problems were also more likely to have a visiting father. [90] Cases with Hispanic caseworkers were also more likely to have a visiting father.

Factors associated with decreased odds of father visits include cases involving older children, cases with the father as perpetrator, cases in which the father had multiple circumstances that could pose barriers to contact, and cases with more experienced caseworkers. In addition, cases in which the current placement type was "other", the child's permanency goal was non-relative adoption as a permanency goal, and cases where the mother resided in the home at the time of the child's removal were less likely to have a visiting father.

Results from a logistic regression on father support[91] are provided in table 4-15. Multiple factors were associated with whether or not the father is supporting the child. In this model, several case and father characteristics, and one caseworker characteristic were associated with father support. With regard to case characteristics, compared to cases in Massachusetts, Arizona cases were less likely to have a father supporting his child. Cases involving sexual abuse and cases in which the permanency goal was non-relative adoption were both less likely to have a father supporting the child. Father characteristics associated with increased odds of supporting his child include whether he was ever married to the mother, whether he expressed an interest in the child living with him, whether the agency had considered placing the child with him, and whether he has visited with the child. Hispanic workers, compared to white workers, had decreased odds of having a father supporting his child.

Discussion

As discussed earlier in this chapter, the lack of previous research on father involvement within the child welfare system means we must rely on our anecdotal knowledge of practice to examine and interpret these findings. Father identification and a father visiting with the child appear to have some association with characteristics of the child, case, and caseworker. Father support appears to have some association with case and caseworker characteristics, as well as father characteristics.

It is important to note again that the lack of data on father characteristics available for inclusion on the father identification regression model (due to not being able to collect this information on unidentified fathers) limits our ability to interpret the findings from this model. Both African American and Hispanic children are far less likely than white children in the sample to have an identified father. Father's marital status and problems or circumstances faced by fathers may explain these differences.

The findings on caseworker characteristics are also difficult to explain. Cases involving male caseworkers or African American caseworkers compared to white caseworkers were both negatively associated with fathers being identified. Urban/rural differences in casework practices may affect the findings on caseworker race and ethnicity. Additional analyses will be conducted as a follow-up to this study in order to examine urban/rural practice differences.

Findings on case characteristics—current placement type and whether the child's mother was in the home—make practical sense. Compared to children in relative foster care, children in non-relative care or adoption/guardianship homes are less likely to have identified fathers. It is not feasible with these data to determine whether the placement type led to differences in casework practice or whether differences in case circumstances led to a different placement types. For example, caseworkers may be able to more easily identify a child's father when the child is living with kin due to greater access to sources of information. Identifying the child's father would presumably be easier in cases in which the mother was in the home at the time of the child's removal ("resident mother" cases constitute the vast majority of our sample) due to her proximity and the worker's ability to ask the mother for information on the father.

While some findings from the visiting father model seem consistent with anecdotal practice knowledge, other findings are more difficult to interpret. Some factors associated with increased odds of the father visiting are easy to understand—when the child's permanency goal is placement with his or her father, the father is visiting with the child or, given that we do not know the timing of events, it could be that when the father visits the child there is a greater likelihood of the permanency goal being reunification with father. Other findings easy to interpret include cases involving fathers who are providing support to their children and fathers who expressed interest in living with their children were both far more likely to have a father who visited his child.

Factors associated with decreased odds of father visits include a variety of case and father characteristics. Cases with a goal of non-relative adoption were far less likely to have a father visiting his child than a case with reunification with the mother as the goal. Cases involving multiple circumstances that pose barriers to contact between the agency and the father are less likely to have a visiting father. Again, this finding is easy to interpret. A father with whom the agency or worker has difficulty contacting would presumably be less likely to be visiting his child.

The negative association between residential mother cases and the likelihood of a father visiting is difficult to explain. Perhaps the relationship between the mother and father in resident mother cases (i.e., cases in which the child's mother was in the home from which the child was removed), is more hostile or less friendly and therefore the father-child relationship was never formed or continued. Perhaps cases with residential mothers are more likely to involve a stepfather or live-in boyfriend that could negatively affect the father-mother relationship. There could also be unique aspects of the non-resident mother cases such as a greater likelihood of a paternal kinship care placement that could affect visitation positively.

The direction of the effects for fathers' problems were not as expected. Fathers whom caseworkers noted as having multiple problems were more likely to be visiting their child than fathers with fewer problems though the effect is not significant. A caveat to this finding is that a number of caseworkers provided "don't know" responses in answering questions pertaining to problem areas of nonresident fathers (e.g., substance abuse, unemployment, domestic violence). Having more problems identified by the caseworker may merely be the result of greater contact with the caseworker. Visiting fathers may, through greater contact with the caseworker, be described as having more problems than non-visiting fathers. Similar problems were encountered in the interpretation of findings presented earlier in this chapter on fathers with whom the agency considered placing the child (see page 112).

Table 4-13. Factors Associated with Father Identification.

Obs = 1,568		
Variable	**Odds Ratio (SE)**	**Sign. * = p < .05 ** = p < .01**
Child Characteristics		
Age	1.08 (0.02)	**
Male	1.30 (0.23)	
Race[a]		
Black	0.53 (0.12)	**
Hispanic	0.35 (0.12)	**
Other Race	0.95 (0.24)	
White (Reference)		
Case Characteristics		
State		
Minnesota	1.35 (0.45)	
Arizona	0.67 (0.18)	
Tennessee	0.77 (0.20)	
Massachusetts (Reference)		
Length of Case	1.00 (0.01)	
Type of Abuse[b]		
Sexual	0.74 (0.31)	
Neglect	0.86 (0.28)	
Other/No Reported Abuse	0.86 (0.37)	
Physical (Reference)		
Perpetrator of Abuse[c]		
Boyfriend/Stepfather	1.00 (0.33)	
Other Individual(s)	0.97 (0.29)	
Mother (Reference)		
Current Placement		
Non-relative Foster Care	0.62 (0.15)	**
Adoption or Guardianship[d]	0.34 (0.12)	**
Other	0.54 (0.16)	**
Relative Foster Care (Reference)		
Permanency Goal[e]		
Relative Adoption or Guardianship	0.70 (0.19)	
Non-relative Adoption	0.86 (0.23)	
Independent Living/Other	0.80 (0.19)	
Reunify with Mother (Reference)		
Residential Mother[f]	2.10 (0.48)	**

Table 4-13. (Continued).

Variable	Odds Ratio (SE)	Sign. * = p < .05 ** = p < .01
Caseworker Characteristics		
Male	0.67 (0.16)	*
Black	0.48	(0.12) **
Hispanic	0.64	(0.21)
Other	0.65	(0.19)
White (Reference)		
Years in Field	0.98	(0.01)
Received Training on Fathers	0.82	(0.16)

[a] Race- Individuals are classified as White or Black if they report only one race. Individuals reporting multiple races are classified as Other. Any individual reporting that they are Hispanic is classified as Hispanic.

[b] Type of Abuse- Any child for whom sexual abuse was reported was classified as being abused sexually. Children who were abused physically but not sexually were classified as physically abused. Children who were neglected but not sexually or physically abused were classified as neglected. Finally, children who were abused in other ways only or not abused were classified as being victims of other or no abuse.

[c] Perpetrator- Any child reported by the caseworker to have been abused by an individual who was not the mother, father, or the mother's boyfriend/stepfather was classified in the other category. This includes cases in which the perpetrator was reported to be another individual and some combination of mother, father, boyfriend, or stepfather. Cases with no identified perpetrator were also placed in this category. Cases in which children were abused by a stepfather or mother's boyfriend are placed in their own category. Cases were classified as stepfather/boyfriend perpetrator when both the stepfather/boyfriend and mother were reported as perpetrators in the case. Mother perpetrator cases are cases where only the mother is reported as a perpetrator. All cases with the father reported as the perpetrator were identified. The father perpetrator cases were not used in the model.

[d] Includes relative and non-relative adoption/guardianship.

[e] Cases with permanency goal of placement with father were perfectly correlated with father identification and were removed from this model.

[f] Residential Mother-The vast majority of mothers in the cases were residing in the home from which the child was removed. However, there were 323 mothers who did not reside in the home from which the child was removed and these mothers are categorized as "nonresident" mothers. See chapter 3 for a more detailed discussion of the two groups.

Similar to the father identification model, findings on caseworker characteristics are again somewhat difficult to understand in the father visiting model. Cases involving Hispanic caseworkers are much more likely to have a visiting father while cases involving workers with more experience are somewhat less likely to have a visiting father.

Some of the findings from the family support model make practical sense (e.g., the positive association between a father providing support and having been married to the mother at some point, a father expressing interest in the child living with him, or being considered for placement). Other findings such as Arizona cases being less likely to involve a father supporting the child are difficult explain. This finding is particularly troublesome given that Arizona cases were far more likely to have a visiting child and support and visitation were positively associated with each other in both models.

Table 4-14. Factors Associated with Father-Child Visitation.

Obs = 242		
Variable	**Odds Ratio (SE)**	**Sign.* = p < .05** **** = p < .01**
Child Characteristics		
Age	0.86 (0.04)	**
Male	2.12 (0.95)	*
Race[a]		
Black	1.02 (0.58)	
Hispanic	4.08 (4.66)	
Other Race	0.75 (0.54)	
White (Reference)		
Case Characteristics		
State		
Minnesota	1.75 (1.54)	
Arizona	5.15 (3.30)	**
Tennessee	1.68 (1.06)	
Massachusetts (Reference)		
Length of Case	1.00 (0.01)	
Type of Abuse[b]		
Sexual	0.74 (0.54)	
Neglect	0.28 (0.22)	
Other/No Reported Abuse	0.31 (0.30)	
Physical (Reference)		
Perpetrator of Abuse[c]		
Father	0.26 (0.19)	*
Boyfriend/Stepfather	0.35 (0.30)	
Other Individual(s)	0.39 (0.32)	
Mother (Reference)		
Current Placement		
Non-relative Foster Care	0.44 (0.26)	
Adoption or Guardianship[d]	1.90 (3.65)	
Other	0.34 (0.22)	*
Relative Foster Care (Reference)		
Permanency Goal	3.70 (2.63)	*
Reunify with Father	7.69 (6.77)	**
Relative Adoption or Guardianship	0.06 (0.06)	**
Non-relative Adoption	1.43 (0.92)	
Independent Living/Other		
Reunify with Mother (Reference)		
Residential Mother[e]	0.09 (0.08)	**
Father Characteristics		
Birth Father	2.47 (2.94)	

Table 4-14. (Continued).

Obs = 242		
Variable	**Odds Ratio (SE)**	**Sign.*** = p < .05 ** = p < .01
No Longer Has Parental Rights	0.24 (0.24)	
Age	1.05 (0.03)	*
Ever Married to Birth Mother	1.11 (0.54)	
Expressed Interest in Child Living with Him	5.19 (3.74)	**
Agency Considered Father for Placement	0.82 (0.43)	
Multiple Circumstances Affecting Contact[f]	0.05 (0.03)	**
Multiple Problems[g]	3.61 (1.61)	**
Provides Support[h]	4.88 (3.06)	**
Mother and Father Have Good Relationship[i]	1.52 (0.75)	
Caseworker Characteristics		
Male	1.39 (0.94)	
Race		
Black	0.97 (0.54)	
Hispanic	5.30 (4.67)	*
Other	1.31 (0.88)	
White (Reference)		
Years in Field	0.91 (0.03)	**
Received Training on Fathers	0.69 (0.35)	

[a] Race- Individuals are classified as White or Black if the caseworker reported only one of these race categories. Individuals reporting multiple races are classified as Other. Any individual reporting that they are Hispanic is classified as Hispanic.

[b] Type of Abuse- Any case for which sexual abuse was reported was classified as sexual abuse. Cases involving physical abuse but no sexual abuse and cases involving physical abuse and neglect are classified as physical abuse. Cases involving only neglect with no sexual or physical abuse are classified as neglect. Finally, cases involving other types of abuse or cases in which the caseworker reported no abuse were classified as other/no reported abuse.

[c] Perpetrator- Any child reported by the caseworker to have been abused by an individual who was not the mother, father, or the mother's boyfriend/stepfather was classified in the other category. This includes cases in which the perpetrator was reported to be another individual or some combination of mother, father, boyfriend, or stepfather. Cases with no identified perpetrator were also placed in the other category. Children abused by a father and stepfather/boyfriend were also placed in the other category. Cases were classified as father perpetrator when both the father and mother were reported as perpetrators in the case. Cases were classified as stepfather/boyfriend perpetrator when both the stepfather/boyfriend and mother were reported as perpetrators in the case. Mother perpetrator cases are cases where only the mother is reported as a perpetrator.

[d] Includes relative and non-relative adoption/guardianship.

[e] Residential Mother-The vast majority of mothers in the cases were residing in the home from which the child was removed. However, there were 323 mothers who did not reside in the home from which the child was removed and these mothers are categorized as "nonresident" mothers. See chapter 3 for a more detailed discussion of the two groups.

[f] An individual is classified as having multiple circumstances affecting contact if the caseworker notes three or more circumstances. Circumstances include living out of state, living out of the country,

incarceration, homelessness, being unreachable by phone, not having adequate transportation, and having a language barrier.

[g] An individual is classified as having multiple problems affecting the child's placement with him if the caseworker notes three or more problems. Problems include homelessness/inadequate housing, unemployment, abuse or neglect, alcohol/substance abuse, criminal justice involvement, domestic violence, lack of child care, and mental/physical health problems.

[h] Provides either financial or nonfinancial support to child.

[i] A father is classified as having a good relationship with the child's mother if the caseworker reported that they are friends, are romantically involved on a steady basis, or involved in an on-again/off-again romantic relationship.

Table 4-15. Factors Associated with Father Support.

Obs = 406		
Variable	**Odds Ratio (SE)**	**Sign.** * = p < .05 ** = p < .01
Child Characteristics		
Age	0.99 (0.04)	
Male	0.68 (0.21)	
Race[a]		
Black	0.64 (0.26)	
Hispanic	0.80 (0.52)	
Other Race	0.95 (0.42)	
White (Reference)		
Case Characteristics		
State		
Minnesota	1.08 (0.66)	
Arizona	0.40 (0.17)	**
Tennessee	0.86 (0.38)	
Massachusetts (Reference)		
Length of Case	0.99 (0.01)	
IV-E Eligible	0.99 (0.41)	
Type of Abuse[b]		
Sexual	0.24 (0.16)	**
Neglect	0.66 (0.30)	
Other/No Reported Abuse	1.39 (0.99)	
Physical (Reference)		
Perpetrator of Abuse[c]		
Father	0.80 (0.37)	
Boyfriend/Stepfather	0.60 (0.32)	
Other Individual(s)	0.71 (0.35)	
Mother (Reference)		
Current Placement		
Non-relative Foster Care	0.69 (0.27)	
Adoption or Guardianship[d]	0.48 (0.41)	
Other	1.93 (0.93)	

Table 4-15. (Continued).

Obs = 406		
Variable	**Odds Ratio (SE)**	**Sign. * = p < .05 ** = p < .01**
Relative Foster Care (Reference)		
Permanency Goal		
Reunify with Father	2.03 (1.09)	
Relative Adoption or Guardianship	0.69 (0.35)	
Non-relative Adoption	0.34 (0.15)	**
Independent Living/Other	1.49 (0.76)	
Reunify with Mother (Reference)		
Residential Mother[e]	1.74 (0.97)	
Father Characteristics		
Birth Father	2.55 (1.59)	
No Longer Has Parental Rights	0.63 (0.26)	
Age	1.00 (0.02)	
Ever Married to Mother	2.63 (0.94)	**
Expressed Interest in Child Living with Him	2.23 (0.86)	**
Agency Considered Father for Placement	2.42 (0.90)	**
Multiple Circumstances Affecting Contact[f]	0.56 (0.20)	
Multiple Problems[g]	0.64 (0.24)	
Has Visited Child During Case Period	3.74 (1.33)	**
Mother and Father Have Good Relationship[h]	1.04 (0.36)	
Caseworker Characteristics		
Male	0.70 (0.26)	
Race		
Black	1.27 (0.65)	
Hispanic	0.20 (0.13)	**
Other	2.24 (1.25)	
White (Reference)		
Years in Field	0.99 (0.02)	
Received Training	1.04 (0.34)	

[a] Race- Individuals are classified as White or Black if the caseworker reported only one of these race categories. Individuals for whom caseworkers reported multiple races are classified as Other. Any individual reported by the caseworker as Hispanic is classified as Hispanic.

[b] Type of Abuse- Any case for which sexual abuse was reported was classified as sexual abuse. Cases involving physical abuse but no sexual abuse and cases involving physical abuse and neglect are classified as physical abuse. Cases involving only neglect with no sexual or physical abuse are classified as neglect. Finally, cases involving other types of abuse or cases in which the caseworker reported no abuse were classified as other/no reported abuse.

[c] Perpetrator- Any child reported by the caseworker to have been abused by an individual who was not the mother, father, or the mother's boyfriend/stepfather was classified in the other category. This includes cases in which the perpetrator was reported to be another individual or some combination of mother, father, boyfriend, or stepfather. Cases with no identified perpetrator were also placed in the other category. Children abused by a father and stepfather/boyfriend were also placed in the other category. Cases were classified as father perpetrator when both the father and mother were

reported as perpetrators in the case. Cases were classified as stepfather/boyfriend perpetrator when both the stepfather/boyfriend and mother were reported as perpetrators in the case. Mother perpetrator cases are cases where only the mother is reported as a perpetrator.

[d] Includes relative and non-relative adoption/guardianship.

[e] Residential Mother-The vast majority of mothers in the cases were residing in the home from which the child was removed. However, there were 323 mothers who did not reside in the home from which the child was removed and these mothers are categorized as "nonresident" mothers. See chapter 3 for a more detailed discussion of the two groups.

[f] An individual is classified as having multiple circumstances affecting contact if the caseworker notes three or more circumstances. Circumstances include living out of state, living out of the country, incarceration, homelessness, being unreachable by phone, not having adequate transportation, and having a language barrier.

[g] An individual is classified as having multiple problems affecting the child's placement with him if the caseworker notes three or more problems. Problems include homelessness/inadequate housing, unemployment, abuse or neglect, alcohol/substance abuse, criminal justice involvement, domestic violence, lack of child care, and mental/physical health problems.

[h] A father is classified as having a good relationship with the child's mother if the caseworker reported that the mother and father are friends, are romantically involved on a steady basis, or involved in an on-again/off-again romantic relationship.

Type of abuse is difficult to interpret. Cases involving sexual abuse were reported to be less likely to have a father providing support than cases involving physical abuse. It should be noted, however, that the group of cases involving sexual abuse is small and likely to be quite different from the sexual abuse cases in the greater child welfare case population due to our case criteria that the child's father not be living in the home from which the child was removed. The small number of cases in this subgroup may skew these findings.

There are several limitations that affect interpretation of findings from the logistic regression models. Most importantly, in the father identification model there are many father characteristics we were unable to include due to their unavailability in cases involving unidentified fathers. Collection of longitudinal data instead of cross-sectional data would allow examination of causality. We also want to examine rural and urban differences and other measures that may impact on the percent of single-female headed households on the agency's caseload. It seems likely that case practices may differ depending upon the extent to which the caseload is comprised of cases involving nonresident fathers.

Child Support Linkage

As discussed in Chapter 1, the study's child support linkage component was designed to explore how child support resources may assist child welfare caseworkers in identifying, locating, and involving nonresident fathers. Topics of interest include paternity establishment, whether locator resources are utilized, and whether child support orders are established and paid. Determining whether paternity has been established is an important first step to locating and involving fathers. ASFA both allowed and encouraged state child welfare agencies to use the Federal Parent Locator Services (FPLS) employed by child support enforcement programs to locate fathers and other relatives. States can also use their in-state child support locate resources to assist child welfare cases. Additionally, determining whether nonresident fathers are providing financial support to their children could be an important component of a father assessment.

Before we present the findings from the data linkage, we draw on the contextual information obtained through discussions with local child welfare administrators (see chapter 2) to present state-specific child support findings from the case-level data collection. We then present findings from the case linkage.

State-specific Child Support Findings

Results of discussions with local child welfare administrators in the four states are generally consistent with findings from the case-level data collection effort. As discussed in chapter 2, state child welfare agencies vary in the ways they establish paternity, both for purposes of involving a father in a case and for purposes of placement opportunities or relinquishment or termination of parental rights. Generally, local administrators said that workers relied on birth certificates, voluntary recognition of parentage and a mother's word. Case-level data confirmed that workers rely heavily on birth certificates (see table 3-13) but also make use of genetic/DNA testing and voluntary paternity documents in many cases. State laws govern voluntary paternity establishment and court proceedings and voluntary paternity establishments are considered court judgments. Additionally for children born after 1993, a father's name cannot appear on a birth certificate unless a voluntary acknowledgement is filed. These records maybe obtained through the child support agency or directly from the court or state vital records office. DNA testing is not necessary for legal paternity to be established and is generally not used when paternity is established through voluntary acknowledgement.

Arizona administrators noted consistently that workers rely on legal departments or clerical staff to find fathers. They also noted uniform access to the State Parent Locator service for a fee when local area searches yield no results. Case level results show overwhelmingly that in comparison to workers in the other study states, Arizona workers reported high levels of use of state parent locator services (77% compared to 3-12% in the other states) in cases with no father identified at time of case opening. Arizona also had the lowest percent of "don't know" responses for this question. Nine percent of caseworkers in Arizona reported not knowing whether state parent locator services were used compared to 19-30% in the other states.

Recouping foster care expenses from birth parents was also discussed with local administrators. Practices varied across states. Massachusetts's administrators had a negative view of the efficacy of a contracted agency responsible for the recouping costs. Minnesota administrators noted the child support office does try to recoup expenses. Arizona caseworkers are responsible for completing a parental assessment and determining how much each parent can pay. Tennessee administrators discussed caseworkers having to ask judges to order child support payments through the enforcement agency. Using case-level data, there was some variation across states with regard to caseworkers noting that seeking financial assistance from the father was part of the case plan (10% in Massachusetts to a high of 21% in Minnesota).[92]

An issue that is of concern when discussing establishing child support orders is whether or not the father has a history of domestic violence, specifically, whether ordering child support may heighten the risk of domestic violence to the child's mother or other guardian. Over the past two decades, Massachusetts has been identified as a state with policies in place to address domestic violence and its overlap with child maltreatment and the impact on families served by child welfare agencies (Findlater et al. 1999). This history of awareness and training may be reflected in the administrator interviews and case-level data. While nearly all administrators in local Massachusetts offices mentioned serving birth parents with a history of domestic violence, the same was not true for the other three states. Administrators in the other states, while mentioning domestic violence, did not do so as consistently as administrators in Massachusetts. In addition, administrators in Massachusetts noted creating separate case plans for each parent in order to not compromise confidentiality or otherwise renew conflict between parents. Domestic violence was identified as a problem area for nonresident fathers in all study states; however, Massachusetts and Minnesota caseworkers were more likely to identify domestic violence (44% of cases in Massachusetts and 43% in Minnesota identified domestic violence as a problem area for the nonresident father, compared to approximately 30% in Arizona and Tennessee).

During the early phases of the study there was discussion of whether child support officials would choose to establish a child support case on a nonresident parent identified through the study's data linkage process. No state decided to pursue such activity; however, screener questions were added to the caseworker questionnaire so that any caseworker concerns about risk to the mother or child would be addressed. Thus, before sending a data file to the child support agencies in each study state, a percentage of cases were removed. Cases in which the caseworker did not know if there was risk were also removed.[93] In each state between 30 and 32 percent of all completed eligible cases were excluded from the linkage.[94]

Child Support Case Match and Data Consistency

The caseworker survey collected data on a number of issues important to the child support field—paternity, locate activities, financial and non-financial support provided by the father. The linkage component was designed to match survey cases with cases from the states' child support administrative data systems. The caseworker survey data was then checked against data in similar fields in the child support data file to determine whether information was consistent and/or complete across systems. While the objective was to determine whether using child support data systems could assist child welfare agencies in identifying and locating fathers, in order to be useful, information available from child support resources would need to be more complete or accurate than information available in the child welfare record. If child welfare workers could access such information, would it supplement or supplant information already available to them? That is, are caseworkers likely to benefit from use of child support resources?

Overall, information on paternity establishment is likely to be more reliable from the child support system than from the child welfare record because it is more reflective of legal paternity than information likely to be available in the child welfare record. Information on the father's location may be more complete and accurate as well. A child welfare caseworker may have information on the father's location but given that workers often rely on information provided by the child's mother (see table 3-17), the data may be outdated, inaccurate, or incomplete. Caseworkers may have little or no information on fathers living out-of-state or those not living in the community.

The caseworker survey collected informal data on a nonresident father's financial support and this makes the comparison of these data across systems difficult to interpret. Child support systems collect information only on official financial support provided by the father to the child. The caseworker survey asked caseworkers if the father had provided financial support to the child during the child's time in placement, not whether there was an established child support order on which he was paying. Thus, the data collected by the caseworker survey cannot be considered a proxy for official child support payments. However, both formal and informal forms of support are generally considered to indicate a father's commitment to his child.

Matched cases

As discussed, a number of cases were removed from this component of the study as a result of caseworkers' response to questions regarding potential risk to mother or child. Once these cases were removed, a separate file was constructed for each state that contained a list of case identification numbers of children in the sample to be included in the child support match process. This file was then sent to each state's child welfare IT specialist who added into the file identifying information on the child and his or her birth parents (to which the researchers did not have access). The file was then sent directly to the corresponding state child support agency where the cases were "matched."[95] The extent to which the child welfare system contained identifiers for the case principals affected whether or not a case could be "matched" with child support information. State policies on referral of foster care and TANF cases to child support agencies also affects this "match."

After the cases were matched, the child support data was merged with the file. Identifiers were again removed to protect families' privacy, and the files were sent back to the researchers. The overall number of cases matched varies greatly across states. Table 4-16 provides the number of cases matched compared to the number of cases sent to child support to be matched. Only 25 percent of Massachusetts cases and 36 percent of Arizona cases matched, compared to all sent cases in Minnesota and Tennessee.

The results shown in table 4-16 mirror information provided by local administrators. Administrators in Minnesota and Tennessee consistently reported sharing information with child support agencies to identify and locate fathers. Tennessee automatically refers cases to its child support agency when a child enters out-of-home placement. Some administrators in Minnesota also noted an automatic referral process when IV-E eligible children come into care. As noted in chapter 2, the relationship between child welfare agencies and their local child support agencies in Arizona and Massachusetts appeared more tentative.

Before presenting findings from the case matching it is important to describe some differences in the child support data received from the four states. Three of the four states (Arizona, Minnesota and Tennessee) were able to provide detail on whether a child support order was attempted, established (if attempted), and paid upon (if established). Overall for the three states, 71 percent of the matched cases had a child support order attempted. Over half (53%) of those orders attempted were established, and of those established, 38 percent had been paid upon. State variation was greatest in the "percent of orders attempted" which ranged from 70 percent in Minnesota to 87 percent in Arizona. However, given the fact that Minnesota had 100 percent of their cases successfully identified across agencies, Minnesota's results are, in fact, superior to Arizona's in terms of orders attempted.[96] There was less state variation in percent of orders established—from 50 percent in Tennessee to 58 percent in Minnesota.

Table 4-16. Results of Child Support Data Linkage – Number and Percent of Cases Included.

	Total # of Cases in the Study Sample	Total # of Cases Sent to Child Support (after caseworker exclusions)	Total # of Cases Successfully Identified in Child Support Files	% Cases Successfully Identified Across Agencies (of total sent)
Arizona	561	387	138	36
Massachusetts	523	361	91	25
Minnesota	344	243	243	100
Tennessee	530	362	362	100
Total	1958	1353	834	62

Child support data also contained information on whether the State Parent Locator Service (SPLS) and Federal Parent Locator Service (FPLS) methods had been used and whether they were successful in providing information on the father's location, generally either his address or that of his employer. Overall in three states (Arizona, Minnesota, and Tennessee), state locate methods had been used in 67 percent of the cases.[97] There was a 10 point range across states (62 to 72%). In 96 percent of the cases in which the state locate methods were used, the methods were successful in locating the father. Federal locator resources were used somewhat less frequently, in 60 percent of the cases. However, these resources were also successful in 96 percent of the cases in which they were used.

Data consistency across systems

Table 4-17 presents findings on the consistency of information across systems. This analysis involved comparing the data from the caseworker survey with child support administrative data to determine if the information was consistent (that is, was the information in the child support file the same as that provided by the child welfare caseworker).[98] Inconsistent data indicates the two sources could be relying on different information. For example, if during the interview, a caseworker noted paternity had been established and data collected from the child support system notes the same result, i.e., paternity established, this was considered "consistent" data. It is important to note however, that we cannot determine the source of the caseworker respondent's information. That is, child support data could very well have been the source of the caseworker's response.

As shown in table 4-17, almost three-quarters of paternity data were consistent across systems. However, in the remaining one-quarter of cases, child welfare workers' responses conflicted with the information contained in the child support administrative data. Overall, data on father location and father's child support matched in 63 and 51 percent of the cases, respectively. As discussed previously, due to the differences in definitions of location and support, interpreting the meaning of inconsistencies in these types of data is more difficult. It is also difficult to interpret state variation except through administrator opinions as discussed above. However, state differences can be presented and may raise questions that future research efforts can examine. While Massachusetts had a small percentage of inconsistent data with regard to paternity, a much greater consistency was found with regard to child support in that state. Arizona's data was the opposite—a high percent of the data was consistent on paternity, but less than a quarter (23%) of the data on child support was consistent.

Table 4-17. Results of Child Support Data Linkage – Percent Consistent.

	% Data Consistency between Caseworker Survey Data and Child Support Data				
	AZ (N=138)	MA (N=91)	MN (N=243)	TN (N=362)	All States (N=834)
Paternity establishment	79	31	76	79	73
Father location[a]	75	44	61	64	63
Child support[b]	23	69	41	62	51

[a] Fathers are considered "located" by child welfare if their location was known at time of placement, or if any of the locator efforts provided information on the non-custodial father's whereabouts.

[b] The caseworker survey definition of child support was whether the caseworker responded "yes" to whether or not the nonresident father ever provided financial support to the child. Reports of non-financial support were not included as "child support" for purposes of these analyses.

Inconsistent and missing data

Inconsistent information is important for two reasons. First, it may mean that child welfare data are inaccurate (e.g., child welfare data indicates paternity has been established but child support data shows paternity has not been established). Secondly, inconsistent data represents information that child welfare caseworkers might benefit from by utilizing child support resources (e.g., child welfare data is missing but the child support system contains data). Breakdowns by type of inconsistency are provided in Table 4-18.

As shown, for all three categories of data—paternity, location, and support—there are cases in which data was available in the child support system yet the child welfare caseworker reported a lack of information. For example, in 17 percent of the matched Arizona cases, child support data shows paternity establishment while the child welfare caseworker reports it has not been established. Similarly, in 9 percent of the Arizona cases, father location is known to the child support system but the child welfare caseworker reported that the father was not located.[99] Overall, paternity and location were more often known by the caseworker and not found in the child support data than visa versa. Perhaps not surprisingly, collection of support was more often noted in the child support system and not reported by the child welfare worker. The category of father support also has the greatest percent of cases in which the caseworker data was missing yet child support data contained such information. However, in Arizona and Minnesota, a significant percentage of cases contained "missing" data on collections in the child support system yet the caseworker respondent reported the father providing support to his child. Again, this may be due to the differing definitions of "child support" between the two systems.

While these analyses are exploratory the findings suggest the need for continued collaboration between child welfare and child support systems. The intent was to determine whether child support data could be helpful to child welfare agencies for locating nonresident fathers. Indeed, with regard to paternity establishment and father location, information available in the child support agency's administrative data system can be useful to child welfare caseworkers. It is also important for assessment purposes that child welfare caseworkers have more complete and accurate information about the status and regularity of a nonresident father's provision of financial support.

Table 4-18. Inconsistent or Missing Data.

	AZ (N= 138)	MA (N=91)	MN (N=243)	TN (N=362)	All States (N=834)
Paternity Establishment					
Inconsistent	%	%	%	%	%
Paternity established by child welfare, not established by child support	4	66	12	9	15
Paternity established by child support, not established by child welfare	17	2	4	11	9
Missing					
Paternity information missing by child welfare, not missing in child support	0	0	2	1	1
Paternity information missing in child support, not missing in child welfare	0	0	7	0	2
Consistent	79	31	76	79	73
Total	100	100	100	100	100
Father Location					
Inconsistent	%	%	%	%	%
Location known by child welfare, not by child support	12	23	6	27	18
Location known by child support, not by child welfare	9	3	4	8	6
Missing					
Location information missing by child welfare, not missing in child support	0	0	0	1	0
Location information missing in child support, not missing in child welfare	4	30	28	0	12
Consistent	75	44	61	64	63
Total	100	100	100	100	100
Father Support					
Inconsistent	%	%	%	%	%
Collection noted by child welfare, not by child support	0	19	7	7	7
Collection noted by child support, not by child welfare	30	4	16	25	21
Missing					
Support information missing in child welfare, not missing in child support	4	8	8	5	6
Support information missing in child support, not missing in child welfare	43	0	28	0	15
Consistent	23	69	41	62	51
Total	100	100	100	100	100

Summary and Conclusions

This study explored casework practices involving nonresident fathers through both qualitative and quantitative research methods. In-depth discussions with 53 local child welfare administrators provide an overview of policies and practices related to fathers and provide state context and across-state variation. Case-level data collection in the four study states provides rich, detailed information on characteristics of the nonresident fathers of the sampled children, case characteristics, and the actions of caseworkers in these cases. Survey data were compared to available child support information to determine if child support information can be of assistance to child welfare caseworkers.

The case-level data collection includes sampled children in foster care who had been removed from households in which their biological father did not reside. While this population of cases allowed for the rich data obtained, it also limits the implications of the findings. Study findings cannot describe how caseworkers interact with fathers who lived in the home with the child prior to removal. Local administrators reported a significant portion of their cases involve nonresident fathers—estimates ranged from 30 to 80 percent of cases. Thus, in some localities, nonresident fathers are the norm. Below, a summary of the study's findings is provided. Findings are presented along the continuum of casework practices regarding nonresident fathers— practices aimed at identifying, locating, and engaging fathers.

Identifying and Locating Nonresident Fathers

This study examined practices used to identify and locate nonresident fathers with regard to the timing of these activities and whether there are certain case, father, or child characteristics that affect when these fathers are sought, how many methods a caseworker uses to search, and whether searches are successful. Caseworker bias was examined by comparing practices used with nonresident mothers and nonresident fathers and by grouping caseworkers according to gender, training, and opinions. Workers reported having identified the fathers in 88 percent of the cases in the study sample, although workers had contacted only 55 percent of the fathers.

Timing of identification

While many administrators reported that caseworkers begin trying to identify a child's father during the investigation phase, most seemed to think that efforts were stronger and more successful early in a case but after the investigation was complete. According to caseworkers, the majority of nonresident fathers had been identified at case opening (68%). It is likely that while most nonresident fathers are identified early, efforts needed to identify a father later become more time-consuming and less successful. Fathers identified and located at the time of case opening were more likely to be contacted by the caseworker and engaged in the case in ways such as visitation with the child.

Factors that may affect practices to identify and locate nonresident fathers

While slightly over half of all identified nonresident fathers had been located at case opening, this varied considerably by whether the identified father was the legal birth father or whether he was an alleged father. Results of our multivariate regression found several significant factors related to father identification. Father identification does appear to be associated with case and caseworker characteristics. Case characteristics associated with father identification include the age and race of the child and current placement type. Cases in which the child was currently placed in a non-relative foster home were less likely than children living with kin to have an identified father. Cases assigned to male caseworkers or African American caseworkers were also less likely to have an identified father.

Cases with a case plan goal of reunification with the mother were more likely than cases with a goal of non-relative adoption to have a father who was located at the time of case opening. However, different case plan goals appear unrelated to caseworkers' methods to locate nonresident fathers except with regard to asking the child for assistance. Children were more likely to be asked to help locate the nonresident father in cases in which the goal was reunification with the mother than in cases in which the goal was non-relative adoption. Differences in locating methods were found when length of placement was taken into account. Caseworkers were more likely to utilize many locating resources—law enforcement and public assistance records, DMV records, phone books, and utility records—for cases involving children in placement a year or more. State and federal parent locator resources were also more likely to be used when children had been in placement more than one year.

There were a few differences found in locating methods utilized by caseworkers when cases were analyzed by whether the child was living with kin or living in a non-kin placement. Not surprisingly, workers were more likely to seek help from the mother's relatives in cases in which children were living with kin. Workers were also more likely to search law enforcement, public assistance records, state and federal parent locator services for help in locating nonresident fathers of children placed with kin.

Caseworker bias in practices to identify and locate nonresident fathers

In order to examine whether there are caseworker biases against nonresident fathers we compared caseworker actions toward nonresident fathers and nonresident mothers and conducted analyses for subgroups of caseworkers. While some comparisons can be drawn between nonresident fathers and resident mothers, as discussed in chapter 3, the sample of "nonresident" mother cases also allowed for comparison of caseworker practices directed at nonresident fathers and nonresident mothers.[100]

A comparison of nonresident mothers and nonresident fathers found that nonresident mothers are more likely to be located at case opening than nonresident fathers. There were some slight differences in how caseworkers attempted to locate nonresident mothers and nonresident fathers. Not surprisingly, public aid records were searched more frequently to help locate nonresident mothers than fathers. Children were asked to help locate nonresident mothers far more often than they were sought to help locate their fathers. Caseworkers reported that not all individuals asked to help identify or locate nonresident fathers are forthcoming with information. Mothers in particular are not always helpful in providing locating information on the father. This finding concurs with other recent research that found that caseworkers noted that mothers often hinder the involvement of fathers in child welfare casework (O'Donnell et al. 2005).

The comparison analyses conducted using different groupings of caseworkers by gender, training and opinions found that caseworkers who received training were more likely than other workers to have cases involving fathers located at case opening. However, caseworker training was not found to be significant after considering other factors associated with father identification. Workers were more likely to seek locating assistance from other workers, the mother's relatives and father's relatives in cases in which the worker reported having received training.

Caseworker gender was examined to determine whether a gender bias exists in relation to identifying and locating nonresident fathers. Previous research found that caseworkers orient services to mothers, regardless of gender of the caseworker (Lazar, Sagi, and Fraser, 1991).

While recent research found that male caseworkers were less likely to express frustration with involving fathers (O'Donnell et al 2005), overall, our comparison group analyses found no significant differences between male and female caseworkers on most of the casework dimensions examined.

More specific analyses of different identifying and locating methods revealed only one significant difference—male caseworkers were less likely to have obtained identifying information from the child. And, as mentioned earlier, male caseworkers were somewhat less likely than their female counterparts to have an identified father case.

Father Involvement

Engaging fathers is an important, but in many cases, difficult task. Administrators perceived the nonresident father population as having a diverse set of needs and experiences. Case level data reinforce this perception though it should be noted that caseworkers were only asked about fathers' problems in cases involving identified fathers who had been contacted.[101] Caseworkers reported a number of circumstances that posed barriers to contact with nonresident fathers including fathers being unreachable by phone, living out of the state, and being incarcerated. The type of relationship the mother and nonresident father had also affects agency-father contact with fathers more likely to have had contact with the agency in cases involving a good relationship with the child's mother. While a substantial group of fathers express interest in having their children live with them or were considered as a placement resource (approximately one quarter of all cases), caseworkers report in many instances a wide range of circumstances and problems that are likely to complicate any efforts to place the child in the home of his or her father.

Administrator and caseworker opinions on father involvement

When local child welfare administrators were asked about potential benefits and drawbacks to father involvement in child welfare cases, they reported that involving fathers may benefit children. However, administrators were quick to caution that this was true only when such involvement poses no safety risk to the children or mothers. Administrators mentioned that even if a father cannot be a placement resource they could offer tangible benefits such as financial support or critical knowledge of the birth family's medical history. While administrators noted fathers as potential placement resources, some administrators mentioned the benefits of paternal kin as placement resources before mentioning the father himself. A small number of administrators noted that involving fathers may make fathers feel empowered and responsible for the care of their children. Almost three-quarters of caseworkers believed that father involvement enhances child well-being, but only a little over half believed nonresident fathers want to be a part of the decision-making process about their children and most reported that nonresident fathers need help with their parenting skills.

Fathers' problems and needs

Nonresident fathers who had been identified and in contact with the caseworker or agency have a diverse set of needs and problems. The most frequently cited problem for fathers was alcohol/drug abuse, a factor in 58 percent of cases in which the father had been in contact with the agency. In slightly over half the contacted father cases, workers cited problems associated with criminal justice involvement.[102] Caseworkers were asked whether services were provided to nonresident fathers to assist them in overcoming the problems identified and whether or not fathers had complied with services. Caseworkers reported offering services to almost 60 percent of the contacted fathers but they reported only 23 percent of those offered had complied with all the services offered.

Examining problems of subgroups of nonresident fathers proved difficult. Comparative analyses of legal and alleged fathers found caseworkers reported more problems for legal fathers than alleged fathers. This may be because legal fathers actually have more problems but another plausible explanation is that the caseworker may have had greater contact with legal fathers, and therefore more opportunity to assess his problems. Caseworkers reported far less "don't know" responses for legal fathers than for alleged fathers.

Father-child visitation, support, and interest in living with children

Caseworkers reported 56 percent of contacted fathers had visited their child but this represents less than one third (3 0%) of all fathers in the sample. As one might expect, more resident mothers than nonresident fathers were visiting with their children. This is likely due to the child having a permanency goal of reunification with mother. However, caseworkers reported that nonresident mothers were also more likely to have visited their child than nonresident fathers (a statistically significant difference). Less than one third (2 9%) of the contacted fathers were reported to have provided financial support to their children representing only 16 percent of all fathers in the sample. Non-financial support was provided by almost one third (32%) of the contacted fathers with almost a quarter (23%) providing both types of support. Clearly, there is a group of nonresident fathers who are visiting and supporting their children. When compared to nonresident mothers, caseworkers noted nonresident fathers were slightly more likely to have provided financial support since the case opened but nonresident mothers were more likely to have provided non-financial support to the child.

Caseworkers reported half of the contacted fathers expressed interest in having their children live with them though this represents only 28 percent of the entire sample. Legal fathers were more likely to express such an interested compared to alleged fathers. Caseworkers also reported nonresident mothers were more likely than nonresident fathers to express an interest in having their children live with them. Interestingly, caseworkers reported similar or greater percentages of problems for nonresident mothers then for nonresident fathers but this could similarly be due to greater contact with the nonresident mother and increased opportunity to assess problem areas.

Caseworker bias against father involvement

Caseworker bias against father involvement has been researched as a barrier to fathers' participation in child welfare casework. Prior research has found that caseworkers do not pay as much attention to birth fathers as birth mothers but fathers also do not respond to outreach efforts as well as mothers (Franck 2001; O'Donnell et al. 2005). Some gender differences among caseworkers were noted (O'Donnell et al. 2005). Our logistic regression models of father-child visitation and father support offer additional research on this topic but do not support the prior findings of gender differences among caseworkers. Caseworker gender was not found to be significant in the father visiting or father support models. In addition, similar percentages of nonresident mothers and nonresident fathers were considered as a placement resource by caseworkers (44% vs. 48%).

While previous studies have noted a lack of training on father involvement (Hairston 1998), in the four study states, caseworker training on fathers appears fairly widespread. More than two-thirds of the caseworker respondents (70%) noted having received training on identifying, locating and involving fathers. [103] Significant differences were found between cases involving workers who did and did not report having received training about fathers. The case plan was more likely to be shared with the father and the agency was more likely to consider placing the child with the father in cases involving workers who reported having received training. Significant differences were also found between cases with workers who received training and those who did not with regard to whether the father expressed interest in having the child live with him (workers with training regarding fathers were more likely than workers who did not receive training to report cases in which the father had expressed such interest), and whether the agency sought financial assistance from the father as part of the plan (workers reporting training about fathers were more likely than other workers to report cases in which this occurred).

Child Support Case Linkage

The linkage of cases between the child welfare and child support systems explored the potential for more extensive use of child support information by child welfare caseworkers. The results indicate that in many cases, child welfare workers do have information on paternity, location, and support that matches the information in the child support agency's files. However, the number of cases with conflicting information is not trivial. Given the importance of paternity establishment and the accuracy of this determination it seems prudent that child welfare workers utilize child support agencies to obtain new information and to confirm the accuracy of their own information about the location and paternity status of fathers of children in foster care.

Data resources specifically designed to provide locate information make it likely that child support administrative data systems have more reliable information about fathers' locations than do child welfare agencies, particularly in cases where the mother has lost contact with the father. And child support systems may be more able to obtain information on out-of-state fathers through the use of the Federal Parent Locator Service. Recent advances in data sharing across states and on a federal level have allowed state child support systems to be a good source of information on nonresident fathers involved in child welfare cases. Information on official child support orders and collection on orders would also be beneficial to child welfare caseworkers as part of an overall assessment of the nonresident father as a placement resource for his child.

Implications for Practice and Future Research

This study has been repeatedly described as an exploratory look at nonresident fathers in child welfare casework. The findings provide a more comprehensive picture of fathers of children in foster care than has been presented previously. And because the case-level data come directly from caseworkers, the picture is from the perspective of the caseworker. While the accuracy of certain types of information can be questioned based on caseworker lack of knowledge or potential bias against nonresident fathers, the perceptions of caseworkers, the front-line workers who have direct interactions with nonresident fathers, are key to understanding how fathers are identified, located and involved in permanency planning and casework. Caseworkers' and administrators' expectations of nonresident fathers, what they can or cannot provide to their children, and where they fit within families served by child welfare agencies is an important component of casework.

While the study's findings cannot define best practices, they can inform practice. In particular, findings indicate a need to:

- **Search for fathers early in the case.** Most successful information gathering about a nonresident father's identity and location occurs very early in the case either as case investigation or other assessment activities. If a nonresident father's identity and location are not determined early on, there is less of a chance he will have contact with the agency.

- **Provide guidance and training to caseworkers on identifying, locating, and involving fathers.** Casework practice related to identifying, locating and involving fathers appears case specific and variable. Agencies and courts should make clear what steps caseworkers should consider when mothers do not know or share information about the child's father. Even when mothers do provide information on the child's father, workers may want to reach out to other individuals (e.g., relatives, former caseworkers) in order to confirm and expand upon the information provided. Significant differences were found between workers who reported being training on fathers and those who did not receive such training in terms of father location and involvement. For example, the agency was more likely to have considered placing the child with father in cases involving trained workers. Overall though, the percentage of involved fathers was low.

- **Agencies may need to examine whether services offered to fathers are designed to engage fathers.** The study found a small percent of nonresident fathers, when offered services, complied with all the services offered. Further attention may need to be focused on how caseworkers present service options to nonresident fathers and how societal expectations play a role in these interactions.

- **Address domestic violence and worker safety concerns.** Caseworkers and administrators expressed a reluctance to involve some fathers because doing so might reintroduce potential abusers into volatile family situations. Administrators also raised concerns regarding worker safety when contacting the fathers of children on the caseload. Unless safety concerns are effectively addressed, both those related to worker safety as well as those related to the safety of the child and mother, efforts to involve fathers are likely to stall. Safety concerns need to be acknowledged and assessed at a case level and, as previously noted, through training. However, that nearly half of the fathers were never contacted by the agency suggests that little assessment of the actual risk presented is occurring.

- **Use child support data more consistently.** Child support information, including father location, paternity, and financial support, can be helpful in considering placements with fathers or other ways in which fathers can play a constructive role in their children's lives. The frequency with which caseworkers sought available information from child support agencies varied by state and was related to administrators' views of the relationship between the two agencies and the ease with which caseworkers (or other staff at the child welfare agency) could request locator services.

- ***Develop models for involving fathers constructively.*** Unless the child has a case plan goal of placement with his/her father or paternal kin, caseworkers are unlikely to know what, if anything, they should be doing to involve nonresident fathers. The case plan was shared with the father in almost all cases in which the father was contacted. However, we cannot determine from these data whether the case plan is mailed to the father or whether the worker meets with the father to share and explain the plan. Caseworkers may offer visitation to the father in some cases but there does not appear to be clear guidance on when, and in what instances, this should be offered. Family court decisions may also vary regarding father involvement. Less intensive forms of involvement such as obtaining the father's medical background and obtaining access to benefits are also not likely to be routine. There is considerable room for programming that engages nonresident fathers on behalf of their children in ways that could extend beyond the child's stay in foster care and supports whatever permanency goal is in the child's best interest.

This report has noted several areas that warrant further research and we hope this study serves as a starting point for such research. Additional research can be conducted using this dataset, which will be available to researchers through the National Data Archive on Child Abuse and Neglect. For example, more detailed state-specific analyses would be helpful in examining how different policies affect casework practice toward nonresident fathers. State and local characteristics (e.g., rural/urban, poverty measures) could be added to the dataset and used in a variety of analyses to examine state and local practice differences. The regression models could be modified to include a different set of independent variables. While not a large sample, children who have a goal of placement with their father could be examined. Case outcomes could also be examined for children reunified with mothers and children placed with fathers.

Other research could include efforts to collect qualitative data to examine the relationship between permanency goals and casework, specifically casework involving fathers. Qualitative research could also examine specific methods of identifying, locating and involving fathers. Further examination of training opportunities for caseworkers and their impact on practice directed at nonresident fathers is also suggested.

In addition to caseworker actions, caseworker expectations of nonresident fathers are important in examining practices and policies. Perhaps equally important is how agency and family expectations of fathers get articulated during agency and family-directed approaches (e.g., permanency planning reviews and family group conferences). Are nonresident fathers expected to be an integral part of family group conferences? Is the expectation that fathers as well as mothers have primary responsibility for the care of their children? Kinship care has become an invaluable placement resource for child welfare agencies but has the focus on kin affected workers' expectations for placing children with nonresident fathers? Are agency expectations such that grandparents and other kin are looked to as placement resources, even before nonresident fathers? Qualitative research methods could be used to explore expectations.

While our findings do not indicate biases in casework practices involving nonresident fathers, low expectations of fathers may be ingrained in agency policies and practices.

Caseworkers reported that nonresident fathers have a wide range of problems and face a variety of circumstances that impact on their ability to care for and visit their children. However, similar problems were also reported for both resident and nonresident mothers. Protocol may dictate that caseworkers invest more heavily in remediation of a resident mother's problems given that returning the child to the mother's care is likely to be the permanency goal. Indeed, the vast majority (84%) of resident mothers were offered services for all reported problems. At the same time, agencies offered more services to nonresident mothers than nonresident fathers (79%** vs. 59%). Societal expectations that mothers know how to care for children and fathers are less capable may also affect these practices. Perhaps workers feel that less effort is needed to help mothers since the expectation is that the mother already knows how to be a mother, she just needs some help getting "back on track."

This study found nonresident fathers less likely than both resident and nonresident mothers to visit their child or express an interest in having their child live with them. Some of these differences could be due to fathers' lack of a prior relationship with the child and additional research should examine this issue. It could also be that caseworkers do not have the same expectations for fathers as they do for mothers. Perhaps nonresident fathers are simply responding to low expectations—expectations that likely mirror those of the community and society in general.

REFERENCES

Anne, E. (2003). Casey Foundation, "The Unsolved Challenge of System Reform: *The Condition of the Frontline Human Services Workforce.*"

Bloomer, S. R., Sipe, T. A. & Ruedt, D. E. (2002). "Child Support Payment and Child Visitation: Perspectives from Nonresident Fathers and Resident Mothers." *Journal of Sociology and Social Welfare, 29(2),* 77-91.

Brown, S. (2004). "Family structure and child well-being: The significance of parental cohabitation." *Journal of Marriage and Family, 66,* 35 1-367.

Bulanda, R. E. (2004). "Paternal Involvement with Children: The Influence of Gender Ideologies." *Journal of Marriage and Family, 66,* 40-45.

Cancian, M. & Meyer, D. (2004). "Fathers of Children Receiving Welfare: Can They Provide More Child Support?" *Social Service Review, 78(2),* 179-206.

Flouri, E. & Buchanan, A. (2004). "Early Father's and Mother's Involvement and Child's Later Educational Outcomes." *British Journal of Educational Psychology, 74,* 141-53.

Franck, E. J. (2001). "Outreach to Birthfathers of Children in Out-of-Home Care." *Child Welfare, 80(3),* 381-99.

Greif, G. L. & Bailey, C. (1990). "Where Are the Fathers in Social Work Literature?" Families in Society: *The Journal of Contemporary Human Services, 71(2),* 88-92.

Greif, G. L. & S. Zuravin, J. (1989). "Fathers: A Placement Resource for Abused and Neglected Children?" *Child Welfare, 68(5),* 479-90.

English, D. (2002). Washington State Office of Children's Administration, Department of Health and Human Services. Preliminary Findings, "*Fatherhood in the Child Welfare System*" Research Progress Report.

Findlater, Janet, E., Kelly, Susan. (1999). The Future of Children, *Winter Child protective services and domestic violence.*

Fix, Michael, & Jeffrey, Passel, S. (2003). "U.S. Immigration—Trends and Implications for Schools." *Presentation to the National Association for Bilingual Education.* Washington, DC: The Urban Institute.

Hofferth, Sandra, L. (2003)."Race/Ethnic Differences in Father Involvement in Two-Parent Families: Culture, Context, or Economy?" *Journal of Family Issues, 24(2),* 185-216.

Hofferth, S. L. & Anderson, K. G. (2003). "Are All Dads Equal? Biology Versus Marriage as a Basis for Paternal Investment." *Journal of Marriage and Family, 65, 2* 13-32.

Kahkonen, P. (1997). "From the Child Welfare Trap to the Foster Care Trap." *Child Welfare, 76(3),* 429-45.

King, V., Mullan Harris, K. & Heard, H. E. (2004). "Racial and Ethnic Diversity in Nonresident Father Involvement." *Journal of Marriage and Family, 66,* 1-21.

Kost, K. A. (2001). "The Functions of Fathers: What Poor Men Say About Fatherhood." *Families in Society, 82(5),* 499-508.

Lazar, A., Sagi, A. & Fraser, M. W. 1991. "Involving Fathers in Social Services." *Children and Youth Services Review, 13(4),* 287-300.

Lerman, R. & Sorensen, E. (2000). "Father Involvement with their Nonmarital Children: Patterns, Determinants, and Effects on their Earnings." *Marriage and Family Review, 29(2),* 137-158.

Marsiglio, W. (1991). Paternal engagement activities with minor children. *Journal of Marriage and the Family, 53,* 973-986.

National Family Preservation Network. (2001). *"An Assessment of Child Welfare Practices Regarding Fathers."* Prepared for the Annie E. Casey Foundation. http://www.nfpn.org/tools/articles/fathers.php. (Accessed June 12, 2005.)

National Resource Center for Family-Centered Practice and Permanency Planning. (2005). *"Findings from the Initial Child and Family Service Reviews,* 2001-2004." Hunter College School of Social Work.

Nelson, Timothy, J. (2004). "Low-Income Fathers." *Annual Review of Sociology, 30,* 427-51.

O'Donnell, J. M. (2001). "Paternal Involvement in Kinship Foster Care Services in One Father and Multiple Father Families." *Child Welfare, 80(4),* 453-79.

O'Donnell, J. M., Johnson Jr., W. E., D'Aunno, L. E. & Thornton. H. L. (2005). "Fathers in Child Welfare: Caseworkers' Perspectives." *Child Welfare, 84(3),* 387-414.

O'Hagan, K. (1997). "The Problem of Engaging Men in Child Protection Work." *The British Journal of Social Work, 27(1),* 25-42.

Pearson, J. & Hardaway, C. (2000). "Designing Programs for Incarcerated and Paroled Obligors." *Welfare Information Network, 1(1).*

Rasheed, J. M. (1999). "Obstacles to the Role of Inner-City, Low-Income, Noncustodial African American Fathers." *Journal of African American Men, 4(1),* 9-23.

Roy, Kevin. (2000). "Fathers on the Margins of Work and Family: The Paternal Involvement Project." *Poverty Research News, 4(2),* Chicago: Northwestern University, University of Chicago, Joint Center for Poverty Research.

Shore, N., Wirth, J., Cahn, K., Yancey, B. & Gunderson, K. (2002). "Long-Term and Immediate Outcomes of Family Group Conferencing in Washington State." *Restorative Practices E-Forum.*

Sonenstein, Freya, Karin Malm, and Amy Billing. (2002). "Literature Review: Study of Fathers' Involvement in Permanency Planning and Child Welfare Casework." Prepared for the Assistant Secretary for Planning and Evaluation, U.S. *Department of Health and Human Services*. http://aspe.hhs.gov/hsp/CW-dads02/index.htm.

Sorensen, Elaine. (2003). "Child Support Gains Some Ground." *No. 11 in Series Snapshots of America's Families III*. Washington, DC. The Urban Institute.

South Carolina Department of Social Services. (2000). "Diligent Search Project, Final Evaluation Report." Columbia, SC: *The Center for Child and Family Studies*, University of South Carolina.

Thoennes, N. (2003). "Family Group Decision Making in Colorado." Protecting Children— Promising Results, Potential New Directions: *International FGDM Research and Evaluation in Child Welfare, 18*, (1-2), 80.

U.S. Department of Health and Human Services, Administration on Children, Youth and Families, (2003). "Executive Summary" *National Survey of Child and Adolescent Well-Being*, One Year in Foster Care Wave 1 Data Analysis. http://www.acf.hhs. gov/programs/opre/abuse neglect/nscaw/

Vogel, C. A., Boller, K., Faerber, J., Shannon, J. D. & Tamis-LeMonda, C. S. (2003). "Understanding Fathering: *The Early Head Start Study of Fathers of Newborns*." Princeton, NJ: Mathematica Policy Research, Inc.

Wilcox, W. B. (2002). "Religion, Convention, and Paternal Involvement." *Journal of Marriage and Family, 64*, 780-92.

End Notes

[1] It is not known how many of the men who are part of the unmarried couples are the biological fathers of the foster children. In addition, an unknown number of "married couple" compositions do not consist of both birth parents. Data were compiled from 31 states (these states had less than 10 percent missing data for this AFCARS field). Many large states, including California, Illinois, and New York, have large amounts of missing data and were not included in the analysis. Urban Institute tabulations of the 1994 National Study of Protective, Preventive, and Reunification Services data, U.S. Department of Health and Human Services, and tabulations of Urban Institute's 1999 National Survey of America's Families calculated 72 percent of children served by child welfare agencies and 80 percent of foster children have noncustodial fathers.

[2] The study is prepared under contract to the Assistant Secretary for Planning and Evaluation and is funded by the Administration for Children and Families, U.S. Department of Health and Human Services.

[3] More information on the sample of fathers analyzed in this study is included in the methodology section of this chapter.

[4] Concurrent planning enables states to seek an adoptive or other permanent placement for a child while pursuing efforts to preserve or reunite the family.

[5] Children's Rights report of results of CFSRs with 22 states for which final reports had been issued as of February 2003, New York City, NY.

[6] We selected only one county-administered child welfare system (in Minnesota) due to the anticipated greater burden in recruiting individual county agencies for participation.

[7] The administrator protocol is available at http://aspe.hhs.gov.

[8] We concluded that although some siblings would have different fathers for whom casework practices might differ, the likelihood of same fathers was high and would thus lessen the number of fathers in the study.

[9] The sampling design is available at http://aspe.hhs.gov.

[10] In Minnesota, our statistician had to modify the design due to a smaller than expected universe of cases meeting our study criteria. Circumstances in Hennepin County, Minnesota, meant that some workers there had to be interviewed on more than two cases. In addition, 18 of Minnesota's 87 counties declined to participate; thus, the first-stage sample frame did not consist of the entire state.

[11] The caseworker instrument is available at http://aspe.hhs.gov.

[12] Adoptive child cases were considered ineligible due to the complexity inherent in determining father relationships.

[13] In Tennessee, we were told all foster care cases are routinely referred to child support to begin the process of obtaining reimbursement for foster care costs. In Minnesota, IV-E cases are automatically referred to child support. Arizona and Massachusetts did not appear to have any established policy of referring foster care cases to child support.

[14] Only cases in which the caseworker responded 'no' to two questions: "Is there any reason why the information you have provided should not be used to facilitate a match with the parent locator services?" and "Do you think locating the father of this child might put the child or the mother at risk of physical harm?" were included in the data linkage.

[15] See later discussion (page 88) for description of relationships.

[16] Tennessee was one of the top 10 states with the fastest growth in immigrant population between 1990 and 2000, with a rate far exceeding 100 percent (Fix and Passel 2003).

[17] Note that some administrators mentioned the benefits of father's kin as placement resources before mentioning the father himself, which may be indicative of the agency's perception of nonresident fathers.

[18] As part of the Brian A. Settlement Agreement, administrative policies and procedures on engaging families require inclusion of all known parents in the permanency planning process. This includes biological parents, legal parents, and alleged fathers. The procedural guidelines specifically mention that "unless contrary to the child/youth's best interest, incarcerated parents must be included in the development of the permanency plan."

[19] In 2004, voters in Arizona passed Proposition 200, which prohibited offering some state and local government benefits to undocumented immigrants. At the time of our interviews, some administrators worried that the proposition would affect child welfare services or services to which the agency could refer undocumented fathers. While the proposition does not actually change child welfare services, it does limit access to some government benefits, such as utility assistance programs, which might be of use to noncustodial fathers providing placements for their children.

[20] As described in chapter 1, ineligible cases included those with resident fathers, adoptive fathers, or deceased fathers.

[21] Identified father cases include cases in which the worker said the father's name was known at case opening and cases in which the worker answered "yes" to whether the agency has identified an alleged father, i.e., does anyone at the agency think they know who the father is, at the time of the interview.

[22] Contact was defined broadly to include in-person, telephone, voicemail or written communication with the caseworker or another staff member.

[23] Cases with fathers who died prior to case opening were considered ineligible and excluded from the sample. A small number (n=25, 1.7% of eligible fathers) died after case opening and are included in descriptive analyses.

[24] Exceptions are noted in the tables.

[25] Tables report weighted percents and unweighted Ns so calculations made by the reader to determine numbers of cases in specific subgroups will provide the estimated Ns which may differ slightly from the actual number of completed interviews for that subgroup.

[26] Cases with deceased mothers (n=46, 2.2% of eligible mothers) remained a part of the sample in order to get information about the nonresident fathers in those cases. Of those deceased, 24 (52%) died prior to case opening and are excluded from subsequent analyses.

[27] Cases with fathers in categories (3) and (4) were not asked about location of father at case opening because the identity of the father was not known at that time.

[28] The caseworker noted no contact yet or did not know whether contact had been made with the father.

[29] The difference between alleged and legal fathers is whether the caseworker reported that paternity had been established in the case.

[30] Anne E. Casey Foundation, 2003. "The Unsolved Challenge of System Reform: The Condition of the Frontline Human Services Workforce."

[31] The reader is reminded that children in the sample were all children who had been in out-of-home care for 3 to 36 months, who were removed for the first time (first placement episode) and who were removed from households in which the father did not reside.

[32] While the majority of children in the sample had siblings, only one child from any sibling group was included in the sample.

[33] This includes children who had been reunified after sampling occurred, as well as children on trial home visits (Massachusetts retains this information in administrative data for 6 months preceding reunification.)

[34] Sampled cases were selected because the child's father was not living in the home. However, during the interim between sample selection and interview, the living arrangement could have changed.

[35] As discussed earlier in the chapter, certain questions were only asked of caseworkers who had been in contact with the parent. Questions about the resident mother visiting with the child were only asked for "contacted mothers." As shown 1,571 of the total 1,635 resident mothers (96%) were "contacted mothers."

[36] We cannot determine from the data whether the financial support provided by mothers was collected through the child support agency.

[37] For study purposes, paternity was established if the caseworker responded in the affirmative to the question. Subsequent analysis of ways in which paternity was established (e.g., genetic testing, signing of voluntary paternity document, father's name on birth certificate, self-declaration by father, default order) did not negate a caseworker's paternity had not yet been established,

[38] While terminology differs between child welfare and child support agencies, for study purposes, fathers for whom the child's caseworker cited "paternity has been established" are considered legal birth fathers; all other fathers are considered to be alleged fathers. The use of the term "birth father" is prevalent in child welfare agencies as the term applied to the biological father of an adopted child. There is no equivalent term used for biological fathers of foster children and thus, survey questions often used the term "birth father."

[39] Fathers identified through consulting birth records are likely to be subsumed in the "identified at time of case opening" category if birth records were consulted at any time in the case preceding placement. The survey does not allow for delineation of this identification method.

[40] Some siblings may have been too young to assist with locating the father. Unlike the "ask child" question, the "ask sibling" question did not consider the age of siblings (i.e., only with cases involving children over 6 were caseworkers asked whether the child was asked about the father's location) because information on sibling age was not collected.

[41] Caseworkers who did respond to this question may be referring to paternal relatives of the study child's siblings. While the father of the study child was not identified it could be that the caseworker believes the child has the same father as one or more of the child's siblings and asks these relatives for help in identifying the study child's father.

[42] Putative father registries are listings of non-legal fathers. This is, the father has been named, but the father has not established paternity.

[43] The question read, "To your knowledge, was the state/federal parent locator services used by your agency to locate the father?" While it is unlikely that child welfare caseworkers could use the service directly, we did not want workers to report on possible child support locate activities undertaken for child support purposes.

[44] Federal data confirm extensive use of the federal parent locator service (FPLS) in Arizona.

[45] This number does not equal the number of "identified" fathers. Identified fathers comprise cases in which the father's name was known at time of case opening and cases for which the agency (at time of interview) had identified a father of the child. The worker may have identified a father but not yet have the father's name in the case record.

[46] "Other information" caseworkers have about fathers included some background and assessment information, criminal history, paternal relative and significant other contact information, and physical description.

[47] A father is classified as having a good relationship with the child's mother if the caseworker reported that the mother and father are friends, are romantically involved on a steady basis, or involved in an on-again/off-again romantic relationship.

[48] Only included cases in which the child was not currently placed with paternal relatives.

[49] Criminal justice involvement was meant to include a wide range of possible involvement including fathers who might have been arrested, were pending trial, incarcerated, or on probation.

[50] Incarcerated at some point since case opening.

[51] Please note the discussion of nonresident mothers in chapter 3.

[52] That is, the caseworker thought he or she had identified the study child's father. Involved fathers are defined as fathers caseworkers reported as visiting with their children frequently (twice a month or more) or supporting their children financially or non-financially.

[53] "Fatherhood Training Curriculum: Principles, Policies and Practices to Engage Fathers in their Children's Lives," National Family Preservation Network, 2005.

[54] It is important to remember that the caseworker respondent is the ongoing or foster care worker. It is not possible to determine whether the caseworker respondent is reporting on whether the father had ever been considered as a resource at some point in the case prior to the worker being assigned.

[55] Caseworkers may supervise a visit, or visits may occur in a supervised visitation center. Parent visitation often differs by whether the child is placed with kin or is placed in a non-kin foster home or other setting.

[56] See footnote on page 75 in chapter 3.

[57] Caseworkers did not know the father's level of education in over 87 percent of alleged father cases and 63 percent of legal father cases. Father's marital status was not known in 45 percent of alleged father cases and 27 percent of legal father cases.

[58] Significant at $p < .01$.

[59] Per communication with Amy Solomon, Justice Policy Center, Urban Institute and Betsey Nevins, Council of State Governments.

[60] Please note the earlier discussion of differential contact rates between alleged and legal fathers. While the percentages are similar for contacted fathers of both groups, the percentages differ across the larger groups, i.e., a caseworker cannot share a case plan with a father with whom there has been no contact.

[61] These questions had low rates of "don't know" responses for both legal and alleged fathers (2% for both questions and types of fathers).

[62] Analyses of the regularity of financial support could not be conducted due to small numbers of alleged fathers.

[63] There were a total of 323 nonresident mother cases.

[64] These figures represent percent of identified nonresident fathers and nonresident mothers who were located at case opening. Caseworkers reported 73 nonresident mothers who had not been located at case opening.

[65] "Don't know" responses constituted 30 percent of the overall responses for nonresident fathers and only 12% for nonresident mothers.

[66] The greatest percent of "don't know" responses was in the category of domestic violence while a prior finding of abuse had the lowest percent of "don't know" responses.

[67] The question was, "We want to know if the child's father has ever had any problems (of the following list) affecting whether his child can be placed with him." That few fathers were considered as a placement resource may affect how caseworkers interpreted the question.

[68] Questions pertaining to visitation were only asked of caseworkers who had contact with the nonresident father or nonresident mother.

[69] The case breakdown between the two groups was nearly equal—48 percent of caseworkers responded "yes" and 50 percent responded "no." "Don't know" responses constituted the remaining 2 percent of responses.

[70] Nonresident fathers of Hispanic origin and non-citizen fathers were both less likely to be considered for placement but the Ns for both categories are small.

[71] The percentage of caseworkers reporting "don't know" responses for both categories was relatively low (less than 15%) and similar for both groups of father cases.

[72] "Don't know" responses were similar for the two groups of cases—13-14 percent for both.

[73] Please note that study criteria called for cases in out-of-home care between 3-36 months; however, we did not eliminate cases if the length of placement fell outside of this range. No placements were less than 3 months but there was a small percentage that are over 36 months.

[74] Significant at p < .05.

[75] Because caseworkers responded to questions regarding multiple cases (See chapter 1 for more detail), the possibility arises that responses to each caseworker's cases are correlated with each other (intraclass correlation). We take intraclass correlation into account by calculating clustered robust standard errors.

[76] See chapter 3, page 56 for gender breakdown for caseworker respondents.

[77] See table 3-2.

[78] The small number of workers (N=133) who neither disagreed, disagreed, or strongly disagreed to the opinion questions made some detailed analyses difficult.

[79] See chapter 1 for a complete description of the sample selection and design, response rates and weighing procedures.

[80] A sample size of 400 was used for the father visitation model and a sample of 844 was used for the father support model.

[81] Many of the variables that may affect father identification could not be included because the information could only be collected if the father was identified. For example, whether the father was ever married to the child's mother was only collected on identified fathers. In addition, questions pertaining to father problems, circumstances that could be barriers to contact with the agency, child support, and questions of whether he had expressed interest in having his child live with him, and whether the agency had ever considered placing the child with him, were asked only if the father had been identified and contacted by the worker or agency. Thus, the father identification model could not include these variables.

[82] Non-financial support was described as provision of clothing, diapers, child care, food or health insurance.

[83] See discussion of resident and nonresident mother cases in chapter 3.

[84] Termination of parental rights was included as a control variable because of the likelihood that it can explain a lot of the variance in which fathers are visiting their children. While a father whose parental rights have been terminated would be less likely to visit his child and in some cases may be legally prohibited from doing so, the cross-sectional dataset does not allow examination of the timing of events. The small percent of fathers whose rights are terminated but visited their children could have done so prior to the termination of rights. In other cases, fathers who no longer have parental rights may still be visiting their children.

[85] Father's race/ethnicity was not included in the model due to its high correlation with child's race/ethnicity. Consideration of placement was included as an independent variable but could also likely be a dependent variable. Caseworkers are likely to decide whether a father should be a placement resource on whether or not he is visiting or supporting his child. Likewise, after a father is considered a placement resource the caseworker might encourage (or actually schedule) visits between him and his child. The survey instrument did not collect data on the timing of these caseworker decisions.

[86] Caseworkers had to report three or more of the problems in order for the case to be deemed a multiple problem case.

[87] A "good relationship" was defined as whether the caseworker responded to one of the following about the nonresident father and birth mother: 1) they are romantically involved on a steady basis; 2) they are involved in an on-again off-again relationship; or 3) they are just friends. Other caseworker responses included 1) they

are hostile toward each other; 2) they hardly ever talk to each other; 3) the never talk to each other; or 4) other. These responses were coded as a "bad relationship."

[88] Other placements included group homes, residential treatment centers, and children reunited with mother.

[89] It is important to remember that the data represent caseworker responses to the questions on visitation. Responses might likely have been different if the questions were asked of the fathers, mothers, or other caregivers.

[90] See page 118. Cases in which the father was considered as a placement resource were more likely to have multiple problems. This is likely due to less "don't know" responses, i.e., the caseworker has had greater access to the father and more time to identify and assess various "problems."

[91] It is important to note that the definition of "support" included both financial and non-financial support.

[92] Caseworkers were asked if seeking financial assistance from the nonresident father was ever part of the case plan. The question did not specify whether the financial assistance would be sought through a child support order established through the child support agency or through informal mechanisms.

[93] Only cases in which the caseworker responded 'no' to two questions: "Is there any reason why the information you have provided should not be used to facilitate a match with the parent locator services?" and "Do you think locating the father of this child might put the child or the mother at risk of physical harm?" were included in the data linkage.

[94] State percentages of excluded cases are as follows: Arizona 31%, Massachusetts 31%, Minnesota 30% and Tennessee.32%

[95] A child welfare case "linked" with information in the child support data system does not equate to a child support order having been attempted or established. Referral to child support could have happened for locate or other purposes. Cases could also have been referred to child support by local TANF agencies.

[96] Overall, Minnesota attempted to establish orders in 70 percent of their cases (100 percent of which were identified in child support files) while Arizona attempted to establish in 31 percent of their cases (87 percent of the 138 cases identified in child support files).

[97] Massachusetts data contained information on whether state or federal locate resources had been used but not whether these efforts were successful.

[98] Matched cases are those in which both sources contained "yes" responses, "no" responses, or "missing" responses.

[99] Father was reported not located at time of case opening and all reported efforts to obtain locate information did not provide information.

[100] See definition of "nonresident" mother in chapter 3.

[101] Fifty-five percent of the entire sample of cases involved fathers who had been contacted by the agency or caseworker (this represents 62% of identified fathers). The frequency and duration of contact was not determined.

[102] Criminal justice involvement was meant to include a wide range of possible involvement including fathers who might have been arrested, pending trial, incarcerated, or on probation.

[103] The question asked of caseworkers was "Have you ever received training on how to identify, locate, or engage nonresident fathers?"

CHAPTER SOURCES

Chapter 1 - This is an edited, reformatted and augmented version of a Congressional Research Service publication, R41431, dated September 28, 2010.

Chapter 2 - This is an edited, reformatted and augmented version of a Congressional Research Service publication, R40499, dated April 7, 2009.

Chapter 3 - This is an edited, reformatted and augmented version of a U.S. Department of Justice publication, NCJ 222964, dated August 2006, revised March 30, 2010.

Chapter 4 - This is an edited, reformatted and augmented version of a U.S. Department of Health and Human Services publication, HHS-100-01-0014, dated April, 2006.

INDEX

G

H

I

J

K

L

M

N

O